Ambiguity and Choice
in Organizations

Ambiguity and Choice in Organizations

By
JAMES G. MARCH and
JOHAN P. OLSEN

with contributions by
Søren Christensen, Michael D. Cohen,
Harald Enderud, Kristian Kreiner,
Pierre Romelaer, Kåre Rommetveit,
Per Stava and Stephen S. Weiner

2. EDITION

Universitetsforlaget
Bergen - Oslo - Tromsø

© Universitetsforlaget 1976 and 1979
ISBN 82-00-01960-8
Cover design by Bjørn˙Roggenbihl

2nd printing 1982
3rd printing 1987

Printed in Norway by
A/S REPRO-TRYKK — BERGEN

Contents

Acknowledgments

We have had a sustained professional and personal contact with the eight collaborators listed on the title page. Although we accept responsibility for the content of this book, we have no hesitation in assigning both specific credit for individual chapters and collective credit to the whole group for the culture of effective collaboration that they sustained and for the main thrusts of the theoretical arguments.

In addition, there is a larger group of friends and associates who have been important to the work. We should like to acknowledge particularly the contributions of Flemming Agersnap, Torben Agersnap, Graham Allison, Ib Andersen, Fredrik Barth, Larry Cuban, James R. Glenn, Jr., Michel Crozier, C. H. Gudnason, Bjørn Henriksen, Gudmund Hernes, Helga Hernes, Knut Dahl Jacobsen, Curtis Manns, Vance Peterson, Kay Schoonhoven, Lee Sproull, Steinar Stjernø, Harald Sætren, Eugene Webb, Karl Weick, David Wolf, and Alice Young.

We have had the support and hospitality of a number of institutions. The University of California at Irvine, Stanford University, the University of Bergen, and the Copenhagen School of Economics have all been hosts for extended periods. On several occasions we have met in the Fossheim Pensjonat at Hemsedal, Norway. The warmth and easy hospitality of the Langehaug family, owners and managers of the inn, set a tone and established a fond memory that has continued.

Parts of the work have been supported by a number of funding agencies. We thank the Ford Foundation, the Spencer Foundation, and the Norwegian Research Council for the Sciences and Humanities for financial support that permitted our collaboration.

Our wives, Jayne D. March and Helene M. Olsen, have smiled on it all with tolerant enthusiasm, knowing that whatever else, they are more important. As they are.

James G. March
Johan P. Olsen

Preface

This book is based on a series of studies of organizational choice in Denmark, Norway, and the United States. It is an attempt to understand how organizations deal with ambiguity – goals that are unclear, technologies that are imperfectly understood, histories that are difficult to interpret, and participants who wander in and out. It is in the tradition of theories of organizational decision making and draws heavily on the works of Allison, Coleman, Crecine, Cyert, Edelman, Hirschman, Lindblom, Simon, Steinbruner, Thompson, and Weick.

Because the problems of ambiguity are very conspicuous in educational institutions, most of the studies are studies of decision making in an educational context. These include the selection of a new dean in an American university (Chapters 6, 15), the location decisions of Norwegian district colleges (Chapter 10) and a new Norwegian medical school (Chapter 7), several important decisions in a Danish free school (Chapters 8 and 16), major decisions in American universities (Chapters 9 and 12), desegregation decisions in San Francisco schools (Chapter 11), participation and reorganization in the University of Oslo (Chapters 13 and 14), and beliefs about power in the Danish Technical University (Chapter 17).

Each of these studies develops a different set of observations of organizations faced with ambiguity. Each attempts to discuss the implications for understanding organizational behavior to be drawn from the cases examined. The sites, issues, and organizations vary. As a result, so do the details of the implications to be drawn. However, there are a number of common themes; and the studies reflect a common set of theoretical concerns developed over several years of collaboration.

The central theoretical themes are outlined in Chapters 1–5. Chapter 1 outlines the basic issues underlying the book by specifying some of the complications in the complete cycle of choice. These complications stem particularly from ambiguity in intentions, interpretations, history, and the organization of decision making. Chapter 2 considers the ambiguity of relevance in organizational problem solving. It examines the ways in which choices, problems, solutions, and participants are connected when goals and technologies are unclear. Chapter 3 looks at the ambiguity of self-interest as an interpretation of participation decisions as individuals allocate time to alternative decision situations. Chapter 4 develops the basic elements of organizational learning and the formation of belief under conditions of unclear goals and technology. Chapter 5 identifies some of the problems posed by ambiguity for the standard normative model of rational decision and suggests some possible modifications in that approach to decision making.

As we point out in Chapter 1, our major effort is in some ways a curious one: We have tried to understand the everyday behavior of organizations as they make decisions. That behavior is familiar to most people who live in modern developed societies. None of the case studies we report will strike usual readers as being "surprising". Yet many of the things we observe seem to be understood badly by our ways of thinking about organizations. We believe this contradiction between what we observe in organizational behavior and the way we talk about organizational behavior is fascinating but often confusing. Our objective is to take a few steps in the direction of talking differently about organizational decision making. Perhaps, reducing the confusion slightly without destroying the fascination.

1. Organizational Choice under Ambiguity

JAMES G. MARCH
Stanford University

JOHAN P. OLSEN
University of Bergen

1.0 Introduction

Organizational choice often involves a curious paradox. The process is both surprising and not surprising. It is familiar to ordinary experiences; it is puzzling for many interpretations of that experience. Very few reports of organizational decision making strike experienced participants in organizations as unusual. At the same time, many common observations about organizations are pathological from the point of view of theories of organizations. What is mundane to experience frequently becomes unexplained variance in the theories. What is standard in the interpretation of organizations frequently becomes irrelevant to experience.

The observations reported in this book are not surprising. Organizations are often observed to do nothing to implement a decision after having devoted much time, energy, and enthusiasm to making it; or to make apparently major decisions with only minor participation by key administrators and significant constituents; or to combine a struggle over participation rights with an indifference to exercising them; or to make argument over ideology without affective action; or to separate the outcome of a major political dispute from the details of the political process involved. Though the examples are new, the stories are old.

Despite their familiarity, the observations are theoretically curious. They appear to be partly inconsistent with several fundamental ideas implicit in ordinary conversations about organizations and decisions in them, as well as several conventional, and highly useful, theoretical treatments of organizations: rational models of individual choice, micro-economic theory, social welfare theory, interest group theories of politics and bureaucracy, theories of power, democratic theories of politics, theories of negotiation and bargaining, theories of planning, management theory.

We wish to examine some aspects of those theoretical ideas and suggest modifications in them. The suggestions are relatively fundamental, but they are not comprehensive. Without attempting a complete reconstruction of ideas about decisions in organizations, we will try to outline some possible perspectives that may make ordinary experience in organizations somewhat more explicable.

Our emphasis is on decisions, but we are impressed by the ways in which the imagery of "decision making" confounds an understanding of organizational phenomena. We will examine below some problems with the standard conception of the choice cycle in organizations and some of the ways in which the organizational settings with which we will be concerned involve substantial elements of ambiguity that is not accommodated well within that conception; but we preface the discussion with the observation that the ideas of "decision" (as an outcome) and "decision making" (as a process) are already confused by a semantic presumption that the latter is connected to the former in some selv-evident fashion.

Choice situations include law-making, price-setting, planning, and a host of other similar things. They are overtly concerned with the allocation of resources and burdens, selection of personnel, designing of new organizational arrangements, policy-programs and the like. Parliaments, courts, universities, firms, political parties, bureaucracies, and hospitals are involved in decision situations frequently. There are social expectations that the main thing taking place in such situations is "decision making".

Explicit decision activities in such situations may have much to do with the outcomes that occur. A choice situation may provide an occasion for problem-solving and conflict resolution, the aggregation of individual and group preferences and power into collective choices. But often the process of decision does not appear to be much concerned with making a decision. Indeed, the activities within a choice situation may be explicable only if we recognize the other major things that take place withing the same arena at the same time.

A choice process provides an occasion for a number of other things, most notably:

- an occasion for executing standard operating procedures, and fulfilling role-expectations, duties, or earlier commitments.
- an occasion for defining virtue and truth, during which the organization discovers or interprets what has happened to it, what it has been doing, what it is doing, what it is going to do, and what justifies its actions.
- an occasion for distributing glory or blame for what has happened in the organization; and thus an occasion for exercising, challenging or reaffirming friendship or trust relationsships, antagonisms, power or status relationships.
- an occasion for expressing and discovering "self-interest" and

11

"group interest", for socialization, and for recruiting (to organizational positions, or to informal groups).

– an occasion for having a good time, for enjoying the pleasures connected to taking part in a choice situation.

The several activities are neither mutually exclusive nor mutually inconsistent. They are aspects of most choice situations and illustrate their complexity. Decisions are a stage for many dramas.

The dramatic complexity is further elaborated by the pervasiveness of ambiguity. By the term *ambiguity* we intend to signify four major kinds of opaqueness in organizations. The first is the ambiguity of *intention*. Many organizations are characterized by inconsistent and ill-defined objectives. It is often impossible to specify a meaningful preference function for an organization that satisfies both the consistency requirements of theories of choice and the empirical requirements of describing organizational motive. The second lack of clarity is the ambiguity of *understanding*. For many organizations the causal world in which they live is obscure. Technologies are unclear; environments are difficult to interpret. It is hard to see the connections between organizational actions and their consequences. The third lack of clarity is the ambiguity of *history*. The past is important, but it is not easily specified or interpreted. History can be reconstructed or twisted. What happened, why it happened, and whether it had to happen are all problematic. The fourth lack of clarity is the ambiguity of *organization*. At any point in time, individuals vary in the attention they provide to different decisions; they vary from one time to another. As a result, the pattern of participation is uncertain and changing.

All organizations confront elements of ambiguity in decision making. For some organizations ambiguity is a dominant condition. In particular, ambiguity is a major feature of decision making in most public and educational organizations; it seems to characterize a wide variety of organizations when they are young or when their environments are changing.

1.1 Limitations in the Complete Cycle of Choice

In order to accommodate these concerns, it is necessary to reexamine some fundamental ideas about organizational choice. They are simple ideas, general in their appeal; but relative to the interplay of events within a decision situation, they are too simple and too seductive.

Consider what might be called the complete cycle of organizational choice. It is a familiar conception, and a useful one.[1]

12

At a certain point in time some participants see a discrepancy between what they think the world ought to be (given present possibilities and constraints) and what the world actually is. This discrepancy produces individual behavior, which is aggregated into collective (organizational) action or choices. The outside world then "responds" to this choice in some way that affects individual assessments both of the state of the world and of the efficacy of the actions.

This conception of choice assumes a closed cycle of connections (Figure 1.0):

(1) The cognitions and preferences held by individuals affect their behavior.
(2) The behavior (including participation) of individuals affects organizational choices.
(3) Organizational choices affect environmental acts (responses).
(4) Environmental acts affect individual cognitions and preferences.

These basic ideas are fundamental to much of our understanding of decisions in organizations. Although frequently subject to criticism, the ideas are implicit in most ordinary conversations about organizations and about important events of policy making. They are the basis for many theoretical treatments, including our own. While we think this conception of choice illuminates choice situations significantly, we want to modify the details of that perspective and explore some specific limitations in a theory based on the closed sequence shown in Figure 1.0.

Figure 1.0. The Complete Cycle of Choice.

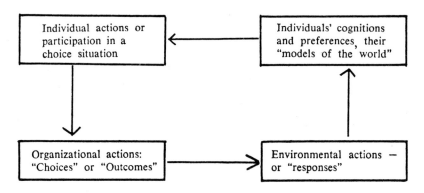

The limitations we will consider are of considerable significance under some situations, of little significance under others. The complete cycle of organizational choice assumes four simple relations. Each of those relations is obviously more complex than the closed cycle represents them to be. More importantly, they are more complex in ways that lead to systematic limitations in the theory. The limitations are particularly important when the cycle is incomplete, when one or more of the connections are broken or confounded by exogenous factors. Under such circumstances, we require a theory of organizational choice that recognizes the loose coupling. We consider each of the four relations, in turn.

1.1.0 Individual Beliefs and Individual Action

Most organization theory is purposive. It assumes that behavior and attention[2] follow belief and attitude. Beliefs and attitudes, in turn, are stable enough so that attention is stable over the course of a choice; and differential levels of attention are predictable from the content of the decision. Decision making activity thus stems from self-interest and is generally attractive so long as the resources being allocated are significant.

Our observations suggest a modification of this view.[3] Instead of stable activity levels we find that people move in and out of choice situations. There is considerable variation among individuals, and over time for the same individual, in terms of the degree and form of attention to decision problems. A step toward understanding this flow of attention, and its connection to individual beliefs and attitudes, is to note that time and energy are scarce resources.

Involvement in decisions is not attractive for everyone in all relevant choice situations, all the time. The capacity for beliefs, attitudes, and concerns is larger than the capacity for action. Under such circumstances, we will observe beliefs and values without behavioral implications. Even given the time and energy, there are alternative choice situations where an individual can present his concerns. The flow of attention will not depend on the content of a single choice alone, but upon the collection of choice situations available. We should not expect that a set of beliefs and preferences will have behavioral implications in any specific choice situation independent of the available claims on attention.

A theory that recognizes time as a scarce resource (Becker, 1965; Linder, 1970) makes attention contextual, subject to resource constraints and alternative "consumption" possibilities. Such a conception assumes some hierarchy of beliefs and preferences, and some hierarchy of choice situations in terms of attractiveness. Individuals are seen to allocate available energy by attending to choice situations with the highest expected return. They do not act in one arena because they are acting in another.

Although it clarifies some aspects of decision involvement, even this contextual version of the connection between values and action is problematic in an organization. It ignores the importance of roles, duties, and standard operating procedures for determining behavior; and it underestimates the ambiguity of self-interest.

Any complex social structure has considerable capability for weakening the connection between individual behavior and individual beliefs and preferences. The potential has produced some affective ambivalence. It has been celebrated as an important device in fighting personal favoritism and establishing equity and equality. It has been portrayed as a major source of organizational inertia preventing progress. Here we are not primarily concerned with a normative evaluation, but with the simple fact that roles, duties, and obligations are behaviorally important to involvement. People attend to decisions not only because they have an interest at stake, but because they are expected to or obliged to. They act according to rules.

Even when they act in self-interest terms, participants in organizations do not appear to act in a way fully anticipated by self-interest theories. They have an abundance of preferences and beliefs. The complexity increases as one moves from interest in immediate, substantive outcomes to long-term effects and to various side agendas (e.g., status) involved in a decision situation. The architecture of these values does not easily lend itself to description in terms of well-behaved preference functions. The behavior apparently stemming from the values proceeds without concern about that fact. Not all values are attended to at the same time; attention focus rather than utility, seems to explain much of the behavior (Cyert and March, 1963). At the same time, beliefs and preferences appear to be the results of behavior as much as they are the determinants of it. Motives and intentions are discovered post factum (March 1972).

We require a theory that takes into consideration the possibility that there may be attitudes and beliefs without behavioral implications, that there may be behavior without any basis in individual preferences, and that there may be an interplay between behavior and the definition (and redefinition) of "self-interest".

1.1.1 *Individual Action and Organizational Choice*

Organizational choices are ordinarily viewed as derivative of individual actions. A decision process transforms the behavior of individuals into something that could be called organizational action. Explorations into the nature of this "visible hand" comprise much of the literature; and most of the theoretical issues are questions of suitable metaphors for characterizing the process. It is sometimes captured by metaphors of deduction (organizational goals, sub-goals, efficiency); sometimes by metaphors of implicit conflict (markets, bureaucracy); sometimes by metaphors of explicit conflict (bargaining, political processes, power). Each of these metaphors accepts the basic notion that organizational choice is understandable as some consequence of individual action. They interpret organizations as instruments of individuals.

Our observations suggest that the connection between individual action and organizational action is sometimes quite loose. Sometimes we observe that the (internal) decision-making process is not strongly related to the organizational action, i.e., the policy selected, the price set, the man hired. Rather it is connected to the definition of truth and virtue in the organization, to the allocation of status, to the maintenance or change of friendship, goodwill, loyalty, and legitimacy; to the definition and redefinition of "group interest". In short, the formal decision-making process sometimes is directly connected to the maintenance or change of the organization as a social unit as well as to the accomplishment of making collective decisions and producing substantive results. A theory of organizational choice probably should attend to the interplay between these two aspects of the internal process.

Sometimes we observe a considerable impact on the process of the temporal flow of autonomous actions. We need a theory that considers the timing of different individual actions, and the changing context of each act. Most theories imply the importance of the context of an act. Typically, however, they have assumed that this context has stable properties that allow unconditional predictions. We observe a much more interactive, branching, and contextual set of connections among the participants, problems, and solutions in an organization.

Sometimes we observe an internal process swamped by external events of factors. Organizational action is conspicuously independent of internal process. The dramatic version – where some external actor intervenes directly, or where some external event completely changes the conditions under which the organization is operating, is well known. In a similar way, macro-theorists of social process rarely feel required to consider the details of organizational phenomena. Theories of the market or long-run social movements have identified important characteristics of the deep structure in which organizational phenomena occur; and it would be foolish for a theory of organizational choice situations not to recognize the extent to which the decision process is part of a broader stream of events. We need a theory of choice that articulates the connections between the environ-

16

mental context of organizations and their actions in such a way that neither is simply the residual unexplained variance for the other.

In general, we need a theory of organizational choice that considers the connection between individual actions and organizational actions sometimes as variable. Organizational action may be determined, or strongly contained, by external forces. Internal process may be related to other phenomena than the organizational choice (i.e., allocating status, defining organizational truth and virtue). The structure of the internal process may be highly time-dependent; changing contexts of the individual acts may produce organizational actions not anticipated or desired by anyone.

1.1.2 Organizational Choice and Environmental Response

The complete cycle of choice assumes a connection between organizational actions and environmental actions. The latter are treated as responses to the choices made in the organization.[4] The notion is a simple one. We assume that there is an enviroment with a schedule of responses to alternative actions on the part of the organization. Voters respond to party platforms or candidate images. Consumers respond to produce quality and price. Competitors respond to challenges. Students respond to curricula. Citizens respond to social experiments. Out of such a paradigm come many of our ideas about organizational learning and natural selection (Cohen and March, 1973; Winter, 1964).

We need a theory of the environment which is less organization centered, a theory where the actions and events in the environment sometimes may have little to do with what the organization does. Environmental acts frequently have to be understood in terms of relationships among events, actors, and structures in the environment, not as responses to what the organization does. As a result, the same organizational action will have different responses at different times; different organizational actions will have the same response. The world of the absurd is sometimes more relevant for our understanding of organizational phenomena than is the idea of a tight connection between action and response.

This independence of action and response is accentuated by our tendency to attempt to explain fine gradations in both. Organizations act within environmentally constrained boundaries. On the rare occasions on which they violate those constraints, the environment is likely to react unambiguously. Most of the time, however, the range of behavior is relatively small; and within that range very little of the variation in response is attributable to variations in the action. Insofar as we wish to explain variations in organizational behavior within the

17

range in which we observe it, we will require a theory that recognizes only a modest connection between environmental response and organizational decision.[5]

1.1.3 *Environmental Response and Individual Beliefs*

Classical theory offers two alternative versions of how environmental actions and events are connected to individual cognition. In the first version, the problem is assumed away. Organizational decision-makers are equipped with perfect information about alternatives and consequences. Since the full cycle is well understood ahead of any individual action there is no learning in the system. In the second version, the connection is understood in terms of a model of individual, rational adaption. Beliefs and models of the world are tied to reality through experience. Events are observed; the individual changes his beliefs on the basis of his experience; he improves his behavior on the basis of this feedback.

Our observations suggest a modification of this view. There is a need for introducing ideas about the process by which beliefs are constructed in an organizational setting. In many contexts the interpretation of an organizational choice process is as important as the immediate, substantive action we commonly consider.[6] Individuals, as well as organizations or nations, develop myths, fictions, legends, and illusions. They develop conflicts over myths and ideology. We need models of the development of belief which do not assume necessary domination by events or "objective reality".

Environmental actions and events frequently are ambiguous. It is not clear what happened, or why it happened. Ambiguity may be inherent in the events, or be caused by the difficulties participants have in observing them. The complexity of, and change in, the environment often overpower our cognitive capacity. Furthermore, our interpretations are seldom based only on our own observations; they rely heavily on the interpretations offered by others. Our trust in the interpretations are clearly dependent on our trust in the interpretors. The degree of ambiguity will be strongly dependent upon the efficiency of the channels through which interpretations are transmitted.

The elaboration of such a theory is particularly germane to the study of organizations. Much of what we know, or believe we know, is based on our interpretation of reports from participants. When we ask a participant to report what happened, we solicit his model of events. When we ask a participant to assess the relative power of various individuals or groups, we ask him to carry out a complex theoretical analysis (March, 1966). It is often true that participants differ in significant ways among themselves or differ in significant

18

ways from the interpretations that we, as outside observers, report. In order to sort out the complications of developing an understanding of participant reports, we need to understand the development of belief structures in an organization under conditions of ambiguity.

This review of some of the limitations of the complete cycle of choice suggests that we can develop some kinds of theories that attend to complications in the relations between individual beliefs and individual action, between individual action and organizational choice, between organizational choice and environmental response, and between environmental response and individual beliefs. Such theories exist in preliminary form already. What might distinguish their use in the study of organizational choice is their linkage to generate some understanding of their interactions in choice situations.

1.2 Reality, Intention, and Necessity

The limitations on the complete cycle of choice also suggest a series of possible confusions in our ordinary ideas about organizational events. The first potential confusion is to assume that what appeared to happen did happen. We do not need to accept a rigidly subjective interpretation of reality to concede that most of what we believe we know about events within organizational choice situations as well as the events themselves, reflects an interpretation of events by organizational actors and observers. Those interpretations are generated within the organization in the face of considerable perceptual ambiguity. Organizational action requires a model of the world. That model itself becomes of interest to us, along with the process by which it is developed and changed.

The second potential confusion is to assume that what happened was intended to happen. It is common to understand organizational actions in terms of intentions, either organizational or individual, to imagine that individuals have intentions and that those intentions are translated into action in a way that makes organizational action some product of individual or group will. Although not everyone gets his way, the primary reason one person fails to achieve an intended outcome is because it is inconsistent with someone else's intended outcome. Thus, choices within an organization are produced by preferences. If something happened, someone wanted it to happen. Different intentions will produce different outcomes. Better intentions will produce better outcomes. The converse position is three fold: First, the flow of individual actions produces a flow of decisions that is intended by no one and is not related in a direct way to anyone's desired outcomes. The process by which individual intentional behavior combines to produce organizational behavior is not one in which shifts in intentions will produce consistent shifts in organizational action. Indeed, much organizational behavior is dominated by rules that exist and are followed without significant impact of individual intentions. Second, individual intent and individual action are sometimes only loosely connected. Much individual behavior is less understandable as a consequence of individual preferences than as a pattern of duty and obligation. Third, the simple process of decision within an organization is often easily swamped by exogenous factors that are much more compelling than are the intentional actions of participants in the process.

The third potential confusion is to assume that what happened had to happen. The presumption is one of classical understanding. Because the objective is taken as explaining why a particular organizational (decision) outcome occurred, the observed events is treated as having an exceptional status relative to events that did not occur. Differences between an observed outcome and alternative possible, but not realized, outcomes are seen as fundamental. In our judgment, this idea is a mistake. Substantial differences in final outcomes are sometimes produced by small (and essentially unpredictable) differences in intermediate events leading to the outcomes. Lawful processes operate subject to essentially chance variation.[7] As a result, an interpretation of an event should include an interpretation of alternative events that could easily have occurred but did not.

All three potential confusions are particularly significant to the study of organizations because they affect both the methods of organizational research and the style of theory about organizations. If what is believed by participants in organizations is a construct subject to being understood in its own right, we require greater sophistication in understanding standard field data. The process by which people in an organization come to believe what they believe about organizational events is demonstrably powerful enough to confound any easy transmutation of beliefs into evidence for the phenomena to which they refer.

If we cannot assume that decision outcomes are necessarily intentional, we are in theoretical trouble. Most organization theories begin with some kind of presumption that individuals and groups pursue objectives and that organizational outcomes reflect that pursuit in some fairly self-evident way. Thus, we are directed to discover who the participants are, what their intentions, beliefs, and resources are. We are encouraged to see revealed preference techniques for identifying intentions or resource distribution techniques for identifying power not as definitional tautologies but as reflection of structure underlying an intentional process. To the extent to which the underlying process

20

is not intentional, the meaning and utility of such procedures shifts, as does our metaphor for understanding events.

If what happened is seen as only one of a number of things that might easily have happened, we require a different historical methodology. In common with most other historians, students of decisions tend to accept the convention that the precision of a realized outcome demonstrates a necessity in that outcome. Relatively few students of decision histories write those histories with an eye to alternative scenarios with prior likelihoods comparable to that of the observed events. The issue is, of course, not unique to studies of organizational decisions and includes a deep challenge to conventional ideology with respect to the relation between theory and data.

1.3 Conclusion

We remain in the tradition of viewing organizational participants as problem-solvers and decision-makers. However, we assume that individuals find themselves in a more complex, less stable, and less understood world than that described by standard theories of organizational choice; they are placed in a world over which they often have only modest control. Nevertheless, we assume organizational participants will try to understand what is going on, to activate themselves and their resources in order to solve their problems and move the world in desired directions. These attempts will have a less heroic character than assumed in the perfect cycle theories, but they will be real.

We have argued that any of the connections in the basic cycle of choice can be broken or changed so significantly as to modify the implications of the whole system. Intention does not control behavior precisely. Participation is not a stable consequence of properties of the choice situation or individual preferences. Outcomes are not a direct consequence of process. Environmental response is not always attributable to organizational action. Belief is not always a result of experience.

In addition, the cycle is frequently touched by exogenous factors outside the control of the internal process. The process is embedded in a larger system. Under relatively easily realized situations, any one of the connections may be overwhelmed by exogenous effects. External factors may dictate individual action without regard to individual learning, organizational action without regard to individual action, environmental action without regard to organizational action, or individual learning without regard to environmental action.

In order to respond to such concerns in a theory of organizations, we require three clusters of interrelated theoretical ideas:

First, we need a modified theory of organizational choice. Such a theory will need to be contextual in the sense that it reflects the ways in which the linkages in the complete cycle of choice are affected by exogenous events, by the timing of events, by the varieties of ways in which the participants wander onto and off the stage. It will need to be structural in the sense that it reflects ways in which stabilities can arise in a highly contextual system. We have tried to suggest the basis for such a theory elsewhere (Cohen, March, and Olsen, 1972).

Second, we need a theory of organizational attention. Such a theory should treat the allocation of attention by potential participants as problematic. Where will they appear? What are the structural limits on their decision activity? How do they allocate time within those limits? Such a theory must attend to the elements of rational choice in attention allocation, to the importance of learning to the modification of attention rules, and to the norms of obligation that affect individual attention to alternative organizational concerns. We have attempted to indicate an outline to such a theory in a forthcoming article.

Third, we need a theory of learning under conditions of organizational ambiguity. The complete cycle is implicitly a theory of learning. What happens when the cycle is incomplete? What is a possible perspective on the development and change of belief structures?

As we pursue these ideas, we will elaborate a number of themes that are familiar to readers of the modern literature on organizational choice. The work we report has a parentage. We owe a particular debt to Allison (1969), Coleman (1957), Cohen and March (1973), Crecine (1969), Cyert and March (1963), Edelman (1960), Heider (1958), Hirschman (1970), Jacobsen (1964), Lindblom (1965), Long (1958), March and Simon (1958), Schilling (1968), Steinbruner (1974), Stinchcombe (1974), Thompson (1967), Vickers (1965), and Weick (1969). Our intentions are conservative. We wish to continue a course of theoretical development, as illuminated by a series of studies of organizational choice situations.

NOTES:

1 This section draws heavily on March and Olsen (1975).
2 The concept of participation is broad. We will use it with reference to activities like seeking information, discussing, proselyting, attending meetings, voting, making speeches, campaigning and competing for offices, with no references

to the motivation for or the effect of the activities. The central criterion thus becomes presence or attendance.

3 Modifications have been suggested by a rather broad range of people. Weick (1969, p. 29) notes that the assumption in organization theory "that once the perceptions of organization members are affected, action consistent with these perceptions will follow automatically" has not been affected by recent work by psychologists interested in how beliefs and values get translated into action. Both Weick (ibid.) and Bem (1970) argue for theories assuming that cognition follows action. The primacy of behavior or praxis over ideas or theory is a classical theme in Marxist theory. Often the point of departure is the statement that life is not determined by consciousness, but consciousness by life (Marx and Engels, 1970. However, the debate between marxists and non-marxists has to some degree detracted attention from the debate among marxists on the role of ideas as a driving force in history. Ibsen reflected some of the complexity when he had Peer Gynt say (on observing a man chopping off a finger to avoid being drafted): "The thought, perhaps — the wish — the will. Those I could understand, but really to do the dead! Ah, no — that astounds me."

4 There are two versions of the theory: The strong organization making the environment adapt to its decisions, and the weak organization being "conditioned" by the environment.

5 Participants in an organization are likely, under a variety of circumstances, to see the connection between action and response as tighter than it is. As a result, one of the major phenomena that we will need to comprehend is superstitious learning within organizations.

6 Vickers (1965, p. 15) is interested in both these two outcomes of choices: "events" and "ideas". He views the Royal Commissions as units which seldom are supposed to make direct choices, but to affect opinions and conceptions or "the appreciative setting" of a certain phenomenon.

7 The idea that some processes may be understandable only up to some distribution is a familiar one. It permeates much of modern physics, biology, and economics. What distinguishes the fields in which it is common is the extent to which they have substantial opportunities to study aggregate effects empirically. Much of the study of organizational decision making is closer to history or clinical practice. The data are more likely to take the form of individual outcomes. In such fields the inclination is strong to treat the outcome as understandable in itself rather than as an instance in a distribution. Yet, it seems unlikely that nature has so neatly divided the phenomena as to ensure that only those processes that generate large numbers of observations are subject to incomplete understanding.

2. People, Problems, Solutions and the Ambiguity of Relevance

MICHAEL D. COHEN
University of Michigan

JAMES G. MARCH
Stanford University

JOHAN P. OLSEN
University of Bergen

2.0 Introduction

As we have observed in Chapter 1, the complete cycle of choice assumes some relatively straight-forward procedure by which individual preferences and cognitions are aggregated into organizational choices. The postulated procedures may be bureaucratic-administrative. By a bureaucratic-administrative procedure we mean some process by which problems are solved. Relevant solutions are associated with appropriate problems and choices are made in order to resolve problems. Alternatively, the postulated procedures may be bargaining-political. By a bargaining-political procedure we mean a process by which coalitions are formed and political bargains struck. Choices are made by forming a group with sufficient power to enforce a joint solution to a problem.

Both procedures assume that criteria of relevance are clear. What issues and solutions are associated with what decisions, and what people participate in what decisions are assumed to be relatively unproblematic. In the case of bureaucratic-administrative procedures, we assume that objectives can be stated reasonably precisely, that a technology associating alternatives with outcomes is reasonably well-known, and that there is a reasonably stable division of labor by which certain individuals and groups specialize in certain decisions. In the case of bargaining-political procedures, we assume that the preferences of the individual participants are reasonably well-specified, that the structure of the political game is reasonably clear, and that participation and power are reasonably stable.

Clear criteria of relevance in decision making tend to make the outcomes of decisions independent of the micro structure of the broader context within which they occur. Clear criteria of what alternatives or solutions are appropriately associated with what problems, and what problems are appropriately associated with what choices, what people appropriately participate in what choices, and what the appropriate distribution of power is all serve to buffer a particular choice from its context. Such criteria provide a tight linkage of choices, problems, solutions, and people.

Although relevance criteria may be quite precise within a decision context, they often are not. In particular, we often have underestimated the extent to which choice situations in organizations involve problematic goals, unclear technologies, and fluid participation.[1]

Preferences are often problematic. It is difficult to impute a set of preferences to the decision situation that satisfies the standard consistency requirements for a theory of choice. The organization operates on the basis of a variety of inconsistent and ill-defined preferences. It can be described better as a loose collection of ideas than as a coherent structure. Preferences are discovered through action as much as being the basis of action.

Technology is often unclear. Although the organization manages to survive and even produce, its own processes are not understood by its members. It operates on the basis of simple trial-and-error procedures, the residue of learning from the accidents of past experience, and pragmatic inventions of necessity.

Participation is often fluid. Participants vary in the amount of time and effort they devote to different domains; involvement varies from one time to another. As a result, the boundaries of the organization are uncertain and changing; the audiences and decision makers for any particular kind of choice change capriciously. No single participant dominates the choice in all its phases.

These three properties have been identified often in studies of organizations. They are characteristic of any organization in part – part of the time. They are particularly conspicuous in public, educational, and illegitimate organizations. Although a college or public organization operates within the metaphor of a political system or a hierarchical bureaucracy, the actual operation of either is considerably attenuated by the ambiguity of goals, by the lack of clarity in technology, and by the transient character of many participants.

A theme running through some recent studies of organizational decisions (Cohen, March, and Olsen, 1972; Cohen and March, 1973) is that choices are fundamentally ambiguous. An organization is a set of procedures for argumentation and interpretation as well as for solving problems and making decisions. A choice situation is a meeting place for issues and feelings looking for decision situations in which they may be aired, solutions looking for issues to which they may be an answer, and participants looking for problems or pleasure.

Such a view focuses attention on the ways in which the meaning of choice changes over time. It calls attention to the strategic effects of timing (in the introduction of choices and problems), the time pattern of availably energy, and the impact of organizational structure and external demands on these. It emphasizes the ambiguity of decision relevance.

When relevance becomes ambiguous, events within choice situations become more context-dependent. What happens in the situation of interest to a student of choice depends on how that situation (and the participants in it) fit into a mosaic of simultaneous performances involving other individuals, other places, other concerns, and the phasing of other events. What happens is often the almost fortuitous result of the intermeshing of loosely-coupled processes.

In this chapter we describe a model of such a decision world. It attempts to capture some of the features of organizational behavior that appear as pathologies within familiar notions of choice and tries to make them understandable in theoretical terms. We call the ideas a garbage can model of organizational choice.

2.1 Garbage Can Decision Processes

Suppose we view a choice opportunity as a garbage can into which various problems and solutions are dumpted by participants. The mix of garbage in a single can depends partly on the labels attached to the alternative cans; but it also depends on what garbage is being produced at the moment, on the mix of cans available, and on the speed with which garbage is collected and removed from the scene.

Although choice opportunities may lead first to the generation of decision alternatives, then to an examination of the consequences of those alternatives, then to an examination of the consequences in terms of objectives, and finally to a decision, such a model is often a poor description of what actually happens. In a garbage can situation, a decision is an outcome or an interpretation of several relatively independent "streams" within an organization.

We will limit our attention to the interrelations among four such streams:

1. *Problems.* Problems are the concern of people inside and outside the organization. They arise over issues of lifestyle; family; frustrations of work; careers; group relations within the organization; distribution of status, jobs, and money; ideology; or current crises of mankind as interpreted by the mass media or the nextdoor neighbor. All require attention. Problems are, however, distinct from choices; and they may not be resolved when choices are made.

2. *Solutions.* A solution is somebody's product. A computer is not just a solution to a problem in payroll management, discovered when needed. It is an answer actively looking for a question. The creation of need is not solely a curiosity of the market in consumer products;

it is a general phenomenon of processes of choice. Despite the dictum that you cannot find the answer until you have formulated the question, you often do not know the question in organizational problem solving until you know the answer.

3. *Participants.* Participants come and go. Since every entrance is an exit somewhere else, the distribution of "entrances" depends on the attributes of the choice being left as much as it does on the attributes of the new choice. Substantial variation in participation stems from other demands on the participants' time (rather than from features of the decision under study).

4. *Choice opportunities.* These are occasions when an organization is expected to produce behavior that can be called a decision. Opportunities arise regularly and any organization has ways of declaring an occasion for choice. Contracts must be signed; people hired, promoted, or fired; money spent; and responsibilities allocated.

Although the streams are not completely independent of each other an organizational choice is a somewhat fortuitous confluence. It is a highly contextual event, depending substantially on the pattern of flows in the several streams. The assumptions that streams are independent and exogenous may be relaxed. Weiner views participants as "carriers" of problems and solutions and discusses the implications of such a modification of the theory (Chapter 11). Christensen (Chapter 16) and Kreiner (Chapter 8) discuss the origins of the four streams and the need for making them a part of the model.

We have focused our primary attention on the consequences of different rates and patterns of flows in each of the streams and different procedures for relating them. The streams of problems, choice opportunities, solutions, and participants are channelled by organizational and social structure. Elements of structure influence outcomes of a garbage can decision process (a) by affecting the time pattern of the arrival of problems, choices, solutions, or decision makers, (b) by determining the allocation of energy by potential participants in the decision, and (c) by establishing linkages among the various streams.

2.2 Organizational Structure

We focus on those aspects of organizational structure that specify rights to participate in a choice opportunity. Such rights are necessary, but not sufficient, for actual involvement in a decision.[2] They can be viewed as invitations to participation. Invitations that may or may not be accepted. In our terms, invitations may be extended either to individuals as decision-makers or to problems and solutions as decision issues. In the former case we talk about the decision structure; in the latter of the access structure.

The decision structure is a mapping of individuals on choice opportunities (or classes of choice opportunities). If we have N potential participants and M classes of choices, then the decision structure is an N–by–M array which shows for every possible participant the choices in which he has a claim to participate (See Cohen, March, and Olsen, 1972). For the simple case in which we assume that each individual either has such a right or does not, there are a larger number (2^{NM}) of possible structures.

Although the number of possible decision structures is large and no simple set of structures will capture the complexity of actual cases, we can identify three major modes of organizing participation rights.

Unsegmented participation. In this structure any decision maker can participate in any active choice opportunity. Thus, the structure is represented by the following array (in which $d_{ij} = 1$ if the *i*th individual can participate in the *j*th choice opportunity):

$$D_0 = \begin{array}{l} 1111111111 \\ 1111111111 \\ 1111111111 \\ 1111111111 \\ 1111111111 \\ 1111111111 \\ 1111111111 \\ 1111111111 \\ 1111111111 \\ 1111111111 \end{array}$$

Hierarchical participation. In this structure both decision makers and choices are arranged in a hierarchy such that important choices must be made by important decision makers and important decision makers can participate in many choices. The structure is represented by the following array:

$$D_1 = \begin{array}{l} 1111111111 \\ 0111111111 \\ 0011111111 \\ 0001111111 \\ 0000111111 \\ 0000011111 \\ 0000001111 \\ 0000000111 \\ 0000000011 \\ 0000000001 \end{array}$$

Specialized participation. In this structure each decision maker is associated with a single choice and each choice has a single decision maker. Decision makers specialize in the choices to which they attend. Thus we have the following array:

$$D_2 = \begin{matrix}
1000000000 \\
0100000000 \\
0010000000 \\
0001000000 \\
0000100000 \\
0000010000 \\
0000001000 \\
0000000100 \\
0000000010 \\
0000000001
\end{matrix}$$

Actual decision structures will require a more complicated array. Most organizations have a mix of rules for defining the rights of participation in decisions. The three pure cases are, however, familiar models of such rules and can be used to understand some consequences of decision structure for decision processes.

A parallel set of observations can be made about the access structure; i.e., the rules that specify the rights of access of problems and solutions to choice opportunities.

Unsegmented access. This structure is represented by an access array in which any active problem (or solution) has access to any active choice opportunity ($a_{ij} = 1$ if the ith problem (solution) has access to the jth choice opportunity).

$$A_0 = \begin{matrix}
1111111111 \\
1111111111 \\
1111111111 \\
1111111111 \\
1111111111 \\
1111111111 \\
1111111111 \\
1111111111 \\
1111111111 \\
1111111111 \\
1111111111 \\
1111111111 \\
1111111111 \\
1111111111 \\
1111111111
\end{matrix}$$

```
1111111111
1111111111
1111111111
1111111111
1111111111
```

Hierarchical access. In this structure both choices and problems (solutions) are arranged in a hierarchy such that important problems (solutions) have access to many choices, and important choices are accessible only to important problems. The structure is represented by the following access array:

$$A_1 = \begin{array}{l}
1111111111 \\
1111111111 \\
0111111111 \\
0111111111 \\
0011111111 \\
0011111111 \\
0001111111 \\
0001111111 \\
0000111111 \\
0000111111 \\
0000011111 \\
0000011111 \\
0000001111 \\
0000001111 \\
0000000111 \\
0000000111 \\
0000000011 \\
0000000011 \\
0000000001 \\
0000000001
\end{array}$$

Specialized access. In this structure each problem (solution) has access to only one choice and each choice is accessible to only two problems (solutions, that is, choices specialize in the kinds of problems (solutions) that can be associated to them. The structure is represented by the following access array:

```
1000000000
1000000000
0100000000
0100000000
0010000000
```

$$A_2 = \begin{matrix} 0010000000 \\ 0001000000 \\ 0001000000 \\ 0000100000 \\ 0000100000 \\ 0000010000 \\ 0000010000 \\ 0000001000 \\ 0000001000 \\ 0000000100 \\ 0000000100 \\ 0000000010 \\ 0000000010 \\ 0000000001 \\ 0000000001 \end{matrix}$$

Actual organizations will exhibit a more complex mix of access rules. Any such combination could be represented by an appropriate access array. The three pure structures considered here represent three classic alternative approaches to the problem of organizing the access of problems to decision situations.

Thus, we may imagine organizational structures varying from unsegmented to highly segmented. In the first case the connections of the four streams are simply a function of timing. Choices, problems, solutions, and energies exist in a time-frame. Choice opportunities become defined by the problems and solutions present at the moment. Problems "choose" among currently available choices. Decision-makers distribute their time and energy to choices and problems in a "fire station» manner (Cyert and March, 1963). In a world in which there is any scarcity in one or more of the streams, the timing of the several flows will affect the outcome importantly.

The complete absence of any segmentation is rare. Both organizations and societies at large seem to change as a result of experience and intention. Problems come to seek connections to choice-opportunities that solve them, solutions come to seek problems they handle successfully. Decision-makers use their energy in areas in which they have success, or about which they have concern, or in which they find pleasure. There is societal segmentation. Even the simplest societies order or institutionalize the four streams somewhat, organizing roles that predominantly deal with specified types of problems in terms of specified solutions.

The same process is observable in organizations. Organizations regulate connections among problems, choice opportunities, solutions, and energy by administrative practice. Hierarchy, specialization, the distribution of information, agenda-building, and the allocation of authority are all devices for regulating the connections among the four streams, and for avoiding unexpected connections between choice opportunities, problems, solutions, and energy. Since an organization can attend to only a limited part of available information, attempts are made to invent mechanisms for increasing sensitivity to some kinds of information and insensitivity to others. Organizational mechanisms are developed for ascribing meaning, relevance, and priority to different types of inputs. Through classifications, categorizations, and recordings, organizations try to provide stability in the ways events are observed, evaluated, interpreted, and combined.

Regulation of the four streams through intention, learning, and segmentation are not mutually exclusive. Segmentation emphasizes the structural rights of participants, problems, solutions; learning and intention address the question whether choice opportunities are attractive for participants, problems, and solutions. In most choice situations we have to consider both aspects.

The less the organizational regulation of the four streams, the less the experience with the situation, and the higher the load on participants, the more important the timing of the four streams for a decision process and its outcome. That is, the process and the outcome will be affected less by the type and character of the choice opportunity than by the problems, solutions, energy, and other choice opportunities present in the same time period. We will experience new and unexpected relationships among the four streams. The opposite will be true in the established bureaucracy with strong organizational devices for connections between the four streams; here the timing mechanism will be of lesser importance for the process and outcome, but very important for the "climate" in the school. Problems become piled up because they cannot be excused in connection with a choice.

Organizational structure is a result of deliberate planning, individual and collective learning, and imitation. These change as a response to such factors as market demands for personnel, the heterogeneity of values, and the distribution of relevant resources. As a result, we need to attend not only to the implications of given structures but also to the conditions that produce one or another. For the most part, this book is concerned with the first question, although we touch on the second in Chapter 3.

2.3 Implications

Elsewhere (Cohen, March, and Olsen, 1972) we have detailed the development of these basic ideas into a computer model which has been examined under conditions simulating a variety of different organizational structures. The garbage can model of choice operates under each of the hypothesized organization structures to assign problems and decision makers to choices, to determine the energy required and effective energy applied to choices, to make such choices and resolve such problems as the assignments and energies indicate are feasible.

For each condition we have computed five simple summary statistics to describe the process:

1. *Decision style.* Within a garbage can process, decisions are made in three different ways:
   (a) By *oversight*. If a choice is activated when problems are attached to other choices and if there is energy available to make the new choice quickly, it will be made without any attention to existing problems and with minimum of time and energy.
   (b) By *flight*. In some cases, choices are associated with problems (unsuccessfully) for some time until a choice "more attractive" to the problems comes along. The problems leave the choice, and thereby make it possible to make the decision. The decision resolves no problems (they having now attached themselves to a new choice).
   (c) By *resolution*. Some choices resolve problems after some period of working on them. The length of time may vary greatly (depending on the number of problems). This is the familiar case that is implicit in most discussions of choice within organizations.

   Some choices involve both flight and resolution (i.e., some problems leave, the remainder are solved). We have defined these as resolution, thus slightly exaggerating the importance of that style. As a result of that convention, the three styles are mutually exclusive and exhaustive with respect to any one choice: but the same organization may use any one of them on different choices. Thus, we can describe the decision-making style of the organization by specifying the proportion of completed choices that are made in each of these three ways.
2. *Problem activity.* We wish to find some measure of the degree to which problems are active within the organization. Such a measure should reflect something of the degree of conflict within the organization or the degree of articulation of problems. We have used the total number of time periods that a problem is active and attached to some choice, summed over all problems.
3. *Problem latency.* A problem may be active but not attached to

any choice. It may be recognized and accepted by some part of the organization but may not be considered germane to any available choice opportunity. Presumably an organization with relatively high problem latency will exhibit somewhat different symptoms from one with low latency. We have measured problem latency by the total number of periods that a problem is active but not attached to a choice, summed over all problems.

4. *Decision maker activity.* To measure the degree of decision maker activity in the system, we require some measure that reflects decision maker energy expenditure, movement, and persistence. We have computed the total number of times that any decision maker shifts from one choice to another.

5. *Decision difficulty.* We want to be able to characterize the ease with which a system makes decisions. Because of the way in which decisions can be made in the system (see the discussion above of decision style), this is not the same as the level of problem activity. We have used, as a measure, the total number of periods that a choice is active, summed over all choices.

These summary statistics,[3] along with a more intensive look at the individual histories of the simulations, reveal eight major properties of garbage can decision processes.

First, resolution of problems is not the most common style for making decisions except under conditions where flight is severely restricited or under a few conditions of light load. Decision making by flight and oversight is a major feature of the process in general. The behavioral and normative implications of a decision process that appears to make choices in large part by the "flight" of problems or by oversight may be particulary important for university presidents to consider.

Second, the process is thoroughly and generally sensitive to variations in load. An increase in the net energy load on the system generally increases problem activity, decision maker activity, decision difficultly, and the uses of flight and oversight. Problems are less likely to be solved, decision makers are likely to shift from one problem to another more frequently, choices are likely to take longer to make and to be less likely to resolve problems.

Third, decision makers and problems tend to track each other through choices. Both decision makers and problems tend to move together from choice to choice. As a result, decision makers may be expected to feel that they are always working on the same problems in somewhat different contexts, mostly without results. Problems, in a similar fashion, meet the same people wherever they go with the same result.

34

Fourth, there are some important interconnections among three key aspects of the "efficiency" of the decision processes we have specified. The first of these is problem activity, the amount of time unresolved problems are actively attached to choice situations. Problem activity is a rough measure of potential for decision conflict in the organization. It assesses the degree of involvement of problems in choices. The second aspect is problem latency, the amount of time that problems spend activated but not linked to choices. The third aspect is decision time – the persistence of choices. Presumably, a good organizational structure would keep both problem activity and problem latency low through rapid problem solution in its choices. In the garbage can process we never observe this. Some structures reduce the number of unresolved problems active in the organization but at the cost of increasing the latency period of problems and (in most cases) the time devoted to reaching decisions. Other structures decrease problem latency, but at the cost of increasing problem activity and decision time.

Fifth, the decision-making process is frequently sharply interactive. Although some phenomena associated with the garbage can are regular and flow through nearly all of the cases (for example, the effect of overall load), other phenomena are much more dependent on the particular combination of structures involved. In fact, the process is one that often looks capricious to an observer. Many of the outcomes are produced by distinct consequences of the particular time phasing of choices, problems, and participant availability.

Sixth, important problems are more likely to be solved than unimportant ones. Early-arriving problems are more likely to be resolved then later ones. The system, in effect produces a queue of problems in terms of their importance – to the strong disadvantage of late-arriving, relatively unimportant problems, particularly when load is heavy. This queue is the result of the operation of the model. It was not imposed as a direct assumption.

Seventh, important choices are much *less* likely to resolve problems than are unimportant choices. Important choices are made by oversight and flight. Unimportant choices are made by resolution. The differences are substantial. Moreover, they are not connected to the entry times of the choices. We believe this property of important choices in a garbage can decision process can be naturally and directly related to the phenomenon in complex organizations of "important" choices that often appear to just "happen".

Eight, although a large proportion of the choices are made, the choice failures that do occur are concentrated among the most important and least important choices. Choices of intermediate importance are virtually always made.

In a broad sense, these features of the decision-making process provide some clues to how organizations survive when they do not know what they are doing. Much of the process violates standard notions of how decisions ought to be made. But most of those notions are built on assumptions that cannot be met under the conditions we have specified. When objectives and technologies are unclear, organizations are charged to discover some alternative decision procedures that permit them to proceed without doing violence to the domains of participants or to their model of an organization. It is a difficult charge, to which the process we have described is a partial response. The detail of the outcomes clearly depend both on features of the organizational structure and on properties of the four streams. The same decision process results in different designs of the structure of organization.

The garbage can process, as it has been observed, is one in which problems, solutions and participants move from one choice opportunity to another in such a way that the nature of the choice, the time it takes, and the problems it solves all depend on a relatively complicated intermeshing of the mix of choices available at any one time, the mix of problems that have access to the organization, the mix of solutions looking for problems, and the outside demands on the decision makers.

Although we have treated the four streams as exogenous for most of our discussion, it should be clear that we view the understanding of the lawful processes determining the flows of those streams as fundamental to understanding what is happening in organizational choice situations. The more complete social theory into which these ideas would be embedded would include ideas on how demographic, social, economic, and political processes affect the extent to which different groups are successful in formulating and diffusing problems and solutions, how the agenda (in terms of choice opportunities) of an organization emerge, and how the distribution of participation in one social institution is related to the distribution in another. While some aspects of some of these issues are dealt with in some of our case studies (Chapter 7, 11, 12, 16), the linkage invites more work.

A major feature of the garbage can process is the partial decoupling of problems and choices. Although we normally think of decision making as a process for solving problems, that is often not what happens. Problems are worked upon in the context of some choice, but choices are made only when the shifting combinations of problems, solutions, and decision makers happen to make action possible. Quite commonly this is after problems have left a given choice arena or before they have discovered it (decisions by flight or oversight).

Though the specification of the model is quite simple the interaction within it is rather complex, so that investigation of the probable behavior of a system fully characterized by the garbage can process and our specifications requires computer simulation. We acknowledge immediately that no real system can be fully characterized in this way. Nonetheless, the simulated organizations exhibit behaviors which can be observed some of the time in almost all organizations and frequently in some, such as universities. The garbage can model is a possible step toward seeing the systematic interrelatedness of organizational phenomena which are familiar, even common, but which have generally been regarded as isolated and pathological. Measured against a conventional normative model of rational choice, the garbage can process does seem pathological, but such standards are not really appropriate since the process occurs precisely when the preconditions of more "normal" rational models are not met.

It is clear that the garbage can process does not do a particularly good job of resolving problems. But it does enable choices to be made and problems sometimes to be resolved even when the organization is plagued with goal ambiguity and conflict, with poorly understood problems that wander in and out of the system, with a variable environment, and with decision makers who may have other things on their minds. This is no mean achievement.

We would argue that there is a large class of significant situations within organizations in which the preconditions of the garbage can process probably cannot be eliminated. Indeed in some they should not be eliminated. The great advantage of trying to see garbage can phenomena together as a process is the possibility that that process can be understood, that organization design and decision making can take account of its existence and that, to some extent, it can be managed.

Finally, it should be observed that although the processes within the garbage can are understandable and in some ways predictable, events are not dominated by intention. The processes and the outcomes are likely to appear to have no close relation with the explicit intention of actors. In situations in which load is heavy and the structure is relatively unsegmented, intention is lost in context dependent flow of problems, solutions, people, and choice opportunities. Indeed, outcomes are frequently sufficiently dependent on elements of exogenously determined timing as to make the differences between what happens and what does not happen deceptively significant.

NOTES:

1 The ideas here draw heavily on Cohen, March, and Olsen (1972).
2 Such a precise statement is, of course, something of a heroic simplification. Rights themselves are almost always conditional and can only be approximated by statements of the form: "Smith has a right to participate in decisions about advertising expenditures."
3 For a discussion of alternative measures, see Cohen, March, and Olsen (1972).

3. Attention and the Ambiguity of Self-interest

JAMES G. MARCH
Stanford University

JOHAN P. OLSEN
University of Bergen

3.0 Introduction

The garbage can model of choice (Chapter 2) suggests a few of the reasons why a theory of organizational choice must attend to the problem of participant attention. Who is attending to what and when become critical features of most of the studies in this book. In this chapter we explore how attention is allocated under conditions of ambiguity.

Individual variations in involvement or activation are, of course, a familiar subject of concern in the study of political and social systems. Analysis of the relation between potential power and activation are important elements of the literature, as is the description of structural or personal limitations on activation. Most students of organizations limit consideration to variations in attention that are stable consequences of properties of the individuals involved, the organization, or the particular decision of interest. Assumptions of stability in the patterns of variation permit a relatively simple theoretical accommodation to variations in attention. For example, in order to use standard ideas of power within an organization, we ordinarily need to make some kind of assumption about stability in attention rates to avoid having the concept of power become intolerably underidentified (March, 1966).

With respect to individuals, some observers note that activity levels for individuals having considerable information about the system are quite different from the levels of those having little information, and that these variations in attention have an impact on the decisions of the organization. Other observers suggest that individuals are arrayed in natural interest groups (in terms of social class, organizational position, etc.) and that although individual attention may be variable, the overall rate for a particular interest group is stable over time.

With respect to organizations, one observation is that position within a hierarchy regulates access to decisions and information, and that attention patterns depend on both. More subtle are the relations between the distribution of decision attention within an organization and the size of the organization, or its age.

With respect to the decision involved, individuals seem to specialize in their attention. Different groups are represented when the discussion turns on budgets from the case when it turns on athletics. Major policy decisions involve a different group from decisions on minor matters.

We believe such observations and theories are useful. Much of the work reported in the volume, however, emphasizes the impact of more complicated variations in participation rates and patterns. We want to understand why people flow in and out of specific choice situations; to explain the frequent observation of non-participation by interested parties; to clarify why established leaders and "powerful people" often do not lead or even attend, while people who seem to be rather peripheral have considerable impact on a choice; and to examine the extent to which the micro structure of attention affects the flow of events.

If we can achieve such understandings, they will be a base for modeling the complexities of highly interactive flows of attention, problems, solutions, and choice situations (Cohen, March, and Olsen, 1972). Once we can model those situations, we can attempt to explore the ways in which the distribution of attention affects the resulting distribution of decisions. It is an ambitious perspective, but it has a few simple beginnings.

The empirical focus is deceptively mundane: The study of time and attention budgets (Stinchcombe, 1974). How do individuals in organizations allocate scarce attention? What do executives do (Mintzberg, 1973; Cohen and March, 1974; Glenn, 1975)? What do ordinary citizens do with their time (Szalai, 1972)? Where are the participants who might have been somewhere else (Weiner, 1973; Peterson, 1975). The deceptiveness lies in the necessity of developing not only the aggregate statistics of time and attention budgets, but also some explanation of the process.

We will distinguish two major components of such an explanation:

First, there is a set of structural constraints on the allocation of attention. Not everything is allowed. The written and unwritten rules of an organization specify who is allowed or required to attend to what and when.

Second, there is a pattern of individual action within the constraints. The structural constraints limit, but do not ordinarily completely specify, the patterns of attention. There are behavioral variations within the constraints.

In the remainder of this chapter we consider some elementary bases for a theory of attention under ambiguity organized in terms of these components of explanation.

3.1 Attention Structures

Attention is regulated by rules. Rules specify who is permitted to attend to a particular choice and who is required to do so; when a decision may be made and when it must be; which factors may be considered relevant and which must be. The rules may be formalized in organizational operating procedures. They may be embedded in statutes. They may be informal norms about legitimate decision procedures. Although they may be unclear in some cases, attention rules are conspicuous features of any choice situation.

In Chapter 2 we described one variety of these rules in terms of access structures that regulate the flow of problems and solutions to choice situations and decision structures that regulate the flow of people. Here we will use the more general term of attention structures to refer to any general set of authoritative rules within which attention behavior occurs. The rules may, as in the case of the access and decision rules described in Chapter 2, specify *upper* limits on attention. Such rules indicate who *may* attend to what, what problems may be attached to what choice, what solutions may be appropriate for which problem. They are permissive in the sense that they exclude some things but do not require anything. Alternatively, the rules may specify *lower* limits on attention, indicating what *must* happen. In the discussion below we will refer to attention structures generally to include cases of both upper and lower limits on attention, distinguishing them when necessary.[1]

As we did in the case of access and decision structures, we will refer to three pure types of attention patterns:

(1) *Unsegemented* structures, where restrictions on attention are homogeneous. In the case of upper limits, anyone may attend to anything, any problems may be attached to any choice, any solution may be appropriate for any problem. In the case of lower limits, everyone must attend to everything, every problem must be attached to every choice, every solution is appropriate for every problem.

(2) *Specialized* structures, where attention is segmented by a partitioning of individuals, choices, problems, and solutions. Some individuals may (or must) attend to some choices, others attend to others. Some problems may (or must) be attached to some choices, others are attached to others. Some solutions may (or must) be viewed as appropriate for some problems, others are appropriate for others.

(3) *Hierarchical* structures, where attention is segmented by a ranking of individuals, choices, problems, and solutions. Low

ranking people may (or must) attend to low ranking choices, while high ranking people may (or must) attend to anything. Low ranking problems may (or must) be attached only to low ranking choices, while high ranking problems may (or must) be attached to any. Low ranking solutions may (or must) be appropriate only for low ranking problems, while high ranking solutions may (or must) be appropriate for anything.

Actual structures will, of course, only approximate these pure types, but they are convenient for our discussion and will permit us to illustrate the major points we wish to make.

The attention structure is important. In a highly segmented structure it may effectively determine major features of the outcomes. For the most part, however, the structure interacts with the way in which individuals and groups exercise participation rights. Individuals engage in decision making. Sometimes they fail to participate even though they are legitimately able to do so. As a result, an understanding of the impact of participation on decisions requires an analysis of how individuals come to the choice situation. Given that they are allowed to be present, when will they be there?

Such questions have different kinds of significance for the different kinds of decision structures. In a highly specialized decision structure, the main consequence of the fact that the right to participate is not always exercised is variation in the time it takes to make a decision. Since only a limited number of individuals can take part in the decision, it will ultimately be made by them; but when it will be made depends on the way in which such individuals allocate their time. Alternatively, if decision time becomes too long, there may be attempts to change existing structures, through a reclassification of problems or participants toward desegmentation.

In a hierarchical decision structure, important decisions (i.e., those only few can attend to) are affected in much the same way as the specialized decisions above. Variation in time allocation results in variation in time spent but not in the values, attitudes, and information brought by participants to the decision. The same individuals will be involved – when they get around to it or structural changes may be proposed. Relatively unimportant decisions, on the other hand, are affected both in timing and in substantive outcome by the allocation of attention to them. Since many different people have the right to participate in them, the mix of participants who engage in the decision, and the mix of problems, will influence considerably the outcome.

The unsegmented decision structure has the same general properties as the unimportant decisions in a hierarchical structure. Since the choices are legitimate arenas for many people, individual time allocation decisions will have considerable impact on outcomes. Typically the attention structure is partly imposed on the organization by its environment, partly adopted consciously within the organization, and partly learned from experience. Attention rules are o modern organizational form of a classic problem in political philosophy, the problem of representation (Pitkin, 1967). In that tradition, we seek to understand the instrumental justification for a particular set of attention rules by asking three broad questions: Why should there be collective decision making? If there is to be collective decision making, why should participation in it be regulated by rules (rather than, for example, by individual decision)? If there are to be rules, what justifies one set of rules rather than another? Since our present interest is not in political philosophy, *per se,* but in understanding organizational behavior, we will limit our attention to asking whether the philosophical justification for political differentiation might help predict variations in the form of attention structures in organizations.

In general, the instrumental justification for governance assumes that there are some costs to any formal system and thus that in order to justify an attention structure one must specify some important benefits to be gained vis-a-vis an alternative of having no collective decision or no regulation of participation in collective decision making. We can identify three major considerations that are familiar to political philosophy and also appear to have behavioral implications:

(1) *Inderdependencies.* To what extent do the actions of one individual or group affect the values of others? For example, the individual instructional decisions of a teacher of introductory mathematics affect the capabilities of a teacher of advanced mathematics to do what he wants more than do the individual instructional decisions of a teacher of introductory sociology; the individual decisions of the foreign ministry and the ministry of war mutually more interdependent than either set is with the decisions of the ministry of culture. The greater the interdependency of individual actions, the greater the likelihood of (justification for) collective decisions (March and Simon, 1958).

(2) *Distribution of competences.* To what extent are competences distributed uniformly among individuals? More precisely, if individuals distribute themselves to various choice situations according to individual calculations of costs and benefits, will the resulting distribution of competences to choices result in the best possible decisions? If, for example, engineering competence is in short supply, people having that competence will have greater time demands on them than will some other people (e.g., social scien-

tists). As a result, some decisions that call for substantial engineering competence might receive rather more participation from others than would be appropriate. The greater the variations in individual competences, the greater the likelihood of (justification for) a relatively segmented attention structure.

(3) *Distribution of values and resources.* To what extent are values homogeneous across individuals? More precisely, if individuals distribute themselves to choice situations according to individual calculations, will the resulting distribution of values to choices result in decisions that are acceptable to dominant interests in the organization? Some people are perverse relative to the dominant concerns (or groups) of the organization. If allowed to do so, they would participate in decisions in which their contribution would be negative (from the perspective of dominant groups). Others might (for personal reasons) want to exclude themselves from decisions in which their contribution would be positive from the point of view of other important groups.[2] Where values are homogeneous, there is no particular likelihood of (justification for) any specific attention structure. Any division of labor is as good as any other. Where values are homogeneous within dominant (legitimate) groups but not throughout the organization, there is a likelihood of (justification for) a segmented structure that excludes deviant values. Where values are heterogeneous within legitimate groups, there is a likelihood of (justification for) relatively unsegmented attention structures.

Variations in interdependencies, competencies, and values will, if we are correct, result in variations in the attention structures within an organization and, thus, in the allocation of attention. We are particularly interested in the impact of ambiguity on attention allocation, however. Suppose that goals and technologies are ambiguous? Under such circumstances most of the instrumental justification (explanation) for segmentation in the attention structure is attenuated. It is hard to be sure about the extent and character of interdependencies; it is not easy to know who has greater competence at what; the magnitude and character of value disagreement is obscure.

Ambiguity appears systematically to reduce the instrumental justification (explanation) for attention structures. As a result, we would expect symbolic, educational, and traditional factors to rise in relative importance (Edelman, 1964). The definition of attention structures under conditions of ambiguity will be somewhat more attentive to discovering and communicating meaning, and somewhat less to decision efficiency, than other situations in which goals and technologies are clear.

The primary meanings associated with attention structures are those connected to personal identity and status and those connected to ideology and causal maps of the world. One of the primary ways by which an individual in an organization defines his person and his place is by reference to attention rights and duties. Where goals and technologies are ambiguous, access to a choice is less significant for the instrumental contribution to be made to values of importance than for what it tells about the person's position. How important am I? What special competences do I have? How does a person like me spend his time?

Where issues of position are important, the attention structure becomes important independent of any consequences for choices. Participation rights are more important than participation. In egalitarian cultures symbolic issues produce a consistent pressure toward relatively unsegmented structures; in cultures or organizations in which there are clear desires for, or beliefs in, differentiated status, there will be corresponding pressures toward relatively segmented structures, preferably hierarchical ones. Where issues of competence are important, the stress will be toward specialized structures. Competence is certified by the right to attend to certain decisions rather than by exhibition of capability.

At the same time, attention structures reflect (particularly under conditions of ambiguity) the efforts of organizations to achieve legitimacy. Those structures that are familiar and normatively approved in a society will tend to be adopted. Structures will diffuse from one organization to another. Structures that are associated traditionally with a particular form of organization will continue to be used in that kind of organization. Attention structures will be established and maintained because they are normatively appropriate.[3]

The studies reported in later chapters in this book are primarily studies of organizations in which attention structures are relatively unsegmented and ordinarily defined in terms of upper limits of attention rather than lower limits. In most of those studies, attention structures limit, but do not closely determine, the decision outcomes. In some cases, however (for example, Chapter 13), there is a conspicuous problem of securing adequate attention; and the primary rules of interest define lower limits on attention. Reluctant individuals are coerced into participation. Since this conflicts with the normal picture of eager participants prevented by attention rules from involving themselves in the choices, it is a good reminder that rules of attention can include stipulations of what must happen as well as what may happen.

44

3.2 The Distribution of Attention

The distribution of attention is particularly problematic under conditions of ambiguity and when traditional norms are predominantely egalitarian. Such conditions lead to relatively unsegmented, permissive attention structures. The constraints on attention do not much limit the distribution. Though almost anything is permitted and few things are required, not everything occurs.

We have tried to interpret the allocation of attention to decisions (within structural constraints) by means of three main themes: First, we examine attention as *rational action*. Attention is a scarce resource; not everyone can attend to everything all of the time. It is easy to overlook the importance of scarcity when one deals with only a single decision or a single choice arena; it becomes obvious when one looks at the mosaic of choice opportunities. A rational theory of attention allocation considers the gains and the costs of attention. Many theories of participation exclude a consideration of the costs of participation, the opportunities thereby foregone. Yet it seems clear that scarcity imposes costs. Some people will not be there by choice; they have better things to do.

Second, we examine the *symbols* of the process. Choice processes are important, independent of the substantive outcomes that result from them. There are pleasures in attending to some things rather than others. There are major connections between the processes of choice and important cultural beliefs about what and who is important. Thus, it will be hard to understand the allocation of attention without some serious concern for the way in which the distribution of attention is connected to the educational, ideological, and symbolic role of choice situations in organizations.

Third, we examine attention as *obligation*. Thinking of attention allocation as a choice, either in terms of substantive outcomes or in response to symbolic values, probably underplays the importance of duty, tradition, and routine. Particularly under conditions of ambiguity, self-interest becomes less clear as a base for action and less powerful as a theory of action. We need to consider the extent to which attention is a duty accepted by virtue of one's role and managed by routine classificatory rules.

3.2.0 *Attention as Rational Action*

Time for decision activity is a scarce resource. Potential participants face a continuous and heterogeneous stream of demands for their attention. Each decision that we study in an organization is only one of many claimants for attention in the lives of the various actors involved. As a result, most decisions in most organizations most of the time involve only a small number of people. Among those people who are involved, the degree of involvement varies substantially, as do the timing and style of involvement. Scarcity is particularly conspicuous for those members of an organization who are most important to, or interested in, decision making. A person who has many interests has less energy to attend to any one of them; a person of many talents has less time to use any one of them; a person with many responsibilities devotes less attention to any one of them.

We can imagine participants deciding how to allocate their scarce time in a standard rational manner, calculating the marginal gain to be obtained (in terms of the individual's own values) and the opportunity costs involved (Becker, 1965). The most familiar propositions in this tradition are the simple, but important, ideas that people who attend to a decision will be disproportionately those (a) for whom the outcome makes a difference, (b) who anticipate that their attention will make a difference.

The first proposition has been used to argue that normative problems of "intensity" of feelings in a political system are ameliorated by variations in participation rates, and to predict a relatively large number of verifiable features of differential participation rates in politics and organizations. The second proposition is the base of interest in "perceived efficacy" as a subjective state of participants, and its impact on decision processes. It is also the basis for the prediction of low participation rates in systems in which there is high trust. High participation rates among individuals who see themselves as efficacious are symptoms of a lack of consensus.

The heart of the idea of rational attention is choice among alternative activities. In part, this is choice among alternative strategies for accomplishing the same personal objectives. Instead of participating in local elections in order to influence the quality of life, citizens can move to a better city. Instead of writing to the company to complain about the quality of a product, consumers can shift to a different product. Instead of exercising faculty rights to control a university through participation, individual faculty members can leave to go to another university. In short, exit can be substituted for voice (Hirschman, 1970). In the present volume, Olsen (Chapter 13) and Weiner (Chapter 11) have examined some aspects of the impact of exit opportunities on decision participation.

In addition, there are competing arenas and competing objectives. An important reason for someone not being one place, is that he is somewhere else. In order to understand the pattern of participation within an organization, we have to understand the context of alternative claims on time. There are almost no decisions that are so important that attention is assured.

46

The result is that even a relatively rational model of attention makes decision outcomes highly contextual. Since every entrance is an exit somewhere else, the distribution of "entrances" depends on the attributes of the choice being left as much as it does on the attributes of the new choice. Substantial variation in attention stems from other demands on the participants' time (rather than from features of the decision under study). If decision outcomes depend on who is involved (a situation that we have suggested is not as universal as is commonly believed), if the attention structures are relatively permissive and unsegmented, and if individuals allocate time relatively rationally, then the outcomes of choices will depend on the availability and attractiveness of alternative arenas for activity. The individuals who end up making the decision are disproportionably those who have nothing better to do. The problems that end up being attached to the choice are disproportionately problems that have no better place to go. The solutions that end up being appropriate for the problems are disproportionately solutions that have no other problems to solve.

3.2.1 *The Symbols of the Process*

Most theories of decision making emphasize the decision process as a procedure for producing outcomes. The outcomes, in turn, have different value to different individuals. Rational models of decision attention focus on involvement in decision making as an instrument for affecting satisfaction by affecting decision outcomes. Decision outcomes, however, are not the only values allocated by a decision process. In particular, there are major symbols associated with the process itself. Status is allocated and acknowledged. Goodwill is collected and earned. Ideology is exercised and reinforced. Information is exchanged. Training takes place. Where the substantive outcome has relatively low salience for many participants or where it is difficult to establish decision efficacy by observing outcome effects, we would expect process pleasures to become particularly relevant.

These effects often make a choice situation into something that is much more easily understood in other terms. Why do people fight for the right to participate and then not spend much time participating? Because most of the status is conferred by the right to participate rather than by the actual activity. Why is there a tendency for major policy decisions to lead to no substantive change? Because the main concern and pleasure are in the symbolic content of the debate and the education rather than in the implementation of the policy.

The symbols of the process confound outcome-oriented rational models of time allocation decisions. They also confound our efforts to understand substantive outcomes. On the one hand, the fact that the right of participation is a source of pleasure even if not exercised places a persistent pressure on the system toward unsegmented and permissive attention structures. This, in turn, means that a relatively large number of people and problems will have the right to engage in a relatively large number of choice situations. The two effects together assure that the combination of persons and problems associated to any choice situation will be highly context-dependent.

At the same time, a relatively large number of participants in any particular choice situation will be more concerned with symbolic and educational issues than with substantive outcomes. Under some conditions we can predict the substantive outcomes of the process even though those outcomes are minor concerns of many participants; but the conditions under which that is possible are not well understood. More generally, it seems likely that a common consequence of making decisions through a process in which most participants are worrying about something else will be decisions that are difficult to anticipate.

3.2.2 Attention as Obligation

Viewing the allocation of attention as a rational choice subject to the constraints of the decision structure is a powerful perspective. This is particularly true if we include in the analysis not only the attributes of our focal choice situation but also the attributes of competing alternative arenas, and if we are attentive to the ways in which the pleasures of the process affect the rationality of participation. We believe, however, that a view of organizational behavior as explicable in terms of individual self-interest constrained by institutional structure fails to capture some significant elements of the phenomena.

Consider the problem of an administrator deciding (rationally) how to allocate his time in a university. As Cohen and March have observed (1974, p. 195), such an administrator faces four fundamental ambiguities:

"The college president faces four fundamental ambiguities. The first is the ambiguity of *purpose*. In what terms can action be justified? What are the goals of the organization? The second is the ambiguity of *power*. How powerful is the president? What can he accomplish? The third is the ambiguity of *experience*. What is to be learned from the events of the presidency? The fourth is the ambiguity of *success*. When is a president successful? How does he access his pleasures?

"These ambiguities are fundamental to college presidents because they strike at the heart of the usual interpretations of leadership. When purpose is ambiguous, ordinary theories of decision making and intelligence become problematic. When power is ambiguous, ordinary theories of social order and control become problematic. When experience is ambiguous, ordinary theories of learning and adaptation become problematic. When success is ambiguous, ordinary theories of motivation and personal pleasure become problematic."

The prevalence of ambiguity makes obvious what is probably more common elsewhere than we appreciate. Action is driven by routines. Individuals attend to decisions when, and because, that is what they are expected to do. Executives spend their time in a particular way because that is a part of the job (Cohen and March, 1974). Time is not so much allocated by decisions as by socialization into and acceptance of roles and by the connection to routine procedures.

Duty obligation, and routine are substantially less evaluative than is the usual concept of choice. The logic is classificatory rather than normative:

Step 1: What am I?   I am the rector.
Step 2: What do rectors do? Rectors go to meetings.
Step 3: What do I do?   I go to meetings.

The complications are complications of cross-classification:

Step 1: What am I?   I am a scholar.
Step 2: What do scholars do? Scholars work in the library.
Step 3: What do I do?   I work in the library.
Step 4: What if I am a rector also? ???

The solutions to the complications tend to be not choices among prior alternatives but new classifications:

Alternative 1: Sometimes I am a rector; sometimes I am a scholar.
Alternative 2: I am a scholar of administration.

The terms of the logic are a bit alien to us. The theory and ideology of individual choice make it difficult to accept both the normative and descriptive validity of duty as a concept. Yet, it seems to us to be an important aspect of understanding the allocation of attention. Nor is it particularly informative to describe a role as a bundle of obligations and routines and decision among roles as the relevant choice. To say that a "choice" to be a boss is a "choice" to do all the things bosses are obliged to do has some truth in it. But it is a bit like saying that a "choice" to be born is a "choice" to die. It is not clear that becoming a boss is a distinct choice located somewhere in time and place; and it is not clear that everything a boss "is" is knowable at the time of the commitment to the role.

The commitment to a self-description with obligations involves elements of choice buried within a deep context of socialization. The boy becomes the man becomes the husband becomes the father becomes the grandfather. The student becomes the graduate student becomes the instructor becomes the professor. Moreover, the obligations change more rapidly than the self-descriptions. College presidents learn and do what a college president does. After they accept the role, some elements of the obligations unfold in ways that are neither dramatically different from prior expectations nor exactly the same. They discover what it means after they know that it is true.

The routines of attention allocation tend to give priority to those things that are immediate, specific, operational, and doable; they tend to ignore things that are distant, general, and difficult to translate into action (March and Simon, 1958). As a result, attention allocation is vulnerable to deadlining, and some things rarely secure attention unless there is nothing else to do. Among the latter are long-run planning, thinking, nonfamiliar problems and ambiguous objectives. Organizations, and the people in them, deal with ambiguity by avoiding it (Cyert and March, 1963; March and Simon, 1958).

The result is a pattern of attention allocation that is heavily normative and often subjectively irrational (Cohen and March, 1974). In terms of our discussion of the complete cycle in organizations (Chapter 1), duty and standard operating procedures associated with duty are major sources of decoupling in the cycle. They give some explanations for the frequent occasions on which individual learning is not translated into organizational action. But from the point of view of a student of attention, duty imposes an element of stability on the system. Although multiple roles produce multiple obligations and the problem of predicting the resolution of inconsistencies, the combinations of role obligations seem likely to be more stable over time than the combinations of self-interests.

This is not to suggest that roles and routines are invariant. They tend to be quite stable in established organizations with experienced, well-socialized people performing socially standardized activities; they are less stable in new organizations with inexperienced personnel doing novel things. Moreover, individuals and situations produce innovations in the specification of obligations and procedures.

3.2.3 The Arithmetic of Attention

Throughout the discussion here we have considered the allocation of attention in terms of autonomous individual responses to scarcity of time. Such a form of the discussion ignores two important complications: First, it ignores a number of ways in which attention may be augmented within a fixed time budget. Second, it ignores the inter-actions among individuals. Both complications are potentially impor-tant.

We have tacitly assumed that an individual has some amount of time available and allocates that time in some way among the alter-native decision situations. Given his position in the organization, his impact in the various areas in which he may participate (under rules) is proportional to his distribution of the time among them.[4] In parti-cular, if he spends no time, he has no impact. The assumption is useful. In conjunction with our other observations, it permits a set of somewhat plausible observations. The assumption is, however, clearly wrong in important ways. We would note four classic ways in which attention is augmented within a fixed budget of time.

First, it is possible to buy attention. Very few people who can earn significant amounts of money in an hour spend many hours beyond the demands of duty in direct participation. They hire a representative.

Second, it is possible to barter attention. There are some gains in efficiency normally if you and I agree that I will attend one meeting and take care of both of our interests and you attend another with the same understanding.

Third, it is possible to organize attention through representation. A designated representative acts for a large number of others not physically present who have provided proxy authority.

Fourth, it is possible to threaten attention. The man who isn't there (but could be) is a threat. The price of his absence is some attention to his concerns and some anticipation of his reactions (Friedrich, 1937).

Because of these complications, a set of ideas that emphasizes the flow of attention is subject to error due to failure to appreciate the significance of the participant who was not there. In the chapters that follow we have on several occasions tried to note the way in which fluid participation is consistent with stability where broad social norms carry an implicit threat of participation.

Interactions among individuals are similarly complicating. Although it is convenient for many purposes to think of attention as a flow of energy from an autonomous individual to an autonomous choice, attention is actually organized in more complicated ways. Person A cannot allocate attention to a meeting unless the meeting exists, and the meeting does not exist unless B, C, and D are also there (i.e., have also allocated attention time to it). X cannot talk to Y unless Y is prepared to talk to X; alternatively, if X coerces Y to talk to him, then Y cannot do other things.

The general problem of interdependence suggests another reason why models of individuals choosing a time allocation by some kind of rational choice are likely to require modification. One person's time allocation is a factor in another person's allocation. Although such a relation does not make the model impossible, it does create some practical, technical difficulties. The difficulties are not only those of the student of time allocation; they are faced also by an organizational participant who wishes to rationalize time. Interpersonal interdependencies are yet another reason why time allocation is likely to become a routine rather than a continuous decision. Routines provide viable solutions to a relatively complicated problem in coordination. Deviation from them by one person produces a chain of difficulties for other persons; and a continuous simultaneous optimal solution to the allocation problem is hard to achieve.

3.3 Conclusion

We began with the observation that attention is important to a contextual theory of choice in organizations. Since time is scarce and there are a large number of claims on attention, the pattern of attention is likely to be hard to anticipate and to change inexplicably. This is particularly true in situations in which the structural constraints on attention are modest – when anything is permitted but nothing is required. Such a situation suggests the necessity for developing a theory that attends to the ebb and flow contending claims on attention.

At the same time, however, we noted that choice situations are not simply occasions for making substantive decisions. They are also arenas in which important symbolic meanings are developed. People gain status and exhibit virtue. Problems are accorded significance. Novices are educated into the values of the society and organization. Participation rights are certification of social legitimacy; participation performances are critical presentations of self.

The complexity involved in attending to simultaneous claims in many different arenas and calculating both substantive and symbolic costs and benefits suggests some of the difficulty in developing a behavioral theory of attention. That complexity itself, however, contributes to the acceptance of routine rules for the allocation of attention. Organizational actors allocate attention in large part according to standard operating procedures associated with concepts of duty, role, and obligation. Their behavior becomes less complex than the situation through the imposition of standard attention rules. Since the rules are contingent ones, the result is still heavily dependent on the flow of events within a broader context; but the rules provide a degree of behavioral stability that is probably greater than the stability that would be observed if individuals were adjusting continuously to shifts in marginal costs and benefits of attention. The rules make the individual actions behaviorally predictable given a particular stimulus, but the flow of stimuli remains highly interactive and contextual.

Such an analysis suggests some limitations on attempts to improve administrative time allocation through deliberate executive action. Although executives and their consultants often note the difficulty experienced in gaining deliberate control over the allocation of attention, they jump too easily to the assumption that the situation is pathological. It is almost impossible for an administrator to make a rational calculation of how he should allocate attention; when he does, he probably underestimates the ambiguity of self-interest; even when he doesn't, there is no reason to assume that a calculation of a rational allocation of attention is systematically better from a general social point of view than is simply following traditional conceptions of administrative role, subject to an occasional marginal adjustment when their perverseness becomes manifest.

NOTES:

1 Much of the political history of western democracies is focused upon the upper limits, or *rights* to attend. The relevance of the lower limits is, however, documented by the difficulties specific organizations as well as political systems frequently have in motivating members to take leadership and responsibility. Dicta emphasizing the duty to participate, as well as the social sanctions for not participating, indicate a set of research questions that a one-sided interest in the upper limit of attention frequently ignores (Olsen, 1971).

2 Note that there are related potentially conflicting rules about representation. It is often argued that when one participates in a *representative* mode, those who are affected by a choice should have a right to participate — to express their interest. However, when the mode is *fiduciary*, those who are affected are excluded — as having too much personally to gain. The former is emphasized when values are clearly in conflict; the latter when they are more shared.

3 Ambiguity does not eliminate the potential for conflict. There are a number of possibilities for considerable disagreement. For example, we can easily imagine differences between an organization that emphasizes differentiated status and a society in which egalitarian norms dominate. Similarly, we can imagine considerable conflict among individuals who compete for symbolic victories, or between individuals who see the world as actually unambiguous (and seek rational attention structures within that framework) and others who are primarily concerned with symbolic values.

4 This is a simplification. Almost all students of power suggest that there is a trade-off between position (status, role, etc.) and presence (attention, participation, etc.). Unfortunately, relatively few of them indicate what the character of that trade-off is, and relatively modest differences in the model make relatively substantial differences in the trade-off surface. Some of the issues are pursued in March and Romelaer (Chapter 12).

4. Organizational Learning and the Ambiguity of the Past[1]

JAMES G. MARCH
Stanford University

JOHAN P. OLSEN
University of Bergen

4.0 Introduction

Organizational intelligence, like individual intelligence, is built on two fundamental processes. The first of these is rational calculation, by which expectations about future consequences are used to choose among current alternatives. Rationality in policy making is typified by planning, analysis, forecasting and the paraphernalia of decision theory and management science; it is the logic of most recent efforts to improve the quality of decision making in public policy (as well as in non-public organizations).

The second process is learning from experience. Through learning, feedback from previous experience is used to choose among present alternatives. Learning in policy making is typified by experimentation, evaluation, assessment, and the paraphernalia of experimental design and control theory; it is the logic of an increasing number of efforts to improve policy making, particularly in areas such as education, social welfare, and social organization.

In the last two decades there has been a considerable examination of the cognitive and evaluative limitations on rationality. Although presumptions of rationality both as an objective and as a reality are still commonly used, the literature is full of attempts to develop the major implications of limitations on the awareness of alternatives, on the precision of information about consequences, and on the clarity and consistency of goals (Simon, 1955; March and Simon, 1958; Cyert and March, 1963; Lindblom, 1965). There is no longer general acceptance of a model of superhuman organizational omniscience in the service of rationality. Instead, there is an inclination to accept the proposition that while organizations are intendedly rational, they frequently act on incomplete or incorrect information and without being aware of all of their alternatives. Similarly, there is no longer general acceptance of a simple view of a well-defined organizational preference function. Instead, there is an effort to accommodate in the theory the frequent observations of inconsistent and conflicting organizational objectives.

In the face of such limitations on organizational rationality, highlighted by recent explorations of apparent failures in analytical decision making, students of policy making have come to appreciate the advantages of trial-and-error intelligence. It is an appreciation that has merit and would certainly have pleased some classical students of politics, but it may be somewhat ill-formed.

Little effort has been devoted to assessing the cognitive and evaluative limitations on organizational learning. As a result, learning is ordinarily understood in terms of a model of simple rational adaptation.[2] Policy makers may have limited abilities to predict consequences or control events, but they are presumed to be able to see what happens and understand why. They can distinguish success from failure. If organizations fail to improve, the explanation is formed in various forms of organizational rigidities that inhibit the adoption of changes even though clearly indicated by experience, or lack of motivation or some other inexplicable failure of the organization to learn.

We question such a perspective. We wish to examine some limitations on learning from experience. We will assume that organizations adapt their behavior in terms of their experience, but that experience requires interpretation. They learn under conditions in which goals (and therefore "success" and "failure") are ambiguous or in conflict, in which what happened is unclear, and in which the causality of events is difficult to untangle. People in organizations come to believe what happened, why it happened, and whether it was good; but the process by which those beliefs are established in the face of a quite problematic "objective" world affects systematically what is learned.

In particular, choice situations provide occasions for argumentation and interpretation as well as decision-making. The ideas, beliefs and attitudes that participants come to hold are important outcomes of the process. Interpretations of the ways in which meanings arise, the ways in which participants in an organization come to "know" or "believe", build on a set of simple theoretical ideas about rational adaptation. Beliefs are modified on the basis of experience in making decisions.

The argument is simple, but the development requires some attention to a number of issues that run through modern theories of organizational decision making and to an assortment of guesses about what might be required to adapt ideas of learning to situations of ambiguity. The strategy is to examine what would happen if a learning style appropriate to a world in which preferences are clear and outcomes unambiguous were extended to a world in which it is hard to determine what happened yesterday, why it happened, whether we liked it, or whether yesterday is comparable to today. Such a strategy does not suggest that organizations are conspicuously foolish in their learning, any more than the idea of limited rationality suggests that they are conspicuously foolish in their rational calculations. Both notions recognize some constraints on human action and some utility in theories of organizational intelligence that consider those constraints.

4.1 Incomplete Learning Cycles

Our general focus is on experiential learning within organizations. We ask how individuals and organizations make sense of their experience and modify behavior in terms of their interpretations of events. Our attempts are in the tradition of efforts to understand organizational behavior in terms of adaptive rationality. That tradition assumes a simple logic of experiential learning: An action is taken; there is some response from the environment; there is some interpretation and evaluation of that response; and then a new action is taken reflecting the impact of the sequence.

The situation is familiar and has been discussed in Chapter 1. It captures some important domains of behavior in organizations. There is a rather large family of models designed to interpret behavior within such a situation. The ideas of the complete cycle are made explicit in the following model by Cyert and March (1963, p. 99):

1. There exist a number of states of the system (organization). At any point in time, the system in some sense "prefers" some of these states to others.
2. There exists an external source of disturbance or shock to the system. These shocks cannot be controlled.
3. There exist a number of decision variables internal to the system. These variables are manipulated according to some decision rules.
4. Each combination of external shocks and decision variables in the system changes the state of the system. Thus, given an existing state, an external shock, and a decision, the next state is determined.
5. Any decision rule that leads to a preferred state at one point is more likely to be used in the future than it was in the past.

We wish to examine what happens when the cycle is incomplete; in particular, to consider the development of belief under conditions of ambiguity.

Some of the more interesting phenomena in organizations occur when one or more of the connections in the complete cycle is attentuated. As we have indicated in Chapter 1, there are a number of ways in which the cycle may be broken. Although it is not necessarily true that the cycle is broken at only one place, we can illustrate the study of incomplete cycles by considering the four incomplete cycles involving only one missing link. The first situation is *role-constrained* experiential learning. In this situation, everything proceeds in the same manner as in the complete cycle except that individual learning has little or no effect on individual behavior. The circle is broken by the constraints of role-definition and standard operating procedures:

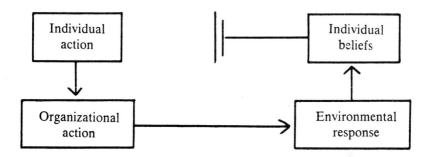

The situation is one that reflects some important dynamics of organizational behavior. One of the conspicuous things about complex organizations (or any complex social structure) is their ability to inhibit the modification of individual behavior on the basis of individual learning. The complication has formed the basis of a number of studies of organizations, most commonly in treatments of organizational inertia; but we do not have a systematic theory of the implications (for the time path of organizational behavior) of a separation of knowledge from action.

The second incomplete cycle is *superstitious* experiential learning. In this situation we assume that individuals within an organization take action, that that action produces organizational behavior, that individuals learn from the apparent environmental response, and that subsequent action is modified in what appears to be an appropriate fashion. The critical feature is that the connection between organizational action and environmental response is severed.

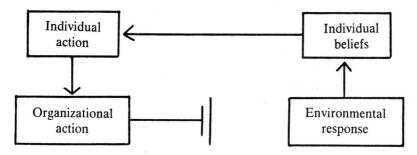

Learning proceeds. Inferences are made and action is changed. Organization behavior is modified as a result of an interpretation of the consequences, but the behavior does not affect the consequences significantly. Although superstitious learning in organizations has not received as much attention as it probably deserves, some discussion of it can be found in Cohen and March (1974). As Hill (1971, p. 75) observes:

> "Many of man's beliefs, not only in charms and magic, but also in medicine, mechanical skills, and administrative techniques probably depend on such superstitious learning."

The third situation is *audience* experiential learning. In this situation the connection between individual action and organizational action becomes problematic. The individual no longer affects (at least in an unambiguous way) organizational action. What he learns cannot affect subsequent behavior by the organization.

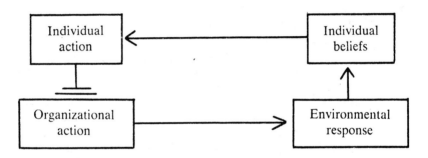

Learning occurs, but adaptation does not (necessarily). Much of our understanding of learning within politics or research falls within this situation, although it has not received much attention within modern organization theory, except in conjunction with the fourth situation below. The connection is a simple one: If adaptation through action is impossible, then adaptation through interpretation becomes conspicuous as an alternative.

Thus, the final incomplete cycle is one of experiential learning under *ambiguity*. In this situation it is not clear what happened or why it happened.[3] The individual tries to learn and to modify his behavior on the basis of his learning. In the simple situation, he affects organizational action and the action affects the environment; but subsequent events are seen only dimly, and causal connections among events have to be inferred.

58

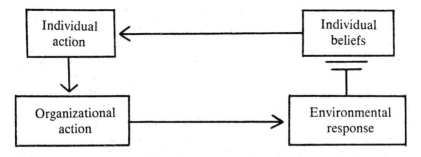

Learning takes place and behavior changes; but a model of the process requires some ideas about the imputation of meaning and structure to events. Such ideas have had little role in the organizational literature.

4.2 Information, Incentives, Cognitive Structures, and Micro Development

The problems of ambiguity in organizations are conspicuous. Nevertheless, the literature on organizational learning is rarely uncoupled from the idea that learning is adaptive. Experience is viewed as producing wisdom and improved behavior. For purposes of studying experiential learning under ambiguity it is necessary to relax such an assumption. Modern organizations develop myths, fictions, legends, folklore, and illusions. They develop conflict over myths. The connection between environmental response to organizational action and individual and organizational interpretation of that response is often weak.

We relax the presumption of improvement but not the presumption of a process of learning. We assume that individuals modify their understandings in a way that is intendedly adaptive. They are, however, operating under conditions in which (a) what happened is not immediately obvious, (b) why it happened is obscure, and (c) whether what happened is good is unclear.

A theory of adaptation under conditions of ambiguity might reasonably include four broad categories of ideas:

First, some ideas of information exposure, memory, and retrieval. Organizations have communication structures through which information is transmitted. As a result, different individuals and parts of the organization "see" different worlds. The occasions for seeking information, as well as where information is searched for, are presumably not random, but varies with both organizational and environmental factors. Organizations have records and other ways of recording history. These records are more or less retrievable at some future date.

How organizational memory functions and how it functions differently at different times and for different parts of the organization are questions that considerably affect the pattern of organizational beliefs. The tendency to use or activate different parts of an organizational memory will vary across individuals as well as organizational subunits.

Second, some ideas about learning incentives. Incentives in learning are usually associated with "motivation", some measure of factors that influence an inclination to accept information and modify behavior. In organizational learning under ambiguity, we confront a different form of incentive. If lack of clarity in the situation or in the feedback make several alternative interpretations possible, what are incentives that might lead a particular person, or part of the organization, to select one interpretation rather than another. For example, what are the incentives for an evaluator of a social experiment to find it a success? Or a failure?

Third, some ideas about belief structure. The development of beliefs under conditions of ambiguity probably accentuates the significance of a pre-existing structure of related values and cognitions. Understandings of events are connected to previous understandings, to the understandings of other people, and to social linkages of friendship and trust. Learning is a form of attitude formation.

Fourth, some ideas about the micro development of belief. It is reasonable to suspect that beliefs, like decisions, are sensitive to the fine detail of the timing, order, and context of information. Suppose, for example, that we think of one process that determines the current degree of salience of various elements of organizational information and another process that relates new information to the structure of existing information. Then modifications in response to experience will depend importantly on the interleaving of those two processes. Similarly, suppose that the elaboration of the meaning of experience is a claim (for time or energy) on a limited capacity system. Then learning will be affected by the characteristics of the other demands on the system.

We do not propose here to specify a theory of audience learning under ambiguity that deals with all of these clusters of ideas. We can, however, illustrate the kinds of considerations that are important by elaborating one version of the ideas about belief structure – that associated with various notions of consistency or balance in belief and perception. The spirit of the effort is strongly in the tradition of Heider (1958), Newcomb (1959), and Abelson (1968).

4.2.0 *An Example – Seeing, Liking, and Trusting*

We assume that organizational participants generally try to make

60

sense of ongoing events and processes. They discover or impose order, attribute meanings, and provide explanations. We wish to identify a simple set of ideas about the ways in which persons in organizations come to learn from experience; how they come to believe what they believe. We are not primarily interested in the ultimate validity of different beliefs. Our focus is on the basic properties of the process by which conceptions of reality might be affected by experience in an organizational setting. We do not attempt to specify all of the detail of that process.

For expository purpose, a distinction is made between beliefs about what a person "sees" and beliefs about what a person "likes". The beliefs about what a person sees include the ways in which the individual defines actions and outcomes, the theories he has about the world, and his interpretations of those theories. The beliefs about what a person likes include the affective sentiments he has, his values, and his tastes. By making this distinction, we will be able to link our ideas to ordinary discourse about fact and value; but it should be clear as we proceed that we do not postulate a fundamentally different process for coming to believe that something exists or is true from a process for coming to believe that something is desirable.

The tightness of the connection between environment response and individual learning hinges on the extent to which the interpretation of events is controlled by six presumptions of ordinary life in unambiguous systems:

> He sees what is to be seen.
> He likes what is to be liked.
> He sees what he expects to see.
> He likes what he expects to like.
> He sees what he is expected to see.
> He likes what he is expected to like.

The first two presumptions reflect the extent to which the processes of perception and preference are effectively self-evident. The second two reflect the intra-personal limitations on perceptions and preferences. The last two reflect the role of social norms. By presenting the six as distinct, we mean to suggest some possible utility in avoiding the dictum that all knowledge is necessarily "social".

An organizational participant sees what is to be seen. There is an ordinary process of perceiving reality. The process is normatively well defined. Through it, an individual establishes reliably what has happened in the phenomenal world. He is able to relate observed events to their future consequences, and to their more stable underlying causes. A correct link can be established between his own past choices and subsequent states of the world (i.e., it is possible to disentangle the effects of own choices and the effects of external factors). There exist some criteria for determining what choice situations are similar. Although much of what we want to discuss relates to other factors, we wish to acknowledge the possibility, and frequent dominance, of what is usually called objective reality.

An organizational participant likes what is to be liked. There are objective interests in the sense that given an individual's position in society (or organization) it is possible to assert that some things are in his interest and others are not, even if that is not his own present awareness. Although such a conception of interest is uncommon in modern social science, we consider it a defensible axiom of a theory that intends to predict actual behavior over time. Indeed, it is the basis of much effective intuitive prediction in social behavior.

An organizational participant sees what he expects to see. We assume that an individual approaches any perceptual situation with expectations. Those expectations may come from experience; they may come from the structure of his beliefs about the world. In either case, the expectations help to control their own realization.

An organizational participant likes what he likes. Individuals come to any particular choice situation with a set of values, attitudes, and opinions. These values are substantially fixed. Changes that occur within an relatively brief time period must attend to problems of consistency with the pre-existing attitude structure. In some cases, the restrictions imposed by this presumption will dominate the behavior.

An organizational participant sees what he is expected to see and likes what he is expected to like. The role of social norms in facilitating the interpretation of events and attitudes is a familiar theme in the analysis of social behavior. Among the best known examples of social provision on precision are the studies of strongly ideological, religious, and political messianistic movements (e.g. Festinger et al. 1956). The phenomenon extends well beyond such cases, however.

In many cases, seeing and liking are controlled by the elemental exogenous forces of objective reality, attitude structure, social reality, and social norms. In the rest of this section, however, we wish to examine situations in which the six elementary presumptions of seeing and liking do not completely determine the interpretation of events, where there is some degree of contextual ambiguity. Under such conditions a different set of assumptions becomes important and some attributes of organizations have significant impact on the development of belief and the process of learning.

Situations of ambiguity are common. The patterns of exposure to events and the channels for diffusing observations and interpretations often obscure the events. In situations where interpretations and explanations are called forth some time after the events, the organizational "memory" (e.g., files, budgets, statistics, etc.) and the retrieval-system will affect the degree to which different participants can use past events, promises, goals, assumptions, behavior, etc. in different ways. Pluralism, decentralization, mobility, and volatility in attention all tend to produce perceptual and attitudinal ambiguity in interpreting events.

Despite ambiguity and uncertainty, organizational participants interpret and try to make sense out of their lives. They try to find meaning in happenings and provide or invent explanations. These explanations and their development over time are our primary focus.

For the present purposes an organization is considered to consist of individuals characterized by:

(a) Varying *patterns of interaction* with each other. The frequency and duration of contacts between any two people may vary. In part this may reflect choice; in part it may be a consequence of organizational structure.

(b) Varying *degrees of trust* in each other. The belief in another person's ability and strength, together with the confidence in his motives, varies.

(c) Varying *degrees of integration* into the organization. A person is integrated to the extent to which he accepts responsibility for the organization and feels that the actions of the organization are fundamentally his actions or the actions of those he trusts. The converse relation with the organization is alienation. We will view an individual as alienated from the organization to the extent to which he does not accept responsibility for it and feels that the actions of the organization are neither his actions nor the actions of others whom he trusts.

(d) Varying *orientations to events* in the phenomenal world. These orientations have four key dimensions: (1) The extent to which the event is *seen*. (2) The extent to which the event is *liked*. (3) The extent to which the event is *relevant* to different interpersonal relations. (4) The extent to which an event is seen as *controlled* by different individuals.

We assume that the individuals in an organization develop their interpretations of events in a way broadly consistent with some hypotheses of cognitive consistency. In a general way, they argue that there are clear interdependencies between cognitive organization (i.e., perceiving someone as causing something, owing something, being close, etc.) and attitudinal organization (i.e., liking or disliking something or someone). The interdependencies with which we will concern ourselves reflect various tendencies toward consistency. We believe that such tendencies capture important aspects of the formation of beliefs in organizations.

5

At the same time, however, it should be obvious that we do not anticipate that the attitude structures we will observe in organizations will exhibit a high degree of consistency on some absolute scale. Ambiguity in the environment, short attention spans, and considerable human tolerance for inconsistency (Bem, 1970) conspire to maintain a high level of incongruence at any one point of time even in a process in which there are substantial efforts toward cognitive structure.

To focus on a simple set of ideas about movement toward cognitive consistency, we make four propositions about seeing and liking:

Proposition 1: An organizational participant will – to the extent to which he is integrated into the organization – see what he likes. To the extent to which he is alienated from the organization he will see what he dislikes.

Thus we assume that the elementary screening devices "used" by the individual in looking at the world tend to obscure those elements of reality that are not consonant with his attitudes. To the extent possible, the individual sees what he wants to see. The result of such wishful thinking is highly dependent upon his integration into the organization. If he is alienated from the organization, he will see evidence confirming his alienation.

Proposition 2: An organizational participant will – to the degree he is integrated into the organization – like what he sees. To the extent to which he is alienated from the organization he will dislike what he sees.

Not only does the individual modify his perceptions to accommodate his attitudes, he also modifies his attitudes to accommodate his perceptions. We assume that individuals discover pleasures in the outcomes arising from worlds into which they are integrated relatively independent of what those outcomes are; and displeasures from worlds from which they are alienated.

Proposition 3: An organizational participant will – to the extent to which he trusts others with whom he has contact – like what they like. To the extent to which he distrusts others with whom he has contact, he will dislike what they like.

Most organizational participants most of the time will not be eyewitnesses to most relevant events. Both what they "see" and what they "like" will be dependent upon available sources of information, which of the sources available they are exposed to, which of those they are exposed to they trust. Learning under such conditions becomes dependent both upon processes like discussion and persuasion, and upon relationships like trust and antagonism. We assume that sentiments diffuse through contact network characterized by variations in trust. They spread positively across trust relationships, negatively across distrust relationships.

The frequency of interaction will be especially important when different trusted people hold different likes. We assume that an organizational participant under such conditions will tend to like what those whom he most frequently interacts with, like.

> Proposition 4: An organizational participant will – to the degree he trusts others with whom he has contact, see what they see. To the extent to which he distrusts others with whom he has contact, he does not see what they see.

Perceptions also diffuse through the contact network, mediated by the trust structure. Individuals (most of the time) have difficulties in "seeing" things different from what a unanimous group of trusted people see.

This elementary set of propositions results in a simple system for coming to believe what one believes, as portrayed in Figure 4.0.

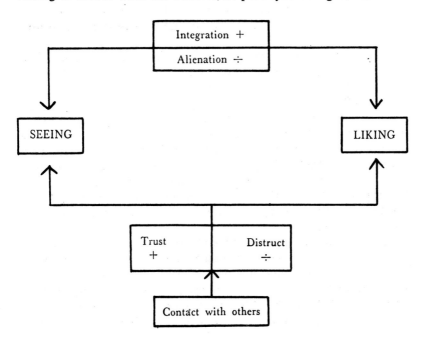

Finally, we need to complete the basic system by adding six propositions that reflect the dynamics of balancing within the organization of life for each participant.

Proposition 5: An organizational participant will come to trust others whom he sees as producing relevant events that he likes and preventing relevant events that he dislikes.

Proposition 6: An organizational participant will come to believe that people he trusts cause events he likes and that people he distrusts cause events he dislikes.

Proposition 7: An organizational participant will come to believe that events are relevant if he agrees about them with people he trusts and disagrees about them with people he distrusts.

Proposition 8: An organizational participant will be active to the extent to which his seeing, liking, and trusting are unambiguous.

Proposition 9: An organizational participant will – to the extent to which the organizational structure and his activity level permit – seek contact with people he trusts and avoid contact with people he distrusts.

Proposition 10: An organizational participant feel integrated into an organization to the extent to which he likes the relevant events that he sees.

Taken together these propositions suggest a view of reality forming that emphasizes the impact of interpersonal connections within the organization and the affective connection between the organization and the participant on the development of belief, as well as the interaction between seeing and liking. In keeping with the balance ideas, the propositions emphasize the organization of belief as vital to the substance of belief, accept a particular form of consistency as an organizing device.

The propositions appear to fit the observations in some case studies. They also seem to fit some more casual observations of organizational life. Their ultimate utility, however, hinges heavily on the extent to which the dynamics they postulate can be used to interpret more subtle aspects of changes in beliefs over time. As a first step toward investigating the properties of the system specified by the propositions,

66

a formal explication of the model has been developed and explored to identify some implications (March and Paté, 1974).

4.3 Conclusion

Organizations and the people in them learn from their experience. They act, observe the consequences of their action, make inferences about those consequences, and draw implications for future action. The process is adaptively rational. If the information is accurate, the goals clear and unchanging, the inferences correct, the behavior modification appropriate, and the environment stable, the process will result in improvement over time.

As we have come to recognize the limitations on rational calculation, planning, and forecasting as bases for intelligence in many organizations, interest in the potential for organizational learning has increased. That interest, however, tends to underestimate the extent to which adaptive rationality is also limited by characteristics of human actors and organizations. The problems are similar to, and probably as profound as, the limits on calculated rationality. We have tried to suggest a few of the complications involved in assuming that organizations "improve" through learning, particularly under conditions of ambiguity.

Despite the difficulties, it is important to study the process of learning in organizations. Individuals try to make sense of their experience, even when that experience is ambiguous or misleading and even when that learning does not affect organizational actions. They impose order, attribute meaning, and provide explanations. We have outlined an application of one set of ideas about cognitive consistency to the question of how ambiguous events in organizations are interpreted, and thus how people in an organization come to believe what they believe.

Some significant understanding of the factors affecting learning from experience will not only be important to the improvement of policy making in an organizational context. It will also be a necessary part of a theory of the full cycle of organizational choice and of the consequences that accrue from breaking the cycle in different ways under different circumstances. Policy analysts interested in designing organizations that can learn intelligently and organization theorists interested in understanding the dynamics of organizational choice share the need for an effective model of organizational learning under conditions of uncertainty about what events happened, why they happened, and whether they were good or bad. Such situations are common in a wide variety of organizations; they are conspicuous in most public organizations, somewhat more concealed in business organizations.

NOTES:

1 This chapter draws substantially on March and Olsen (1975).

2 A recent exception is Axelrod (1973), March and Cohen (1974) discuss the relevance of superstitious learning as an organizational phenomenon, see also Weick (1969). Olsen (1970) shows that a decision-making process is a process of interpretation as well as a process of choice. Thompson (1967) has a very interesting discussion of how organizations keep score: "Even if we concede that organizations sometimes maximize, the organizational question is whether the organization has any way of knowing that it has done so. And how does it assess itself on the ultimate question, its fitness for the future" (p. 84).

3 Ambiguity here refers to an "objective" assessment of the situation (in practice the assessment of the researcher). The individual participants may view the situation as quite unambiguous, though they disagree about the content of that interpretation.

5. The Technology of Foolishness

JAMES G. MARCH
Stanford University

5.0 Choice and Rationality[1]

The concept of choice as a focus for interpreting and guiding human behavior has rarely had an easy time in the realm of ideas. It is beset by theological disputations over free will, by the dilemmas of absurdism, by the doubts of psychological behaviorism, by the claims of historical, economic, social, and demographic determinism. Nevertheless, the idea that humans make choices has proven robust enough to become a major matter of faith in important segments of contemporary western civilization. It is a faith that is professed by virtually all theories of social policy making.

The major tenets of this faith run something like this:

> Human beings make choices. If done properly, choices are made by evaluating alternatives in terms of goals on the basis of information currently available. The alternative that is most attractive in terms of the goals is chosen. The process of making choices can be improved by using the technology of choice. Through the paraphernalia of modern techniques, we can improve the quality of the search for alternatives, the quality of information, and the quality of the analysis used to evaluate alternatives. Although actual choice may fall short of this ideal in various ways, it is an attractive model of how choices should be made by individuals, organizations, and social systems.

These articles of faith have been built upon, and have stimulated, some scripture. It is the scripture of theories of decision making. The scripture is partly a codification of received doctrine and partly a source for that doctrine. As a result, our cultural ideas of intelligence and our theories of choice bear some substantial resemblance. In particular, they share three conspicuous interrelated ideas:

The first idea is the *pre-existence of purpose*. We find it natural to base an interpretation of human choice behavior on a presumption of human purpose. We have, in fact, invented one of the most elaborate

69

terminologies in the professional literature: "values", "needs", "wants", "goods", "tastes", "preferences", "utility", "objectives", "goals", "aspirations", "drives". All of these reflect a strong tendency to believe that a useful interpretation of human behavior involves defining a set of objectives that (a) are prior attributes of the system, and (b) make the observed behavior in some sense intelligent *vis-á-vis* those objectives.

Whether we are talking about individuals or about organizations, purpose is an obvious presumtion of the discussion. An organization is often defined in terms of its purpose. It is seen by some as the largest collectivity directed by a purpose. Action within an organization is justified (or criticized) in terms of the purpose. Individuals explain their own behavior, as well as the behavior of others, in terms of a set of value premises that are presumed to be antecedent to the behavior. Normative theories of choice begin with an assumption of a pre-existent preference ordering defined over the possible outcomes of a choice.

The second idea is the *necessity of consistency*. We have come to recognize consistency both as an important property of human behavior and as a prerequisite for normative models of choice. Dissonancy theory, balance theory, theories of congruency in attitudes, statuses, and performances have all served to remind us of the possibilities for interpreting human behavior in terms of the consistency requirements of a limited capacity information-processing system.

At the same time, consistency is a cultural and theoretical virtue. Action should be made consistent with belief. Actions taken by different parts of an organization should be consistent with each other. Individual and organizational activities are seen as connected with each other in terms of their consequences for some consistent set of purposes. In an organization, the structural manifestation of the dictum of consistency is the hierarchy with its obligations of coordination and control. In the individual, the structural manifestation is a set of values that generates a consistent preference ordering.

The third idea is the *primacy of rationality*. By rationality I mean a procedure for deciding what is correct behavior by relating consequences systematically to objectives. By placing primary emphasis on rational techniques, we implicitly have rejected – or seriously impaired – two other procedures for choice: (a) The processes of intuition, by means of which people may do things without fully understanding why. (b) The processes of tradition and faith, through which people do things because that is the way they are done.

Both within the theory and within the culture we insist on the ethic of rationality. We justify individual and organizational action in terms of an analysis of means and ends. Impulse, intuition, faith, and tradition are outside that system and viewed as antithetical to it. Faith may be seen as a possible source of values. Intuition may be seen as a possible source of ideas about alternatives. But the analysis and justification of action lie within the context of reason.

These ideas are obviously deeply imbedded in the culture. Their roots extend into ideas that have conditioned much of modern western history and interpretations of that history. Their general acceptance is probably highly correlated with the permeation of rationalism and individualism into the style of thinking within the culture. The ideas are even more obviously imbedded in modern theories of choice. It is fundamental to those theories that thinking should precede action; that action should serve a purpose; that purpose should be defined in terms of a consistent set of pre-existent goals; and that choice should be based on a consistent theory of the relation between action and its consequences.

Every tool of management decision that is currently a part of management science, operations research, or decision theory assumes the prior existence of a set of consistent goals. Almost the entire structure of micro-economic theory builds on the assumption that there exists a well-defined, stable, and consistent preference ordering. Most theories of individual or organizational choice behavior accept the idea that goals exist and that (in some sense) an individual or organization acts on those goals, choosing from among some alternatives on the basis of available information. Discussions of educational policy, for example, with the emphasis on goal setting, evaluation, and accountability, are directly in this tradition.

From the perspective of all of man's history, the ideas of purpose, consistency, and rationality are relatively new. Much of the technology currently available to implement them is extremely new. Over the past few centuries, and conspicuously over the past few decades, we have substantially improved man's capability for acting purposively, consistently, and rationally. We have substantially increased his propensity to think of himself as doing so. It is an impressive victory, won – where it has been won – by a happy combination of timing, performance, ideology, and persistence. It is a battle yet to be concluded, or even engaged, in many cultures of the world; but within most of the western world, individuals and organizations see themselves as making choices.

5.1 The Problem of Goals

The tools of intelligence as they are fashioned in modern theories of choice are necessary to any reasonable behavior in contemporary society. It is difficult to see how we could, and inconceivable that we would, fail to continue their development, refinement, and extension. As might be expected, however, a theory and ideology of choice built on the ideas outlined above is deficient in some obvious, elementary ways, most conspicuously in the treatment of human goals.

Goals are thrust upon the intelligent man. We ask that he act in the name of goals. We ask that he keep his goals consistent. We ask that his actions be oriented to his goals. We ask that a social system amalgamate individual goals into a collective goal. But we do not concern ourselves with the origin of goals. Theories of individual organizational and social choice assume actors with pre-existent values.

Since it is obvious that goals change over time and that the character of those changes affects both the richness of personal and social development and the outcome of choice behavior, a theory of choice must somehow justify ignoring the phenomena. Although it is unreasonable to ask a theory of choice to solve all of the problems of man and his development, it is reasonable to ask how something as conspicuous as the fluidity and ambiguity of objectives can plausibly be ignored in a theory that is offered as a guide to human choice behavior.

There are three classic justifications. The first is that goal development and choice are independent processes, conceptually and behaviorally. The second is that the model of choice is never satisfied in fact and that deviations from the model accommodate the problems of introducing change. The third is that the idea of changing goals is so intractable in a normative theory of choice that nothing can be said about it. Since I am unpersuaded of the first and second justifications, my optimism with respect to the third is somewhat greater than most of my fellows.

The argument that goal development and choice are independent behaviorally seems clearly false. It seems to me perfectly obvious that a description that assumes goals come first and action comes later is frequently radically wrong. Human choice behavior is at least as much a process for discovering goals as for acting on them. Although it is true enough that goals and decisions are "conceptually" distinct, that is simply a statement of the theory. It is not defense of it. They are conceptually distinct if we choose to make them so.

The argument that the model is incomplete is more persuasive. There do appear to be some critical "holes" in the system of intelligence as described by standard theories of choice. There is incomplete information, incomplete goal consistency, and a variety of external processes impinging on goal development – including intuition and tradition. What is somewhat disconcerting about the argument, however, is that it makes the efficacy of the concepts of intelligent choice dependent on their inadequacy. As we become more competent in the techniques of the model, and more committed to it, the "holes" become smaller. As the model becomes more accepted, our obligation to modify it increases.

The final argument seems to me sensible as a general principle, but misleading here. Why are we more reluctant to ask how human beings might find "good" goals than we are to ask how they might make "good" decisions? The second question appears to be a relatively technical problem. The first seems more pretentious. It claims to say something about alternative virtues. The appearance of pretense, however, stems directly from the theory and the ideology associated with it.

In fact, the conscious introduction of goal discovery as a consideration in theories of human choice is not unknown to modern man. For example, we have two kinds of theories of choice behavior in human beings. One is a theory of children. The other is a theory of adults. In the theory of childhood, we emphasize choices as leading to experiences that develop the child's scope, his complexity, his awareness of the world. As parents, or psychologists, we try to lead the child to do things that are inconsistent with his present goals because we know (or believe) that he can only develop into an interesting person by coming to appreciate aspects of experience that he initially rejects.

In the theory of adulthood, we emphasize choices as a consequence of our intentions. As adults, or economists, we try to take actions that (within the limits of scarce resources) come as close as possible to achieving our goals. We try to find improved ways of making decisions consistent with our perceptions of what is valuable in the world.

The asymmetry in these models is conspicuous. Adults have constructed a model world in which adults know what is good for themselves, but children do not. It is hard to react positively to the conceit. The asymmetry has, in fact, stimulated a rather large number of ideologies and reforms designed to allow children the same moral prerogative granted to adults – the right to imagine that they know what they want. The efforts have cut deeply into traditional child-rearing, traditional educational policies, traditional politics, and traditional consumer economics.

In my judgment, the asymmetry between models of choice for adults and models of choice for children is awkward; but the solution we have adopted is precisely wrong-headed. Instead of trying to adapt the model of adults to children, we might better adapt the model of children to adults. For many purposes, our model of children is better. Of course, children know what they want. Everyone does. The critical question is whether they are encouraged to develop more interesting "wants". Values change. People become more interesting as those values and the interconnections made among them change.

One of the most obvious things in the world turns out to be hard for us to accommodate in our theory of choice: A child of two will almost always have a less interesting set of values (yes, indeed, a *worse* set of values) than a child of 12. The same is true of adults. Values develop through experience. Although one of the main natural arenas for the modification of human values is the area of choice, our theories of adult and organizational decision making ignore the phenomenon entirely.

Introducing ambiguity and fluidity to the interpretation of individual, organizational, and societal goals, obviously has implications for behavioral theories of decision making. The main point here, however, is not to consider how we might describe the behavior of systems that are discovering goals as they act. Rather it is to examine how we might improve the quality of that behavior, how we might aid the development of interesting goals.

We know how to advise a society, an organization, or an individual if we are first given a consistent set of preferences. Under some conditions, we can suggest how to make decisions if the preferences are only consistent up to the point of specifying a series of independent constraints on the choice. But what about a normative theory of goal-finding behavior? What do we say when our client tells us that he is not sure his present set of values is the set of values in terms of which he wants to act?

It is a question familiar to many aspects of ordinary life. It is a question that friends, associates, students, college presidents, business managers, voters, and children ask at least as frequently as they ask how they should act within a set consistent and stable values.

Within the context of the normative theory of choice as it exists, the answer we give is: First determine the values, then act. The advice is frequently useful. Moreover, we have developed ways in which we can use conventional techniques for decision analysis to help discover value premises and to expose value inconsistencies. These techniques involve testing the decision implications of some successive approximations to a set of preferences. The object is to find a consistent set of preferences with implications that are acceptable to the person or organization making the decisions. Variations on such techniques are used routinely in operations research, as well as in personal counseling and analysis.

The utility of such techniques, however, apparently depends on the assumption that a primary problem is the amalgamation or excavation of preexistent values. The metaphors – "finding oneself", "goal clarification", "self-discovery", "social welfare function", "revealed preference" – are metaphors of search. If our value premises are to be

74

"constructed" rather than "discovered", our standard procedures may be useful; but we have no *a priori* reason for assuming they will.

Perhaps we should explore a somewhat different approach to the normative question of how we ought to behave when our value premises are not yet (and never will be) fully determined. Suppose we treat action as a way of creating interesting goals at the same time as we treat goals as a way of justifying action. It is an intuitively plausible and simple idea, but one that is not immediately within the domain of standard normative theories of intelligent choice.

Interesting people and interesting organizations construct complicated theories of themselves. In order to do this, they need to supplement the technology of reason with a technology of foolishness. Individuals and organizations need ways of doing things for which they have no good reason. Not always. Not usually. But sometimes. They need to act before they think.

5.2 Sensible Foolishness

In order to use the act of intelligent choice as a planned occasion for discovering new goals, we apparently require some idea of sensible foolishness. Which of the many foolish things that we might do now will lead to attractive value consequences? The question is almost inconceivable. Not only does it ask us to predict the value consequences of action, it asks us to evaluate them. In what terms can we talk about "good" changes in goals?

In effect, we are asked either to specify a set of super-goals in terms of which alternative goals are evaluated, or to choose among alternatives *now* in terms of the unknown set of values we will have at some future time (or the distribution over time of that unknown set of future values). The former alternative moves us back to the original situation of a fixed set of values – now called "super-goals" – and hardly seems an important step in the direction of inventing procedures for discovering new goals. The latter alternative seems fundamental enough, but it violates severely our sense of temporal order. To say that we make decisions now in terms of goals that will only be knowable later is non sensical – as long as we accept the basic framework of the theory of choice and its presumptions of pre-existent goals.

I do not know in detail what is required, but I think it will be substantial. As we challenge the dogma of pre-existent goals, we will be forced to reexamine some of our most precious prejudices: the strictures against imitation, coercion, and rationalization. Each of those honorable prohibitions depends on the view of man and human choice imposed on us by conventional theories of choice.

Imitation is not necessarily a sign of moral weakness. It is a prediction. It is a prediction that if we duplicate the behavior or attitudes of someone else, the chances of our discovering attractive new goals for ourselves are relatively high. In order for imitation to be normatively attractive we need a better theory of who should be imitated. Such a theory seems to be eminently feasible. For example, what are the conditions for effectiveness of a rule that you should imitate another person whose values are in a close neighborhood of yours? How do the chances of discovering interesting goals through imitation change as the number of other people exhibiting the behavior to be imitated increases?

Coercion is not necessarily an assault on individual autonomy. It can be a device for stimulating individuality. We recognice this when we talk about parents and children (at least sometimes). What has always been difficult with coercion is the possibility for perversion that it involves, not its obvious capability for stimulating change. What we require is a theory of the circumstances under which entry into a coercive system produces behavior that leads to the discovery of interesting goals. We are all familiar with the tactic. We use it in imposing deadlines, entering contracts, making commitments. What are the conditions for its effective use? In particular, what are the conditions for coercion in social systems?

Rationalization is not necessarily a way of evading morality. It can be a test for the feasibility of a goal change. When deciding among alternative actions for which we have no good reason, it may be sensible to develop some definition of how "near" to intelligence alternative "unintelligent" actions lie. Effective rationalization permits this kind of incremental approach to changes in values. To use it effectively, however, we require a better idea of the kinds of metrics that might be possible in measuring value distances. At the same time, rationalization is the major procedure for integrating newly discovered goals into an existing structure of values. It provides the organization of complexity without which complexity itself becomes indistinguishable from randomness.

There are dangers in imitation, coercion, and rationalization. The risks are too familiar to elaborate. We should, indeed, be able to develop better techniques. Whatever those techniques may be, however, they will almost certainly undermine the superstructure of biases erected on purpose, consistency, and rationality. They will involve some way of thinking about action now as occurring in terms of a set of unknown future values.

5.3 Play and Reason

A second requirement for a technology of foolishness is some strategy for suspending rational imperatives toward consistency. Even if we know which of several foolish things we want to do, we still need a mechanism for allowing us to do it. How do we escape the logic of our reason?

Here, I think, we are closer to understanding what we need. It is playfulness. Playfulness is the deliberate, temporary relaxation of rules in order to explore the possibilities of alternative rules. When we are playful, we challenge the necessity of consistency. In effect, we announce – in advance – our rejection of the usual objections to behavior that does not fit the standard model of intelligence.

Playfulness allows experimentation. At the same time, it acknowledges reason. It accepts an obligation that at some point either the playful behavior will be stopped or it will be integrated into the structure of intelligence in some way that makes sense. The suspension of the rules is temporary.

The idea of play may suggest three things that are, in my mind, quite erroneous in the present context. First, play may be seen as a kind of Mardi Gras for reason, a release of emotional tensions of virtue. Although it is possible that play performs some such function, that is not the function with which I am concerned. Second, play may be seen as part af some mystical balance of spiritual principles: Fire and water, hot and cold, weak and strong. The intention here is much narrower than a general mystique of balance. Third, play may be seen as an antithesis of intelligence, so that the emphasis on the importance of play becomes a support for simple self-indulgence. My present intent is to propose play as an instrument of intelligence, not a substitute.

Playfulness is a natural outgrowth of our standard view of reason. A strict insistence on purpose, consistency, and rationality limits our ability to find new purposes. Play relaxes that insistence to allow us to act "unintelligently" or "irrationally", or "foolishly" to explore alternative ideas of possible purposes and alternative concepts of behavioral consistency. And it does this while maintaining our basic commitment to the necessity of intelligence.

Although play and reason are in this way functional complements, they are often behavioral competitors. They are alternative styles and alternative orientations to the same situation. There is no guarantee that the styles will be equally well-developed. There is no guarantee that all individuals, all organizations, or all societies will be equally adept in both styles. There is no guarantee that all cultures will be equally encouraging to both.

Our design problem is either to specify the best mix of styles or, failing that, to assure that most people and most organizations most of the time use an alternation of strategies rather than perseverate in either one. It is a difficult problem. The optimization problem looks extremely difficult on the face of it, and the learning situations that will produce alternation in behavior appear to be somewhat less common than those that produce perseveration.

Consider, for example, the difficulty of sustaining playfulness as a style within contemporary American society. Individuals who are good at consistent rationality are rewarded early and heavily. We define it as intelligence, and the educational rewards of society are associated strongly with it. Social norms press in the same direction, particularly for men. Many of the demands of modern organizational life reinforce the same abilities and style preferences.

The result is that many of the most influential, best educated, and best placed citizens have experienced a powerful overlearning with respect to rationality. They are exceptionally good at maintaining consistent pictures of themselves, of relating action to purposes. They are exceptionally poor at a playful attitude toward their own beliefs, toward the logic of consistency, or toward the way they see things as being connected in the world. The dictates of manliness, forcefulness, independence, and intelligence are intolerant of playful urges if they arise. The playful urges that arise are weak ones.

The picture is probably overdrawn, but not, I believe, the implications. For societies, for organizations, and for individuals reason and intelligence have had the unnecessary consequence of inhibiting the development of purpose into more complicated forms of consistency. In order to move away from that position, we need to find some ways of helping individuals and organizations to experiment with doing things for which they have no good reason, to be playful with their conception of themselves. It is a facility that requires more careful attention than I can give it, but I would suggest five things as a small beginning:

First, we can treat *goals as hypotheses*. Conventional decision theory allows us to entertain doubts about almost everything except the thing about which we frequently have the greatest doubt – our objectives. Suppose we define the decision process as a time for the sequential testing of hypotheses about goals. If we can experiment with alternative goals, we stand some chance of discovering complicated and interesting combinations of good values that none of us previously imagined.

Second, we can treat *intuition as real*. I do not know what intuition is, or even if it is any one thing. Perhaps it is simply an excuse for doing something we cannot justify in terms of present values or for refusing to follow the logic of our own beliefs. Perhaps it is an inexplicable way of consulting that part of our intelligence that is not organized in a way anticipated by standard theories of choice. In either case, intuition permits us to see some possible actions that are outside our present scheme for justifying behavior.

Third, we can treat *hypocrisy as a transition*. Hypocrisy is an inconsistency between expressed values and behavior. Negative attitudes about hypocrisy stem from two major things. The first is a general onus against inconsistency. The second is a sentiment against combining the pleasures of vice with the appearance of virtue. Apparently, that is an unfair way of allowing evil to escape temporal punishment. Whatever the merits of such a position as ethics, it seems to me distinctly inhibiting toward change. A bad man with good intentions may be a man experimenting with the possibility of becoming good. Somehow it seems to me more sensible to encourage the experimentation than to insult it.

Fourth, we can treat *memory as an enemy*. The rules of consistency and rationality require a technology of memory. For most purposes, good memories make good choices. But the ability to forget, or overlook, is also useful. If I do not know what I did yesterday or what other people in the organization are doing today, I can act within the system of reason and still do things that are foolish.

Fifth, we can treat *experience as a theory*. Learning can be viewed as a series of conclusions based on concepts of action and consequences that we have invented. Experience can be changed retrospectively. By changing our interpretive concepts now, we modify what we learned earlier. Thus, we expose the possibility of experimenting with alternative histories. The usual strictures against "self-deception" in experience need occasionally to be tempered with an awareness of the extent to which all experience is an interpretation subject to conscious revision. Personal histories, and national histories, need to be rewritten rather continuously as a base for the retrospective learning of new self-conceptions.

Each of these procedures represents a way in which we temporarily suspend the operation of the system of reasoned intelligence. They are playful. They make greatest sense in situations in which there has been an overlearning of virtues of conventional rationality. They are possibly dangerous applications of powerful devices more familiar to the study of behavioral pathology than to the investigation of human development. But they offer a few techniques for introducing change within current concepts of choice.

The argument extends easily to the problems of social organization. If we knew more about the normative theory of acting before you think, we could say more intelligent things about the functions of management and leadership when organizations or societies do not know what they are doing. Consider, for example, the following general implications.

First, we need to reexamine the functions of management decision. One of the primary ways in which the goals of an organization are developed is by interpreting the decisions it makes, and one feature of good managerial decisions is that they lead to the development of more interesting value premises for the organization. As a result, decisions should not be seen as flowing directly or strictly from a pre-existent set of objectives. Managers who make decisions might well view that function somewhat less as a process of deduction or a process of political negotiation, and somewhat more as a process of gently upsetting preconceptions of what the organization is doing.

Second, we need a modified view of planning. Planning in organizations has many virtues, but a plan can often be more effective as an interpretation of past decisions than as a program for future ones. It can be used as a part of the efforts of the organization to develop a new consistent theory of itself that incorporates the mix of recent actions into a moderately comprehensive structure of goals. Procedures for interpreting the meaning of most past events are familiar to the memoirs of retired generals, prime ministers, business leaders, and movie stars. They suffer from the company they keep. In an organization that wants to continue to develop new objectives, a manager needs to be relatively tolerant of the idea that he will discover the meaning of yesterday's action in the experiences and interpretations of today.

Third, we need to reconsider evaluation. As nearly as I can determine, there is nothing in a formal theory of evaluation that requires that the criterion function for evaluation be specified in advance. In particular, the evaluation of social experiments need not be in terms of the degree to which they have fulfilled our *a priori* expectations. Rather we can examine what they did in terms of what we now believe to be important. The prior specification of criteria and the prior specification of evaluational procedures that depend on such criteria are common presumptions in contemporary social policy making. They are presumptions that inhibit the serendipitous discovery of new criteria. Experience should be used explicitly as an occasion for evaluating our values as well as our actions.

Fourth, we need a reconsideration of social accountability. Individual preferences and social action need to be consistent in some way. But the process of pursuing consistency is one in which both the preferences and the actions change over time. Imagination in social policy formation involves systematically adapting to and influencing preferences. It would be unfortunate if our theories of social action encouraged leaders to ignore their responsibilities for anticipating public preferences through action and for providing social experiences that modify individual expectations.

Fifth, we need to accept playfulness in social organizations. The design of organizations should attend to the problems of maintaining both playfulness and reason as aspects of intelligent choice. Since much of the literature on social design is concerned with strengthening the rationality of decision, managers are likely to overlook the importance of play. This is partly a matter of making the individuals within an organization more playful by encouraging the attitudes and skills of inconsistency. It is also a matter of making organizational structure and organizational procedure more playful. Organizations can be playful even when the participants in them are not. The managerial devices for maintaining consistency can be varied. We encourage organizational play be permitting (and insisting on) some temporary relief from control, coordination, and communication.

5.4 Intelligence and Foolishness

Contemporary theories of decision making and the technology of reason have considerably strengthened our capabilities for effective social action. The conversion of the simple ideas of choice into an extensive technology is a major achievement. It is, however, an achievement that has reinforced some biases in the underlying models of choice in individuals and groups. In particular, it has reinforced the uncritical acceptance of a static interpretation of human goals.

There is little magic in the world, and foolishness in people and organizations is one of the many things that fail to produce miracles. Under certain conditions, it is one of several ways in which some of the problems of our current theories of intelligence can be overcome. It may be a good way. It preserves the virtues of consistency while stimulating change. If we had a good technology of foolishness, it might (in combination with the technology of reason) help in a small way to develop the unusual combinations of attitudes and behaviors that describe the interesting people, interesting organizations, and interesting societies of the world.

NOTE:
1 This chapter is based on March (1972).

6. Choice in an Organized Anarchy

JOHAN P. OLSEN
University of Bergen

6.0 Introduction

In this chapter three models of organizational choice are examined. Each model emphasizes a different aspect of decision-making behavior, (a) the intellectual aspect, (b) the socio-political aspect, and (c) the artifactual or non-decision aspect. An attempt is made to continue recent efforts at reconciling these models (Cyert and March, 1963; Thompson, 1967, Robinson and Majak, 1967; Allison, 1971; Cohen and March, 1974) by proposing some conditions under which each of the three models might be adequate. These propositions are illustrated by a study of a specific choice within one American academic organization.

Consider the following three models of choice in complex organizations:

(1) *"Rational decision" (entrepreneurial) models.* In the framework of these models events are explained as the willed product of the activity of the decision maker(s) maximizing some utility function. The intellectual aspects of this activity are emphasized, the linking of means to ends. An occasion for choice is taken as given and value consensus is established before the decision (often by treating the organization as *one* person – the entrepreneur or manager). In this way organizational choice is seen as a product of (a) predetermined preferences (with well-defined rules for comparing different criteria), (b) predetermined alternatives (with search treated either as infinite or as being evaluated in terms of calculable costs and expected returns at the margin), and (c) known techniques for relating preferences and alternatives (e.g., maximization of expected utility). The "rational decision" model assumes that participants know what they want and have the knowledge and power to get it (at least on the average). Some efforts have been made to modify the way in which preferences or alternatives are treated. In particular, "bounded" rationality (Simon, 1955) was an important modification of the rational decision-maker model. For

the most part, however, these efforts have been directed at understanding the ways of relating means and ends – the *intellectual* aspects of decisions.

(2) *Conflict resolution (coalition-bargaining) models.* In these models (as in the previous ones), we assume a close connection between the desires of the decision makers and organizational events. However, here the organization is seen as consisting of rational individuals and subgroups with *different* interests, perceptions, demands, and resources. The prototypic situation is one in which some participants will be better off if a decision is made but where no single alternative will satisfy *all* participants. Furthermore, no single participant alone can force a decision. The participants engage in a bargaining process, using threats, bribes, trades, and compromises as devices for establishing a combination of participants and participant demands that is consistent with resources. The central questions are: 1) What coalitions will be formed? 2) How will they divide the resources? The criterion of viability does not presume a value consensus (at least not in the same sense as is presumed in the decision model). The coalition structure is problematic; in some forms of the model the alternative coalitions are also.

(3) *Artifactual (non-decision) models.* The most important difference between these models and the two classes previously mentioned is that events are not the realization of individual purposes, not even in the compromised way of the conflict resolution model. While both rational decision models and conflict resolution models view the organization mainly as a vehicle for production of decisions, the basic premises of the artifactual model are quite the opposite. The automatic and unconscious aspects – or what Robinson and Majak (1967) have called the "quasi-mechanical" aspects – are dominant. The outcome is seen as an unintended product of certain processes having dynamics of their own. "Decision" in these models is a *post factum* construct produced by participants or onlookers.[1] Events happen, and if they are afterwards described in a systematic fashion as decisions, it expresses more man's ability to form *post factum* theories of his own behavior than his ability to make goal oriented decisions through established structures and processes.

Although models of these three types are sometimes viewed as mutually inconsistent, we find it more fruitful to assume that each has its own place depending on the nature of the organizational situation and the kind of phenomena we wish to understand. The decisive matching of models to situations will be empirical, but we will propose some hypotheses specifying conditions under which each model seems likely to provide a useful framework for understanding organizational events.

6.1 Theoretical Concerns

The main thrust of our argument comes from two simple ideas: First, every participant in any organization is a part-time participant. Second, every decision opportunity in any organization is an ambiguous stimulus.

Part-time participants. Only in very rare situations will a decision command the attention of all the potential participants. The statement appears obvious; but students of decision-making often seem to err in assuming that *their* focus on a decision is matched by a similar focus by the members of the organization.

Every participant constantly faces the personal problem of allocating his attention among competitive claims on his time. On the one hand, it may be assumed that many decision-makers in contemporary organizations are overloaded, that organization tasks alone can consume more time than many participants have. On the other hand, participants also must play other roles as members of families, neighborhoods, friendship groups, and as members of local, national, and (sometimes) international communities. As a result, the character and outcome of any decision process in an organization is dependent on other demands on the time of different participants, including both potentially quite extraneous outside demands and "irrelevant" internal demands. We propose that an important aspect of any decision is the attention pattern for participants potentially concerned with the decision; and this pattern is only to a limited degree a function of the properties of the decision itself. It depends heavily on other decisions and other concerns that are currently activated.[2]

When actors are part-time, a theory must attend to the process of activation. We will be interested in (a) the number of participants activated, (b) the types of participants activated, (c) the way they perform (generating solutions, testing solutions, reacting) and (d) the turnover among participants.

Ambiguity. An organization is not simply a vehicle for solving given problems or for resolving conflict through bargaining. It is also a collection of choices looking for problems; issues and feelings looking for decisions-in-process through which they can be mediated; and solutions looking for questions. An organization is not only an instrument, with decision processes related to instrumental, task-directed activities. It is also a set of procedures by which participants arrive at an interpretation of what they (and others) are doing, and who they are.

This view of an organization as a mixture of issues, activities, feelings, and choices, each generated in part from extraneous factors, makes every choice opportunity an ambiguous stimulus. What is being decided is itself to be determined through the course of deciding it. We will be especially interested in the complexity of the definitions (e.g., multidimensionality of goals, the number of decision-making variables, the existence of algorithms for manipulating means-end connections), and the stability of the definition over time.

We believe that a choice among the three alternative models of organizational choice will prove to be dependent on both the process of activation and the process of definition. Most decisions in most organizations most of the time are probably made by relatively few people who, because of special expertise or for other reasons, are expected to focus on certain issues and generate solutions. Their decisions are made on the basis of a set of procedures that make the outcomes widely acceptable most of the time. We expect these people to establish stable values and beliefs related to their tasks and to deal with those tasks in terms of a comparatively stable definition of the situation, including implicit expectations of the demands of others, less activated, people. We also expect that the complexity of their "model of the world" will be adjusted to their capacities for analysis and decisions. The "rational decision" model – with its emphasis on the intellectual aspects of choice – will be particularly appropriate for a situation in which relatively few participants of the organization are activated and where the definition of the decision situation (i.e., which values, beliefs, and procedures are relevant) is stable and not too complex.

On the other hand, the conflict resolution model – with its emphasis on the socio-political aspects of choice – seems likely to be particularly appropriate in a situation where several relatively part-time participants are activated, where the group of participants is relatively stable, where there is agreement over the issues involved in the choice, but where there is disagreement over the values that should be used to resolve the issues.

Finally, the artifactual model – with its emphasis on the non-decision aspects of choice seems likely to be particularly appropriate in a situation where both activation and definition of the situation are changing, where several participants are activated (in generating solutions, testing solutions, and reacting), where the definition is complex, involving many values and decision-making variables, so that the situation is difficult to analyze and it is difficult to see and compare the consequences of the existing alternatives.

This brief review suggests, not that one model will be particularly appropriate for one organization and a different model for another, but that each model will probably apply to any organization under appropriate circumstances. A complete examination of the factors that affect the activation of participants and the definition of a choice

85

situation in a complex organization is beyond the scope of the present study. However, as a prelude to the present case study, we wish to call attention to four conspicuous variables that will be considered in more detail in our study of a university decision: Decision-time, organizational slack and the management of slack, style of the decision process, and external demands (or load) on participants.

Decision-time. The time it takes to make a decision has often been studied as a dependent variable in the investigation of individual and organizational behavior. Less commonly considered is the extent to which decision-time itself is a critical feature of a decision and affects both process and outcome. We ask how time affects the definition of a choice situation and the activation of participants to a decision. Our basic hypothesis is a "garbage can" model. It is assumed that each choice opportunity is an open receptacle into which any currently unresolved issues may be dumped (an assumption which will be modified and elaborated later). In general, the longer a choice remains unresolved, the greater the potential range of issues that are defined as relevant. Similarly with respect to the activation of participants, everything else being equal, the longer the time taken to reach a decision, the greater the potential number of participants who are activated. The longer the decision time, the broader the involvement in the decision.[3]

The more time a decision takes, the more participants and issues; as a result, the more complicated the situation. However, the more complicated the situation, the more participants will tend to postpone the decision and to avoid early commitment or find it difficult to agree, and the less attractive will be the role of taking leadership and generating solutions.[4] In such situations we would suggest that the impact of institutionalized deadlines would be especially important.

In suggesting that the ambiguous stimulus of a choice situation serves as a garbage can for issues and participants, we have ignored the extent to which there are competing choices.[5] As is well known to any organizational tactician, new choice opportunities attract some of the garbage from old choices. Thus, our consideration of the effects of time as an independent variable must include a specification of the temporal spacing of choice opportunities (and the amount of time devoted to them). If a decision requires (or is made to require) an extended period of time and no alternative choice situation arises during the same time period, the resulting choice will become a very general problem encompassing a wide range of issues – the garbage can will be filled to overflowing.

Thus, at one extreme we have an organizational setting in which there are (a) many alternative choice opportunities, (b) few issues and problems, and (c) rapid decisions. In such a setting any particular

86

choice will be made in terms of a narrow range of issues, and a narrow range of participants. As the number of choice situations decreases, or the decision time increases, the choices become broader, both with respect to the range of issues and problems defined as relevant and to the range of participants. These propositions are substantially independent of the explicit *a priori* content of the choice. The organizational meaning of the choice is provided in large part during the decision process.

Either the number of alternative choice opportunities or the number of issues may change over time. The model suggests that if the number of alternative choice opportunities decreases or the number of issues increases during the decision period, we would observe essentially the same phenomenon of broadening in meaning and active participants that has already been described. On the other hand, if the number of alternative choices increases after a choice has accumulated a set of issues and participants, we would predict that the number of participants involved in the choice would decrease almost immediately. The number of issues associated with the choice, however, would decrease more slowly (primarily because activation has a certain cost of time and energy, while an issue after it is raised may follow the choice, e.g., as a written document, without any such costs). As a result, the choice would become one associated with a relatively broad range of issues but commanding the attention of only a relatively narrow range of participants. However, over time we may expect that the issues and problems most central to the participants still active, will tend to dominate the definition of what the choice is all about (Weiner, 1972).

Organizational slack and the management of slack. Cyert and March (1963) have proposed that slack (the difference between existing resources and activated demands) in an organization will absorb a substantial share of the potential variability in an organization's environment. Slack permits the leadership to stabilize activation of participants and definitions of the situation by using parts of the reserve. We will be interested in the consequences of different degrees of slack for the activation and definition processes. The close connection to decision time is clear: The more slack, the easier (in general) to find a satisfactory solution and, therefore, the less the delay. But we may also derive some predictions that are independent of the time dimension. Since an organization in a given situation will not necessarily know the existing level of slack, but has to act in order to clarify the relationship between demands and resources, we have to consider not only "real" slack but also perceived slack. Perception of slack depends on existing procedures for the generation and coordination of demands and choice alternatives in the organization.

In organizations with a great amount of slack we expect few attempts to define general organizational values and beliefs in operational terms. We expect fairly frequent use of inconsistent premises for decisions in different parts of the organization. The inconsistencies are, in effect, buffered from one another by the slack. We would suggest that decisions made under a high degree of slack will not significantly change the "models" of the world which are governing organizational choices. On the other hand, we expect that organizations experiencing reduced slack will start processes designed to reduce inconsistency, and to clarify values and beliefs. The process increases the possibility that conceptions of the organization and its environment will change.

The underlying mechanisms are simple: The greater the amount of slack, the less difficulty the various potential participants have in routinely satisfying the demands. Thus, the greater the slack, the fewer the number of people activated in a decision. When slack is reduced, more people will be activated. We may draw a parallel to the process which develops when the solvency of a bank is questioned. If such a rumor produces a rush to get one's money back (demand that the organization fulfill the contract), this will make it necessary for others to do the same, and it will make it more and more difficult for the bank to meet the demands. As we move from a high slack to a low slack position, the insolvency metaphor suggests that there will be an organizational transition as follows:

(a) When there is a great amount of slack, decisions are made with minimal participant involvement; they are made by the relatively full-time "management", acting as though they were solving problems.

(b) When slack is reduced some of the relatively part-time participants are activated. They orient their demands to the "management" who continue to try to make the decisions by manipulating slack or somehow increasing total resources.

(c) When slack is further reduced (or time passes without the "managerial" strategies of (b) working successfully), more part-time participants are activated and it becomes obvious that there is no way all the demands can be met. As the participants confront each other with an overt conflict of interest, the "managerial" style of leadership is replaced with a "political" style; and the terms of the organizational coalition are renegotiated.

Such a transition, of course, will expose organizational procedures learned under one set of circumstances (i.e. high slack) to the cruelties of a different set (i.e., low slack). We would expect the usual problems

88

of organizational relearning on the part of all participants. The styles that they have come to believe are unconditional attributes of "good" management are exposed as attributes whose "goodness" is conditioned by the current and historical position of the organization with respect to slack.

Style of the decision-making process. As we have noted earlier, an organization may react to a given choice opportunity in several different ways; each style having a different degree of legitimacy in (most parts of) our culture:

In an *entrepreneurial* style. In this style it is assumed that objectives are shared (at least at some level) and that the problem is to identify an alternative that satisfies the shared criteria. This analytical or problem-solving, style (March and Simon, 1958) secures its legitimacy from widespread social acceptance of the postulates of rationality.

In a *political* style. In this style it is assumed that participants disagree over goals and a solution is sought that does not require operational commonality of goals. The political style secures its legitimacy either from its adherence to Pareto optimal solution or from widespread social acceptance of both the postulates of politics and the distribution of political power within the system.

In a *non-decision* style. In this style it is assumed that "choices" are the relatively extraneous product of a set of simultaneous independent activities, with little management or planning of either the entrepreneurial or the political manner. For the most part, the non-decision style appears to have no normative legitimacy and to be subject to normative attack both from those who believe in the necessary legitimacy of rationality and from those who believe in the necessary legitimacy of politics.

The emphasis on style has always been an important part of organizational governance. It is often assumed that people accept the policy content because they accept the legitimacy of the process through which this content is reached. In organizations with strong norms toward "rationality" we expect that only the entrepreneurial decision-model with its analytical, non-conflict, approach will be regarded as "legitimate". The other two models will be regarded as pathological. Organizations with strong norms of "equality" among participants can accept a "democratic" political process but not one that exposes power and status differences. Universities are apparently institutions with strong "rationality" and "equality" norms.

March and Simon (1958) predict that since most political processes have the potential of being disruptive for an organization (by placing strains on the status and power system), organizations will approach all decisions as if they were analytical problems. Even where it is obvious that bargaining takes place, attempts will be made to conceal it in an analytical framework. We expect this to be more true for established leaders than for their opponents, and more true in some organizations than others. Sometimes affecting the style-perceptions of potential participants may be a major tool for affecting the outcome of the choice.

Analytical processes are related mainly to enlarging resources or discovering new alternatives (e.g., search-behavior). We would expect that focusing on a common problem and trying to solve it will ordinarily have an integrating effect on an organization. Also, since value agreement is assumed (and therefore the definition of the situation somewhat stable), the research process will be defined as a technical, "neutral" operation. Those involved will normally be a few relatively full-time participants with special expertise in the field; the majority of potential participants will remain effectively inactive.

In bargaining, or "political" situations, the competition element is explicit: Whose values and beliefs will be accepted as a basis for decision? Who will get what part of the resources and burdens? Typically, the participants seek to resolve the issue by "political" activity. These may include redefining the issue, bringing in new aspects and activating other questions, issues, and feelings which tend to strengthen one's partisan position; or mobilizing (activating) one's constituency, inducing potential supporters among the participants to become active, eventually trying to prevent the opponent from doing the same.

These two devices are closely interrelated. For example, in situations where current contenders try to activate people, a necessary "price" may be the modification of the definition of the choice to be made. Sometimes this is done by including new values and beliefs, but often by simplifying the problems – popularizing them in order to make them more easily "understood". Such modifications by management make it particularly vulnerable to attacks both upon procedures and individuals. Coleman (1957) has noted that complaints about maladministration are used commonly to extend community conflicts. We would suggest that such a tendency toward attacks on individuals and procedures is a general phenomenon in organizations moving from a problem solving to a political mode of decision-making.

We may come to the same predictions from a much less rational basis. While problem-solving situations seem to have an integrative effect on an organization, a bargaining situation seems to have (at least in the short run) a polarizing effect. In particular, the bargaining mode exhibits a tendency for a participant to talk more and more with others with whom he agrees and less and less with those with whom he disagrees. Such a tendency, in turn, has important consequences for the definition of the choice situation. With polarization of interaction, we obtain segmentation of information. Also, participants will be more "free" to read their own meaning into the situation and the importance of fictions and rumors will increase, due to lack of check against reality. The differences among the various pictures of the actual situation grow as the several participants come to depend increasingly on information generated and processed within their own subgroups.

When a choice situation comes to be viewed generally within an organization as a political situation, we should expect such a view to be self-confirming. Perceiving a choice as being basically political will tend to weaken inhibition on latent conflict, thereby further linking the definition of the situation to a conflict-bargaining model.

In non-decision, or artifactual, choice situations, the style is always vulnerable to attack. Despite their generality, the procedures are not recognized as normatively legitimate. When a choice situation comes to be viewed generally within an organization as being met in a non-decision style, dissatisfied participants will immediately question the legitimacy of the style, raise questions with respect to the organizational raison d'etre, attempt to change the leadership style to a more acceptable form, or leave the organization. Thus, artifactual procedures for making choices represent the organizational version of a commonly observed combination – behavioral attractiveness and normative illegitimacy.

External demands on participants. Any organizational activity depends on a certain amount of liquidity of resources, the time, energy, and attention of potential participants being one important resource. Therefore, we have asserted that any choice opportunity must compete for the attention of organizational participants. This competition comes from other issues, choices, and feelings both inside and outside the organization. The level of attention to any specific decision in an organization will depend on the relative pressure of other claims for attention. For example, a participant facing serious problems in one organization (e.g., his family) will be less likely to become highly involved in a choice situation in a second one (e.g., his work organization).

The idiosyncratic aspects of external demands on individual participants may be important in individual cases, but our primary theoretical concern is with the statistical properties of the distribution of claims on attention. Under what circumstances are the average external demands relatively high? Under what conditions relatively low? What are the consequences of variations in the average attention load on participants?

If we assume that most participants are operating most of the time at (or near) their capacity, increasing the average load will have some obvious effects. It immediately decreases the amount of energy (per person per unit of time) available for any one problem. As a result, either the length of time taken to reach a decision must be increased in order to obtain the same amount of attention to the problem, or the number of persons involved must be increased (with attendent multiplier effects on average load), or the total amount of attention to the problem must be reduced. The activation patterns are affected by any of these routes, either directly or through decision delay.

The average load on potential participants is particularly susceptible to three sets of factors:

(a) Properties of the participants. Relatively "important" participants tend to be more heavily loaded than relatively "unimportant" ones. "Importance" here refers to the mix of attributes most commonly associated with social and organizational status. One interesting possible consequence of this differential loading stems from the fact that when a choice situation is defined as an important one, it tends automatically to involve relatively important people. As a result of the high average load on such people, "important" decisions have difficulties securing much attention.

(b) Properties of the environment. When the environment of an organization is generating many problems, the attention load of its participants increases. The result is translated into effects within the organization as participants direct their attention to meeting the outside demands. These properties of the environment are frequently seasonal (e.g., variable loads produced by seasonal variations in weather problems, tax problems, children problems, etc.) or life-cyclic (e.g., variable loads associated with stages in the life-cycle of participants).

(c) Properties of the organization. Organizations may be characterized in terms of their load autonomy. An organization with high load autonomy is one in which the various participants control their activities within and outside the organization to a predetermined level. The pure case is the employee who successfully assigns his work problems to 40 pre-determined hours a week and his other problems to the 128 other hours. The closer to load autonomy the organization comes, the less sensitive organizational behavior is to the external load problems, and the more sensitive to a build-up in internal problems. Under such circumstances, an increase in problems within the organization must be accommodated within the pre-determined time and cannot be buffered by some excess capacity within the time allocated to other organizations. Similarly, an increase in problems external to an autonomous organization has little internal effect. Universities, in common with many organizations of professionals, appear to have relatively low load autonomy. Thus, increases in internal load may be accommodated by using external time. The price paid for this is the converse: Increases in external load affect internal operations immediately.

In general we suggest that decisions involving high load participants will have problems of getting attention until a *deadline* is approached. If a deadline is set as a part of the choice, this becomes an important decision in itself. If deadlines are externally set, the importance of the artifactual element increases. Working with only "important issues", and being overloaded, decision-makers will attend to choices only when they have to – often probably because they do not want others to make the decision. At the same time, variations in load affect the definition of a choice. The higher the load, the more important is easily available information and the more important a "mating theory" of information (Cyert and March, 1963, p. 80). Also, the higher the load the more the ability of external groups to produce information affect the content of organizational choices (Jacobsen, 1965), and the more important is the phenomenon of uncertainty absorption.[6]

As will become obvious below, the choice of these four variables – time, slack, style, and load – is not fortuitous. We believe the basic model is substantially correct and that it provides a good basis for understanding the phenomena to be reported in the study below when considered in the light of the four variables. The choice studied was distinguished particularly by: An extended decision time, at least partly due to extraneous reasons; an organization undergoing an apparent reduction of slack, from a high slack position to a lower slack position; a decision style that changed from a predominately (perceived) problem-solving style to a predominately (perceived) political style; heavy external demands on almost all of the major participants.

6.2 The Setting of the Study

On July 1, 1969, a new dean was appointed to a school at one of the campuses of a major American public university. His appointment culminated a search for a new dean that began on September 27, 1968, with the announcement by the previous dean of his intention to resign. The appointment was made by the Chancellor of the campus on the recommendation of the Academic Vice-Chancellor. It was approved by the President of the university and the Board of Trustees. This study reports that nine-month decision process as observed, analyzed,

93

and understood by a visiting foreign student of organizations.

Opened in 1965, the campus had an enrollment in 1968 of about 4,000 students and some 250 faculty. The campus was organized into eight schools along broad disciplinary lines. Each school was headed by a dean who was administratively responsible to the Academic Vice-Chancellor. By 1968 the university faced growing financial stringency in both operating and capital budgets and increasing tension over student and faculty unrest.

The present study is focused on one of the eight schools on the campus. In the academic year 1968–1969 this school had 48 faculty (13 of these being part-time) and accounted for about 15 percent of the total campus student enrollment (both in terms of "majors" and in terms of course enrollments). Twelve of the 34 full-time faculty members were new in 1968–1969. The school engaged in both undergraduate and graduate teaching and research over a domain represented by about six recognized academic disciplines.

In the university catalogue, the school emphasized that "the program, faculty, and students differ substantially from conventional counterparts elsewhere". An outsider would not be left in doubt that most insiders viewed the scool as something very special, crusading for innovation. The school's 10-year plan also states as its goal, "to achieve as rapidly as possible a national reputation" and "to provide educational leadership"in the relevant disciplines. This should be done not through an imitative strategy but through exploiting special competence to develop national preeminence in areas that had not been developed at the major institutions. These statements clearly reflect the high level of aspirations among the faculty in the school.

The ideology had its counterpart in the organizational patterns, breaking away from traditional departments, having flexible and fragile programs[7] with a certain amount of contempt for bureaucratic procedures, and emphasizing a feeling of community with personal relationships among faculty members and between faculty and students. While in some areas (e.g., curriculum decision) the organization model clearly was one of "anarchy" with a great amount of freedom for the student and the individual faculty-member (or subgroups), the school in other ways had a strong "power-center". The school's ideological father, being dean from the start, combined the formal authority of the dean's position with a certain amount of charismatic leadership for a majority of the faculty. He played the major role in developing the "vision" of the school and its place in the academic world, providing explanations for events taking place inside and outside the school, and in formulating goals for the future. The absence of other important formal administrative positions (lack of department chairmen, the associate dean position was defined as a

94

minor one and occupied by a young assistant professor) also strengthened the dean's position.

A much used style of decision-making was that the dean would *consult* with the faculty, formulate, and often innovate the decision alternatives, actively mobilize support for one alternative, and then *announce* it. This combination of a highly centralized decision-making in some cases with an extremely decentralized process in others had two important consequences. On the one hand it provided a situation where the school, as an organization, had taken few important *joint* decisions; on the other hand it can be said to have put the full professors in a "relatively deprived" position compared to their colleagues in traditional departments. Either the dean would take the decision, or each faculty member or small groups would do it; in neither case were the formal differences between tenure and non-tenure members the same as in more traditional departments.

One important domain for the dean was the management of external relations, in particular the protection of the faculty from other university authorities and the defence of autonomy for the school in all academic matters. In general, the posture of the school had produced an external reputation of the school as an innovative, maverick institution on the campus, supported by the administration of the campus but not universally loved by representatives of other schools. This in a way provided a "we-against-the-rest-of-the-world" feeling (especially among the junior faculty). At the same time, there was also some internal tension, the most important being between the dean and one of the program directors.

Thus, we are focusing upon a school not organized along traditional disciplinary lines, without traditional departments, and with a somewhat special authority and decision-structure. The faculty clearly had high aspirations and expectations. Now they were confronted with an unexpected situation, i.e., the ideological father of the school resigned. There was no ready-made procedure for replacing him. The choice was perceived as a very important one. Furthermore, given that the school, for several reasons, wanted to focus on candidates outside the school, the choice would potentially provide a confrontation of the image of the school dominant in the school itself and the image of the school among potential dean candidates.

Data about this process were obtained in four ways:

(a) Participant observation. The author had the opportunity to participate in all meetings of the search committee[8] (also meetings between the committee and the candidates), and in the two general faculty meetings. He was present in the organization throughout the time period covered by the decision, was recognized as an "outsider", and was accorded the access of a foreign scholar.

(b) Numerous interviews during the whole period. The author interviewed all of the important participants several times during the course of the decision. In total these interviews represented about 400 hours of direct discussion about the process.

(c) Analysis of written material. Written material about the school, its plans, and its organization were collected and examined. In addition, written memoranda during the course of the decision were collected.

(d) A general questionnaire. A detailed structured questionnaire was administered to all faculty during the process (last week of March through first week of April). Thirty-five of the 48 faculty members answered this questionnaire. All of the tenured, full-time faculty answered the questionnaire, as did 76 percent of the non-tenured, full-time faculty and 52 percent of the part-time faculty. Three of the respondents effectively provided no information, they neither had opinions of the process nor had taken active part in it. From responses to the questionnaires it was obvious that the non-respondents were clearly on the periphery of the decision, and that the major reason for not answering was the fact that they had nothing to say.

We can present a brief chronology of the events, starting September 27, 1968, with the announcement by the dean of his intention to resign and ending with the appointment of the new dean on July 1, 1969.

Date	Event
9/27/68	The dean announces his intention to resign.
11/8	Faculty meeting, general discussion.
11/11	First meeting of the search committee (appointed by the Vice-Chancellor).
11/14	The search committee meets. Proposal for building a list of candidates and discussion about how to approach candidates.
11/18	A candidate visits the campus on the initiative of a group outside the committee. An "episode" between the candidate and a section of the faculty in one of the programs (Program A).
11/20	The committee decides to accept this candidate (not willing to let this part of the faculty have a veto). The episode produces a general discussion of how to present new candidates to the faculty. The only committee-

Date	Event

member from outside the school no longer attends meetings.

12/3 No definite answer from the accepted candidate. The search committee agrees on a list of "active candidates" and decides to make some new contacts.

12/10 Committee meets. No definite answer from the accepted candidate. Some other candidates approached, but with negative result. Two decisions on procedure: Not to call (use telephone) but make personal contacts. Relaxing the rule that the candidates should be approached sequentially.

12/10 A non-tenured faculty member proposes to some of his colleagues a "party cluster" among the junior-people, to assure that each has an opportunity to meet dean candidates.

12/13 Search committee meets. For the first time members ask for the candidates' publications. Further screening dates. The student member's last meeting. She leaves the university and no new student-representative is appointed.

12/14–12/28 No formal meetings, but consultations. Sometimes parts of the search committee meet. Still waiting for definite answer from the first accepted candidate. Approaches to other possible candidates turn out negative.

1/28/69 One committee-member (full professor, new 1968–69) proposes the establishment of regular departments. Bargaining goes on between this committee-member and some of his colleagues on the one hand, and the dean on the other, regarding the possibility of organizing a department or a committee on a given subject.

1/29–2/8 Committee inactive. An initiative and power vacuum seem to exist. The dean takes over in the beginning of February. During a meeting (in the home of the dean) between the dean, the associate dean, and the chairman of the search committee, 29 candidates are proposed. The list is very soon reduced to 6 candidates, and after some consultations the dean decides to invite three candidates to the campus. All three come.

2/24 A memorandum on the school's future organization by one tenured faculty outside the search committee, (written on the initiative of the dean), is circulated. One

Date	Event

point raised is the power of the new dean, opening the possibility for making this a decision variable. Meanwhile, and before the three candidates come to the campus, there seems to be a strong opinion among some faculty members that the three invited candidates are not "good enough".

2/24–3/14 The three candidates visit the campus, talk with the dean, faculty, search committee, and university administration.

2/28 The committee-member who had proposed the introduction of regular departments, resigns from the search committee. Exchange of highly emotional and personal memoranda between the dean and one of the program directors (Program B), former associate dean. This episode is closely related to a rumor (real or asserted) that the dean and the chairman of the search-committee are "playing games" in inviting three "unacceptable" candidates to the school in order to pave the way to the deanship for a (named) associate professor, already a faculty member.

3/6–3/17 A new candidate is introduced. He is visiting the campus by accident. During a meeting with one program director (B) and the Vice-Chancellor, his candidacy is proposed. Later he states that he will not accept.

3/7 The chairman of the search committee takes the initiative, sending the list of all proposed candidates to the members of the search committee in order to see if an agreement is possible. No result.

3/12 One of the programs (B) gathers behind an "inside" candidate, the first associate dean of the school, now primarily in another school on campus, but a member of the program proposing him.

3/17 A general faculty meeting. Five candidates mentioned – among them the chairman of the search committee (a member of Program A). A majority vote for the inside candidate proposed by Program B. The faculty votes; 16 for the Program B candidate, 3 for the committee chairman, 1 for either of these, and 2 for recycling the search process. The graduate students vote; 6 for the Program B candidate, 1 for the committee chairman, 1 for one of the outside candidates and

	1 against all the candidates. The junior fellows (under-graduates); 1 for one of the outside candidates, 1 for recycling and the rest for people who are not "official" candidates. No "hot" debate. The dean will not give his opinion on the different candidates.
3/18–4/1	The Vice-Chancellor consults with parts of the faculty. Different reasons are discussed among faculty as to why the majority candidate is not proposed for appointment. Among many faculty members the most important and surprising factor is seen to be the fact that the dean – when reporting to the Vice-Chancellor – said he did not agree with the choice made by the majority. A set of other solutions are discussed (acting dean, new candidates from outside, etc.). The chairman of the search committee comes in focus as main candidate. After this, the Vice-Chancellor, dean, and the chairman of the search committee again consult with (some) faculty.
4/17	Another member of the search committee withdraws from all administrative work in the school; this because of new procedures for faculty evaluation proposed by the dean the previous day.
5/1–5/31	Informally, the faculty know that the committee chairman will be the new dean. The official announcement has to wait (the Vice-Chancellor says) for the final decision by the administrative board of the university. One of the programs (A) – to which the new dean belong – decides to go further toward an "anarchy" organization, one other program (B) reacts by stating that they want to keep the existing structure of the program. The third program (C) does not react at all. A general faculty meeting discussing the future of the school is boycotted by most of the people in Program B. Some controversy between the director of this program and the new dean and between the director and the Vice-Chancellor.
7/1	The new dean is formally appointed.

6.3 Analysis of the Decision

The analysis starts at the point when the dean had made his decision to resign, the school had a choice opportunity, and a committee had been appointed. The analysis ends with the official announcement of the choice of a new dean, excluding the implementation phase. The process will be divided into three parts, (a) a committee-centered phase, (b) a dean-centered phase, and (c) a Vice-Chancellor-centered phase. This is more an analytical construct than a reflection of clear-cut breaks in the events. The search committee phase started November 11, 1968. Roughly, it continued to the end of 1968; Januar 1969, was some kind of "vacuum" situation. The dean-centered phase started in the first days of February and went on to March 17 when the Vice-Chancellor phase began.

We begin with a description of the four variables: time, perceived slack, perceived style governing the decision, and external load, when the process started. From these four variables we make some interpretations of activation and definition processes. These interpretations will then be related to the events actually taking place. Then we discuss the relationships between the states of activation and definition and the three models of decision-making presented above. Finally, we attend to some observations on the outcomes of each choice: (1) the dean-candidate(s) selected, and (2) the state of the organization after the choice.

6.3.0 *The Search Committee-Centered Phase*

Although *slack* had been reduced (budget-cuts, student unrest, etc.), the perceived slack was very high among a majority of the faculty – especially among junior faculty. The school was viewed as a "swinging place" which would make its mark in the professional world. The wishes of the 10-year plan could be clearly seen behind this definition of the situation. Instead of discussing a choice under scarcity, the school started out with a high level of aspiration, focusing on highly visible scientists, "stars" in their fields – and people with standing offers from some of the best American universities. This level of aspiration, which also has to be viewed in connection with the fact that the dean himself was a man of this class,[9] was clearly expressed in the first faculty meeting (November 8). Besides being an outstanding academician, an acceptable candidate had both to be able to make educational and organizational innovations and to fit some "style" criteria connected to the unusual organization of the school.

Everybody seemed to take it as given that the choice should be, and was, approached in a problem-solving style. The assumption was that the committee was endeavoring to find a dean whom everybody could accept. There was (during the first month) an assumed value consensus closely related to protect the school and its somewhat special character.[10] In interviews we were told that since values were shared and since all the people in the school were intelligent, there was no problem delegating the decision to others.

The *load autonomy*, at least in the short run, was low for most potential participants. The dean and the chairman of the search committee, especially, besides teaching, research, and administrative work in the school, were heavily involved in national and international professional organizations, national research councils and major foundations. As a result, the external load was rather high for key people.

Given this description of the situation – slack perceived as high; problem solving perceived as the style dominating the decision; heavy external load; and time not yet a relevant variable, we would expect the process of definition to go on without well defined criteria, and without strong attempts to make the different criteria consistent. It should be expected that the somewhat non-operational definition of a good dean already established in the school would be central, and that the choice would be influenced only slightly by other issues, sentiments, values, and beliefs. Concerning the *process of activation* we would expect that few of the potential participants would activate themselves and that the people participating would do it in a part-time manner. We would expect search behavior to be emphasized. But also, we would expect the patterns of search to reflect the desire of the participants to avoid search costs, that most of the activity would be concentrated around the "defined experts" – the search committee.

We then turn to what actually took place in the search committee-centered phase. During this first phase 75 candidates were mentioned in the committee. By the end of the period, 10 of these candidates had been judged acceptable for the deanship. In addition, we had a group of 9 "active" candidates. These were people discussed in more than one committee-meeting and put on a special list but never asked to be dean. The third and biggest category was the "passive candidates". These were candidates who were discussed in only one committee-meeting or who were mentioned but never discussed.

The search for candidates started with a "brain-storming" procedure for resource-persons, people who could be used to find candidates. In the first committee-meeting, 19 informants outside the school were proposed, however, only 9 were ever contacted. Six of these proposed candidates. This has to be viewed in connection with the fact that brain-storming in the committee and with a few senior faculty members outside it, gave 65 (out of the 75) candidates the first three days. Only one of the people later asked to be dean and one of the "active" candidates were not proposed during this period.

The dean position has traditionally been a resource that could attract people who otherwise would not come. This obviously was the way some faculty members now perceived the situation. From the very day the dean resigned they had candidates whom they would accept immediately. We find (as did Caplow and McGee, 1958) that a majority of the candidates had close relationships with the school *before* the search started. This connection being of increasing importance when we go from the "passive" to the "active" candidates and further to the people asked to be dean.

Consider the following four criteria for "nearness":

(a) Has the candidate earlier been approached about the possibility of being a faculty member of the school? Nine out of the ten people asked to be dean, 6 out of the 9 active candidates, and 20 out of the 56 passive candidates had already been approached about the possibility of becoming faculty members.

(b) Has the candidate been quoted in the professional work of the members of the search committee?[11] Here we find an important difference between the dean and the others. In the work (written or edited) of the committee-members, the highest number is six candidates quoted. In the work of the dean, however, nine out of the ten people asked to be dean, seven out of nine active candidates, and 40 out of 56 passive candidates are quoted in his two latest books. Since one of these is a volumnious reader we have also compared it with similar readers in the field (same number pages, ± two years in date of publication). Again the difference is very clear. The reader coming nearest to that edited by the dean has quotations from four of the people asked to be dean, from five of the active candidates and 20 passive candidates. The other two readers each mention one of the people asked to be dean, one active candidate and six and 12 of the passive candidates.

(c) Does anybody in the committee know the candidates' professional work?[12] All the ten people asked to be dean, eight of the active, and 34 of the passive candidates' professional production were known (as defined) by at least one member of the committe when the search process started.

(d) Does anybody know the candidates personally?[13] Nine of the people asked to be dean, eight of the active candidates and 40 of the passive candidates were known personally by at least one member of the search committee when the process started.

This concentration on candidates "near" the school has the consequence that the participants could avoid search-cost and uncertainty. The important job for the committee was more to scale down the list of candidates than to find candidates, more a search for consequences than a search for alternatives. The criteria for nearness also played an important role in reducing the number of candidates. This can be

102

viewed as a process having two important steps: (1) Reduce the list to 19 candidates, (2) Reduce this again to 10 people approached about the possibility of becoming dean.

The first phase may be described by means of a simple model, built on the following three questions (the data were garthered through interviews). (1) Does at least one committee-member know the candidate's professional, written work? (2) Is there at least one committee-member, who knows the candidate's professional, written work, willing to accept him immediately as dean when his name is proposed for the first time in the committee? (3) Is there anybody expressing very negative opinions about the candidate when his name is mentioned for the first time in the committee?[14]

Predicting that a candidate will be activated if one can answer "yes-yes-no" on the three questions we are wrong only in 7 out of 75 cases (Table 6.0). Four candidates should have been activated following the model but were not. They were all people of very high reputations, national leaders in their fields. One possible reason for not activating them may be a learning process in the committee. After approaching several of the people in this high status category and getting negative answers, the probability of getting people of this type must have appeared small. Three candidates were activated but should not have been according to the model. At least one of them was explicitly activated for very special reasons related more to his career outside than inside academic affairs.

Table 6.0. Comparison of the model's prediction of which candidates would be activated in the committee, with those who were in fact activated

	The model predicts	
	Should be activated	Should not
Activated in the committee	16	3
Not activated in the committee	4	52

The next phase, picking those among the activated candidates to whom the dean position should be offered, can be described by Tables 6.1. and 6.2. As shown in Table 6.1. the committee, with only one exception, approached all the activated candidates whom two or more committee-members wanted to accept as dean immediately. This describes the outcome as a result of a pure "voting" situation with weak demands for consensus. (The committee never used any explicit voting procedure, although each member made some tentative rankings of candidates once). Table 6.2. shows that a model assuming that candidates *known personally* by two or more committee members will be chosen from among the activated candidates, predicts correctly 14 times out of 19.

Table 6.1. Treatment for the activated candidates related to how many committee members were willing to accept them immediately as dean

Number of committee members that want to accept the candidate as dean immediately	Candidates	
	Asked to be dean	Activated but not asked to be dean
Five	3	0
Four	1	0
Three	3	0
Two	3	1
One	0	5
None	0	3

Table 6.2. Treatment of activated candidates related to the committee member's knowledge about them as persons

The committee members knowledge about the candidates as persons	Candidates	
	Asked to be dean	Activated but not asked to be dean
Two or more know the candidate as a person	7	2
Less than two know the candidate as a person	3	7

Several possible rules do *not* improve the predictions in the model. Giving the participants different "power" weights makes no improvement. This fact does not of course mean that each member of the committee had the same influence. However, it appears that information in this phase is the most important resource, so that "power" considerations beyond these differences do not improve our model. In addition, adding information about support for a candidate outside the committee (among faculty members, among informants) does not improve predictions. Some candidates had support outside the committee, (e.g., proposed as candidates from 2–3 different sources but no support inside). Candidates in this category were never activated. This stresses the importance of *where* in an organization search is located, and a part of the explanation may simply be that the committee's "memory" did not provide exact information about who had supported whom.[15] Finally, considering the *strength* of preferences within the committee does not improve predictions.

Since introducing these different weights into the model does not improve the predictions, we may speculate that this type of information presumes a different kind of decision process than was used. The work on scaling the list of candidates down can be described as a "sounding out" process used to test the degree of support for a certain candidate (Thompson and McEwan, 1958, Olsen, 1972). Very rarely did any committee-member present strong opinions when a candidate was presented for the first time, and when it happened, it was always in connection with candidates who obviously had no support at all in the committee. The usual procedure in the committee would be to mention tentatively general sentiments and let the other members respond. At least 10–12 candidates who one or more of the committee-members (in the interviews) said they would accept as dean immediately, were never strongly fought for in meetings, presumably because there was little support or a somewhat negative response when the candidate's name was first mentioned.

The emphasis on using existing information rather than producing new, and the predictive value in our models of the distribution of information about a candidate, make it necessary to take a closer look at the distribution of knowledge among the participants. Table 6.3. shows very marked differences in the degree of information among the committee-members.[16] The effect was that the most "senior" people, with highest external demands on their time and energy, had to do most of the job. Another factor was working in the same direction. The school and the committee would not have liked to be rejected openly too many times. It was, therefore, necessary to approach candidates in a somewhat informal way. The belief was that a positive answer was more likely if the man inquiring was of the same status as the candidate, and knew him already. Thus the number of people making contact with candidates was substantially reduced.

Table 6.3. The committee members' knowledge about the written production of the candiates and about the candiates as persons

Knowledge about the written production*	Committee members				
	A	B	C	D	E
High	32	25	11	15	10
Middle	24	20	11	11	11
Low	19	30	53	49	54
Knowledge about the candidates as persons					
High	31	33	7	5	4
Middle	18	14	6	3	5
Low	26	28	62	67	66

*The categories used are explained in footnotes 12 and 13.

This situation poses an interesting dilemma for the organization. One important condition for obtaining information (and ability to take initiative and control) seems to be participation in meetings and decisions away from the campus. But this again imposes strong constraints on the time and energy these participants can devote to decisions on campus.

The analysis so far reveals two important tendencies. First, concerning activation, our data can be understood by referring only to the existing information and preferences in the committee. We do not have to assume anything about activity outside the committee. Also, the patterns of search clearly reflect a situation where those participating (the committee-members) wanted to avoid search-costs and uncertainty. Second, concerning definition, we do not have to refer to any explicit goals or criteria in the committee in order to understand how the candidates were treated. These two tendencies, which are consistent with our expectations, are supported by what was observed directly.

Faculty members mentioned several *dimensions* which were important, but the meaning and relative importance of each dimension was never clarified. The faculty meeting emphasized that the new dean had to be an academic leader in his field. He had to be fully established and not a person trying to escape into administration from an unsuccessful academic career. He should be young, 40 years or less, and he had to take most aspects of the school as given: Keep the "anarchy" and not introduce departments; be permissive inwards, but strong outwards; have strong interests in interdisciplinary and quantitative work; and keep the mathematical requirements.[17] By and large the faculty reacted conservatively, wanting to protect what was already established.

The search committee first accepted this vague definition, but soon found it impossible to discuss these criteria in the abstract. The discussion went on with little explicit comparison between candidates and criteria and between different candidates. As a committee the group did not attempt to reach value consensus before ranking candidates. Preferences among candidates were stated, but few reasons given. Trade-offs among criteria were never discussed seriously (as the economic man-model would demand), and levels of aspirations (e.g., how much interdisciplinary orientation would be "satisfying") were never clarified in any intersubjective way (such as the "administrative man"/satisficing man-model would demand). In the interviews, however, it was indicated that the criteria mentioned above were those considered.[18] No other issues, feelings or sentiments were related to the choice.

Concerning activation, the general lack of involvement of people outside the committee can be indicated in several ways. Only eight tenured and five non-tenured faculty members ever proposed any candidate, and only 3–4 faculty members outside the search committee seemed to activate themselves in order to campaign for a candidate.

106

Potential participants outside the school (e.g., administration, faculty senate, students) never activated themselves. The problem was seen as an internal one for the school. This is reflected both in the composition of the committee, and in the fact that the only outside member neither tried to play an important role nor attended the committee meetings after the first few. The only occasion on which an outside initiative *was* taken (November 18) was viewed as an attempt to find a unilateral solution to the problem by one group, instead of "talking oneself into consensus". The letter from a junior faculty proposing a "party-cluster" which should offer its services to the search committee, did not have any effect.

To summarize, the process of definition was characterized by multiple and ambiguous (but probably stable) goals. Although few other issues, values, beliefs, and sentiments were connected to the choice, the relationships between alternatives and consequences were uncertain. Taken together, this ambiguity and uncertainty made the definition quite complex. The process of activation was characterized by a fairly small and stable group of participants (the committee), but people activated in a part-time manner, emphasizing already existing or easily available information and a "talking-oneself-into-consensus-style".

The summary indicates a set of conditions that do not fit any of the three models of choice perfectly. The definition was too complex for a rational decision-model, the values and beliefs too unclear to provide a pure bargaining situation, and the rational elements too strong to let artifactual aspects dominate. Although the participants as a committee could not "maximize" or "satisfice" in the way these models demand, they could clearly *avoid* outcomes obviously not wanted.

We have described the selection among candidates as a pure voting model with low demands on consensus and with a veto to each committee-member. In this way each person becomes a "hurdle" for each candidate (and not as "satisficing" theory proposes, that a candidate has to pass a certain level on each of the relevant goal-dimension stated by a joint committee). However, we should also consider some artifactual aspects. The analysis should take into account that the committee could easily have been successful, i.e., the outside candidate could have accepted the job. His nonacceptance was more related to things taking place outside the school, than to the behavior of the committee. (While there were different opinions among faculty members as to what degree the "episode" had any effect on the candidate's decision not to accept the deanship, several factors outside the school *were i*mportant.)

We might speculate about the consequences of early success. Probably, the search committee would have been judged a success, the faculty would have found its dominating "model of the world" reinforced (including the high quality dimension), and some important conflicts would probably have been avoided. We mention these as a brake on our tendency to over-interpret events having substantial "chance" elements. Nevertheless, the committee did fail to find a dean. At the end of this phase the school had to face the fact that the committee had accepted ten candidates for the deanship, but that none of these had indicated interest.

To understand *why* the committee did not succeed we take into account several factors reducing the likelihood of success: (a) the dean position had lost some of its value, due to the student unrest, budget cuts, etc. (b) One candidate early in the process said that he might accept the deanship. Consistent with the theory of "satisficing" this slowed down the process in an important stage. (c) Given the crusading ideology of the school a general and fast lowering of the level of aspiration was difficult. It would have had important implications for the participants image of both themselves and the school. (d) Using a formal committee was against the expectations in the school. Most faculty believed the dean would make the decision. This decreased their own activity. The dean, however, decided not to be the godfather of his successor (for reasons which cannot be explained within our model). He took part, but did not run the process. Given the history of the school this was a difficult role to play. It also was difficult for others to believe that this was the role played. (e) Several faculty-members who usually were "leaders" in the school, were for different, extraneous reasons not active. (f) The style of management, with low degree of activity and emphasis on "talking-oneself-into-consensus" more than imposing a solution upon someone, turned out to be inefficient when applied across several disciplines with rather little overlapping information about potential candidates. (g) The important role the most overloaded people had to play, reinforced the tendency of low activity.

Looking at the *consequences* of not finding a dean, we get an illustration of man's need and ability to form or invent "explanations" after the fact, and thereafter use these constructs as if they were facts as a point of departure for new actions or non-actions. The process of organizational learning showed a general tendency to presume more post fact certainty in events than existed. While we observed a set of events which had ambiguous and uncertain aspects, the explanations invented after the fact were basically derived from a rational, deterministic model of choice. Although the events were too obscure to be described by any simple model, the basic question was *who has been running the process?* The possibility that nobody had governed the process did not seem to give a satisfactory explanation. Later – in a rumor – the inactivity in the first phase was explained as a planned plot.

Some explained the failure as a level-of-aspiration phenomenon. The question was raised whether the school's quality had been overrated. It was "discovered" that the written production, especially that of the younger faculty, had not been as great as thought; that the school and the campus did not score as high as often implicitly assumed on criteria like quality of library and computer facilities; that the social environment of the campus had developed in a more negative direction than expected. Some asked if the school really was as interdisciplinary as one had believed (saying that most people were publishing in the journals of their discipline, that few interdisciplinary research projects had been started, etc.). The perceptions of slack changed in important ways.

The other reaction was one of perceived decision *style*. The faculty members proposing candidates found that their candidates would not accept or were not accepted. There was some bitterness because it was believed that their candidate(s) had not been approached at all or in an inadequate way. One of the committee-members openly stated that he had misused his time participating in the committee. And from some people in the school it was said that the whole search process was "screwed up". Certainly the definition of the choice opportunity as a question of problem solving had started to change. The fact that the dean a little later took the initiative was perceived by some people as proof of the "politicing" going on. (However, others would say that the dean was the only one able to find a solution.)

6.3.1 *The Dean-Centered Phase*

During the last part of the search-committee phase and the first part of the dean-centered phase it became clear that the choice would require time. This was important because some very significant issues now had to be confronted, especially promotion of faculty and the reorganization of the school – both as a function of predetermined time-limits. These issues were handled by the programs and the dean, and not converted into school choices. In our terminology, garbage was coming up, but no alternative cans. The majority perceived the *style* to be a political one. The level of mutual trust had been lowered, and the choice could not be managed in a problem-solving way. The organization had to operate on a reduced level of *slack* and assume scarcity. When the dean took over, the job was placed with the person having the highest external *load* on his time. At the same time, time-demands (i.e., search costs) increased. Given these changes from the first phase, our model predicts some important differences in the definition and activation processes.

109

Concerning the *definition* of the choice, we would expect the "garbage can" to become filled with issues and sentiments. We would expect an *expansion* of issues and feelings defined as relevant, that new issues would be connected to the choice, and especially that person and process directed criteria (the maladministration aspect) would be focused on. Also, we would expect a clarification of values and beliefs among the different participating groups, making visible differences in opinions concerning where the school ought to go and how to reach stated ends. The changes in the range of issues and problems perceived relevant, and the clarification and search for consistency between different criteria used, should also be accompanied with a higher degree of activation of the participants than in the first phase. We should expect new leaders to arise. Especially as a conflict begins encompassing the basic values of the organization, it will be difficult for any member to keep out. In sum, we would expect both more people to be activated and that some more than before would be activated in a full-time manner.

The dean's point of departure was a "rational decision" definition of the situation. The school would have to discover future academic leaders before the market (a definition increasing the element of gambling and of search-costs). Also one should take a step toward more emphasis on the candidates' ability to deal with people (the "community"-aspect).

The problem solving-approach, however, was very soon abandoned. An important new aspect was that the whole problem of the school's organization structure was opened up for debate when a member of the search committee and program B proposed traditional departments along disciplinary lines introduced. The anarchy-aspect was the only question formally voted upon in the faculty-meeting (November 8). At that time is was given unanimous support. Thus, the proposal to introduce departments certainly aroused excitement in the school, and an associate professor (and in practice the administrative leaders of program A for some time) stated that "centralized authority as ordinarily embodied in the departmental chairman is an inadequate model for our needs". A decision by the program B director to introduce a standing committee in a special field – a proposal not supported by the dean – emphasized the importance of the whole organizational question – an issue taken as given in the first phase.

The questions of organization were related to the person of the ideological father of the anarchy-model, the dean. The changes in attitudes and feelings surrounding the decision came out in the open most clearly in an exchange of memoranda February 28. Said the dean in a memorandum:

110

The following extraordinarily destructive rumor has been planted within the School in the last day or so ... (the dean) and ... (the chairman of the search committee) are playing a devious game of inviting unacceptable dean candidates in order to pave the way for the appointment of ... (the faculty member writing a memorandum against departments) as dean. That is a lie.

The same day the chairman of program B reacted by denying that he had circulated any rumor and saying that there was no rumor. The program director made it quite clear that he was not a great admirer of either the dean or the candidate proposed in the rumor. Especially the leadership style of the dean was attacked.

The third memorandum on this date came from the faculty member who had proposed the introduction of traditional departments. Withdrawing from the search committee he told the Vice-Chancellor and the faculty:

I don't understand the current behavior of my colleagues. I am particularly distressed with the power politics that has engulfed the school. The actions of the search committee have been few and singularly unsuccessful. My contributions to the effort have been uniformly unrewarding.

The emphasis on organization and person criteria, obviously had a maladministration aspect. The importance of this aspect was expressed in other ways, too: A rumor was circulated, but always denied by everybody when confronted by it, that the chairman of the search-committee had been inactive in order to get the deanship himself. The search-committee in general was said to have forgotten the "second best candidates". When the top people had said no, three candidates belonging to a much lower level had been invited to the campus. The dean was attacked for usurping power. The way he had acted when inviting the three candidates was indicating that the dean was playing games and not taking the choice seriously enough.

Thus, for one group (among them the dean), the activity among senior people in program B was an attack on the anarchy-ideology of the school and its laissez-faire spirit. At the same time the people "attacking" would say that their actions were the results of the fact that the school did not follow its own ideology of "letting every flower bloom" (e.g., the resistance against letting the subgroup form their own committee). In the same way as the motives of the people in program B were questioned, they – on their side – were sceptical of the real motives of the dean and some of the people in program A. The question was raised as to whether the dean believed any longer in making the school an elite institution which was an important part of the school's ideology. It was argued that the group around the dean was now trying to escape the judgement of the external, professional market. Like many lesser colleges one would use internal judges and define as good what one was doing in the school. While the school had had a deep commitment to excellence through deviance, the tendency seemed to be more and more deviance for the sake of deviance, it was said.

So far we have described how new issues, sentiments and criteria were related to the choice. It may be added that the open struggle made it very important for some people simply to reestablish peace in the school. The other side of the coin was that some of the criteria earlier defined as very important (e.g., brightness, defend the quantitative orientation and mathematical requirements) receded into the background. Finally we should observe that for a large group in the school the decision cannot be understood as a choice among the candidates. Rather, they were making votes of confidence in people campaigning for candidates, one reason being that this group would not have, and could not easily get, first hand information, enabling them to choose directly between the candidates.

Thus, we find some cleavages concerning the values and goals that should govern the school. Both main groups, that around the dean, i.e., the "establishment" in the school, and the "opposition" would say that they were defending important parts of the ideology of the school. For the people in program B, productivity – as measured by existing professional criteria in the market was most important. In order to reach this end, and also for recruiting purposes, they felt they had to have some degree of organizational structure in the school. They had less patience with the community aspect (warmth, love, and care) which also had been an important part of the ideology of the dean. Within the group around the dean, on the other hand, some made this community dimension an important end in itself and some stressed the human style and the "anarchy"-organization as important conditions for being good scientists. This group was less satisfied with existing criteria for success in the professional market, often talking about innovation and new criteria. These cleavages by no means were clear to everybody. Mostly they were known among the active people. For the other both the memoranda crises and the fact that the dean was against the program B-candidate were big surprises.

A second major aspect of the situation was the communication blockages and the low degree of joint and reliable information. This has been seen in the importance of rumors, the fact that different groups had very different perceptions of and interpretations of what was going on[19], and that they had little information about the consequences of different acts (i.e., taking an outsider or an insider as dean, having an acting dean, the "value" of the three outside candidates, etc.).

One important reason for this somewhat unclear and uncertain situation was that the dean did not give his opinion on whom he preferred as the new dean. This confused many of his "constituency" and made them act in ways they would not have done if they had known the dean's preferences and how he perceived the situation. Even if the dean took the initiative to get the three candidates to the campus, he never stated any preference for any of them nor tried to build a coalition in order to have one of them accepted. This silence was interpreted wrongly among some of his followers as a negative attitude toward the three candidates and made them act according to this. Also the candidate pushed by program B, and voted for by a majority of the faculty present in the meeting March 17, was a close friend and former student of the dean, indeed had been his first appointment. The two of them had been the founders of the school. The dean had been active in encouraging the candidate's promotion a year or two earlier, the two of them were collaborators on a research grant. Most faculty members knew about this close relationship, and albeit older faculty members would mention that the dean and the candidate had had some fights (during the period when the candidate was associate dean), it probably never occurred to the majority that the dean would not support the candidate.

The disagreement over values combined with a high degree of uncertainty made the conflicts take a somewhat special character. We observe a situation with a general lack of solutions, i.e., candidates. Also, while maladministration and personal aspects came into the forefront, people emphasizing different values ended up voting for the same candidate. Consider the lack of candidates. In the questionnaire we asked: "In the best of all worlds (with no constraints) whom would you want as dean for the school?" *None* apart from the dean were mentioned by more than one respondent. The five candidates presented to the final faculty meeting (March 17) were not mentioned by anyone. The dean was the first choice of $2/3$ of the non-tenured faculty, and $1/3$ of the tenured. The latter support came from programs A and C.

We find nearly the same pattern in the attitudes toward having the dean continue. A majority of the junior faculty strongly wanted the dean to continue, although those from program B would not (like those from A and C) trust his judgment to the degree that they would change their opinions about *other* candidates. Among the tenured people there was some support for the dean himself, but not so strong that they would change their opinions of other candidates. Again the most negative attitudes are found in program B.

Furthermore the faculty was presented with a list of names including all the candidates asked to be dean, a sample of the "active" and "passive" candidates along with some people not discussed at all as candidates in the search committee. Each respondent was asked whom he would accept as a dean immediately from this list, whom he wanted to consider as dean, whom he might consider only if someone made a strong case for the candidate, and whom he would not accept under any circumstances.

Again we find that few candidates would have a chance to be accepted if voting took place without any management of the decision. Only three of the 42 mentioned were given a positive answer by 50 percent or more of the faculty (answering "accept as dean immediately" or "wish considered as dean"). All these three are "stars" and were among the first five the search committee itself approached and asked to be dean.

The response further illustrates the loose relationship between values held and candidates accepted. For instance, while most faculty emphasized the importance of having a young, innovative dean, they were only willing to accept immediately fairly old, well established scientists with a "star" reputation. One of those most frequently accepted had just reached the retirement-age and had withdrawn from his university. Again we see that knowledge about style and personal aspects of the candidate were not known, and that choices from our list basically were made on professional reputation.

Consider also the relationships between the stated values and the five candidates actually chosen between. The faculty members were asked to rank each of the candidates along a five point positive-negative dimension, to rank order the candidates for the deanship, and to rank order the candidates along the eleven criteria most frequently used in the discussions going on.[20] In the questionnaire the eleven criteria were mentioned, and the faculty members were asked directly which of these (or other criteria) were the most important for them choosing a dean.

By looking at the direct answers on which criteria are the most important, we find interesting differences between the programs in the School. In program A, "defend the school", interdisciplinary orientation and ability to innovate, are mentioned most often. In program B, ability to recruit good faculty and interdisciplinary orientation are at the top; and in program C, "defend the school" and ability to innovate.

These differences are clearer when we look at the simple correlations between the different criteria and (a) total ranking, (b) degree of positive-negative attitude, and (c) the correlations for the relationships among the different criteria themselves (Tables 6.4. a–c). Obviously

114

Table 6.4a. A simple correlation matrix for relationships between total ranking of five dean candidates, ranking of the candidates on a general positive-negative dimension, and ranking of the candidates on eleven specified criteria. Answers given by faculty members of program A.

	Total ranking of candidates	Positive-negative to candidates in general	Reestablish peace	Recruit good faculty	Inter-disciplinary	Introduce departments	Change math. requirements	"Bright"	Deal with people in school	Innovative	Sympathy own work	Professional reputation
Defend the school	.625	.376	.020	.400	.728	.764	.648	.296	.177	.532	.489	.487
Professional reputation	.274	.037	−.111	.730	.640	.371	.449	.386	1.63	.539	.352	
Sympathy own work	.726	.518	.523	.669	.664	.395	.650	.281	.664	.483		
Innovative	.410	.190	.237	.546	.727	.440	.582	.440	.131			
Deal with people inside school	.554	.429	.469	.427	.299	.243	.113	.164				
"Bright"	.273	−.134	.060	.283	.368	.196	.358					
Change math. requirements	.485	.390	.312	.497	.645	.515						
Introduce departments	.538	.374	−.026	.284	.671							
Interdisciplinary	.475	.364	.147	.732								
Recruit good faculty	.452	.296	.271									
Reestablish peace	.304	.215										
Positive-negative in general	.675											

Table 6.4b. A simple correlation matrix for relationships between total ranking of five dean candidates, ranking of the candidates on a general positive-negative dimension, and ranking of the candidates on eleven specified criteria. Answers given by faculty members of program **B**.

	Total ranking of candidates	Positive-negative to candidates in general	Reestablish peace	Recruit good faculty	Interdisciplinary	Introduce departments	Change math. requirements	"Bright"	Deal with people in school	Innovative	Sympathy own work	Professional reputation
Defend the school	.735	.740	.655	.788	.390	.045	.655	.313	.522	.575	.306	.682
Professional reputation	.788	.740	.520	.920	.496	-.061	.628	.446	.602	.337	.386	
Sympathy own work	.494	.497	.413	.440	.171	-.501	.628	.099	.413	.117		
Innovative	.549	.535	.735	.416	.788	.337	.469	.181	.682			
Deal with people inside school	.894	.812	.947	.708	.628	-.035	.788	.468				
"Bright"	.512	.525	.446	.468	.181	.093	.446					
Change math. requirements	.867	.788	.788	.735	.496	-.114						
Introduce departments	-.061	-.056	-.035	-.088	.363							
Interdisciplinary	.575	.474	.549	.496								
Recruit good faculty	.920	.860	.682									
Reestablish peace	.867	.836										
Positive-negative in general	.908											

Table 6.4c. A simple correlation matrix for relationships between total ranking of five dean candidates, ranking of the candidates on a general positive-negative dimension, and ranking of the candidates on eleven specified criteria. Answers given by faculty members of program C.

	Total ranking of candidates	Positive-negative to candidates in general	Reestablish peace	Recruit good faculty	Interdisciplinary	Introduce departments	Change math. requirements	"Bright"	Deal with people in school	Innovative	Sympathy own work	Professional reputation
Defend the school	.871	.874	-.350	1.000	.871	.936	.807	.936	.229	.871	.056	.936
Professional reputation	.743	.786	-.286	.936	.807	.871	.871	.871	.293	.807	.182	
Sympathy own work	-.007	-.067	-.133	.056	-.196	-.133	-.070	-.007	-.133	.133		
Innovative	.871	.963	-.029	.871	.807	.936	.743	.743	.486			
Deal with people inside school	.357	.432	.743	.229	.164	.421	.229	-.029				
"Bright"	.679	.698	-.607	.936	.936	.871	.871					
Change math. requirements	.486	.609	-.414	.807	.936	.871						
Introduce departments	.807	.874	-.221	.936	.936							
Interdisciplinary	.614	.698	-.479	.871								
Recruit good faculty	.871	.874	-.350									
Reestablish peace	-.029	-.010										
Positive-Negative in general	.963											

117

most criteria are highly interrelated, making the possibilities for spurious correlations high.[21] The correlations between total ranking of candidates and where they are placed along a five point positive-negative scale, is very high for two programs (B = .908 and C = .963). For the third program (A) it is somewhat lower (.665). We use the total ranking of the candidates.

Some interesting patterns appear to exist. The criterion "least probable to introduce departments" is among the four strongest correlated with total ranking for two of the programs (A–C) and slightly negatively correlated for the third one (B). This is a difference we have seen earlier in the verbal discussion and it supports what has been said there. However, the fact that the correlation is very near zero for program B, tells us that the question about introducing departments has not been important for everybody in this program. (Running a regression analysis for program B, "introduce department" does *not* enter the equation until step 5, with an increase in r^2 = .001 and a beta-coefficient = .0475.)

There are similar important differences between the programs for the criteria "ability to innovate" which is on top for program C but among the four lowest for the two other programs; "reestablish peace" which is among the four highest for program B and among the four lowest for programs A and C; "sympathy with own work", the highest for program A, among the four lowest for the other two programs; "deal with people", among the four highest for programs A and B, among the four lowest for program C. Finally we may note that "brightness", which was so important in the first part of the search, is among the four lowest criteria for two of the programs.

Thus, *program A* emphasizes sympathy with own work and ability to defend the school and take little interest in the candidate's professional reputation and his brightness. *Program B* finds recruitment abilities, ability to deal with people inside the school, keeping the math requirements and reestablishing peace most important, while as a group not attending to whether the candidate was likely to introduce departments and his sympathy with the respondent's own work. Finally, *program C* underline ability to defend the school, being innovative, recruiting-abilities, and not being likely to introduce departments, while being little interested in the candidate's sympathy with own work and his abilities to reestablish peace in the school. The differences between the departments found so far, are given some further support when we run a multiple regression analysis[22] (Table 6.5.).

The pattern found for program A is consistent with the general picture of this program as mainly a gathering of "longshots", people doing somewhat strange things, which could turn out to be very

Table 6.5. A stepwise multiple regression analysis of the relationships between total ranking of dean candidates and ranking of candidates on several criteria for each of the three programs in the school

Program	Beta-coefficient
Program A:	
Sympathy with own work	.6800
Ability to defend the school against the outside world	.4498
Least probable to introduce departments	.3343
Ability to innovate	.1596
Interdisciplinary orientation	— .8092
	$r^2 = .860$, sign. on 0.001 level
Program B:	
Ability to recruit good faculty	.5765
Deal with people inside the school	.4856
	$r^2 = .982$, sign on 0.001 level
Program C:	
Ability to defend the school against outside world	.9713
Ability to innovate	.6093
Interdisciplinary orientation	— .7240
	$r^2 = .966$, sign on 0.01 level

important but with a high probability of failure. This part of the faculty would need a dean who accepted their type of work and did this so strongly that he would be willing, and also able, to protect them against the outside world. An important condition for working as they did was a loose structure, and introducing departments would reduce these opportunities. It is somewhat surprising that "ability to innovate" does not have a more important explanatory power. But to a certain degree some people in this program did not demand of the dean that he should be innovative, but that he should let the faculty members themselves innovate.

Another plausible "explanation" is to see values and attitudes as a function of "the life phase" of the program. The people in program A were (in general) those hired first. In this phase "innovation" meant to build up the research and teaching they wanted and to hire faculty they would like – often their friends. After a while these people became "the establishment". Organizational innovation then could mean changing relationships *among* the people in this group, *or* it could mean hiring new people and new groups. If so, these people would be rivals for resources.

In this framework we can understand that the majority in program A now wanted protection more than innovation (even if the verbal support of "innovation" could not be abandoned). This interpretation is supported by the fact that the faculty reacted conservatively in the first faculty meeting; wanting to keep what had been established. It is also supported by the fact that the people now claiming resources in order to build up new groups primarily could be found outside this program. In short the referent of the word "innovation" in this framework is not some intellectual construct or ideal, but some preferred allocation of resources (money, love, promotions, added positions). Emerging groups say they favor innovation and that the established group is not truly for innovation. Groups which are established will either stop saying they want innovation or claim that they themselves are the institutionalized, permanent innovation.

The pattern found for program B is consistent with the view that the members of this program to a lower degree than the other faculty viewed the school as a unique place. The immediate acceptance of the criteria of the academic marked-place was higher, the felt need for protection against these criteria smaller. The emphasis on recruiting has also to be seen in relation to the fact that people in program B felt a strong need for building new research groups and recruiting new faculty. Consistent with the life-phase-explanation, these people started to claim that they were the people proposing something new – the people really wanting innovation. The emphasis on the new dean's ability to deal with the people inside the school may reflect the attack raised on "maladministration" in general in the dean-centered phase.

We should remember that program C really was a residual of people either wanting to work alone (and therefore primarily wanting peace and protection) or people still not established in any group, but looking for some group or program (and therefore wanting innovation). Such an explanation would relate the research-style and the "entrepreneur" ambitions of the faculty with the "life phase" argument.

Compared to the search committee-phase we have seen an expansion of issues and problems defined as relevant. Differences in values and beliefs were "discovered". Basically these differences can be understood as functions of the programs (and the formal positions of the respondents). The relevance of the programs have been related to the different "life-phases" of these programs.

At the same time, it is not easy to discover any close relationship between this differentiation in values and the choices made. As the garbage can model suggests, the decision became a choice of world views, perspectives for the future, and an assortment of individual and group issues that were currently important. The most important conflicts took place in a period where no solutions (i.e. candidates) were present. Furthermore, it was discovered that the concepts and criteria for choice most central in the discussion, did not help much when confronted with choice alternatives. Ability to innovate became problematic both because it was very difficult to say who would be innovative, and because it was problematic what kind of innovation one was talking about. Professional reputation worked well as long as one discussed "stars" with an accepted reputation over several fields. When this category of candidates was left, one had to ask reputation among whom, what kind of reputation.

To understand the (lack of) relationships between criteria and candidates chosen, we attend to some negative findings. When using the programs as the basis for our correlation-matrices and regression analysis, there are clear patterns and differences. This is not the case when we use "voted for the program B candidate" – "voted for others" as our basis.[23] This is in a way given from the fact that people from all programs voted for this candidate. But the observation tells us that the discussed criteria and goals (so important in the "rational decision" model and the "bargaining coalition" model) were not of much help for the participants when they were confronted with the choice among candidates. The situation was simply too complex and obscure. This is again consistent with the observation that for many faculty members the choice was one among indirect criteria, that is more choosing among people campaigning for a candidate, (whom to believe and trust) than a direct evaluation of the candidates against the respondent's own preference structure.

During this phase activation increased only slightly. Given the mentioned changes in our four independent variables, time, slack, style, and load, we expected that on the average more people would be activated in the choice during the dean-centered phase than in the search committee-centered phase. However, we should not forget that it was against the "culture" of the school to be *too* active – one should talk oneself into consensus. Moreover, most potential leaders had heavy external demands on their time and energy, and the energy demands increased as one left the "star" candidates. We have already seen that the search process went from "private" to "public". In the first phase people outside the committee were told very little about what was going on, and few outsiders asked the committee members for information. In the second phase important parts of the discussion took place in public. Faculty, students, and outsiders could follow the memorandum crises.

In the search for candidates, the patterns in the dean-centered phase are consistent with a wish for a reduction of search costs and uncertainty. The three candidates invited to the campus (February 24 – March 14) all had clear criteria of "nearness". One had recently been a visiting professor at the school and had been reviewed for a faculty position, one had a long work period with a group of the faculty, and the third had also recently been reviewed for a faculty position. The offer to a candidate visiting the campus by accident

121

(March 6-7) and the final step – focusing on internal candidates – certainly is consistent with the desire to avoid search costs.

Just as we find little search for remote candidates, we also note little energy being used to learn about the consequences of different choices. In spite of the fact that arrangements were made for all faculty members, graduate students, and junior fellows as representatives of the undergraduates to meet the outside candidates, approximately 40 percent of the faculty members did not meet two of the candidates (Table 6.6). This lack of interest apparently was partly connected to the view that none of these three candidates was good enough to be accepted. Some also gave as their reason for not meeting the candidates that it was impossible to get any reliable information from a short meeting with a candidate. (The somewhat higher number for the third candidate was occasioned by the fact that he had just stayed in the school for a whole year and had friends among the faculty).

Table 6.6. The faculty members' contact with the dean candidates from outside

Candidates	Did meet	Did not meet
1	24	8
2	19	13
3	20	12

Remembering the importance of intellectual and professional criteria, it is somewhat surprising (but quite consistent with the lack of reading during the first phase) that 70 percent–75 percent of the faculty had read nothing of the written production of the three outside candidates (Table 6.7). We have to remember that "nothing" here means not even "looked briefly at 1–2 articles". Only one or two

Table 6.7. The factulty members' reading of the scientific production of the dean candidates

Candidates	Read nothing	Some reading*	Read carefully the major part of written production
Outside:			
1	23	6	3
2	25	6	1
3	25	7	0
Inside:			
1	14	13	5
2	17	14	1

*This category includes the following answers: "looked briefly at 1-2 articles", "read carefully 1-2 articles", and "looked briefly at the major part of written work". The five categories were given in the questionnaire.

faculty members started reading parts of the production of the three candidates *after* they were proposed as candidates. We also find that the level of knowledge about the written production of the inside candidates is rather low.

Both the data on meeting candidates and reading their scientific production could reflect more the irrelevance of the measurement used than a low degree of activation. However, this explanation is not supported by the data on the interaction among the faculty (Table 6.8). Asking the faculty members whom they had been talking to about the deanship, we use (a) how people report their own activity, and (b) what each faculty member's activity has been, as reported by his colleagues.[24] Only eight persons, two of them non-tenured, report that they had been talking with ten faculty members two times or more during the process. For ten respondents, nine of these non-tenured, there had been *no* contacts or the choice had been discussed with only one other faculty member. For 70 percent of the respondents their contacts had been limited to five or less faculty members. Using others report on activity, the group of people talking to ten or more decreases to five, while the percentage of non-active increases. Also, the cross-program contacts at this point involved only a small group (5 persons). For the others interaction relevant for the dean-choice was highly

Table 6.8. Frequency of contact among faculty members with reference to the choice of new dean

a) Degree of activation of faculty: Each faculty member reporting his own activity:

Number of faculty members talked to two or more times		0	1	2	3	4	5	6	7	8	9	10	11	12	13	14	15..28
Respondent's status	Tenured:	0	1	3	1	1	1	0	1	0	0	1	2	2	0	1	0 0
	Non-tenured:	3	6	2	2	1	1	0	1	0	0	0	0	0	0	0	1 1

b) Degree of activation of factulty: Each member ranked from the reports of *other* participants:

Number of faculty members talked to two or more times*		0	1	2	3	4	5	6	7	8	9	10	11	12	13	14
Respondent's status	Tenured:	3	1	2	4	0	0	0	0	2	1	0	1	2	1	0
	Non-tenured:	5	11	4	4	1	2	0	0	1	1	0	0	1	0	0

*The total number is 47 because one faculty member was absent during the whole process and therefore was not included on the list.

concentrated around people belonging to their own program (Olsen, 1970, pp. 106–107).

While faculty was not really involved, this was even more true for some other groups. The students were never really activated. No new representative was appointed when the student member of the search committee left the campus, and the students never made any attempt to get representation or by other means to influence the choice in any important way. This did not appear to be a consequence of a deliberate, planned withdrawal of students from participation in the decision. Students simply were inactive. Neither were people from outside the school activated. The campus and university administration played a minor role, as did faculty from other schools.

Potential leaders did little to activate their constituencies.[25] The initiative to gather program B behind an inside candidate was the only strong attempt to generate a solution by managing the process. This type of initiative was never taken by people in the other two programs. While four tenured and one non-tenured faculty member ranked one of the outside candidates as number one for the deanship, this candidacy was never pushed. The same can be said about candidate five (Table 6.9). Even though six faculty members ranked the candidate as number one, and eleven as number two, nobody tried to build a coalition behind him, and nobody even talked about him in the faculty meeting (March 17).

Table 6.9. The faculty ranking of the five candidates for the deanship

Ranking of the five candidates:

	Tenured faculty						Non-tenured faculty						Total faculty					
	1	2	3	4	5	NA	1	2	3	4	5	NA	1	2	3	4	5	NA
Candidate 1	1	2	4	2	1	4	2	1	2	4	1	8	3	3	6	6	2	12
Candidate 2	4	2	1	2	3	2	1	1	4	1	3	8	5	3	5	3	6	10
Candidate 3	0	0	2	2	3	7	0	1	3	3	3	8	0	1	5	5	6	15
Candidate 4	7	0	1	2	0	4	7	4	0	0	1	6	14	4	1	2	1	10
Candidate 5	1	6	2	1	1	3	5	5	1	1	1	5	6	11	3	2	2	8

The lack of leadership was very visible in the meeting. During the one hour and thirteen minutes of discussion only one person talked for five minutes (after being asked if he would "talk for" the program B candidate). One talked for three minutes, and four for two minutes. The rest of the discussion was short comments or questions. The type of activity was close to what we have called "reacting". Being in a room with the stated purpose of making a (rational) decision on whom the faculty should recommend for the dean position, people had to do something even if they were without information and (many of them) clearly confused. Potential leaders did not give much information; the dean would not, the chairman of the search committee was absent since he was a candidate, the director of program A was absent, the member of the search committee proposing traditional departments did not take initiative, and the director of program B did not take the lead (the two latter obviously could see that their candidate would win if no new initiative were taken). Very early in the meeting the dean stated that if people would not talk he would not detain them there but dissolve the meeting.

Summarizing the data on activation, we see some important differences from the committee centered-phase. The choice went from a private to a public arena, more people became involved, some new people tried to gain leadership, and a certain polarization in interaction took place. However, we also observed that the activity to a limited degree was focused on generating solutions. Several faculty members had candidates they never campaigned for. The people trying to generate solutions in "opposition" to the candidates the dean had proposed were full-time, tenured people with desires for expansion, who held the belief that they would not be supported by the dean. They belonged to the same program and held regular meetings. In this way the program meeting was an already established device for communication and "interpretation" of what was going on, and a device for interest-aggregation, and coalition building (in the same way as a traditional program would have worked). For the junior people in program B there was on the one hand the definition given via the program meetings, on the other hand their trust in the dean as the leader of the school. They ended up with wanting the dean to continue but not being willing to change their minds about *other* candidates.

The other two programs did *not* work this way. Program C being a residual one, did not in fact operate as a program; and program A had the handicap that two of the potential leaders were involved (one as a dean candidate and one mentioned in a rumor as a candidate). Thus for the junior faculty of these two programs the confusion was even greater. Given their lack of knowledge concerning candidates and the lack of clear cues from potential leaders, they simply did not know what to do, and (most of them) stayed inactive. A majority of the junior faculty would have changed their votes if they knew the preferences of the dean. If he had wanted to campaign for a candidate, the probability of this candidate being accepted would have been very high.

However, to understand the behavior of the junior faculty (and the students) it is not enough to look only at the activity and lack of activity of the leaders. During the period involved the students and junior faculty (and also the university administration) had other choice opportunities of some importance. In particular the firing of three junior faculty members in another school on campus produced rallies and a confrontation in the Academic Senate between many of the tenured faculty on the one side and many of the junior faculty and students on the other. Also the general tensions between the political authorities in the state and students (and some faculty) were competing for attention with the choice of a dean.

Thus, several factors worked in order to reduce the level of activity. We have to consider external load and opportunities, the general confusion about means-ends relationships, and that the lack of departments made the (potential) lines of conflict more obscure. Also, while the style of "sounding out" was attacked when it became clear that it did not produce an acceptable result, this style was highly celebrated before the process started. It was against the ideology of the school to be very active. Finally, probably the most important single factor for understanding the level of activation was the dean's decision not to be the godfather of the new dean.

In general, we found that the dean-centered phase was characterized by:

(a) instability; there were multiple, ambiguous, and changing goals. Important information blockages strongly reduced the degree of shared information and produced wide gaps in perceptions and interpretations both of events taking place and of means-ends relationships. The lack of trust was apparent, and this aspect, together with other issues and feelings, contributed to making the definition of the choice *complex* and *unstable*.

(b) more people being activated, but the majority only in a reacting way. The degree of management was still small, and we observed a shift in who tried to generate a solution (from the dean, to the senior people of program B). There was an increase in activation and an unstable (and not too active) management group.

From this description we should, on the basis of our model, expect the artifactual elements of the process to be the dominant ones. In fact the outcome of this phase: (a) a majority – consisting of groups emphasizing different goals – in favor of the program B candidate and (b) a school where a majority became very surprised and confused when discovering that they had voted against the preferences of the dean, is difficult to understand without using an artifactual framework. The dean did attempt to approach the question in a problem solving way. This approach was unsuccessful, which is consistent with the changes in perceptions of slack and style, the time the decision took,

126

and the load at the end of the search committee-centered phase. The attempts to make the situation one of bargaining and coalition building were strongest in the period when some senior people in program B tried to get the dean to accept a new department or a committee, when the new dean's power position was opened up for discussion, and when the role of the associate dean was made problematic. We may also speculate whether program B proposed the candidate because they believed the dean would support him, and also, if the dean's attitude toward this candidate was affected by the fact that he (the candidate) was proposed by the "opposition" in the school.

However, as the contact decreased between the leaders in program B on the one hand, the dean and the chairman of the search committee on the other hand, the artifactual elements grew in importance. They were clearly seen in the faculty meeting. At the same time, the process is artifactual only within certain limits or within a certain set of candidates. This set was partly determined by the fact that the school now primarily focused on inside candidates. Besides reducing uncertainty and search costs, turning to insiders made it possible to avoid a "confrontation" with (some part of) the environment.

6.3.2 *The Vice-Chancellor-Centered Phase*

The choice was now taken out of the school. Coming to the office of the Vice-Chancellor the choice was placed in a completely new environment of choices, issues, feelings, and procedures. The style governing the decision should be influenced more by the general experiences from previous decisions of the Vice-Chancellor than by what had occurred earlier in the process. We would expect the definition to reflect the differences in planning horizon between the school and the campus administration. And we would expect the activation to be influenced by the existing programs and procedures for solving problems in the campus administration.

Given that the dean had said that he did not agree with the majority in the faculty meeting, it was difficult to see any slack in the system. Time was running on, but it took some time before the faculty in general knew that the dean had informed the Vice-Chancellor that he was not in agreement with the recommendation made. Therefore, the period in which the choice was visible was reduced. Finally, the load on the Vice-Chancellor in this period was very high, given the events in the university as whole and its environment. A number of important choices were in process (e.g., an important crises in a service unit on campus, the student unrest connected to the firing of the three junior professors, the development of a planning and budgeting system, etc.).

9

In this period the administration was very busy putting out "fires" as they developed. On the other hand, the organization now had a deadline.

This phase is the most difficult to report. Most events took place in closed meetings, and with very few exceptions with only two persons present. Often those two would not agree on what had happened – what had been said and done – and why. Nevertheless, this phase clearly differed from the two preceding phases along important dimensions, and even a tentative analysis of the data available will shed some light on the general model in this study.

One "extraneous" factor played an important part in what occurred in this phase. Time was running short, and the "hunting season" for candidates outside the school was over. It would be impossible to get new candidates from outside to take over before the fall term started. In this way the rules for hiring produced a "frozen" situation, limiting the choice alternatives in the Vice-Chancellor phase to the following: (a) the faculty candidate (program B candidate), (b) the chairman of the search committee, (c) the three outside candidates, and (d) appointment of an acting dean and recycle the process.

These few alternatives very soon were reduced to only two, the faculty candidate and the chairman of the search committee. The resistance against having an acting dean and starting a new search process was strong. The people who emphasized the need for reestablishing peace in the school were against having a new search. Those stressing the need for a strong protector against the outside world did not believe an acting dean could play this role. The senior people in program B were against all alternatives except the candidate they had proposed and for whom a majority of the faculty present had voted. Finally, no one had a strong candidate for the position of acting dean. (The dean very late in the process rejected an offer to continue while the search went on.) The three outside candidates had not received any strong open support among the faculty, even though one might have according to the answers given on the questionnaire. No one campaigned for any of the three candidates, and the Vice-Chancellor never seriously considered appointing any of them. Thus, the decision situation was frozen, with only two real alternatives, which meant an enormous reduction in the uncertainty and complexity of the choice. The search was concentrated on clarifying the consequences of the two alternatives.

From the Vice-Chancellor's point of view both candidates were acceptable. Thus, the consequences focused on were primarily consequences for the organization and its ability to work in the future. The Vice-Chancellor obviously wanted to play the problem-solving game rather than openly make a choice under scarity. An attempt was made

128

to remove the choice from the public to greater privacy, with personal consultations and very little information leaking out before the Vice-Chancellor and the Chancellor had made their choice. Information on the process came out very slowly; first, the chairman of the search committee was now a strong candidate, and later that he had already been chosen as dean.

Being a member of the school (and program B) the Vice-Chancellor had good relationships with all the active participants in the dean search when the process started.[26] He got information from all factions, and could list fairly reliably the consequences of the different alternatives. The fact that he did not take the voting by the faculty as the final decision, but opened up for new discussions and deliberations, clearly produced a very negative reaction (and a reduction of trust), especially among senior people in program B. It became obvious that the Vice-Chancellor had to decide whose preferences he would satisfy, and to what degree.

Looking then, at the definition of the choice, it is important to remember that there was no agreement among faculty members as to why the Vice-Chancellor acted as he did. We will not be able to say how important the different criteria were, but we can at least mention some factors, showing how the definition changed.

(1) The campus had just had a crises in the (service) unit the faculty candidate was leading. During this crises he had done a very good job. However, the situation was still problematic, and appointing the leader of the unit as dean in another school, the Vice-Chancellor said, could ruin the unit, which was a very important one for the whole campus.

(2) The dean, reporting the result of the faculty meeting, said that he did *not* agree with the choice made by the majority.

(3) Opening up a new discussion, the Vice-Chancellor was informed that he would have resignations if he rejected the recommendation made by the faculty.

(4) In important ways the choice was also related to the division of labor between the schools and the administration. Four deans had resigned during the last six months, and for the Vice-Chancellor it was of some importance to find procedures that could be used in the future. The Vice-Chancellor hoped that the schools could solve their leadership problems themselves. That is, he would give some testing criteria candidates would have to meet, rather than generate a solution himself; he certainly also wanted a dean who could keep peace in the school and who would not produce more "fires" (problems) which the administration would have to cope with later.

(5) Finally, most of the criteria so important in the first phase receded into the background, partly because both candidates were "satisfactory" on most of these dimensions, and partly because it was very difficult (or impossible) for the Vice-Chancellor to construct some trade-off scale for the different dimensions. The criteria of "war and peace", and probably also the crises in the mentioned unit, were very visible. Here again information could be gathered fairly easily through consultation.

To connect these factors different "theories" developed. One of the most popular theories was that the Vice-Chancellor simply had accepted that the dean should have a veto in deciding who should be his successor. Another assumed that considerations related to the future of the service unit had been the most important single factor. No serious effort was ever made to provide a definitive answer to the question.

However, it is important to see that the definition of the choice was very different from the preceding phases, and that it, as suggested by the garbage can model, was highly dependent on the issues and problems present at the moment at the Vice-Chancellor's office. In defining his problem, the Vice-Chancellor took into account the effects the choice alternatives would have on other parts of the campus, while so far only consequences for the school (and the people inside it) had been evaluated. Again the candidate selected aroused less dislike than the way he was selected and the meaning which thereby was connected to the choice (e.g., the dean had gotten his way). As shown in Table 4.9 the differences in the faculty preferences between the two candidates (4 and 5) were not very big. The people ranking the program B candidate as number one, most often would rank the committee chairman as number two. Also, we have seen that the choice moved from a "public" arena back to privacy again, with high degrees of uncertainty (for most of the people in the school) about what was really going on. This, together with the fact that the situation was "frozen" with only two alternatives, made the possibilities for redefinition from people other than the Vice-Chancellor, more difficult. For the "managers", however, the complexity of the choice was reduced when the process went from a dynamic one to a static one.

The patterns of *activation* were organized around the Vice-Chancellor, the dean, and the chairman of the search committee, all trying to get information on how faculty members would react on the different choice alternatives, and later, building a coalition supporting the latter's candidacy. The initiative clearly was in the hands of these three people, the others more or less giving information in a passive way. The attempts from some tenured people in program B to constrain the actions of the Vice-Chancellor by threatening to resign were the only exceptions. During the consulting period all the formerly active people had an opportunity to state their views (at least to one of the three organizers of the process in this phase). No formal meeting was arranged. The people most strongly supporting the program B candidate had shown a strong vote for him and knew they could not do better in a new voting situation. For people wanting to get the chairman of the search committee as the new dean, it would be important to show that the support to the program B candidate was not as clear as the voting result seemed to show. This type of information could be conveyed to the Vice-Chancellor without arranging any formal meeting. At the same time consultations prevented the open confrontation a formal meeting would have produced.

To summarize the Vice-Chancellor phase, we find a relatively stable and simple definition of the situation and a small and stable group of decision-makers. The alternatives were very soon clarified, the consequences could be outlined, and the relevant goals were few. It is thus consistent with our expectations that this phase was the one closest to a "managed" decision process. The Vice-Chancellor can be looked upon as attempting to maximize peace and the organization's ability to work in the future. However, the main reason for getting such a stable and frozen situation was artifactual, namely the deadline provided by the rules for hunting seasons in American universities. From the faculty's point of view the computer crises could also be looked upon as an artifactual element.

For the Vice-Chancellor an emphasis on the relevance of the computer crisis would make it possible to define the problem as a technical one (both candidates are qualified for the deanship, but we need the program B candidate for other important purposes). Emphasis on the fact that the dean disagreed with the faculty decision, would stress the "political" aspects. Still, however, the Vice-Chancellor could calculate fairly well in a "rational decision" manner what the consequences would be. The bargaining aspect was a minor one. In the "frozen" situation most people had very little to bargain with. The threat of resignations could be included in the Vice-Chancellor's decision model.

We will not follow up here the question of the school's readiness for new choices. As indicated in the chronology the new dean had to take with him some of the "garbage" from the decision-making process through which he was appointed. The "state of the organization", including the changes in the level of trust, the general conceptions of the organization etc., were – at least – as important an outcome of the choice process as which person was chosen as dean.

6.4 The Decision-Making Framework Revisited

If we consider the selection of a new dean as one choice opportunity, the definition of the choice has to be characterized as complex and changing. The process involved multiple, inconsistent, ill defined, and changing goals. Decision-makers could neither reduce all goals to a single index, nor could they in advance define what would be a "satisficing" solution. The concept of a (predetermined) goal has very limited value both for predicting behavior and for the actors in the process.[27] Nevertheless, people at each stage had some sort of preferences and they had feelings, often very strong ones. Besides goal-ambiguity the process was characterized by a high degree of uncertainty about potential alternatives and strategies, and about other peoples' preferences, strategies, and calculations. The means-end connections were not very well understood. Behavior by others could not easily be predicted. The uncertainty was increased by the paucity of attempts to provide "explanations" or interpretations of what was going on. The ambiguity and uncertainty make the meaning of "rationality" more problematic.

With respect to activation, the selection of a dean involved several participants. Most of them were part-time; most of them engaged in testing alternatives or reacting rather than trying to generate a solution themselves. The small group of people trying to find a solution changed over time and was relatively passive. Most of the time they avoided comparing candidates, using a "sounding out" technique. They did little searching, relying mainly on already existing information.

We have suggested that "choice" under such circumstances will be best understood in the framework of an artifactual or non-decision model. The final outcome should not be viewed as a product of any conscious selection among alternatives based on some definition of their consequences in relation to a more or less clearly defined scale of preferences. We find it difficult to interpret the decision or the state of the organization at the end of the process as the product of any single "rational" decision-maker maximizing some utility function, or as the willed product of any winning coalition. The artifactual model deemphasizes the "willed", "rational", "logical", "strategic", and "calculated". It gives decision-makers (and their "power") a less heroic role and directs our attention to other aspects of the situation.

Moreover, our data indicate some complications with interpreting the events studied. It is tempting to assume implicitly that what happened in some sense "had to happen" and to attempt to explain the unique events. At least in this case, such a strategy seems misguided. There certainly is "lawfulness" about the script that was followed. But it belongs to a family of possible scripts, and there appear to be strong "chance" elements influencing the branching that occurred within the possible scripts. "Chance" here is used less in the sense of a purely random element than in the sense of a critical branch in the development of the history that was determined by factors largely independent of the main factors we are examining.

One obvious example of such "chance" elements: A possible dean, who was apparently acceptable, was identified very early in the process. He expressed interest but was deeply involved in a rather complicated legal situation on his current job. He ultimately became unavailable for the job apparently because of these outside factors. Had he been appointed to the job as a result of the early approaches, many of the events in our story would have been quite different.

A second example: The choice of a new dean never became a student power issue despite the fact that it occurred at a time of high student activity with respect to involvement in university decision-making. Student leaders were already heavily involved in another choice opportunity – the firing of three assistant professors in another school on the campus. If the choice had become a matter of student power, it might have changed the story.

Finally: We do not need much imagination to suggest that the process could have continued. We may speculate on the conditions under which the administrative board of the university would have been involved (and the press or politicians). In the case studied, we would suggest that the administrative board could have been activated on the question of "radicalism" or support to radicalism, or that the board could have found the choice an opportunity to activate such questions. We may also speculate that such a redefinition of the choice could have evoked an answer from other groups in the university connected to the question of academic freedom. Thus, the choice which started as a question of finding the best person given some consensus values "could" have ended up as a question of law and order versus academic freedom. At the time of our decision, however, these groups (like the students) were focusing on other choices and events taking place at other campuses in the same geographical area.

We believe the process could easily have been changed fundamentally or ended at several different points. Rather small perturbations could have changed the story and resulted in alternative scripts, which would have produced:

(a) *Different deans.* There is no reason to believe that the final choice of dean was a necessary result of the process we have described. Most obviously, the process could have produced, and almost did produce, a dean very early in the story.

(b) *Different "winning coalitions".* Since both the groups of participants and their organization changed over time – at least in part in response to outside factors of load and attention – any particular termination of the choice would have resulted in a particular group of participants making the decision. In our view, this would have been substantially fortuitous.

(c) *Different mixes of values fulfilled.* Values, like decision-makers, drifted in and out of the process. An "arbitrary" ending at one point rather than another would have resulted in a different value mix.

(d) *Different interpretations by members of the organization.* The participants in the process generally attempted to understand it. For the reasons we have indicated, those interpretations were different at different points in the history. Alternative endings would have reinforced alternative interpretations.

(e) *Different conceptions of the school.* Closely connected to the interpretations of the process were the implications of those interpretations for the conception held by the participants of the organization. An early choice, for example, would have reassured many participants about the quality of the school in a way that the actual process did not. Likewise, an early choice would in general have had an integrating effect by affecting the social "climate" in the school (characterized originally by a feeling of unity, trust, friendship, etc.).

Two general theories are required to deal with this type of organizational choice situations. First, we need to understand the way individuals in organizations "learn", i.e., how events and processes are interpreted, and how these interpretations are related to future behavior. This case indicates that we need a theory that does not assume that experience produces wisdom and improve behavior. One such theory, which allows individuals and groups to develop myths, fictions, folklore, and illusions, under specified conditions, is presented in Chapter 4.

Second, we need a theory of organizational choice that is consistent not only with the actual historical record of our case study, but also with the alternative possible histories that (we believe) could easily have been written under trivially different conditions. We believe that the "garbage can", where an organization is seen as a meeting place for streams of problems, solutions, participants, and choice opportunities, (Olsen, 1970; Cohen, March, and Olsen, 1972) is one such theory. That theory both captures a significant portion of the process involved in this case study, as well as having a potential for describing decision-making in organizations with ambiguous goals, unclear technologies, and part-time participants.

134

NOTES:

1 The modest place "artifactual" models have in organization theories should not be taken as proof of their lack of importance or relevance. Some examples where such models are used should be mentioned: James Coleman's study of community conflict (Coleman, 1957). Norton Long's very stimulating article "The Local Community as an Ecology of Games" (Long, 1958). Joanne Woodward's research on the development of new business firms (Woodward, 1965). Gamson's "utter confusion" theory for coalition building (1969). The explanations given by Cyert and March of how a research project developed (Cyert and March, 1963, p. 2). Trow tells us that "the rapid expansion of American Higher Education is not the product of any governmental decision, or indeed, of any 'decision' anywhere, but the outcome of a large number of trends and forces in the larger society", (Trow, 1962, p. 239). Needless to say, most studies in this volume underline the relevance of "artifactual" models.

2 Because of the part-time character of participation, it becomes difficult to specify the relevant participants in advance, and the time-demands of decisions becomes important. We need distinctions between more or less time-consuming ways of activation. A first approach to this problem may be to differentiate between:
   (a) Activities focused on generating alternatives and having them accepted (e.g., problem-definition, information-seeking, agenda-building, coalition-building).
   (b) Activities focused on generating criteria for choice, that is generating criteria for testing alternatives (e.g., stating demands, comparing alternatives with demands).
   (c) Activities which can be described more as reactions than actions. In such a situation (e.g., a faculty meeting) the participant will not himself take any initiative, but confronted with a certain organizational setting, he will be strongly expected to act (vote, give his opinion) even if he has no interest in the choice, has no information, etc. The distinction between behavior focused on generating candidates and behavior producing criteria or constraints on the choice is derived from Simon's distinction between generating and testing elements or organizational goals (Simon, 1964).

3 To be sure, the issue is confounded empirically by the opposite effect. That is, we should also expect that the greater the number of issues and participants activated, the longer the decision will take.

4 Thus, the number and types of participants activated will be a product of several sub-processes of activation and de-activation. Some important aspects are:
   "an exhaustiveness-effect": The longer time a choice takes, the more costly in time and energy. Therefore, some participants will de-activate themselves.
   "a visibility-effect": A major reason why some people may not be activated is simply that they do not know what is going on. On the average, the longer the choice time, the more visible the choice opportunity, and the more people activated.
   "a cummulation-effect": As people with interests contrary to your own activate themselves, one will be in danger of coming into a relatively deprived situation. Organization tend to call forth organization. If people organize on one side of an issue, their opponents will organize on the other.
   "a flight-effect": The more a choice opportunity becomes a garbage can for an increasing number of people and issues, the less the chance that a decision

will be reached, the more likely that people will make attempts to get into other choice opportunities and solve their problems there. Consider also political entrepreneurs with a primary goal of getting a reputation as "problem-solvers". Very likely they will find such overloaded choice opportunities non-attractive, and will try to make success spending their energy in other arenas.

Certainly this list could be multiplied.

5 The fact that the production of "garbage" is not independent of the number of decisions, has also been ignored. We may expect that the more decisions, the higher the probability of a high garbage-production.

6 Uncertainty absorption takes place when inferences are drawn from a body of evidence and the inferences, instead of the evidence itself, are communicated (March and Simon, 1958, p. 165).

7 The three programs were led by directors. One of the programs, in fact a residual one, formally had the dean as director, but did not in fact operate as a program.

8 The committee consisted of one full professor from outside the school, and the following insiders; three full professors, one assistant professor, and one student. We may note that none of the program directors were included, even though program A asked the Vice-Chancellor to appoint their leader as a member of the committee.

9 Both Caplow and McGee (1958, pp. 45—46 and 103—105) and Haas and Collen (1963—64, p. 51) have given data showing a general tendency among faculty to assign unrealistically high ratings to their own institute in comparison with competing institutes. New institutions may have a special problem, that is, the environment will rate it lower than its real quality, simply because of a time lag in professional reputation (Thompson and McEwen, 1958, p. 24).

10 The fact that none of the program directors were members of the committee, albeit one had been proposed by a group of faculty members, is the only indicator opposing this view.

11 In all quantitative references to "the committee" this means the committee minus the member from outside the school and the student member. They never took any active part and left the committee before the most important events took place. On the other hand, the dean is included because he took part in most meetings.

12 We originally used three categories: *Low knowledge:* Not read anything written by the candidate, no good indirect knowledge about his writing from trustworthy sources. *Middle knowledge:* Read one or two articles, good indirect information from trustworthy sources. *High knowledge:* Read more than 1—2 articles. "Know" is here defined as middle or high knowledge.

13 We originally used three categories: *Low knowledge:* Never met the person, no good indirect knowledge about him as a person from trustworthy sources. *Middle knowledge:* Met the candidate very briefly, indirect knowledge from trustworthy sources. *High knowledge:* Met the person several times in personal meetings and talked to him. "Know" here means middle or high knowledge.

14 The willingness to give people "veto" if they express very negative attitudes toward a candidate is consistent with the finding of Caplow and McGee (1958, p. 133) who noted a high sensibility toward sharply negative opinions in hiring procedures. However, only six persons were vetoed by means of this rule.

15 During the committee-centered phase written information was of little

importance. An attempt to write a paragraph about each candidate of interest very soon broke down. It is important, however, to stress that no candidate had any general support outside the committee.

16 Approximately the same distribution of knowledge is found for each sub-group of candidates (those asked to be dean), the "active" and the "passive" candidates, (Olsen, 1970, pp. 55 and 56). If we defined "know" as only "high knowledge" (notes 12 and 13) the differences among the committee members will increase.

17 Consider the ways in which professional and personal knowledge are transmitted. For professional qualities there is a well developed network of journals making it relatively "cheap" in a time-energy perspective to get this type of knowledge. Concerning knowledge of personal properties we found the following three major channels for diffusion of knowledge: One was a national center for advanced study. Thirty-eight out of the 75 candidates had visited this center, 14 the same year as one or the other of the two best informed committee members. Seven of the 10 people asked to be dean had attended the center — 4 of these the same year as the two committee members mentioned. Also, 5 of the 9 active candidates had been at the center. Another important source of information seems to be membership in the informal national science cadre represented by national committees in the profession, research councils, foundations and especially in committees making "site visits" in connection with applications for grants. Six out of the 10 people asked to be dean had been members of such committees together with the two best informed members of the search committee. The third important channel seems to be participation in hiring — firing procedures. Again "senior" people, well established in the discipline were participating much more than junior people, giving them a much higher level of information.

18 Asking each committee member directly who among the candidates they knew, they would accept as dean immediately, and the reasons for this, the most important reason for all committee members for refusing a candidate was that he was not good enough intellectually (mentioned 22 times). Too narrow professional interest was mentioned 9 times, "not strong enough as a leader" 8, too old 6, while not innovative in the future and too autocratic were each mentioned 3 times.

19 To give on more illustration: In the questionnaire the respondents were asked, "Given an activity-scale from 1 (very inactive) to 7 (very active), where do you think the dean has been on the scale during the search process (how active has he been), and where do you think he should have been (how active should he have been)?" The distribution of responses were:

	Degree of activity:						
	(very inactive)					(very active)	
	1	2	3	4	5	6	7
The dean *was:*	0	3	4	3	2	7	3
The dean *should have been:*	4	0	2	4	2	5	7

(10 and 8 respondents respectively did not hold any opinion.)
The leaders of the opposition perceived the dean as very active (6 or 7 on the scale) and indicate that he should not have been active at all (1 on the scale). The followers of the dean are spread all over the scale concerning how active he had been but express a strong wish that he had been more active. Asking the same question of the chairman of the search committee we find the unanimous opinion that he should have been more active.

137

20 The criteria mentioned were: defend the school against the outside world, professional reputation, sympathy with your own work, ability to innovate, deal with people inside the school, "brightness", least probable to change math requirements, least probable to introduce departments, most positive to interdisciplinary work, able to recruit good faculty, able to reestablish peace in the school. Analyzing the responses it is important to have in mind that the people responding on these questions are the faculty members most active among those answering the questionnaire (who again have been more active than the people not answering the questionnaire).

21 Also, it is important to remember that the faculty members have to choose between *candidates,* that we may describe candidates with our variables, but that a variable might be very highly correlated with total ranking of candidates without being important for the ranking given (the variable might be unimportant, or a given faculty member may rank a candidate as number one in spite of the fact that he is scoring high on a certain variable; that is, the criteria is not of such negative importance that it prevents the candidate from being ranked as number one).

22 The use of a regression technique on a material like ours is problematic from the point of view of statistical theory. However, our confidence in the results is greatly strengthened by the outcomes of the other analytical techniques used. Thus, although none of the techniques used would be sufficiently in itself, their common agreement tends to validate the results. A special problem is the effects of "interdisciplinary orientation" which for two programs turns from highly positive to strongly negative (A/C) and for the third program from highly positive to zero (B). After living in the school for one year it is impossible to believe that interdisciplinary orientation should be negatively correlated with total ranking for any of the programs. It is possible to assume that the change is an effect of the regression technique itself. In principle we may also argue that these numbers are reflecting a situation where five candidates are given, where all the candidates would be said to be interdisciplinary oriented, and where the *differences* in interdisciplinarity would not be critical for the choice at hand. (See note 21.)

23 Other categories which do not give any clear patterns are new-old faculty, tenured-non-tenured, and positive-negative toward the dean.

24 The consistency between the two types of information is fairly good. It should be remembered that in Table 6.8a we have only the people answering the questionnaire, while in 6.8b we have reports on all faculty members present in the school during the search period. Comparing Tables 6.8a and 6.8b supports the view that it is the people on the periphery of the decision who have not answered the questionnaire. The reason for using the criterion "talked with two times or more" is to avoid casual exchanges of few words in the corridor, etc.

25 The outburst (among leaders) of person and process oriented criteria could be viewed in connection with the need which a majority had for indirect clues. When a decision process comes to votes of confidence in leaders and a question of lining up behind some of them, we may expect that one way of affecting who lines up behind whom would be to affect the image of ones opponents. A less Machiavellian interpretation, with less emphasis on "strategic" thinking, would be to suggest that as tension and conflict grow, decision makers will lose some of their capacity to think clearly about the problems at hand. Under such conditions decision makers (a) are less aware of the complexity of their environment, (b) consider fewer alternatives, and

138

(c) choose alternatives more impulsively with less adequate review of their consequences (Pruitt, 1966, p. 396).

26 The Vice-Chancellor had been chairman of the department (at another university) who had hired the director of program B in his first job. They were close personal friends. The director of program B also had been chairman of the search committee which had "discovered" the Vice-Chancellor when that position was vacant two years earlier. However, the Vice-Chancellor had also been active in order to get the chairman of the search committee to the school. Also, the person mentioned in the rumor as a dean candidate was a former student of the Vice-Chancellor and was his friend. In short this seems to be an exception to the rule that my friend's enemy is my enemy.

27 These goals were relevant more for selecting the set of candidates considered (which certainly was a biased sample of all the scientists in the respective fields) than for choosing within this set. Thus, even if participants were unable to state clearly what they wanted, they to some degree were able to state what they did not want and to avoid some outcomes. The fact that the process ended up as a choice between the chairman of the search committee and the first associate dean of the school also indicates that an "artifactual outcome" clearly is different from a random one.

7. Decision Making under Changing Norms

KÅRE ROMMETVEIT
University of Bergen

7.0 Introduction

All polities routinize some activities. Governmental policies become the products of large scale organizations enacting preestablished programs or standard operating procedures. These programs coordinate behavior through establishing stable roles and role relationships around a simplified model of the world (i.e., what is problematic, what solutions should look like, what information is relevant, etc.). Both the social relationships and the values and beliefs built into the substantive models take into consideration the expectations and power of environmental groups not involved in the everyday activity of the organizations. The predictability is high. Well known solutions are imposed on well known problems by people who are perceived to be the experts.

In this chapter, we examine a situation where standard operating procedures were challenged. On such occasions an organization is not simply a vehicle for solving well-defined problems as efficiently as possible. We see competing definitions of the problems, the best solutions, expertise, and the rules of procedure. Where established programs and social relationships are challenged, outcomes are not limited to the immediate substantive outcomes. They also establish future social relationships and definitions of the situation.

In the language of the garbage can model such situations involve temporary desegmentation of the decision-structure and the access-structure for problems and solutions (Cohen, March, and Olsen, 1972). So far the work on the garbage can model has concentrated on tracing the effects of different degrees and combinations of segmentation. In this chapter we focus on the conditions for desegmentation. Especially we are interested in the relationships between desegmentation and changes in the normative structures, or basic value-priorities in a polity. In a political system where the normative structure remains stable, we expect the relationships between politicians, bureaucrats, experts, and "clients" to be clearly defined and built upon stable expectations as to what each group may demand and will get from others. When changes occur in the normative structure, we may expect changes in the role relationships and also in the policy outcome. We may speculate about the nature of such changes. Classical administrative and democratic theory, assuming a clearcut division of labor between politicians and bureaucrats, suggest that changes in standard operating procedures may be instantaneous. A central planning unit or a renegotiated coalition may simply replace an established routine. Experience with organizational inertia, however, make us believe that this type of change will be the exception rather than the rule. Here it is suggested that the garbage can model at least under some conditions may be an adequate description of decision making in a polity experiencing challenges of established routines.

We will illustrate one situation where established standard operating procedures were challenged. We focus on the decision-making processes concerning the location of Norway's third medical school, where new definitions of the problems involved were raised, new participants activated, and the outcome so clearly suggested by existing standard operating procedures *not* selected.

7.1 The Setting

In March 1968 the Norwegian parliament decided to establish two new universities – one in Trondheim and one in Tromsø.[1] "This is definitely the most important event in the history of northern Norway", the mayor of Tromsø claimed in an interview the next day.

Although this was an important event in both cities, there was additional reason for celebration in Tromsø. The question of where to locate the country's third medical school had been the most hotly debated issue in the discussion preceding the parliament's decision. As this issue had been decided in Tromsø's favor, this was perceived as an important proof of a certain minimum public investment in Tromsø. The establishment of a medical school necessarily meant investments in buildings and equipment, and was (at least by some) seen as leading to a more general rise in the standard of health services in the northern part of Norway.

Although giving priority to building a medical school in Tromsø, the parliament's decision included a commitment to establish a fourth medical school in Trondheim at some future date. The timing was left indeterminate and dependent on the development in Tromsø. Shortly after the parliament's action, it seemed likely that this "decision" in fact would result in the parallel construction of two new medical schools in Norway. Paralleling the construction of the university hospital in Tromsø, the region of Trøndelag (where Trondheim is located) was setting up a regional hospital which clearly was meant also to function as a university hospital.

141

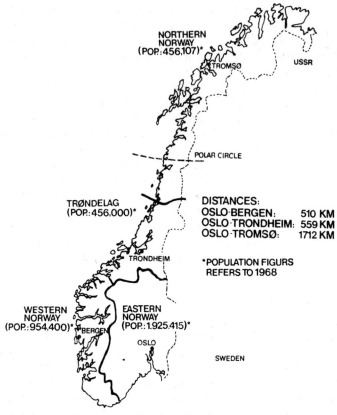

NORTHERN
NORWAY
(POP.: 456,107)*

TROMSØ

USSR

POLAR CIRCLE

TRØNDELAG
(POP.: 456,000)*

DISTANCES:
OSLO-BERGEN: 510 KM
OSLO-TRONDHEIM: 559 KM
OSLO-TROMSØ: 1712 KM

*POPULATION FIGURS
REFERS TO 1968

TRONDHEIM

WESTERN
NORWAY
(POP.: 954,400)*

BERGEN

EASTERN
NORWAY
(POP.: 1.925.415)*

OSLO

SWEDEN

Fig. 7.0. Map of Norway, showing the location of the two existing medical
schools, the two new alternatives, and the population density in each region

This series of events represented a two-fold break with what only a
short time before had seemed most likely. First, the fact that the third
medical school was located in Tromsø rather than in Trondheim. At
the beginning of the time-period studied here, Trondheim clearly had
been the dominant alternative – and in fact the only alternative
considered – for the location of the medical school. Professionally, the
city could claim a fairly large scientific milieu, in medicine as well as
the natural and technical sciences. Politically, the region had well
established contacts with the national bureaucracy and the relevant
political authorities. Second, instead of one medical school encompassing only the clinical part of the education, two medical schools
were established – Tromsø starting up with a full-fledged program
from 1973 of, and Trondheim expected to start with the clinical part
shortly thereafter.[2] In a memorandum from the Ministry of Finance

(November 1966) it was made clear that the further expansion in the capacity of the medical education had to be limited to the construction of only *one* new medical school. Regardless of what alternative was finally decided upon, this had to be limited to the clinical part of the education.

The discrepancy between "the final outcome" and what only a short time before had seemed to be the likely outcome, is our point of departure. "Likely" here refers to what one should expect given established programs and standard operating procedures in the Norwegian polity, and we ask what were the processes that generated the unexpected outcomes? What were the conditions under which these processes operated?

7.2 The Data

Data were collected over a 1½ year period, starting in the fall of 1969. It included several kinds of activities: (a) An extensive examination of the largest newspapers in Tromsø, Trondheim, and Oslo over the 10-year period starting in 1960. (b) Forty-two lengthy interviews with 36 persons. These persons all had been central in the process at hand, and were selected on the basis of names of people/ institutions appearing in the written material so as to make up a rather comprehensive selection of all those participating. The interviews, which were unstructured, were systematically used to confirm (or disconfirm) the information given by other informants or obtained through the written material. (c) Reading of personal notes and letters made available by some of the persons interviewed. (d) Examination of the archives in the participating institutions, containing public documents as well as more confidential notes and reports. (e) Participant observation at several meetings taking place in 1969/70.

The empirical data from these studies will be presented in the following way: over six periods of time (within a ten-year span), we will try to trace the streams of participants, problems, solutions, and choice-opportunities. A more detailed description and analysis has been given elsewhere (Rommetveit, 1972). The present discussion is simplified, but it captures the most important elements of the process as it is reported in the longer treatment.

The four columns listed on the following pages (Table 7.0) were established as follows. The list of participants in the different time periods suggested itself: Through the examination of the different kinds of data reported above marked differences in the types[3] and numbers of participants became apparent. The entries in the columns for definition of problems and definitions of solutions rely heavily upon the different kinds of written material – what did the main groups of participants in each period perceive as problematic and what solutions

Table 7.0. A brief outline of the sequence of events

Time period:	Participants	Definition of problems	Definition of solutions	Choice opportunities
1. Pre-conception period 1960	–A few politicians within the Labour Party and the Ministry of Education –Local politicians in Trondheim and health administrators	–Strengthening of the economic basis of the different regions –Need for expansion of hospitals	–Building a university in Tromsø –Building a university in Trondheim	
2. The social economist involvement 1960–62/63	–Politicians and bureaucrats within the Labour Party, the Ministries of Education and Finance	–How to meet the expected increase in the demand for higher education? –How to get qualified teachers for a planned elementary school reform? –How to avoid spreading the resources on too many places	–Expansion of existing universities, giving college courses in Tromsø and giving priority to Tromsø as the 4th university city in Norway	–Long-term planning being introduced
	–Directorate for Public Health	–Lack of medical doctors	–Revision of hospital plans in Trondheim to include facilities for medical education	–Plans for the regional hospital in Trondheim to be approved
	–Leaders of the scientific institutions in Tromsø	–How to get adequate housing facilities and qualified personnel?	–Start giving college courses	–Inquiries from Ministry of Education concerning possibilities for giving courses at college level
3. Committee period 1963–65	–Trondheim-committee –Brodal-committee, representatives from medical faculty in	–How could the existing activities at the scientific institutions be coordinated? –How to expand educational capacity for medical doctors—for	–Establishing a university also encompassing a medical faculty –Expand at the existing faculties, and establish a new school where the facilities	

Table 7.6. (contd.)

Time period:	Participants	Definition of problems	Definition of solutions	Choice opportunities
	–Tromsø-committee	–How to legitimate the building of a university and a medical school in Tromsø? –How to lower the speed of expansion in the Oslo-region and thus better the health-service in other regions—including Bergen?	–Produce data by setting down a subcommittee consisting of high-status members of the medical profession –Produce arguments favoring expansion in the periphery, i. e. Tromsø.	
	–Subcommittee recruited from medical faculty in Bergen			
4. Departmental stage 1965–67	–Bureaucracy in Ministry of Education	–Expand the capacity in higher education	–Universities in Trondheim and Tromsø, but medical school (clinical part) located in Trondheim—in line with the arguments of the overwhelming majority of medical experts	–Routine handling of committee proposals, writing draft for parliamentary bill
	–Directorate of Public Health	–How could the expansion in medical education be done in the best possible professional way?	–Expansion of existing medical schools, establishing of a new school (clinical part) in Trondheim	–Committee proposals (see period 3) and draft for parliamentary bill to be commented upon, in line with ordinary bureaucratic routine
	–Political leadership in Ministry of Education (change of government in 1965)	–Work for regional re-distribution of goods—or at least demonstrate an image in this direction	–Universities in Trondheim and Tromsø but medical education (clinical part of it) to Tromsø	–Parliamentary bill on building of universities and expansion of capacity in medical training to be presented
	–Politicians and represent-atives from scientific institutions in Tromsø	–How to secure this good for Tromsø and Northern Norway?	–Put on political pressure, present this as a joint demand from the whole northern part of Norway	–The different proposals put forward

Table 7.0. (contd.)

Time period:	Participants	Definition of problems	Definition of solutions	Choice opportunities
5. Formal decision-making period 1967–68	Members of parliament: -- primarily representing the regions (around Trondheim and Tromsø) -- primarily representing the political parties	How to secure the goods for own region? How to reach a compromise?	Expansion of the frames earlier given: Tromsø to have the first medical school (clinical part)—but also a second school to be established in Trondheim after the development in Tromsø made this possible	Parliamentary bill to be decided upon
	Members of medical faculty/profession in Oslo	How to reform medical education?	Make plans for integrated medical education, clinical and basic training given already from the first year of study	The issue of the location of the third medical faculty
	University committee in Tromsø	How to secure this good for Tromsø and Northern Norway?	Put on political pressure, produce arguments, present this as a joint demand from the whole Northern Norway	Parliament's discussion of location issue
	University committee in Trondheim	How to secure the medical school for Trondheim?	An expansion of existing frames necessary: Rather than one medical school, two would be necessary	Parliament's discussion of location issue
6. Implementary period 1968–70	Ministry of Education	Small market of candidates for leading the work in Tromsø—strong political commitment created	Accept the conditions put forward by the governing board in Tromsø	Plans for educational program in Tromsø to be approved

Table 7.0. (contd.)

Time period:	Participants	Definition of problems	Definition of solutions	Choice opportunities
	-Professor of Medicine, University of Oslo	-How to reform medical education	-Accept the job of making plans for a medical school at a place where this could be done from scratch	-Asked by the Ministry of Education to make plans for the medical study in Tromsø
	-Directorate for Public Health	-To delay the expansion in Tromsø	-Stick to its earlier programs	-Plans for hospitals to be approved
	-Government Board of the new university	-How to get started before the expansion in Trondheim took all resources—economic and personnel?	-Starting up with integrated medical education in provisory housing facilities as soon as possible	-The criticism raised from Directorate of Public Health, the competition from Trondheim
		How to get the central authorities to stick to their former decision? How to keep up enthusiasm among the planners involved?		
	-Students	-How to create a more democratic university?	-Strong involvement in reform plans for University in Tromsø—including medical education	-Governing board for the new university to be set up
	-Regional authorities in Trondheim -- represesentatives from scientific institutions	-To get the regional hospital built	-Continue the building of the regional hospital, making this fit for medical education	-The parliament's decision (see period 5)

were put forward in answer to these problems? Both these columns report perceptions as they were recorded in each time period. The last column, "choice opportunities", contains entries of a different kind: Through bureaucratic routine or external events (external to the choice situation here analyzed) an institution, a group of people or an individual is presented with an opportunity where some kind of reaction is expected – either as a matter of routine or as an event presenting a legitimate opportunity to activate oneself. What represents a choice opportunity thus is heavily dependent on such factors as deadlines and established procedures.

The sequence of events is divided into six time periods on the basis of the main differences in participants and their definitions of problems and solutions – as these differences could be inferred from the data.[4]

The story revealed by a persual of the table can be summarized briefly: At an early stage, paralleling the social economists' first attempt at more extensive planning within the sector of higher education, the problems of meeting the expected demand for higher education were preeminent. Capacity problems dominated the standard operating procedures for three strong governmental organizations: The ministry of education (meeting the demand for higher education), the Directorate of Public Health (meeting the demand for medical doctors), The ministry of finance (emphasizing the scarcity of resources, and the priorities between education and other sectors of public policy). In terms of all these three standard definitions of what was problematic, Trondheim would be the best solution. The different scientific institutions in Tromsø first got involved in order to solve their most pressing problem: lack of economic resources and personnel. When representatives from the medical faculty in Bergen were activated, their concern was as much for hindering further strong expansion in Oslo as getting a medical faculty established in Tromsø. When the new Minister of Education entered office in 1965, his concerns seemed to be to establish a clear political posture regarding the question of a regional redistribution of goods within Norway. This was one of the most hotly debated issues in Norwegian politics – and an issue of growing importance within the whole 10-year period considered. The primary reason for the dissent among members of the medical profession in Oslo was to reform existing programs for medical education in Norway rather than to establish a medical faculty in Tromsø. Students were activated on the "democracy"-issue. The Parliament made a compromise by expanding the framework. However, later events made this expansion much larger than expected by most members of the Parliament. This was at least partly due to a very active board at the University of Tromsø "using" the present concern with regional redistribution in its bargaining with the authorities.

148

Rather than one process and one outcome, we have a series of different processes and outcomes – in short, a series of different problems, solutions, and participants being hooked on and off the choice situation more specifically under scrutiny, i.e., the location of the medical school. We may thus speak of an "economic-planning" arena, a "regional policy" arena and a "medical" arena, all partly independent of but nevertheless having relevance for the question of where to locate Norway's third medical school.

The choice situation was one in which several participants were activated for a shorter or longer period of time, where several definitions of the problems involved existed simultaneously and over time, where perceptions of the likely outcome of the different alternatives varied, and where disagreement existed as to the values that ought to be used to resolve the issues.

The decision-process resulting was characterized by a sequence of locally understandable steps heavily dependent upon special features of the moment in which they occurred. In order to understand the larger process resulting from the chaining of these steps, it will be argued that emphasis has to be placed on tracing the impact of the broader normative structure.

Our task is twofold. First, we say something about the basic properties of the decision-making process within the desegmented political structure. Second, we discuss more in detail this desegmentation of the political structure, and especially the connections between the changes in the normative context of public policy making in Norway and the desegmentation of the decision- and access structure of the choice.

7.3 The Process as a Garbage Can

The location of the universities and the medical school was a major political decision involving major actors in the Norwegian political system. It seems obvious that the outcome was not a product of standard operating procedures of the relevant public bureaucracies. It also seems obvious that the final outcome of the whole process can not be understood as the willed product of a single actor or some winning coalition. Models of individual rational choice or of bargaining-coalition building (see Chapter 6) can be used to interpret different actions within any specific period. These kinds of models do not, however, enable us to explain how the sets of apparently rational actions add up to a result different from what most participants expected only a short time before. Even in 1967 none of the participants was planning an expansion even close to the scale which only 1½ year later was taking place. Furthermore, none of these models seems to take into account the continuous shifts in participants' definitions of problems and definitions of solutions.

Our data are good enough to exclude some models (standard operating organizational procedure, individual rational choice, bargaining-coalition building model). We think the basic features of the process come close to that of the garbage can. However, the data do not allow us to give a full description in terms of this model (that would demand more knowledge about the alternative choice-opportunities the participants had during the period). What they do allow us, is to point out some aspects of the process which clearly overlap with those predicted by the garbage can model.

Consider the decision ambiguity, the partial irrelevance of the immediate substantive outcome of the process for many central participants, and the competitive activation of participants. The content of the decision was not always clear. The interpretation changed over time and from one set of participants to another. Different participants emphasized different aspects of a specific decision – depending on which aspects were relevant for the respective arenas of primary interest. After the formal Parliamentary decision in 1968, there was substantial rewriting, reinterpretation and supplementing of the formal decision made. Even four years later it was not clear what the "final" outcome would be.

For at least some (perhaps most) of the key groups the explicit decision seemed to be of little importance "per se". While interested in certain aspects of the decision, the relevance of the decision otherwise largely disappeared once the decision was made. The outcome of the battle was important less for the immediate outcome that resulted than for the implications this outcome had for contemporary battles within other arenas or future battles involving the same participants. When the political leadership in the Ministry of Education came out in favor of locating the medical faculty in Tromsø this had clear symbolic effects in terms of indicating the interest in regional development. However, it was done without any thorough inquiries into actual consequences this location would have for the medical care in the region. It was made without more detailed knowledge of the approved plans for expansion at the hospital in Tromsø. Also it was made without any well-founded ideas of what the likely regional consequences of starting up a project of this magnitude would be (Rommetveit, 1972, p. 124). Similarly, the representatives from the medical faculty in Bergen had their primary interest within a more limited medical arena where the competition with the faculty in Oslo for scarce resources continually was going on. They wanted to reduce the speed of expansion in Oslo. The activation of this group within the larger arena represented a rational act on its behalf, but the interest

150

was as much in a victory as in the specific content of the victory. To the group of dissenting members from the medical faculty in Oslo, activated in the formal decision making period, the location issue merely presented an incidental opportunity to come forward with their reform plans for the existing educational programs.

The plans for a reform of medical education could have found an outlet at the existing faculties or in Trondheim. However, possibilities for success there were lower than in Tromsø. This ironically was due to exactly the reasons upon which the established part of the medical community based its argument in favor of Trondheim: the rather small and limited milieu in Tromsø relative to Trondheim. The plans for reform here had a larger probability for success exactly because this "handicap" also meant there existed fewer established constraints (traditions, existing programs, power groups with vested interest, etc.) for a reform. The relative absence of this kind of constraints made Tromsø a better arena for innovation, while considerations emphasizing rationality and efficiency in further expansion within the medical education lead to exactly the opposite conclusion as to where to locate the medical school.

A series of "rational acts" by participants became connected to the "larger" arena in a way that makes it difficult to explain the outcome within this arena. We are left to conclude that there existed a rather complex connection between the processes analyzed and the "final outcome". Many games were being played simultaneously in different arenas. They were related to one arena, or one choice-situation in a way neither planned nor managed by anyone (individual or group of participants). Players entered and left in terms of definitions of the situation that often had little to do with the establishment of a medical faculty in Tromsø.

One of the central features of garbage can situations is that "decision opportunities are fundamentally ambiguous stimuli". This seems to be generally in accordance with the present empirical data. However, if a dominant participant should be involved in a decision process dealing with problems such as these, it seems unlikely that this ambiguity would arise. An important precondition for applying the garbage-can model to the analysis of more encompassing social structures, thus seems to be that the different interests or power groups involved are of roughly comparable strength.

7.4 Desegmentation in a Political Structure

We now attend to the question of how it was possible for Tromsø to arise as an alternative to Trondheim, when the standard operating procedures of several strong public agencies were selecting the latter location? In order to understand this we have to study the ways in which changes in the normative context in Norway produced important changes in the relationships among bureaucrats, experts, and politicians.

Tromsø became an alternative when regional redistribution values became central in the general political discussion in Norway. Table 7.1 shows the significance given to regional development as a political issue in three parliamentary elections covering this period.[5]

Table 7.1. The significance given by voters to regional development as a political issue compared to other policy areas in three elections

Policy area/year	1957	1965	1969
Economic policy	72	14	7
Social policy	37	28	26
Regional development policy	9	27	59
Defence and foreign policy	12	14	22
Other political areas	75	86	88
Total*	205%	169%	202%
N =	429	1751	1595

*Adds up to more than 100 percent because more than one answer allowed for.
Source: Valen & Martinussen, *Velgerne og de politiske frontlinjer*, Gyldendal, Oslo 1972.

What consequences did this shift in normative orientation have for the location? The lack of resources necessary to establish a medical school had been an obstacle to locating the medical school in Tromsø. However, what within a "capacity" frame of reference was perceived as decisive arguments *against* Tromsø, within a regional redistribution definition of the situation represented strong arguments *in favor of* locating the medical school in the same place. All the economic and professional arguments earlier in favor of Trondheim, now could be seen as equally decisive arguments in favor of Tromsø.

We may suggest a "Matthew-effect of public administration". Given that a public agency is trying to solve a capacity problem without a specified clientele (e.g., produce as many student places as possible for a certain amount of money), it will always try to use already existing resources. Those who have will get more ... Trondheim became the "natural" solution – not Tromsø. Only when a capacity problem becomes more specified in terms of clientele, (social, regional, etc.) will those who do not already have resources, who are not already strong, have a chance.[6]

In Norway we may expect redefinitions and changes in the normative structure to have a stronger immediate impact upon politicians than upon the bureaucracy or the professional experts.

Politicians, bureaucrats, and experts are patently interdependent figures in the political system. As argued by Parsons (1947, p. 58), a bureaucratic decision may be based upon two different sources of legitimacy: professional knowledge (technical competence) and legal authority. The bureaucracy consequently can be seen as being dependent upon experts as well as politicians as sources of legitimacy. At the same time, politicians obviously are dependent upon the bureaucracy and the experts. They ordinarily do not have a detailed understanding of different technical fields.

Politicians are also dependent on their political bases – the constituencies and the parties. Constituency and party may be seen as two different sources of rewards in the Norwegian political system. Within such a model, politicians can be seen as operating within a dualistic reward system trying to maximize the total reward sum.[7] A politician can express a predominantly localist orientation – the source of reward mainly being his constituency: or he can express a more cosmopolitan orientation where the national party represents the source of reward. The better organized and the more centralized a party is, the stronger the cosmopolitan orientation of its parliamentarians can be expected to be. The national party, in turn, operates somewhat bureaucratic, and consequently is more vulnerable to professional values.

In the Tromsø decision the primary group of experts was the medical profession. Both sides used arguments based upon medical insight to justify their positions. Both relied on members of the medical profession. In fact, persons having a medical degree made up exactly 50 percent (29 out of 58) of the total membership in the nine committees somehow dealing with this issue during the course of decision. The dominance of this group is especially clear in the periods from 1964 to 1967/68, when this percentage was as high as 92 percent (24 out of 26).

During the first period the medical professional values were not challenged. Regional policy was a realm of policy apart from the issue of expanding the capacity of medical education. As the normative structure changed, uncertainty was created in the role relations and in the meaning of a medical school decision. Politicians and bureaucrats no longer were as dependent upon the dominant groups within the profession (basically located in Oslo). Values having to do with a "just" distribution of goods between the center and the periphery also became of central importance, making the idea of "expertise" more obscure.[8]

If all members of the medical profession had defined the problems and solutions in the same way, and as the majority did, it is unlikely that the project in Tromsø could have materialized. Within the profession, however, different groups had diverging objectives which could be furthered by providing professional legitimacy to the political and administrative authorities.

The disagreement among the professionals probably was a necessary condition for political intervention, but also the converse can be said to be true. The possibility for political intervention gave some point to the disagreement between the medical communities in Oslo and Bergen. The question of the location of the medical school represented an occasion for exercising antagonisms and testing strength between the two rivals. If a redistribution of goods could not be accomplished within the profession, then entering the larger political system represented a new opportunity.

Where formerly the relations among politicians, experts and bureaucrats were clearly prescribed and founded upon an accepted set of values, leaving open only a capacity-definition of the problems, these relations during the process became rather complicated as a consequence of the changes taking place in the normative structures within society. The values up to now accepted as the basis for means-ends relations were degraded, the role of the expertise became problematic and dissenting groups within the medical profession perceived this as an opportunity to realize their diverging views. This in turn made possible the activation of new groups, which could claim special insight in this field. Little agreement existed as to the relevant values upon which to base the decision, and no clear monopoly of expertise could be claimed. The professional values hitherto dominant were degraded relative to the regional redistribution values now becoming of central importance on the political scene. "Regionalism" was a problem capable of entering a previously highly segmented decision area.

We may speculate about the long term effects of the choice upon the segmentation of decision- and access-structures in the Norwegian polity. On the one hand regional arguments have been legitimized in choice situations dealing with the location of a university and a medical school. This type of arguments is probably more likely to be used in the future. On the other hand the standard operating procedures were by no means "defeated". Joining with local resources in Trondheim, they produced a medical school there.

Looking at Tromsø there are indications of a reestablishing of earlier segmentation. It seems clear that the degree of freedom enjoyed and the possibilities existing for "entrepeneurial" activity have been severely restricted since this study was completed. The University of Tromsø is now much more integrated into the regular programs for higher education and the norms of the medical experts. Regional redistribution values have wandered elsewhere and the decision arena involves the more conventional competition for scarce resources to be divided among the four universities. The variety of views is also reflected among the different interests within the new university in Tromsø. The process has returned to a highly bureaucratic one dominated by questions of professional expertise and scarce economic resources. In certain respects the circle has been closed.

NOTES:

* A slightly different version of this chapter appeared as an article in Acta Sociologica, Vol. 17, no. 3, 1974.
1 As seen from Figure 7.0 Trondheim is located in central Norway, 559 kilometers from the capital, Oslo. It has been the site of the Norwegian Technical University since 1910, and also had other institutions offering graduate instruction in the humanities and natural sciences. The location of Tromsø is more peripheral — above the Arctic Circle, and about 1700 kilometers from Oslo. The two existing medical schools are located in Oslo and Bergen.
2 While this was being written, the Ministry of Education announced that medical students would be accepted at the University of Trondheim begining in 1973. Thus, the two new medical schools would start their teaching activities simultaneously.
3 Mainly differences which could be drawn between the institutional and the professional background of the participants.
4 The differences as they here are presented probably are much more clear-cut than perceived by the participants. The division into six different time periods represents an analytical post hoc construct. The value of this depends on the degree to which the differences in characteristics emphasized are helpful in structuring our understanding of the empirical data.
5 These figures are not directly comparable as they refer to different samples and as the questions were not identical. Thus even though the trend is clear the absolute differences between the figures ought not to be given great importance.
6 This argument is illustrated in an excellent study of Norwegian agricultural administration in the end of the 19th century (Jacobsen, 1964). The principle that you have to contribute something yourself in order to get something from the public has a long tradition in Norway (Seip, 1959).
7 A thorough elaboration of this point is carried out in Hernes (1971).
8 Jacobsen (1968) has defined expertise as a triadic relationship: A person is an expert to the extent others expect him to have special insight in a particular field. Other people or groups determine whether a person or group possesses expertise, a crucial factor often being whether a profession in practice deals with the group of clients whose interests are involved. For a discussion of these relations, see Eckhoff (1967, p. 10).

8. Ideology and Management in a Garbage Can Situation

KRISTIAN KREINER
Copenhagen School of Economics

8.0 Introduction

It is a fundamental tenet of our usual interpretation of organizations that the impact of management attempts depends on the extent to which those attempts are seen as legitimate by participants.[1] Most modern theories of leaderskip build on the idea that the relation between the leaders and the led depends on the extent to which the activities of the leaders are consistent with the basic ideology of the organization. Deviation from the norm is assumed to lead to resistance from followers and, thus, increased chance of leadership failure.

There is ample evidence that participants react to leaders in terms of the legitimacy of their behavior. Unless prohibited, verbal and social sanctions that are highly visible (or audible) are provided by followers for deviant leaders. An important part of organizational decision-making is the continous definition and redefinition of what is legitimate. Where, as in many advanced societies, power (and thus leadership) are counter-ideology, sanctions are part of the routine accoutrements of positions of authority.

At the same time, it is less clear what connection there is between illegitimacy and effectiveness of leadership acts. It has been observed that actions that are illegitimate, and sanctioned as illegitimate, may nonetheless be tolerated if the leader has high standing in the group. Thus, illegitimate behavior may be particularly likely among highly-regarded and effective leaders. Management that violates group ideology will be criticized, but accepted.[2]

This connection between ideological expression and action is further confused in a decision process that tends to separate process from outcome. Where process and outcome drift apart, feelings about appropriate mangerial behavior are reflected in the rhetoric surrounding the process; but they are buffered from outcomes. Feelings about appropriate results are reflected in rhetoric surrounding the outcomes; but they are buffered from the process.

A typical case of the latter situation is a business firm in which ideology emphasizes profit as a measure of performance but where the connection between managerial behavior and profitability is small. Under such circumstances most rhetoric and sanctions will be applied in terms of results.

The converse case is also interesting. Where ideology emphasizes aspects of managerial behavior (e.g., democratic leadership) and those behaviors have only modest impact on outcomes, there will be relatively little connection between the legitimacy of leader behavior and its apparent effectiveness. In this chapter, we explore such a possibility.

We discuss different techniques of management in an organization characterized as being a direct democracy. The organization is an experimental free-school in Denmark (see Christensen, Chapter 16). No formal authority-differentiation exists; all adult members (parents and teachers) of the organization are invited to participate in the decision-processes as equals. Our aim was to examine management success and failure in an ideological organized anarchy. Despite the ideology of the organization, we fund little apparent correlation between the legitimacy of the form of management and the apparent success of the attempt.

8.1 The Organization

8.1.0 *Formal Structure*

During 1971–72 we made observations of the decision-making processes in an experimental free-school in Copenhagen, Denmark. One of the decisions made during this period was to change the pedagogical structure of the school, and it is this decision which is the focus of this chapter. During the course of this decision, the research group was present at every important meeting except one, conducted extensive interviews, and drew upon a detailed questionnaire completed by parents and teachers.

The decision was made by *the open assembly* – the formal governing body of the school. All 170 parents and 10 teachers of the school were invited to the open assembly's monthly meetings. A chairman was elected each time, but there existed no rules for the procedure of the meetings. Subject to the approval of the participants present, the assembly could discuss and decide upon everything. Normally, the meetings were structured by an agenda, put together by the school board and mailed to all members.

The six members of the *school board,* all of them parents, were elected by the assembly. They served for two year terms. Normally, the elections were not contested, the usual problem being one of finding enough candidates willing to serve rather than choosing from among competitors. The main function of board members was administrative, but they also served as a link between the assembly and the board of teachers.

A system of collective leadership existed among the teachers. In order to exercise this, *the board of teachers,* consisting of all teachers, met once a week. The planning of teacher activities was to take place here. In day-to-day matters, individual teachers had considerable autonomy. During the observation period there were six grades, among which the approximately 110 children were distributed according to age. Most teachers were assigned to a specific grade. The parents from each grade met occasionally with the teacher(s) in order to discuss class-specific problems. These *class meetings* had no formal authority to make decisions.

8.1.1 *Pedagogical Structure*

The children were divided into six different grades. Most of the time was spent in these groups. Although a time schedule did not exist officially, most grades seemed to follow some plan of activities. Subject to a few limits, children were allowed to leave the group in order to take part in outdoor activities. During two afternoons each week the grade-structure was replaced by a workshop structure: Every teacher offered an activity, and the children could choose among these according to their own desires – at least in principle. In practice, due to an overwhelming interest in the cooking class, children were distributed among the workshops by the teachers.

8.1.2 *The Ideology*

The school was founded by a group of parents in reaction to the public school system. The founders believed that:

(a) The hierarchical structure of the public schools resulted in a situation in which parents had little influence on the kind of education provided their children. This dissatisfaction developed into the concept of a parent-governed school, which further developed into a direct democracy. An attempt was made to avoid status and authority differentiation.

(b) The high priority given by the public schools to intellectual development produced more harm than good for the children. In the view of the founders the children would, by their own drive, demand such education when they were ready for it. To force them to learn to read before they themselves demanded it would disturb their natural development, or at least be a waste of energy. This idea manifested itself in a high priority for playing, as play was believed to develop creative and social abilities. In the appliction form to the school it was clearly stated that the children should not be expected to read as early as children in the public schools.

The ideologies were real, but they were not completely fulfilled in practice. Even though the formal authority distribution was eliminated, there existed clear differences among the members with regard to their influence on the development of the school. This was the perception of the members as well as the observers. Of the approximately 200 members, only 27 members were mentioned in our questionnaire as being influentials. Further, of these 27, a group of six was mentioned on the average ten times more often than the remaining group on the average. Thus, there seemed to be a high degree of concensus in the perception of a power-distribution. In addition, even though the official policy was not to force the children to acquire intellectual abilities – and this policy was often praised at the assembly meetings – quite a few parents felt unhappy about it. Their complaints were aired to the teachers privately or at the class meetings.

8.1.3 Description of the Choice-situation

Like many organizations of this type, we think that the school could be described as an organized anarchy (Cohen, March, and Olsen, 1972). By this we mean:

(1) No consistent set of preferences existed to be applied to actual choices. Instead, a number of highly valued symbols (e.g., democracy, Marx, children's right to self-determination) were used. However, the implications of the symbols for any choice were uncertain and subject to much interpretation from the participants.

(2) The knowledge about the technology, in the realm in which decisions were to be made, was vague. Thus, questions about which solutions solved which problems, or which consequences should be taken into consideration, were matters of individual judgment.

(3) The participants were not assigned to different decisions through rules or obligations. Although there were fairly stable differences in participation, it was hard to predict who would participate in a given choice. Whether a member would participate was at least partly a result of outside time and energy demands (e.g., childcare, work).

Normally about 40 parents participated in an assembly meeting. In our questionnaire, only a few stated that they never participated (mainly parents with no children in the school at the moment) and only a few stated that they always participated. The series of meetings, which we will describe shortly, attracted about 80 parents on the average. They were well-attended. Attendance varied within single meetings; typically quite a few participants left before a meeting was concluded.

In general, the decision-structure and the access-structure placed few limitations on the way in which problems, solutions, and participants were connected to choices. In fact, the ideology encouraged members to participate and encouraged the participants to air their concerns in open debate.

The load these meetings put on the members' energy was not very high. Almost no preparation was required. The amount of written material distributed in advance was usually modest. In our case, three meetings were held within one month. There were numerous requests for more meetings.

8.1.4 *The Dynamics of the Decision-process*

We expect a decision-process to exhibit some kind of dynamic by which it moves toward a conclusion. This may be through the solution of problems, or through some other logic by which the decision process produces a decision. The process secures its major meaning from the outcomes it generates. In contrast, choice-opportunities in the school we studied seemed to contain little of these dynamics.

We think that there are at least three reasons for this:

(a) Many of the problems were highly discussable but hardly solvable. A long ideological discussion of creative training may serve as an example. Creative training had always had a high priority among the educational goals for the school. At one point, however, one of the members persuaded the participants to focus on the fact that industry made use of exactly such abilities. Since presumably none of them wanted to educate children for capitalist society, the concept of creativity needed some kind of reformulation. The ensuing discussion was long, but without conspicuous results.

(b) Members of the school were urged to participate. Intrinsic in the democratic ideals was the idea that as many as possible should make the decisions. Furthermore, the assembly was perceived not only as an arena for discussion, but also as a social center for the school, a place to meet each other, and in some important respects, a church.

(c) Status and power-reputation were distributed according to activity at the assembly meetings. It appeared to be more virtuous to have one's definition of the choice accepted as definitive than to make compromises. Thus, there were disincentives for participants, seeking status and power-reputation, to sacrifice a preferred definition of the situation, even if the symbolic intransigence limited the chances of a decision.[3]

8.1.5 *The Main Participants*

We have already mentioned that six members of the school were commonly perceived to have more power than other members. Since these six members normally played a central role in the assembly meetings, and did so in our case, we describe them briefly on a number of dimensions. Using data from our questionnaire, we can state that:

(a) All of them had high seniority in the organization. In fact all but one had participated in the founding of the school.
(b) Each attended the assembly meetings every time or almost every time.
(c) All but one rated themselves as belonging to the most active third of the participants at the essembly meetings.
(d) All but one rated themselves av belonging to the most radical group in the school.
(e) Their circles of private acquaintances were dominated by other free-school members (from 50 percent to 85 percent with an average of 75 percent), rather than outsiders.

One of the six was a teacher at the school. The others were a psychology student, bookbinder, architect, artist, and public school teacher. The four last mentioned parents all had children in the third grade; and the public school teacher and the bookbinder were members of the school board. All of them seemed to be well trained in meeting behavior and to be in the possession of some oratorical gifts.

These six members seemed to agree on most issues. Often the "enemy", whom they fought at meetings was not easy to discover. In particular, they were concerned with "the conservative parents who force the school in direction of intellectual over-emphasis". Often their meeting activity seemed to be a kind of educational performance in which public virtue was demonstrated and reinforced.

At times, however, confrontations did occur. The usual opponents in these confrontations belonged to a rather unstructured group, the members of which could be described as fairly active at the meetings but without great power-reputation. Often they seemed to be regarded

161

as less radical than the leadership, but whether this was a result of real differences or just derived from the fact that they opposed the leading radicals, we are unable to answer. In such confrontations, many (maybe most) participants played on-looker roles. They did not participate in the debate, but only in the voting procedures.

8.2 The Events

8.2.0 *The Decision*

By 69 votes to 6, the assembly decided to change the pedagogical structure. The main idea was to dissolve the existing grades and to have a considerable proportion of the teaching take place in workshops. The decision represented a general frame for action rather than a specific set of mandated actions. A lot of questions were still not settled: How much time should be spent in workshops? How much freedom should children have in their choice of activity? What should the workshops contain? All these questions were to be worked out in seven small groups as specified in the school board's plan for the implementation. These groups were to consist of teachers as well as parents.

8.2.1 *The Antecedents*

The situation, in which this choice-opportunity appeared, was from all sides described as a crisis. The teachers had major troubles with their collective leadership, as well as personal problems among themselves. Some parents were dissatisfied with the school. Some of the children were playing outdoors most of the time; others complained of being bored. The teachers were too busy with their own problems to do much of anything about them.

The problems among the teachers led to a discontinuation of the normal collaboration between the two teachers in the third grade. Consequently, a newly-hired teacher was left alone in what was generally regarded as the most difficult grade. At a class meeting for the third grade, parents tried unsuccessfuly to persuade the teachers to reallocate some teacher hours back to the grade.

In the course of this process the idea of a new pedagogical structure was born. Dissolution of the grades would also solve the problem for the third grade. One of the parents from this grade wrote a paper, in which he discussed different pedagogical goals and structures. He submitted the paper to the school board. Using the construction of a new school as the occasion, the assembly leaders placed the paper on the agenda for the regular meeting in the assembly on October 8, 1971.

8.2.3 *Highlights of the Process*

The main events we wish to consider took place over a period of about one month in 1971. It was a relatively crowded month, as the following table (Table 8.0) suggests:

Table 8.0. Time-line of decision

Date	Arena	Agenda	Events
1971 Oct. 8	Assembly	Paper on pedagogical goals and structures	1) general discussion of the paper 2) airing of dissatisfaction over teachers and structure 3) teachers complaints of cross-pressure regarding the priority of intellectual education 4) vote on the priority of intellectual, social, and creative training. By 31 votes to 16 the meeting refuses to make any priority at that time
Oct. 11	School board	The cross-pressure on the teachers	1) it is decided to cancel all class meetings for a period of three months 2) the members agree to draft a proposal for a new pedagogical structure and to present it in the assembly as soon as possible
Oct. 21	Extra-parliamentary meeting	The crisis of the school	1) due to the autumn holidays not all invited show up in the home of the originator 2) the teachers present attack the meeting, which they say is violating basic, democratic principles in the school 3) exchange of viewpoints
Oct. 29	Assembly	School boards proposal for a pedagogical structure	1) presentation of the proposal 2) general discussion, no agreement on whether to discuss goals or structure 3) group discussion. The groups can decide themselves what to discuss 4) School board demands final decision on their proposal. Many objections. The school board threatens resignation 5) a vote shows a small majority in favor of a final vote 6) a guiding vote shows near unanimity for the proposal 7) the school board agrees to postpone the final vote one week
Nov. 2	Extra-parlimentary meeting for "the silent majority"	Meeting with head-of another free-school with workshop structure	1) Initiative taken by four couples from the third grade; approximately 30 members attend 2) the speaker has positive experiences with the structure, and he is thus able to relieve worried parents

163

Table 8.0. (contd.)

Date	Arena	Agenda	Events
Nov. 5	Assembly	Final decision on the proposal	1) School board presents the implementation plan 2) general discussion, in which all concerned are referred to as being taken care of by the group 3) Final decision; the proposal is accepted by 69 votes to 6

8.3 Efforts at Management

The description of the events shows the clear properties of a garbage can decision process. The course of decision was erratic. Problems, solutions, choice opportunities, and participants wandered in and out of a relatively unsegmented structure. Activities within the process were organized by those flows more than by any clear internal logic.

At the same time, it is also clear that various participants tried at various times to manage the process. Interventions were made with the intent of controlling the flow of events. Some interventions were successful; some failed. The management attempts varied in style. In particular, some were consistent with the decision making ideology of the school; others were not.

We wish to consider five efforts to manage the process leading up to the vote to change the pedagogical structure in the school. They were the five identifiable occasions on which an initiative was taken during the time period covered by this report:

(1) A proposal to vote on the priority of pedagogical goals (October 8).
(2) The school board decision to cancel class meetings for three months (October 11).
(3) The meeting of a group of parents and teachers to reach private agreement (October 21).
(4) The development of a new implementation plan (October 29).
(5) The imposition of a deadline under threat of resignation (October 29).

8.3.0 *A Vote on Goals*

At the end of the first meeting in the assembly (October 8) a vote on the priority of different educational goals was proposed. The idea was to assert whether intellectual, social, or creative goals should be given precedence. The proposal was made in a situation which was characterized by confusion. The preliminary paper contained two different topics, one concerning the goals and the other the pedagogical structure. While nobody objected to a change of the structure, one group of parents felt that the goals had to be considered and probably changed prior to any change in the structure. Thus, not only was there no concensus about what to do; no concensus existed about what to discuss, either.[4]

The immediate occasion for the priority proposal was a challenge from the teachers. Following rather sharp attacks by some parents, the teachers answered by claiming that parents made inconsistent demands on them. While the low priority for the intellectual training was never doubted at assembly meetings, teachers reported receiving many complaints at class meetings and privately from parents on their children's inadequate performance on intellectual subjects. An unidentified group of "reactionary parents" was accused by the teachers of having forced a departure from the school's ideals.

The priority proposal was more or less a codification of existing ideology. One of the original reasons for the foundation of the school was to escape the (in the founders' view) over-emphasis on intellectual training in the public schools. To give this a lower priority than social and creative training was not something new. An acceptance of it would probably reinforce some basic beliefs and attitudes of the parents.

Almost no effort was made to argue in favor of the content of the proposal. The discussion was entirely about whether or not to vote on it at all. The prime argument for taking a vote was that this was a way of ensuring that equality was maintained. A recent issue in the assembly had been that very few people participated in the debates. This was perceived as contradictory to the democratic ideals of the school. Voting had become a recognized way of ameliorating the situation and inhibiting the development of inequality in power.

The proposal was more or less a codification of an already accepted ideology; popular reasons were given for taking the vote; the proposer was an important leader in the school; and the proposal was supported not only by most teachers but also by the most high-status parents. Nevertheless, there was opposition to taking a vote. Indeed, the assembly ultimately refused to vote on the priority proposal.

The only expressed reason for the opposition was that the three goals were so much inter-connected that it made no sense to make priorities among them. The argument, of course, has merit in principle; but it is not the kind of argument that normally was persuasive in the group. What appears to be true is that this proposal had a context. It was seen in connection with another proposal which was made (but never came to a vote either). It had for some time been believed that a group of parents wanted a division of the school. In their view, the school had grown too big. Consequently, since no members could be excluded, they had adopted a strategy of attrition. The idea was that the assembly should be induced to make radical enough decisions so that the school would become unacceptable to the more conservative parents. For example, one of the members of this group proposed that instead of making a ranking of the goals, all intellectual training should be abandoned for a period of three months. At least some participants saw the priority-proposal as connected to the desire for a division of the school. Such an interpretation was facilitated by the attack on the "reactionary parents" by the teachers.

In this context, the assembly refused to vote to establish a goal priority. The management attempt, which could have led to a less complex definition of the choice by excluding some ideological concerns, failed to succeed apparently because of circumstances which had less to do with the proposal itself than the context in which it was made and the supporters it attracted.[5]

8.3.1 *The Cancellation of Class Meetings*

Three days after the refusal of the assembly to vote on priorities the school board met. At this meeting, two things were decided: First, the members of the board agreed to draft a proposal for a new pedagogical structure, and to seek its approval in the assembly as soon as possible. Second, the board agreed to cancel all class meetings for a period of three months. The cancellation was an implicit bargain. Although the "terms of trade" were never clearly specified, we think that the cancellation of the class meetings was an attempt by the board to make an exchange with teachers.

While the number of teaching hours in the school was fixed through legislation, the number of hours the teachers were expected to use on meetings with the parents (both at class meetings and assembly meetings) was determined internally and informally. Normally, four or five class meetings were held during a year for each grade. During this period, where many assembly meetings were held and where the teachers met frequently to work on their own collaboration problems, teachers felt a heavy overload. Cancellation of class meetings was viewed as a relief.

Just what the board expected to receive in return was never made explicit. One possibility, however, is the removal of an "extraneous" concern. Since parental cross-pressure on teachers was most conspicuous in class meetings, the cancellation made the pressure less obvious. Teachers would be less likely to keep that garbage in the can at the next meeting. Since the issue of cross-pressures had diverted attention from the pedagogical structure, the implicit side bargain was to permit it focus on pedagogy in return for avoiding further parent-teacher confrontation in class meetings. The cross-pressure issue was in fact not mentioned again in the assembly. If our interpretation is correct, the teachers kept their part of the bargain.[6]

By making the decision to cancel class meetings without consulting the assembly, the board violated some widely-shared norms in the school. The decision was never made public as an explicit decision. Instead the board suggested to the teachers that no class meetings should be held for three months.[7] Since teachers were responsible for calling meetings, they simply were not scheduled. No protest was recorded from the parents. Apparently, they did not know about the decision.[8] The lack of class meetings elicited no comment. The high activity level in the assembly, in combination with the background of irregularity in timing of class meetings, obscured the management-attempt.

The trade was successful.[9] A move that in spirit (implicit bribe) and in style (secret) violated the norms of the group appears nevertheless to have modified the flow of problems into the choice situation.

8.3.2 The Extra-Parliamentary Meeting

On October 21 the originator of the discussion in the assembly (the architect) gathered all teachers and a few parents to an informal meeting in his home. This meeting was called after the first, rather chaotic, meeting in the assembly. In the assembly the teachers had shown little interest in discussing the pedagogical structure. In fact, they had agreed privately to neglect this discussion and to concentrate on their own problems of internal collaboration. Their reluctance to participate was a source of concern. It was widely believed that the teachers' commitment to the decision was of great importance. They were acknowledged publicly as the experts and several times were urged to state their opinions and preferences.[10] They resisted.

We view this extra-parliamentary meeting as an attempt to change the arena in which the actual decision was to be made. Only a few parents (mainly rather high-status members and mainly third grade parents with a supposedly relatively homogeneous view of the situation) were invited. As a result, the possibility of reaching a conclusion among the parents was much higher in this group than in the assembly. The pressure these parents, in turn, could put on the teachers for changes was consequently much stronger. If the extra-parliamentary meeting had reached some kind of an agreement, the discussion in the assembly would probably have been different. A proposal supported by the teachers and the high-status parents would be very likely to be adopted.

In order to persuade the teachers to participate in the meeting, the crisis-nature of the situation was stressed. Something had to be done soon, and the teachers had to do it. The unusual situation justified the unusual procedure. This seemed to be the reasoning of the architect, who justified his action in terms of "honest concerns about the future of the school". Although the teachers to a certain extent agreed, they nevertheless defeated the effort by arguing emphatically that the meeting violated basic democratic principles in the school, symbolized by the assembly. It was asserted that such concerns should be dealt with in an assembly meeting and not in informal groups. The appeal to legitimacy made it impossible for the group to operate. The arena of the choice was still the assembly where the teachers still refused to participate.[11]

In order to understand this outcome, we have to consider what was happening in the board of teachers. The immediate problem the teachers faced was a conflict between the third grade teacher on the one side and the rest of the teachers on the other. What started out as a collaboration-problem between two teachers in the third grade, increased during the autumn to a crisis. Several of the teachers were looking for jobs at other schools. Feelings were high. The teacher in the third grade was isolated. In fact, during this period all the other teachers were working to get rid of her.

In an organization where symbols like "reason", "solidarity", and "tolerance" were highly valued, this was not an easy task. The conflict seemed to be based more on personal antipathy than on pedagogical inconsistency. Since they could not expect to get any help from the parents with this problem, they refused to inform anybody about it. They needed time to work out this problem (i.e., to find good reasons) without involvement of the parents.[12]

Teacher participation could come only at the cost of other things. They were not generally opposed to a change of the pedagogical structure; but the work in the board of teachers was so much more vital for them, that no attention could be paid to the decision process in the assembly. That the reason for the teachers' resistance was one of timing rather than lack of concern is suggested by the fact that as soon as the third grade teacher was fired, the teachers immediately started working on a new pedagogical structure.

The attempt to change the arena for the choice failed. The conflict between the teachers distracted them and left little time for participation in the political maneuvering and post-decision implementation that the extra-parliamentary meeting would have required. In their resistance, they appealed to major symbolic themes of the school. As a result, an illegitimate effort at management was unsuccessful.

168

8.3.3 *The Implementation Plan*

At the November 5th meeting in the assembly, the school board presented its plan for implementation of the proposed pedagogical structure. Part of the plan called for the formation of seven small groups of parents and teachers. Since the proposal was a framework only, quite a few questions remained to be settled. The official task of these groups was to work out the details.

In fact, the groups appeared to be designed to provide seven new, specialized-access garbage cans. Almost all of the concerns expressed during the process were referred to the small groups for discussion. The action was a log-roll. If the school board proposal were accepted, the resistant parents would have their concerns considered in more attractive arenas. For two reasons, these new arenas were more attractive than the assembly:

(a) The groups had restricted access and decision structures. The different groups had names that identified specific questions they were to consider. Participation was specialized. No one could participate in more than one group. Individuals were likely to get a favorable result in the areas they most cared about, at the risk of loosing out in less important areas.

(b) The number of participants in each group was small. One of the acknowledged disadvantages in the assembly was that many individuals felt uneasy about addressing such a large audience, particularly when there was conflict. Consequently, a large "silent majority" was believed to exist. For them the new arenas must have seemed more attractive.

The design of these alternative arenas was a part of the decision on the pedagogical structure. It preserved the illusion of assembly policy making, but would have made the actual decisions highly decentralized. In the former sense it supported the ideology; in the latter it was not consistent with the general belief in the doctrine of collective discussion and decision.

8.3.4 *Imposing a Deadline on the Choice*

By a vote on October 29, a deadline of one week was imposed on the decision. The action was demanded by the school board members as the price of avoiding their collective resignation. Even then it was approved by only a very small margin. The management technique was the overt threat of withdrawal.

The threat by the school board and the time limit were neither very popular nor perceived as legitimate. A good deal of protest was raised. It was, however, futile. The realities favored the board. Election to the school board was not very attractive (as suggested by the difficulties in finding candidates for the seats). The work was timeconsuming. The present members did the job well. The threat was effective despite its illegitimacy.

The imposition of a deadline enforced by the threat of resignation and in conjunction with a log-roll, produced the final decision almost without resistance. Only one participant protested strongly against the procedure used by the school board at the November 5 meeting when the decision was made formally.

8.4 Discussion

We have described decision making in a standard garbage can situation. Various symbolic and substantive problems were exercised. Participants wandered in and out. The definition of what was being decided changed over time. The process was guided by the often casual temporal connections among problems, solutions, participants, and choice opportunities.

In the midst of this, there were efforts to direct the process. Individuals and groups, particularly the leaders of the school, tried to control the process by various moves. These attempts varied significantly in terms of their consistency with widely-shared norms of legitimate decision behavior.

We have examined five such efforts (Table 8.1) and have tried to indicate for each attempt how it related to the ideology of the school and whether it was successful.

Table 8.1. Five attempts at management in an ideological organization

Attempt	Management method	Ideological legitimacy*	Outcome
(1) Vote on goals	Priority setting	High	Failure
(2) Class meeting cancellation	Private trade	Low	Success
(3) Extra-parliamentary meeting	Caucus	Low	Failure
(4) Implementation plan	Log-roll	Intermediate	Success
(5) Deadline	Threat	Low	Success

* As assessed by the writer on the basis of comments made by participants and consistency with the explicit ideology of the organization.

The data are thin enough and subjective enough to make any interpretation problematic. Nevertheless, it is hard to see in this sequence of management attempts any sign that the likelihood of success of the attempts is positively related to their ideological purity. The ideology was real. The complaints about violations were intense.

The commitment to the ideas was important. But the flow of events in the process dominated the rationality and ideology of the stages. The efforts at intentional management and the debates over their legitimacy were educational. They provided a serious training in the values of the group. But the connections between legitimacy and effectiveness were tenuous and confused by the ways in which the process confounded attempts to understand outcomes as intended.

Our observations, moreover, seem to suggest that the time perspective is important. Individual phases of a decision-process might be described as fairly intentional in the short term; but the process taken as a whole is better described in terms of a garbage can model. Within the time frame of our study, the broader the time perspective, the better does the garbage can description fit.[13] Indeed, our story has no end. Class meetings were resumed after less than two months, and the decision to change the pedagogical structure was never implemented. In order to suggest the continuing garbage can nature of the process, we include the following epilogue.

8.5 Epilogue

Although management seemed to move the choice opportunity to a decision, the process did not end. Fourteen days after the decision, and prior to the formation of the seven small groups, the teachers informed the school board that they had excluded the third grade teacher. This offended the board severely, first of all because they had been left totally unaware of the severity of the problem; secondly because the board, not the teachers, had the authority to take such a step; and thirdly because they disagreed with the exclusion.

A new crisis was defined, which (along with the Christmas holidays) diverted all attention from the pedagogical structure for several months. Urged by the school board, the assembly finally decided to invite the excluded teacher back to the school, although she already had a new job and was not expected to (and did not) accept the invitation.

Since the third grade was left without any teacher, the teachers merged the third and fourth grade. Later on fifth grade was added. The pedagogical structure was changed, but not in accordance with the assembly decision. The seven small groups were never formed. Thus, in the end, none of the efforts at management produced outcomes as apparently intended.

Once diverted, attention never turned to the implementation of the great November decision. Through the merging of the third grade with the fourth and fifth grade, the problems for the third grade parents, who played such an important role in the case, were solved. A new big issue arose, namely the construction of a new school. The architect, who initiated the structure-discussion was also the chairman of a committee, the task of which was to provide more space for the school. The architect, projected a building which consisted of only one big room, not very suitable for a workshop structure. This project was discussed and accepted in the assembly with no mention of the pedagogical structure mandated in November.

Problems, solutions, participants, and choice opportunities continue to flow. Interpretations and discussions continue to illuminate the belief structure. And the connections between the two continue to be loose.

NOTES:

1 Many of these discussions take as their point of departure Weber's distinction between power (Macht) and authority (Herrschaft). In the latter obedience depend upon the belief of the subordinate that the orders given are legitimate — that they are justified and that it is correct to obey. Weber make the distinction between charismatic, traditional, and legal-rational forms of authority, and thus links different organization structures. (Weber, 1964, pp. 324–391).

2 Notice the anomaly: Leaders are expected to be more conforming than others with respect to many norms; but successful leaders earn "idiosyncracy credit" (Hollander, 1958).

3 This statement is based, in part, on reasons for perceiving participants as powerful, given in our questionnaire.

4 These were only two of the major concerns aired at the meeting. "The nature of parental government" and "the working conditions for the teachers" were two other examples.

5 To underline the very unusual situation, we can add that this was the only time during our observation period that the powerful parents were on the loosing side in a vote.

6 The teachers had, in the meantime, privately agreed that since they controlled the implementation of a decision, they would rather delay the implementation than involve themselves in open conflict with the parents at the assembly.

7 In fact, the decision remained valid for only one and a half months, because of the situation created by the teachers' exclusion of one of their colleagues.

8 Another explanation could be that they did know but did not care too much. However, the fact that class meetings normally attracted many more parents than did assembly meetings, makes this explanation less likely.

9 Although the cross-pressure issue never was raised again, all ideological concerns were not eliminated. In this respect, the attempt was less successful.

10 This was in some sense contradictory to the basic concept of a parent-governed school, which also was used by the teachers as an excuse for being quiet.

11 This discussion might leave a picture of the teachers as guardians of the ideology. We have several reasons to believe that they made a virtue of necessity. First, they indicated in interviews that the concept of parent-government was almost empty. Second, the discussion in the board of

teachers gave the impression that they consciously avoided any action which could tax some of *their scarce energy*. And third, this form for informal consultation was not as unusual as the teachers made it. If the group had fulfilled its task, the problems in relation to the assembly could have been solved through a limitation of the information about the procedure. Actions were in fact taken in order to keep the meeting secret. Although a report existed, nothing was ever published, and for the first time during the observation period, we were not invited.

12 This tactic was based on correct estimates of parental attitudes. When the teachers finally informed the school board that they refused to collaborate further with the third grade teacher, the reaction was very negative toward the teachers. (See epilogue.)

13 The time frame of this study is short relative to studies that might cover several years (or longer). We have no reason to suppose that the garbage can model will necessarily improve without limit as time perspective lengthens. It is quite possible that longer run perspectives could lead to useful descriptions that are neither intentional nor garbage cans.

9. Decisions, Presidents, and Status [1]

MICHAEL D. COHEN
University of Michigan

JAMES G. MARCH
Stanford University

9.0 Introduction

Elsewhere (Cohen, March, and Olsen, 1972) we have examined in some detail the character of a garbage can decision process. That general perspective is basic to many of the studies reported in this book. Essentially, we have argued that any decision process can be viewed as a channeled confluence of four streams: problems, choice opportunities, solutions, and participants. The garbage can model calls attention to six main attributes of a decision system affecting decisions:

(1) The load on the system. As the load increases, so also does the number of decisions that are made by flight or oversight.
(2) The timing of problems, choices, solutions, and participation. Which problems and solutions are attended to in the context of which choices depends on when they appear and who is available to participate.
(3) The distribution of time. Those problems, solutions, and attitudes that are persistently present are attended to more consistently than are those that are sporadic.
(4) Structural channels limiting the flows. Rules limiting the flow of problems to choices (the access structure) or the flow of participants to choices (the decision structure) change the process and the outcomes.
(5) The garbage can context. The movement of problems to particular choices affects not only the choices to which they move but also the choices they leave alone. Decisions are made by "flight" and "oversights".
(6) The pleasures of the process. Problems and solutions are debated (at least in part) for the positive rewards associated with the debate rather than for the decision outcomes.

Taken collectively, these attributes of decision making in organizations suggest a heavily time-dependent decision process. The process

174

is one in which major changes can occur for what seem to be rather fortuitous reasons of timing; it is a process in which much of the behavior seems to be directed toward exercising problems in the context of choices rather than solving them; but it is also a process in which many outcomes are dominated by stable structural and time distribution factors. The three properties appear to be inconsistent insofar as they suggest a simultaneous consequence of unpredictability and stability. They are, in fact, interrelated and joint consequences of the system.

Some of the discussions in this book focus particularly on the impact of time sequencing on events; others focus on the overt process of argumentation that characterizes garbage can situations; others examine the sources of stability in garbage can processes. The present chapter continues the later treatment. We attempt to identify the stable underlying logic of some major classes of decisions within American higher education. Against the background of that explication of the sources of stability in decisions and the role of presidential leadership in them, we examine the question of executive power in organized anarchies and the status certification consequences of formal decision procedures.

9.1 The Logic of Choice in American Colleges

American colleges and universities are organizations with unclear goals and technologies and fluid participation. Opportunities for choice in higher education can easily become complex "garbage cans" into which a striking variety of problems, solutions, and participants may be dumped. Debate over the hiring of a footbal coach can become connected to concerns about the essence of a liberal education, the relations of the school to ethnic minorities, or the philosophy of talent. At the same time, there are conspicuous sources of decision stability within the college structure. Some people consistently spend more time than others. Some problems are always there. There are important structural and normative constraints on the access and decision structures. The culture is one that rewards the performances of participation. Relatively light loads on the system produce relatively frequent decisions by "flight" or "oversight". In order to understand university decision making adequately we need to supplement an awareness of the opportunities for time-dependent complexity with a look at the occasions and ways in which choices are driven in a relatively consistent, relatively stable way. We require a look at what we will call the logic of decision in universities.

Any such examination is, of course, subject to gross overgeneralization. It is quite unlikely that New York University or the University of Illinois will operate in the same way as Ripon College or California Lutheran College. Size and wealth make substantial differences. Such an examination is also subject to simple error. The search for the "real" decision logic is a difficult and often dubious activity, typically contaminated with ideological mythology. Without denying these problems, we want to try to describe our impressions of the ways in which decision outcomes are produced in some key areas of university internal governance, and particularly our impressions of the role of major administrators in them.

The analysis is essentially an interpretation of data available to us from the literature and a series of interviews with presidents, chief academic officers (i.e., academic vice-presidents, deans of the college, etc.), chief business and financial officers (i.e., business and financial vice-presidents, treasurers, business managers), and assistants to the president. These interviews were made in a 42-school sample and included 41 presidents, 39 chief academic officers, 36 chief business and financial officers, and 28 assistants to the president.[2]

We consider four domains of decision that are important within a modern American college:

1. *The operating budget.* The distribution of financial resources among the departments.
2. *Educational policy decisions.* The establishment of curricula and academic organization.
3. *Academic tenure decisions.* The granting of indefinite tenure to individual academic personnel.
4. *Planning.* The development of long-run plans for capital expenditures, academic development, and institutional growth.

We asked presidents to nominate another president whom they viewed as successful, and we then asked for the criteria on which the nomination was based. The results in Table 9.0 indicate that presidents consider fiscal matters, educational policy, and the quality of academic personnel to be important aspects of their success (along with growth, quiet on campus, and the respect of their constituencies). Planning is traditionally an important function of executive leadership. These four domains do not include all of the decisions made within the university or college that might concern a president or other active participants. Indeed, some presidents probably devote at least as much time to landscaping and parking. But the four domains are easily recognized by students of colleges as some of the more important activities of educational governance. They form the justification for a· significant number of meetings, a substantial amount of paper, and a perceptible level of political and bureaucratic energy.

176

Table 9.0. Evidence of success cited by 35 choosing presidents**

Criteria	Total mentions	% of 83 mentions	% of 35 respondents who mentioned each criterion	Estimated % of total mentions among all presidents
Fiscal	6	7.2	17.1	6.6
Educational program	8	9.6	22.8	10.0
Growth	9	10.8	25.7	13.7
Quiet	11	13.2	31.5	10.3
Quality of faculty	8	9.6	22.8	11.6
Quality of students	2	2.4	5.7	3.1
Respect of faculty	8	9.6	25.7	8.7
Respect of students	6	7.2	17.1	4.9
Respect of community	7	8.4	20.0	7.9
Other	18	21.7	–	23.2
Totals	83	99.7	*	100.0

*Does not total 100 because respondents could mention more than one. "Other" percentage was not calculated as it could be mentioned more than once by a single respondent.

**This estimate is made by applying weights which correct for the bias introduced into the sample by stratification.

We asked our respondents to describe briefly the processes involved in making operating budgets, academic policy, and academic personnel decisions. We asked them to characterize the long-run plan in the college, what it covered, and how it was developed. We asked them to focus particularly on the role of the president in these activities. The summary descriptions that follow are based primarily on the responses we received.[3]

9.1.0 *The Operating Budget*

The operating budget in American colleges and universities can be described in terms of three fundamental accounting flows.

I. The *enrollment cycle* flow. The rate and pattern of enrollment in the college and in the departments depend on the educational program in the school, its reputation, its competitors, and the level of demand for education relative to the supply. Resources come to the university because of the student enrollment. In private universities, the main flow is normally through direct tuition charges to the students and their families. Secondary flows from families (donations) and sometimes legislatures (subsidies) depend largely on maintaining or increasing student enrollment. In public colleges and universities, the main flow is from legislatures reacting to the number of students enrolled, with secondary flows from tuition and federal subsidies. Resources coming to the university from the student enrollment flow are then distributed by the university to the departments in the operating budget.

II. The *institutional reputation* flow. Presidents and others seek support for the institution from outside agencies. They claim certain properties for the institution (e.g., age, prestige, innovativeness, poverty, uniqueness) as justification for support; or they offer to provide such properties if given the support. Resources come to the school as a function of the cogency of its appeal and the availability of outside resources. The outside agencies include foundations, legislatures, and major donors. Through endowment, current administrations reap the benefits of past reputations. These resources are then distributed to the departments in the operating budget.

III. The *research reputation* flow. Departments, laboratories, institutes, and individual research workers solicit funds from research support institutions. These are primarily institutions of the federal government (e.g., National Institutes of Health, National Science Foundation, National Aeronautics and Space Administration, the several cabinet-level departments). To a lesser extent they are private foundations (e.g., Ford Foundation, Carnegie Corporation, Sloan Foundation, Rockefeller Foundation). The size of the flow depends on the availability of resources within the particular domain of the department and on the nationally recognized research strength of the department or individual research worker. The resources come directly to the research group, with a fraction flowing to the university generally as overhead.

These three major flows are shown in Figure 9.0. We have emphasized them as accounting flows because we think the administrator's role in operating budget decision making is strongly conditioned by the mundane relationship between income and expenditure. (See Simon, 1967.) That fact has been somewhat obscured by the traditions of governmental budgeting with respect to public institutions of higher education. Within those traditions it sometimes appears that income is an "act of God" – or at least of legislatures. But the administrators with whom we talked were quite aware that legislators were de facto parents and that perhaps 90 percent of the public operating budget is determined by the student enrollment and by some standard formulas, that is to say, by implicit tuition charges.

The dynamics of the flows are such as substantially to restrict

178

Figure 9.0. Major accounting flows determning operating budgets in American colleges and universities

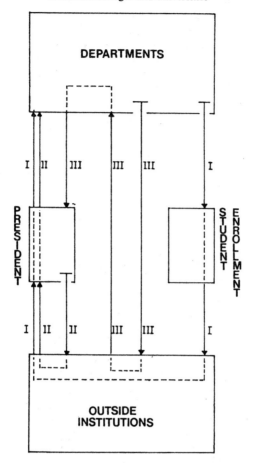

presidential influence over the main thrust of the operating budget. Consider first the *enrollment cycle.* We observed two major styles of dealing with income received from student enrollment: (1) Direct payment of the tuition or some major fraction of it to the department or school involved. (2) Payment to the college and then reallocation on some basis to the departments. Since the departments control enrollments (through the classic departmental control over academic "pricing" – curriculum requirements, grading, and teaching formats), it is hard to see how there can be any really significant differences between the two alternatives in the longrun. Control over departmental enrollments gives the departments enormous leverage in the internal bargaining.

179

The bargaining leverage is attenuated, however, under certain conditions. For example, if the demand for education within the college is strong, and if the amount of teaching delivered per unit of resources is fixed, the flow of resources can be used to influence the flow of enrollment. *If* an academic administrator can increase the number of faculty in a department, and *if* that increase does not change the average teaching productivity in the department, he can produce a redistribution of enrollment within the college without changing the overall enrollment. The internal reallocation of resources modifies the implicit prices (e.g., the teacher/student ratio or degree requirements) charged by the various departments in the direction of lowering the prices in the favored departments. If a strong demand for educating in the college assures that "outside" competition will not be able to take advantage of the new internal prices, some students will shift from one department to another. Thus, the enrollment flow is brought into equilibrium at a new position determined by the arbitrary reallocation of resources.

The restrictions are rather severe, however. On the one hand, most colleges cannot presume the unconditional student enthusiasm that makes external competition with respect to programs largely irrelevant. On the other hand, among those colleges with strong student demand, only a handful can assume that an increase in resources for a given department will lead that department to increase its attractiveness to students (rather than the obvious alternative of increasing its attractiveness to faculty by reducing teaching load).

A second attenuation of the bargaining leverage of departments on enrollment occurs in choices between departments that are largely interchangeable from the point of view of student demand. One might suspect that the total student demand for courses in sociology and social psychology is more stable than the demand for either one of them, that the total student demand for courses in English and comparative literature is more stable than the demand for either one of them. Waves of students shift fairly easily from one to another as the number of courses offered, the size of classes, and the popularity of teachers change. As a result, it is easier to use a short-run arbitrary flow of resources to increase English enrollment at the expense of comparative literature (and thus to make a stable shift in relative emphasis) than it is to induce a stable shift from physics to English. In this respect, an organization with a large number of departments works in favor of administrative influence.

A third attenuation of departmental leverage is the frequent inability of academic departments to act strategically – particularly during periods of relatively strong outside demand for faculty. In order to use the enrollment cycle as a bargaining device the department must be

180

prepared to endure some short-run dislocations. It must be prepared to increase enrollment systematically to produce future resources, a procedure which requires coordination within the department and a willingness to incur current costs in anticipation of future benefits. Heavy turnover in faculty, or rules of faculty equality, make such a strategy difficult to adopt since the benefits are unlikely to be realized by the faculty bearing the costs.

In general, the student enrollment flow provides an administrator with little flexibility. He must, for the most part, ratify the market and approve the allocation of resources in the way dictated by enrollment. He may make marginal variations in that pattern. He may occasionally help to get a new department started. He may, under some conditions, be able to intervene in such a way as to affect demand, for example, by encouraging reduction of requirements so that (under "free trade") a new distribution of enrollment might emerge. He may be able to exploit the difficulties departments have in looking more than one year ahead. With some understanding of the system, in fact he can probably do more than most academic administrators do. But he acts within a rather tight set of constraints.

The *institutional reputation* flow is in direct contrast with the enrollment cycle. First, it is minor for most institutions. Second, it is the flow most subject to top administrator influence. Third, it has a much less dynamic character.

Operating budget resources from the institutional reputation flow (along with their close cousin, the endowment) are minor factors in the budget of most American colleges and universities. However, even at schools at which such resources are quite minor, presidents tend to view them as very important. They are the resources that give the president the greatest sense of control over expenditure. Along with endowment income, they tend to be "his" resources.[4] As the obvious spokesman for the whole institution, the president receives them. Although they are frequently received with commitments on their use, some fraction of them are "free", and some fraction of the committed resources go into already budgeted activities and thereby free other funds.

The relative stability of the institutional reputation flow stems from a long lag in the process. The pattern of expenditures undoubtedly affects the magnitude of the flow, but rarely within the tenure of one president. Changes in the institutional reputation of a college and university attributable to one president normally affect the flow of resources to a subsequent one. In the normal tenure of a president, the major opportunity for increasing the flow is through merchandising the college, through persuading outside institutions that the college is better than is currently believed or that it might become better.

Presidents do that and some have their successes; but it is hard to look at the statistics on endowment over time without concluding that the institutional reputations of American colleges and universities change a good deal more slowly than do their presidents.

Internally, of course, the smallness of the short-run effects of presidential action on presidential resources through the institutional reputation flow increases presidential independence. Within rather wide boundaries the institutional reputation operating funds can be distributed arbitrarily whitout affecting the flow of those funds in the succeeding few years. Such a result stems, in large part, from the basic ambiguity within a college of objectives and technology, which can make almost any course of action plausible.

This does not mean that presidents can be capricious. There are other influences on their behavior, and more claims on the money than there is money. In fact, with ambiguous criteria and slow feedback, we might reasonably predict that presidents and other administrators would turn heavily to *social* validation of their resource allocation decisions. A pattern of expenditures becomes legitimate because a large group of people believe it is legitimate. Despite the fact that the intrinsic constraints are weak – indeed because of that fact – presidential behavior is remarkably uniform.

The *research reputation* flow has been the subject of considerable investigation and grief over the past few years. Like the institutional reputation flow, the research reputation flow is a small one for most colleges. Where it does exist, the administrator is characteristically a minor figure. He does not initiate proposals. He rarely intervenes in them, indeed, rarely sees them. College presidents with whom we talked did not view themselves as having any significant year-to-year control over that part of the operating budget. Some wished they might have such control but did not view it as a serious possibility except through the "bloc grant" proposal that were gaining some popularity in granting agencies and Congress prior to 1969. The enthusiasm of presidents for institutional grant funding is well documented in the recommendations of such bodies as the Association of Land Grant Colleges, which are technically associations of colleges but actually associations of college presidents.

Not only is the flow outside the control of the president, it is also a leverage on funds under his control. Outstanding faculty at major institutions control substantial resources directly through research grants; they can and do use that control and the threat of departure (with consequent loss of funds and reputation) as a device for influencing the allocation of other resources. In recent years at major universities the teaching load in physics has very rarely been as great as the teaching load in French.

182

This research reputation flow is of critical importance to the president of any large, well-known American university. It represents a substantial part of his annual operating budget. It is a basis for attracting and retaining high-quality faculty. It is a primary sign of success as a president. In many terms that the president recognizes as valid, major research grant recipients have higher status than do presidents within the academic community.

The annual operating budget is largely determined by these three flows. But the impact is not the same in all colleges. In fact, we think we can characterize most American colleges and universities rather simply in terms of the extent to which their operating budget depends on the three flows. We will identify four basic budgeting types.

Type A is the university for which the enrollment cycle is relatively unimportant. For most purposes these universities draw upon the institutional reputation and research reputation flows in order to develop their budgets. Income from students is significant, but the colleges are largely shielded from the consequences of enrollment demand by the strong general demand for attendance. Basically, these are the prestigious private universities of the United States, representing about 1 percent of the four year colleges and universities in the country. In terms of numbers this is clearly an insignificant group. In terms of reputation it includes the giants of American private education.

Type B is the university which relies heavily on both the enrollment flow and the research reputation flow with little (or substantially less) coming from the institutional reputation. These are the major public universities and some private universities in the United States. They represent a major locus of growth in American higher education in the period from 1950 to 1965.

Type C is the college for which research reputation is relatively unimportant. These are the prestigious, small colleges in the United States. Their budgets rely heavily on income from the enrollment cycle and on institutional support and endowment. In terms of numbers of schools and numbers of students, this type is not very common, but it includes the best-known private, liberal-arts colleges in the country.

Type D is the college or university for which the enrollment cycle accounts for virtually all the income and operating budget allocations. This is the mean, mode, and median of American higher education. It includes most of the schools and most of the students. In these schools the enrollment market dominates budgeting. Sometimes, for some of them, the demand for education has served to blunt the obviousness of the "customer"; but for most of them most of the time, the budgeting problem is one of finding a set of allocations that produces an

183

educational program that attracts enough enrollment to provide the allocations.

Table 9.1 shows our estimates of where these types of schools are found in a sixfold division of colleges and universities by size and wealth. What this and our earlier remarks may suggest is the awkwardness of talking about governance at all. Insofar as large parts of the

Table 9.1. Types of mixes of accounting flows in operating
budgets, by type of schools

Type of school	Relatively rich	Relatively poor
Large	Type A	Type B
	Type B	Type D
Medium	Type A	Type D
	Type B	
	Type C	
	Type D	
Small	Type C	Type D
	Type D	

budget, for example, research budgetary items, are not so much decisions as collections of independent agreements assembled for the convenience of the accountants into a common document, we need to reconsider the meaning of decision in a university context. Insofar as other large parts of the budget are embedded in the long-run complications of the enrollment cycle, we need to describe a process that is heavily constrained by "market" factors.

We are also left with some possible interpretations of the problems of budgetary control confronting American college presidents. In particular, we should note:

1. Strong research reputation in the faculty makes weak budget presidents. On the whole, that means that most of the better known academic institutions will have "weaker" presidents than the less known institutions, and presidents who transfer "up" into such schools will find themselves "weaker" than they were before.

2. Prestige in the institution makes weak students. Where the demand for entrance is strong, the policy-making force of the enrollment cycle is blunted.[5]

3. Public universities make weak budget presidents. The president of a public university must simultaneously negotiate the appropriations for his operating budget from the legislature or some intervening body and negotiate the allocation of that budget among his departments. The simultaneity and public character of those two negotiations restrict him seriously.

184

In general, the operating budget of an American university is heavily constrained by accounting procedures, particularly the very elementary requirements of the enrollment cycle. As a result, there are many things that an administrator cannot do. The administrators with whom we talked were aware of this, particularly within Type D schools. At the same time, administrators seemed to be somewhat less aware of, or somewhat less interested in, the flexibility the system did offer them. So long as the constraints are met, there is the potential for rather substantial discretionary action. For example, we suspect that many presidents fail or are not willing to distinguish sharply shifts in the operating budget that will disturb the *total* enrollment from shifts that will disturb only the internal allocation of that total enrollment. The former are problems; the latter are opportunities.

9.1.1 *Academic Policy Decisions*

By training, background, and basic commitment, college presidents are academic in orientation. Studies by Ferrari (1971) and Bolman (1965) indicate that over 80 percent of all presidents have been faculty members. It is natural, therefore, that presidents should have a special concern with academic policy decisions. Most presidents take pride in the academic program of their school and see themselves as performing an important supportive role with respect to that program. They accept credit for new programs and recent changes which they have initiated or supported.

For the most part, however, and particularly in the larger schools, college presidents do not appear to have much to say about academic policy. Indeed, the term policy is probably somewhat misleading if it conveys a notion of systematic collective decision-making. The set of activities that are subsumed under the general term academic policy are the organization of academic departments, the organization of the educational program, degree requirements and alternatives, courses and course assignments, patterns of student education. To describe these as resulting from anything approximating high-level decision based on policy would be wrong. Presidents and their chief academic subordinates concede that much of the structure of academic policy is determined in the individual departments – realistically, often in the individual classroom.

Formally, academic policy is almost always portrayed as the responsibility of the faculty. By the standard academic constitution, the faculty is granted control over degrees and educational programs. The traditions of faculty control are embedded deeply in the culture of academe. Except in some minor ways, college administrators show little desire to question that tradition. They accept the mythology of

185

"the faculty" even when the size and diversity of the institution clearly makes talking about "the faculty" no more sensible than talking about "the students".

At the same time, the presidents recognize that even in a small, liberal arts college the collective decisions of the faculty rarely do more than condition slightly and ratify the actions of the departments and individual teachers. Academic "policy" is the accretion of hundreds of largely autonomous actions taken for different reasons, at different times, under different conditions, by different people in the college. This collection of actions is periodically codified into what is presented as an educational program by the college catalog or a student or faculty handbook.

Consider as a first example of academic policy the academic expectations of faculty and students. What are legitimate programs? What is a legitimate workload? What are legitimate quality and quantity expectations?

These simple working conditions of education are viewed as being primarily the concern of faculty and students. Their importance to parents, or to employers or governmental licensing agencies (particularly in the case of professional education) is, for the most part, secondary. As a result, most colleges leave the conditions of education to informal bilateral negotiations between students and faculty. These negotiations take place daily in the classroom, each term in the enrollment and grade lists, and continuously in student-faculty interaction. The results of the negotiation may be formally ratified by the appropriate faculty body, but they often exist simply as a shared understanding within the community. Teachers who enjoy teaching and students who enjoy being taught form enclaves. Teachers who do not enjoy teaching and students who do not enjoy being taught form other enclaves.

The latter coalition is a frequent one. Suppose that a group of faculty views teaching as a job. That is, as something one does in order to be able to do something else (e.g., play golf, sit in the sun, do research). And suppose a group of students views studying as a job; that is, as something one does in order to be able to do something else (e.g., earn a living, sit in the sun, do research). Under such conditions one would expect the bilaterally negotiated educational program to include:

(a) A joint agreement to assert that both teachers and students are working very hard.
(b) A joint agreement to restrict work.

Such agreements are common in American higher education, as they

186

are throughout noneducational work situations. Given the basic organizational situation, the surprise is not that work restriction is practiced, but that work is. If faculty and students had the purely and narrowly selfinterested goals of which they are sometimes accused, educational programs would consist in the minimally acceptable external facades.

Negotiated work levels are not responsive to conventional bureaucratic interventions. Presidents and others have criticized the resistance of informal agreements to change. The criticism sometimes misses the point. The outcomes of bilateral negotiation between faculty and students are little affected by policy proclamations by presidents or academic councils, although they may be ratified, somewhat inhibited, or modestly stimulated by such machinery. Significant changes appear to result (as for example at Berkeley and San Francisco State College) from widespread shifts in faculty and student attitudes. These shifts lead to direct renegotiations at the classroom and department levels that collectively modify the nature of the academic program.

For example, the bilateral bargains between faculty and students appear in recent years to have been renegotiated at some schools in the direction of reducing the traditional scholarship demands on students and faculty and increasing the political demands. Politically acceptable faculty are allowed by students to substitute new criteria and styles of scholarship for·those conventional within their disciplines. Politically acceptable students are allowed to substitute ideological development, political activity, or unusual terms of scholarship. These renegotiations of the educational program involve a small minority of students at American colleges and universities, but at a few institutions the number has apparently been large enough to result in appreciable change in the overall educational program.

Whether such changes are viewed as attractive or unattractive, they illustrate the process by which academic policy is actually affected. American college administrators have generally been unwilling or unable to participate significantly in the broad attitudinal changes that underlie such shifts. For the most part, college presidents have not felt they had either the mandate or the platform for producing shifts in the demands that students and faculty make on each other, and have been more inclined to try to make modest bureaucratic limitations on the process than to participate in it.

Consider a second example of academic policy: the structure of general educational requirements (commonly called breadth requirements) imposed on students. This set of rules, by which the claims of liberal education are satisfied, is a persistent source of minor conflict within a college or university and occasionally erupts into a major dispute. Our impression is that faculties struggle with such questions, trying to capture some idea of what a good education is. But since that question is one which few reasonable men can answer with confidence, the outcomes are dominated by three somewhat more mundane considerations:

(1) The willingness of students to be coerced into taking courses they would not choose to take independent of the requirement. Students place limits on the proportion of their total studies that can be directed in this way, on the difficulty of the courses that are required, and on the subject matter that may be included. These limits become increasingly compelling as the overall demand for education declines.

(2) The enrollment needs of various departments. As we have noted above, the enrollment cycle is a major factor in resource allocation. Normally, one cannot have a large French department without large enrollment in French. One cannot support many graduate students as teaching assistants in political science without large enrollments in introductory political science courses. One cannot justify many science laboratories without substantial enrollments in introductory laboratory science courses. An awareness of the virtue of French, political science, and chemistry as elements of a liberal education is facilitated by an awareness of the benefits of enrollments.

(3) The desire to have small classes. To have many small classes, the college or university must ordinarily have some large classes that can be taught using modest faculty resources. Two devices of educational policy are used together to accomplish this – required courses and a structure of prerequisites that force enrollments in a few introductory courses. Both are justified – appropriately – in terms of educational considerations. There are reasons why one might require that an educated man have exposure to subjects outside his major field and why one might expect a student to study elementary material before he studies advanced material. However, practical considerations of university life almost certainly amplify such beliefs, so that some prerequisites and some breadth requirements are less educationally relevant than they are argued to be.

We do not mean to suggest that these considerations are illegitimate. The point is simply that though educational policy discussions are couched in terms of the educational needs of students, they tend to be substantially influenced by the necessities of organizational life in a university. When the chairman of the department of history argues for a required course for all university students in the history of some

188

nonwestern society, he need not examine the relative importance of the education (which he believes in) and the implied growth of the history department (which he also believes in). What is good for history is good for the university.

The result is that educational policy, insofar as it is a matter for the general faculty, tends to be a fairly straightforward "log-roll" among the major faculty groups. The price of a requirement in humanities is a requirement in natural sciences. The major participants will not ordinarily see it that way, of course. Policy is negotiated without clear distinctions between nobility and necessity.

We observed little inclination among administrators to participate in this log-rolling. For the most part, they did not see their interests as being heavily involved; nor did they often have a clear program that was much differentiated from the natural outcome of the log-roll. Thus, the two most conspicuous recent trends – the overall reduction in breadth requirements and foreign language requirements – have not been affected significantly by administrative action (although through the enrollment cycle such changes have substantial effects within a college or university).

The "major" decisions of academic policy that produce administrative activity are rarely heroic. Presidents sometimes involve themselves moderately in questions of instructional calendars (e.g., quarter versus semester) or in questions of new academic departments or schools (e.g., Black Studies) or in questions of schoolwide curriculum requirements. In general, the president's role has been relatively unimportant in recent years except in a few cases where he has entered the educational policy arena with limited objectives. Typically this has been because educational policy has produced an effect on those things that a president considers immediately important – most notably quiet on the campus, the financial position of the school, and the reputation of the president among his constituents.

Although presidents are educators by experience and by identification, they are not educators by behavior. They notice the anomaly. One of the most reliable complaints of an American college president is the degree to which he is removed from educational matters. He is committed to success in his job. He does not consider academic policy achievements as a major factor in the evaluation of his success. He does not feel he has any serious leverage. He is a nostalgic realist.

9.1.2 *Academic Tenure Decisions*

Academic tenure, as it has existed for the past 30 years, is a major organizational commitment. Assuming that a faculty member ordinarily receives tenure sometime during his thirties, a tenure decision is essentially a 30 year contract. At present prices the face value of the contract, quite aside from other commitments, is somewhere from $ 400,000 to $ 1 million in salary alone. As college administrators have discovered under conditions of budget restrictions, academic salaries are both the largest part of the college budget and one of the parts least susceptible to short-run downward modification.

In addition, tenure is an important symbolic act. Actions on tenure and beliefs about those actions form a major basis for the faculty reward structure within a college. The widespread belief that tenure depends on research productivity has conditioned not only a whole generation of academic workers but also a large number of contemporary theories of academe and its ills. It has been used as an excuse and explanation for bad teaching, bad manners, and bad research.

Whether the excuses, explanations, and beliefs are correct may perhaps be questioned, but it is impossible to question their ubiquity. Moreover, the ritual of the decision process is carefully designed to maintain the beliefs. Each year thousands of department chairmen solicit tens of thousands of letters supporting the claims to tenure made by members of their staff. These letters and other supporting documents are processed through a typically complex series of assessments by faculty committees, departments, deans, executive committees, and provosts until they arrive at the president's desk. At each stage, the process is made to appear more powerful than it is in at least two senses: (1) The rate of moving to tenure is almost certainly higher than believed. (2) The "failures" are rarely real failures. They succeed later (often at a different school) and often become at least as distinguished in research as those who "succeeded" originally.

In the past quarter century college presidents have operated under conditions that have made the substance of tenure decisions relatively less important to them than the associated ritual. There are at least seven clear reasons for this:

First, most of the costs of the long-term contract in a tenure decision are borne by subsequent administrations. Although presidents concern themselves with long-term consequences for the institution – often more than others within the organization – it is natural for those costs to be somewhat less pressing than some others.

Second, with a high turnover of faculty, the contract is really not an 30 year one. This is particularly true for a school where faculty members are likely to have options for movement.

Third, with continued inflation and flexible salary schedule the contract is not as expensive a commitment as it appears nor as absolute.

Fourth, with rapid growth, tenure decisions of the past represent

190

a smaller part of the institution's total commitment than would be true under stable conditions. So long as growth is maintained, tenure commitments are balanced by expansion of the nontenured staff, and do not preclude further tenure commitments.

Fifth, in some cases the costs have seemed to be largely borne by the federal government through research grants. A senior research star is a good financial investment, not a net cost. Not only can substantial elements of his salary be funded extramurally, he brings additional funds to support others. Although this situation has directly affected only a small minority of the tenure decisions within American colleges and universities, it probably has contributed to a belief that tenure decisions are not, in fact, as costly as they appear to be.

Sixth, with a shortage of qualified faculty and an active market for faculty, there appears to be no way of maintaining a faculty without granting tenure rather liberally. The alternative, in principle, is higher salary. In many cases, the institutional structure of salary schemes make such a tradeoff difficult. Even where it does not, few presidents are likely to want to save future dollars by paying present dollars.

Seventh, the president has no basis for believing that his judgment is better than the process. Moreover, even if he believes he knows better, he knows that he has no good way to demonstrate the superiority of his judgment in any reasonable length of time.

We would expect presidents of some schools to be more concerned with the substance of tenure decisions than presidents of others. Presidents of schools where turnover of faculty is low and where growth is modest or nonexistent would involve themselves more directly in tenure decisions than would presidents of high turnover and rapidly growing schools. Although our data from interviews are not adequate to a firm text of such ideas, we believe that they are generally consistent with such conclusions. Relatively active presidents tended to be in the very small handful of prestigious institutions of stable size and the larger group of stable-sized, low-prestige colleges off the major academic market place.

Most of the presidents we interviewed had never rejected a tenure recommendation that came to them through the internal faculty and administrative reviewing process. The overall rejection rate – at the final approval point – appears to be no more than 5 percent and probably closer to 1 percent. Some presidents, though by no means all, tried to involve themselves earlier in the process in order to develop a consensus before the time for their formal action arrived. This was much more characteristic of presidents in small schools than of those in large ones. In larger schools, presidents typically viewed their role in tenure decisions as ratifying the actions recommended by chief academic officer and the appropriate faculty-administrative committees. This would break down seriously only in the occasional case in which some major part of the president's constituency became activated. Recently this has almost exclusively involved student protest against the refusal of tenure to a popular teacher and community-trusted protest against the granting of tenure to a politically unpopular professor. Spectacular as such cases sometimes are and as difficult as they may become for a president, they have been and still are infrequent.

We have argued, however, that this situation is based on the seven key reasons listed above. The last 25 years have been a special era in the history of American higher education that appears to be ending or to have ended. Growth rates have slowed considerably. As a result, market demand for faculty and faculty turnover appear destined to be reduced.[6] The rate of growth of research support has declined. All of these factors are likely to increase presidential activity in tenure decisions. Through him, both symbolically and perhaps directly, local and internal factors seem likely to become somewhat more important than they have been (e.g., teaching, university service, good collegue-ship) and cosmopolitan, national, and professional factors somewhat less important. We are likely to have an increase in the number of complaints about "cronyism" or "personal favoritism" and a decrease in the number of complaints about a professor's primary allegiance lying with his outside professional groups.

Although it is hard to imagine that academic tenure decisions will become a major source of attention for most presidents, the ritual consider actions associated with tenure will continue to be important. The reputed quality of the faculty and the research standing of the school (two important dimensions to many presidents) can be influenced by creating a climate of belief in the importance of research. This climate has been constructed by emphasizing the research basis through a system of reports, market offers, research "stars", and the like. For most purposes, the accuracy of a "publish or perish" characterization of the concrete tenure rules is less critical than a wide acceptance of research productivity as a norm of the system.

We would expect to find presidents concerned that the dogma of research be reinforced by the litany of promotion procedures. As the pressures upon presidents have changed (e.g., from students and from sources of funds), we can expect the dogma and the litany to be revised, and the perceived reasons for tenure decisions to shift. With research, teaching, and service standards vague and uncertain, it is particularly important that the president announce that they are being used. And this is not simply a strategy of deception. It is also a recognition that if one is going to influence such diffuse things as the research identity of an institution, the influence will come about in large part by changing the pictures of people within the institution of what they are good at and what those who are rewarded are good at. A general acceptance of teaching dogmas will probably produce more teaching, even though the changes in peoples' beliefs are almost certain to be greater than the changes in their behavior.

9.1.3 *Planning*

Planning is a primary responsibility of executive leadership and is so certified by traditional administrative theory and by innumerable modern treatments. In our interviews, we never heard an administrator deny the importance and virtue of planning within the college. In many cases they observed that this had not been a function that was well performed within the college previously. In some cases they observed that it was not a function that was easy to perform. But the fundamental value of planning was asserted by all, and in approximately the same terms by all.

Most administrators accepted two basic organizational axioms with respect to planning:

1. A primary responsibility of leadership is that of providing, broad, general direction to the organization.
2. Orderly direction requires a clear specification of objectives, an identification of alternative routes to those objectives, and a choice among those alternatives.

In short, one must have a plan.

Moreover, it was generally accepted that the plan should be comprehensive. It should involve academic planning, fiscal planning, physical planning, personnel planning, research planning, and organizational planning in an integrated and consistent master plan. The frequently recited stories of physical planning that proceeds without attention to the academic plan of the university are seen as horror stories.

Despite this unanimous acceptance of the importance of planning, we saw little evidence of planning in American colleges and universities – at least planning in the terms indicated above. At each of the colleges in our sample we asked presidents and their chief subordinates whether their college had a "plan". We also asked what role the plan played in current decisions. The answers varied somewhat across four main alternatives:

1. Yes, we have a plan. It is used in capital project and physical location decisions.
2. Yes, we have a plan. Here it is. It was made during the administration of our last president. We are working on a new one.
3. No, we do not have a plan. We should. We are working on one.
4. I think there's a plan around here someplace. Miss Jones, do we have a copy of our comprehensive 10-year plan?

Most schools had a capital-physical plan of some sort, and most of these were subject to relatively continuous review and revisions. Few people were completely satisfied with such planning. Nearly everyone agreed that it rarely took adequate account of "academic" considerations. It was often felt that actual decisions were essentially independent of the plan. There were persistent problems in identifying a rational basis for a particular plan. Nevertheless, such plans were reasonably well-accepted and reasonably institutionalized.

In a similar way, many schools had fiscal plans of one sort or another. It was not uncommon to find plans for future operating budgets. Plans for fiscal problems associated with income uncertanties (e.g., endowment earnings, grant income, tuition/enrollment) were common, particularly among nonpublic institutions. In public institutions legislative-administrative tactics seemed to make it impossible to develop serious contingent plans for alternative levels of public appropriations. Plans to deal with cash flow difficulties (particularly associated with heavy dependence in tuition income) or with the short-term investment of temporary sources of cash were common. Long- and medium-range budget planning, however, seemed to be very modest and hyper-routine. Other fiscal planning was, for the most part, "technical" in the sense that it did not ordinarily involve considerations beyond the maintenance of the best financial position possible for the institution.

Some schools have academic plans. Some of these are voluminous – the natural consequence of asking each department to prepare a plan and then binding all the documents together without editing. Few administrators thought the academic plans were useful in decision making. On the whole academic plans seem to suffer from two conspicuous administrative problems: (1) They often had no connection to any decisions that anyone might be called upon to make. (2) They rejected the idea of scarcity. At best they were lists of what the various academic departments wished Santa Claus would bring them. At worst, they were fantasies, neither believed in nor intended to be believable.

Presidents believe in comprehensive planning, but do virtually none of it. How do we understand such an inconsistency and what are its consequences?

We believe that the phenomena of planning – and the corresponding administrative attitudes – are the striking consequences of the inconsistencies between universities as organizations and the models of organizations with which administrators are familiar. Plans, in their usual form, particularly long-run comprehensive plans, presume substantial clarity about goals, substantial understanding of the basic technology of the organization, and substantial continuity in leadership. Universities have none of these, except – possible – in the capital-physical-fiscal-planning area. Presidents frequently come to the presidency from outside the organization and are frequently succeeded by someone from outside the organization. Their terms are short relative to the length of time involved in a "plan". Except for their chief officers in business-finance, their main subordinates will remain in office for an even shorter period. Boards of trustees are rarely organized to maintain continuity in anything more than general fiscal policies. Presidents emphasize the importance of making a mark on the institution. They have little stake in continuity with the past. They may hope for continuity with the future, but they would have to be extraordinarily naive to expect their successor to spend much time "implementing" someone else's plan. Despite the obeisance paid it, comprehensive planning has little reality for presidents in the form in which we usually conceive it.

Long-run planning in universities is something other than long-run planning. In particular, we would identify four major things that plans become:

1. Plans become *symbols*. Academic organizations provide few "real" pieces of feedback data. They have nothing closely analogous to profit or sales figures. How are we doing? Where are we going? An organization that is failing can announce a plan to succeed. An institution that does not have a reactor can announce a plan for one, and is probably valued higher than a university without such a plan.
2. Plans become *advertisements*. What is frequently called a "plan" by a university is really an investment brochure. It is an attempt to persuade private and public donors of the attractiveness of the institution. Such plans are characterized by pictures, by ex cathedra pronouncements of excellence, and by the absence of most relevant information.
3. Plans become *games*. In an organization in which goals and technology are unclear, plans and the insistence on plans become an administrative test of will. If a department wants a new

program badly enough, it will spend a substantial amount of effort in "justifying" the expenditure by fitting it into a "plan". If an administrator wished to avoid saying "yes" to everything, but has no basis for saying "no" to anything, he tests the commitment of the department by asking for a plan.

4. Plans become *excuses for interaction*. As several students of planning have noted, the results of the process of planning are usually more important than the plan. The development of a plan forces some discussion and may induce some interest in and commitment to relatively low-priority activities in the departments/schools. Occasionally that interaction yields results of positive value. But only rarely does it yield anything that would accurately describe the activities of a school or department beyond one or two years into the future. As people engage in discussions of the future they may modify each other's ideas about what should be done today, but their conclusions about what should be done next year are likely to be altered in the interim by changes in personnel, political climate, foundation policy, or student demand.

The side benefits of plans seem enough to sustain talk of planning and a modest level of activity, but not enough to motivate either intense administrative involvement or a community-wide commitment to execute what has been written. As long as education is a process particularly sensitive to the character and individual interests of those who teach and those who study, the direct rewards of planning activity both for presidents and for others can be expected to remain relatively low.

9.2 Presidential Power

The examination we have made of the logic of decision in four areas of college decision making suggests some complications in the idea of executive power. The American college president plays a far from dominant role in these four conspicuous areas of college decision making. He is important. He has power. The processes, however, have logics that he cannot alter, and normally does not want to alter.

It is unlikely that we can determine how much power the American college president has or should have. Such questions require a specification of a model of executive/administrative power that has proven impossible to make. (See March, 1966.) However, we can consider some possible reasons why the president's power is an issue and a problem, and we can examine some implications of those reasons. To do this, we will assert that the following propositions are plausible without detailed argumentation or evidence:

1. Most people believe in a simple force model of organizational choice. That is, they believe that power (force) is distributed among participants and that decisions are approximated by the weighted average of individual wishes (where the weights are the power indices of the individuals).
2. The simple force model of organizational choice accounts for a good deal less of the variation in outcomes than is believed. There are other factors that are relevant in important ways.
3. The president is both perceived to have and, in fact, does have more power than most (perhaps all) other participants in college or university decision making.
4. Power, the interpretation of power, and the assessment of individual leadership behavior are considered against the background of an egalitarian ideology within the United States.

Notice that the second point is not a direct argument that "power" is distributed more "equally" than is commonly believed. The argument is that a simple force model is incorrect, that there are substantial "nonpower" factors in decisions. Since these are somewhat independent of "power" as reflected in the standard model, they are as less likely to help the "strong" in direct proportion to their strength. Thus, in effect they equalize apparent power.

The decision processes we have described are not easily characterized in simple "force" terms. Decisions are typically not made by a confrontation of well-organized factions, with victory to the strongest. The factions are not well-organized. They are rarely all activated at one time. They rarely have any significant staying power. As a result of egalitarian norms the American college president is faced with a set of beliefs about the amount of power he should have and the amount of power he does have that assure some resentment toward him. In addition, given perceptions of power and the force-independent features of the processes, he is faced with a disparity between his potential power and beliefs about his power that assure his disappointment and the disappointment of others. He is resented because he is more powerful than he should be. He is scorned and frustrated because he is weaker than he is believed capable of being. If he acts as a "strong" president, he exposes his weakness. If he acts as a "democratic" president, people consider him timid. For the most part, his behavior has only modest impact on beliefs about presidential legitimacy or power.

We can illustrate the situation very simply. In Figure 9.1 we plot perceptions of power against hierarchical position within the organization. We have simplified considerably by assuming that there is a linear relationship between power and hierarchical position and that the "total power" perceived within the system is fixed, but neither of those simplifications is critical to the argument.

The horizontal line represents the *evaluative* norm within the university. We have portrayed the simple case of a pure egalitarian ideology. The steep line represents the *cognitive* norm within the university. It reflects the attribution of power within the organization. The intermediate line is the *behavioral* situation (the exerciseable power) within the university. It is more steep than the evaluative norm (assertions 3 and 4) and less steep than the cognitive norm (assertions 1 and 2).

Since he is at the top of the hierarchy, the president is represented by the three endpoint values in Figure 9.1: his *legitimate* power (point *c*), his *actual* power (point *b*), and his *perceived* power (point *a*).

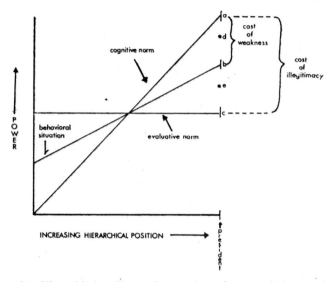

Figure 9.1. Hierarchical position and perceptions of power within the university

From this it is easy to see that the president is subject to two major costs with respect to power: The first costs are the costs of illegitimacy – the difference between the perceived power of the president and his legitimate power (a–c). According to our assertions, these costs will always exist. The second costs are the costs of weakness – the difference between the perceived power of the president and his actual power (a-b). According to our assertions, these costs will also always exist.

The costs of illegitimacy are realized in resentment toward the

198

office and the person holding it, in pressure to reduce the power of the president, in motivational assumptions about the behavior of presidents (e.g., "power-hunger"). The magnitude of the costs of illegitimacy depends on the extent to which the power model of the university is accepted and the extent to which norms of equality apply.

In general, we would expect to find the degree of acceptance of the power model to increase with the degree of conflict in the organization, the size of the organization, the average pleasure derived from politics by participants in the organization. We would expect the acceptance of norms of equality to increase with the degree of differentiation between hierarchical status orders and other (e.g., professional) status orders, with the opportunities for exit from the organization provided within the environment, with the degree of public control of the institution, and with the recency of presidential accession to the office.

The costs of weakness, on the other hand, are paid in criticism for timidity, in disappointment among supporters, and in reduced self-esteem. The magnitude of these costs depends on the extent to which the power model is accepted and the actual power of the president (or, in effect, the number and scope of other factors in decisions). We would expect the actual power in these terms to increase with the slack in the system. Slack serves as a buffer from exogenous forces. We would expect the actual power to increase when other participants become more dependent on the organization, for example, when exit opportunities decline. We would expect power to increase as the social significance of universities decreases.

This kind of analysis provides an interpretation of one familiar sequence of university events. If slack declines at the same time as the social importance of universities and conflict in them increases, complaints about presidential timidity will increase at a more rapid rate than complaints about presidential illegitimacy (which may in fact decline). Objections to presidential weakness will be particularly notable in large, public institutions. If subsequently the opportunities for exit by other administrators, students, and faculty decline, complaints of both kinds decline; but the decline is most notable with respect to perceptions of weakness of presidents. Presidents become both stronger and more legitimate, particularly the former.

We can add to the analysis in Figure 9.1 by considering the president's own perception of the ditribution of power. In general, we would expect presidents to see their power as somewhat more than that presumed by the egalitarian norm and as somewhat less than that believed by non-presidents. What difference does this make?

In our discussion we have assumed that the president's perception of his power has no direct effect on either legitimate power or perceived power. However, it could affect actual power. If the president sees his own power as greater than it actually is (say at point d), the cost of weakness will still be (a–b) (since his perception cannot change the facts in a positive direction). If, on the other hand, he perceives his power as less than it actually is (point e), he will generally not realize all of his actual potential power. The costs of weakness are, in fact either (a–b) or (a–e), which ever is larger. Presidents who underestimate their power and act in terms of that underestimate will not affect their costs of legitimacy (unless the perceptions of power are actually a function of events as well as models) but will affect the costs of weakness.

If the president overestimates his power, he will think he can do something that, in fact, he cannot. If the president underestimates his power, he will think he cannot do something that, in fact, he can. Generally, the former errors are more conspicuous, both to the president and to his audiences, than are the latter. As a result, we would expect ordinary learning to lead the president to reduce his estimate of his own power (though he may easily still overestimate it).

Combining these observations, we obtain the following kind of progression: A president is more likely to overestimate his power in early years of the presidency than in the later years. This occurs because he is coming to the presidency from the universe of non-presidential beliefs about presidential power (which tend to be high), because he has high hopes, and because a honeymoon with his audiences makes the costs of illegitimacy less conspicuous. The result is a large power-expectation gap for the president and a large number of errors of attempting to do things he cannot. Over time, the president reduces his estimate of his power as he learns from the errors. His learning reduces the power-expectation gap, decreases the frequency of those errors, increases the (less conspicuous) errors of timidity, and increases the cost of weakness. At the same time, familiarity with the president as president raises the legitimacy of his position among his constituencies, with a resulting decline in the costs of legitimacy. According to this analysis, presidents should ordinarily experience systematic increases in the complaints about their timidity over time and systematic decreases in the complaints about their illegitimacy.

Presidents are not the only actors in the college scene who experience the phenomena we have indicated. In particular, student leaders, faculty leaders, and trustees can be located on Figure 9.1 in a similar way. If we are substantially correct, the costs of weakness and the costs of legitimacy are less for them, but some of the same phenomena obtain. They will generally find themselves less powerful than they expected and less powerful than their constituents expect them to be.

9.3 The Certification of Status

We have argued that several key domains of academic decision are subject to a logic that makes the official procedures for decision only marginally relevant to decision outcomes. Choices are made, but much of the activity in formal choice situations does not directly affect them. As a result, beliefs about the power of major participants are predictably confounded. We need to add a final note on the decision procedures themselves.

A system of university governance is a system for simultaneously making and validating decisions, exercising problems, and certifying status. The first of these functions dominates most discussions. We identify the system of governance as the procedure by which major decisions are made: Who is allowed access to the university – as student, faculty member, trustee, donor, employee? How are the scarce financial resources of the university allocated? How do the participants in the university use their time? What are the formats and rules of the teaching function? What research is done?

Governance as problem exercising is also familiar to readers of this volume. Several of our discussions have considered the conditions under which formal decision procedures become opportunities for exercising problems, rather than solving them. Where access and decision structures are relatively open in an organized anarchy, many decisions will be made; but if there is a moderate load, most of the decision energy will be spent attending unsuccessfully to problems collected in attractive garbage cans.

The status certification function of governance is less commonly discussed. For many participants, the process and structure of university governance are more important than the outcome – at least within wide ranges of possible outcomes. Participation is not a means but an end. Academic institutions easily become *process*-rather than *output*-oriented. Goals provide scant evidence on whether the output of the decision process within academe is desirable, but participation in the process is a conspicuous certification of status. Individuals establish themselves as important by virtue of their rights of participation in the governance of the institution.

To illustrate the phenomenon, consider the implications of the following simply hypothesis: Most people in a college are most of the time less concerned with the content of a decision than they are with eliciting an acknowledgment of their importance within the community. We believe that some substantial elements of the governance of universities can be better understood in terms of such a hypothesis than in terms of an assumption that governance is primarily concerned with the outcomes of decisions. Presidents are more insistent on their

201

right to make a decision than on the content of the decision. Faculty members are more insistent on their right to participate in faculty deliberations than they are on exercising that right. Students are more insistent on their right to representation on key decision bodies than they are on attending meetings. Boards of trustees are more insistent of defining the scope of their authority than they are on using it.

Much of the argument is over the symbols of governance. Who has the right to claim power? Since the main symbols of power and status are participation and victory, the university decision-making system is crowded with instruments of participation and platforms for claims of victories: select committees, faculty senates, ad hoc groups, reviews, memoranda, votes, meetings, rallies, conferences. The system is typically not crowded with actual participation except where validation of status positions is involved. Unless some highly symbolic conflict can be arranged, it is often hard to sustain student and faculty interest in the activities of a committee whose existence they apparently consider a matter of some importance. The situation has been illustrated well in recent years by instances of distinguished faculty, who rarely before had attended a general faculty meeting, coming to a meeting to discuss whether students should be allowed to attend.

As a system for making decisions, the standard college governance system is open to a number of vital challenges. It is not clear that it has a major role in the outcomes of decisions; that anyone seriously wants it to have such a role; that it is constituted in such a way as to make such a role feasible. The formal structure of governance does, however, provide some gradations of deference and a forum for debating the rights to participation. Not everyone receives as much deference as he might like. Arguments over scarce deference can be just as ferocious and just as serious as arguments over "real" resources. Universities, like countries, may struggle for a long time to decide the participation rights of member groups. But by providing numerous parallel decision system with numerous levels of overlapping committees, titles, and responsibilities, universities are relatively efficient in reducing conflict over status resources.

By calling attention to the importance of status, we do not intend to demean it. That academic man cares more for his self-respect than for his material well-being (if he does) may not be entirely a vice. And if he does, he may perhaps be excused the luxury of fighting more for the former than for the latter. Moreover, the right to participate is a necessary prerequisite to making the threat to participate; and the threat to participate is, at least in principle, a prime device for exerting influence over the course of events without being present (see Chapter 3). Although we do not believe that claims for status are generally

202

explicable as conscious efforts to construct a basis for subsequent threat, they have that potential whether intended or not.

Least of all should persons concerned about the substance of university decisions scorn a concern by others in the allocation of status. Such variations in concern form the basis for one of the most common of organizational exchanges – the exchange of status for substance. As Dale Carnegie (1936) has observed, the most natural coalition in the world is between someone who wants to sell pots and pans and someone who wants to be admired. In a world in which most people care more about their self-esteem than they do about what pots and pans are bought, anyone who has the opposite scale of values is in strong trading position. In important ways, universities are such a world. A person who is interested in changing a university may have some chance of doing so if he is willing to accord status to others within the community and is able to prevent the decisions in which he is interested from becoming garbage cans for collectively insatiable status concerns.

For the same reasons, concerns about participation status probably contribute to general stability of decision outcomes. Status concerns can become a problem to be discussed in the context of almost any choice. In classic garbage can terms, they may effectively prevent almost any specific choice from being made; but they leave most things untouched. They force the commitment of large shares of decision energy to the problems of constitutional rights. Much of the machinery and many of the participants are constrained to discuss those problems. This leaves little time or energy to overcome what we have called the logic of choice.

9.4 Conclusion

By examining the reports from college administrators on decision making in American colleges and universities, we have tried to elaborate the garbage can view of decision making in an organized anarchy. In particular, we have tried to suggest how the logic of decision in four key areas of university action provides a stability that is significantly independent of the detailed timing in flows of problems, solutions, choices, and participants. The flows are channeled by the terrain.

The results lend support, though in less elegant form, to Stava's (Chapter 10) discussion of the way in which an elaborately political and explicitly complex process in Norway led to a series of decisions rather closely approximated by a simple normative rule; to March and Romelaer's (Chapter 12) discussion of the impact of consistent participation in decision making in a university; and to Kreiner's (Chapter

8) and Christensen's (Chapter 16) discussions of the interplay between curriculum decision making and curriculum in a Danish free school.

Such a view, however, poses some problems of interpretation of executive power and of the functions of governance. We have argued that a serious view of the decision process in universities is inconsistent with a simple force model of power. This supports Enderud's (Chapter 17) contention that a focus on beliefs about power is necessary in order to interpret individual reports on a power distribution. Inconsistencies between the model of power in organizations held by many participants and the model we have outlined yield predictions about the development of beliefs about college administrators that seem to us to have some face validity. For example, standard descriptions of the presidential role tend to be heroic in their view of presidential importance. The portrait of reality we have sketched implies a more limited presidential role. A president probably has more power than other single individuals but he faces a poorly understood and rather tightly constrained managerial world. His ability to control decision outcomes is often less than expected by those around him and by himself. This leads to a predictable set of beliefs about presidential power and the exercise of it.

Finally, we are led to draw some implications of our interpretation for understanding the events that take place within formal decision arenas. Kreiner (Chapter 8), Christensen (Chapter 16), Olsen (Chapter 13), Weiner (Chapter 11), and Enderud (Chapter 17) have all observed ways in which the right to participate in decisions appears to be more important than actual participation and ways in which formal decision procedures are ritual confirmation of those rights. Such observations are consistent with at least some interpretations of a long stream of literature on organizational participation and alienation and recent examinations of the symbolic elements in political life.

In contemporary American colleges, a widely-shared egalitarian ideology contributes to making status a prime scarce resource and thus to making the certification of status a major concern. This, in turn, lends stability to many streams of decision outcomes by creating a heavy problem load on a system with modest decision energy.

NOTES:

1 This chapter borrows extensively from a longer discussion of some of the issues of leadership in organized anarchies (Cohen and March, 1974).

2 The sample is stratified into six categories. "Relatively wealthy" schools are defined as those in the top fifth of the distribution of 4-year colleges by income per full time student. All others are designated "relatively poor". Schools are classed as "large" if they have 9,000 or more students, "medium" if they have between 1,500 and 8,999 full time students, and "small" when the student body is 1,499 or less. Seven schools were drawn randomly into

each of the 3 x 2 = 6 sample cells. Further information on sampling and estimating procedures can be found in Cohen and March (1973).

3 We are indebted particularly to Nancy Block and Jackie Fry for their work in listening to the tapes, responses, and providing summaries and transcripts of those responses to control our faulty memories.

4 At some of the best-endowed universities, endowments flow directly to the subunits in the university rather than to the president. Although those presidents tend to be enthusiastic about the "each ship on its own bottom" ideology, they are also aware of their substantial irrelevance to the expenditures stemming from such independent sources.

5 There are many interpretations of the strong positive correlation between prestige of an institution and student unrest. Most of them, correctly in our view, stress factors that have rather little to do with conditions on the campus except as a pretext. We wish simply to add the observation that a school that has 10 outstanding applicants for every place in the freshman class is unlikely to feel enrollment cycle pressure to be attentive to student needs or desires.

6 For a discussion of some of the faculty personnel consequences of the end of growth see McNeil and Thompson (1971).

10. Constraints on the Politics of Public Choice*

PER STAVA
University of Bergen

10.0 Introduction

Both organization theorists and political scientists are inclined to use actions as independent variables. The set of actions considered relevant are those intended to influence the events to be explained. The result has been a tendency to overlook the role of non-action elements, like material or symbolic "structures", i.e. elements which are stable over the time span we study. This chapter reports an attempt to examine the relative explanatory power of several alternative models of political decision-making. The event of primary concern is the location of six new district colleges in Norway. We will also briefly look into the location of Norwegian universities. On the whole, the results suggest that we might wish to consider more favorably some theories where the independent variables refer to structures.

10.1 The Decisions

In 1968 the Norwegian system of higher education consisted of four universities (Bergen, Oslo, Tromsø, Trondheim), and some specialized colleges. In a series of decisions made between 1968 and 1970, and generally perceived as major policy decisions the Norwegian parliament authorized the addition of six district colleges.[1] The establishment of the three first district colleges was discussed by the Storting (parliament) on June 20, 1969. The colleges were located in the counties of Vest-Agder, Møre og Romsdal, and Rogaland. The establishment of three more district colleges was discussed by the Storting on May 29, 1970. The colleges were placed in the counties of Nordland, Oppland, and Telemark.

The need to establish a set of new colleges was not seriously contested in the political system. Most of the participants apparently regarded the district colleges as important for the nation's educational system and for the development of the country in general. District colleges were, at the time of their establishment, regarded as a means to absorb the great influx of students. After a period of decline in student figures (1950–54), the number more than quadrupled from 1954 to 1968 (from 5,673 to 24,115).[2] The opinion was that neither the existing institutions nor the addition of two more universities in 1968 could solve this problem of capacity. Also, it was stated that the country did not have resources to establish more new universities in the foreseeable future, (until about 1990). To this dilemma the district colleges were almost unanimously welcomed as a good solution. They are cheaper to establish and operate than the universities (e.g., because they were not intended to do research). The intention is to establish 12 district colleges in the country.

The district colleges were welcomed also because of the presumed benefits for the country in general. The parliamentary committee discussing the issue, stated that "the district colleges may – in the committee's opinion – contribute essentially to cultural and economic growth and development in the districts".[3] In the parliamentary debate the following quotation is rather representative:

"I regard this recommendation ... as very important ... because we have now reached the tiny beginning of a new kind of school that may become of great importance to our country. It will be exciting to see what ability the school has to release cultural efforts in the districts, and what significance it will have for occupational life, industry and trade."[4]

Unlike the decision to establish the colleges, the issue of location was debated at length, was the subject of considerable political activity, and was a matter of considerable governmental attention. Crudely stated, two dimensions were involved. First, in which counties and municipalities should the district colleges be located; secondly, should the colleges be a means to promote rural development (i.e., should some schools be located in rural areas). Along both dimensions activity was considerable and conflicts at times rather acute.

Counties and municipalities were mainly interested in the first dimension, whether they could get a district college. A district college was regarded as an important resource. Local groups activated themselves by forming deputations to the Ministry of Church and Education or to the parliamentary committee. They prepared reports arguing for a district college in their county or municipality.

There was pressure from more tangential groups. A committee (The Action Committee for District Colleges) was actively promoting district colleges for rural areas. The committee sent letters to Norwegian municipalities inviting them to state their opinion on the issue, sent letters to the government, held press conferences, and distributed pamphlets. The newspapers followed the development and reported the major events. Quite a few letters were sent to the newspapers, and many of them discussed the location issue.

By every external sign this was an important political issue involving important stakes and activating important political and social interest groups. In the Storting it was noted that over the past years no other case had received so much interest from outsiders.

10.2 Some Alternative Theories

Suppose we wish to understand the processes involved in major political decisions of the type described above. We suggest four broad types of theories about the way scarce resources are allocated: democratic theories, interest group theories, decision process theories, and legal-bureaucratic theories.[5]

For the most part, *democratic theories*[6] argue that the society allocates resources by attending to voters (or potential voters), each substantially equal to the other. Thus, democratic theories assume that resources are allocated essentially by counting heads, and that individual voters pursue individual self-interest.

In democratic theories we assume that there is an "electorate" delimited according to some specified criteria of formal position within the system (e.g. membership). This electorate either decides policy directly or chooses a representative body to decide in its name. Decisions are made according to certain procedures: (1) Whenever policy choices are made or representatives elected, the alternative selected and enforced is the alternative most preferred by the electorate. (2) In this choice process, each member of the electorate is assigned an equal value. (3) In choosing among alternatives, the alternative preferred by the.greater number is selected.

Interest group theories[7] mostly argue that certain interests in society are better organized for exerting pressure and are better financed than other interests. As a result, these groups receive a greater share of the resources. It is presumed that groups are of critical importance for understanding politics. "Through these formations a society is experienced by its members, and in this way it must be observed and understood by its students" (Truman, 1965, p. 43).

The groups make claims upon each other. The claims most relevant for explaining public policies are those made upon government groups. Not all groups are equally effective in making claims upon the government, however, and public policy is determined by the configuration of effective claims concerning the actual policy. This configuration may be accounted for by three main clusters of variables:

208

(1) internal characteristics of the groups, (2) the groups' differential strategic position in society, and (3) characteristics of the government. With knowledge of these main factors and their dynamic interaction it is possible to understand politics and explain policies.

In *decision process theories*[8] it is presumed that policy is the outcome of a choice made by one or several decision-makers. Which choice is made is determined by the situation in which the decision-maker finds himself. This situation is, in turn, largely caused by the processes preceeding the choice. It is impossible, then, to predict policies without knowing the details of the preceding processes. Different processes will result in different choices, and hence policies.

The behavior of the decision-maker may be accounted for with the knowledge of three main sets of variables, which set of alternatives does he consider, what does he perceive the consequences of different alternatives to be, and which goals does he seek to realize. "To explain any sequence of political actions, therefore, the analyst must ascertain who made the key decisions that gave rise to the action and then assess the intellectual and interactive processes whereby the decision-makers reached their conclusions". (Rosenau, 1967, p. 195.)

Legal-bureaucratic theories[9] mostly argue that resources are allocated within a political system according to some universalistic rules applied in a neutral way and in accord with the *prima facie* needs of the society. It is assumed that decisions have two main characteristics, they are formally neutral and they are rational. They are neutral in the sense that the necessary value premises for the decisions are given or treated as given. If the decision-makers have to establish the value premises themselves, they usually resort to generally accepted values (e.g., in western culture, such values as justice, equity, equality). The proof of the neutrality of the decisions is (in many cases) that they can be subsumed under general, "objective" rules. It is these rules that determine the decisions, and not the fiat or personal preferences of the decision-makers.

The decision should also be (formally) rational. This means that they are intended to realize goals. The goals, however, are given, in accordance with the neutrality requirement. Often they are given in the form of general rules or other prescriptions. Rational decisions, then, mean decisions taken in accordance with what the prescriptions demand, i.e. correct application of rules to concrete cases.

From these brief statements of the four classes of theories it should be evident that democratic theories, interest group theories and decision process theories locate the explanatory variables in actions. Actions may be taken in more or less structured environments, but these structures are secondary in importance to actions. Legal-bureaucratic theories on the other hand focus directly on structures, on (relatively) stable rules. Intentional action is assumed not to interfere with the application of rules to concrete cases.

10.3 Some Specific Models

Like all theories, the four classes of theories discussed in the previous section contain concepts that are not operational. One cannot there-fore, determine directly which, if any, of the four theories best explains the location of district colleges. In order to do so, we establish a set of connections between the theories and the location decisions. Such a connection is provided by specific models. The empirical testing proceeds from the models, but the interesting interpretations of the results of this testing are probably in terms of the more general theoretical concepts.

In this section we present eleven models, relate them to the four classes of theories, and suggest which models may be regarded as specifications of which theories.

Models belonging to two main classes are considered here:

(1) *Power models.* In these models we assume that those areas of the country having the greatest power will receive the greatest rewards from the political system. In particular, we assume that colleges will be distributed to the "powerful". We consider five alternative measures of the power of a geographical unit:

    a) *Total population.* The greater the population, the greater the power.

    b) *Total number of eligible students.* The greater the number of students eligible for college, the greater the power.

    c) *Total parliamentary representation.* The greater the number of representatives in the parliament, the greater the power.

    d) *Total personal and business income.* The greater the total income, the greater the power.

    e) *Per capita personal income.* The greater the per capita income, the greater the power.

In each case, we assume that geographical units in a country compete for resources by using their power. This power comes from population, political representation, active clients (stu-dents), or wealth. Resources are assumed to be distributed disproportionately to the powerful geographical units.

(2) *Weighted distance models.* In these models we assume that the political process locates colleges to minimize the summed distance between politically relevant clientele and the nearest college.[10]

The substance of the models lies in the alternative weighting schemes. They represent alternative ideas of the relevant clientele for the political process. We have considered six alternative schemes:

a) *Equal weights.* Each geographical unit is equal to each other one.
b) *Total population.* Each unit is weighted by its population.
c) *Total number of eligible students.* Each unit is weighted by its numbers of students eligible for college.
d) *Total parliamentary representation.* Each unit is weighted by the per capita personal income in the unit.
e) *Total personal and business income.* Each unit is weighted by the sum of its personal and business income.
f) *Per capita personal income.* Each unit is weighted by the per capita personal income in the unit.

Before examining how each of these models performs in predicting where in Norway colleges will be established, it may be well to examine the relationship between these models and the more general verbal theories suggested in section 2.

Democratic theories generally assume that the relevant factors are formal positions within the system. In a general way, they are consistent with either power models or weighted distance models that are tied to the total population (voters) or official legislative status (parliamentary representation). Thus, these theories are consistent with power models (a) total population, and (c) total parliamentary representation and the corresponding weighted distance models (b) and (d).[11]

Interest group theories generally emphasize the resources available to groups. In these terms, the obvious interest groups are related to counties and the obvious resource is money. Thus, such theories are relatively consistent with the models linked to total or per capita income, i.e., power models (d) and (e) weighted distance models (e) and (f).[12]

Decision process theories generally assume that it is impossible to predict or understand social choice without attention to the micro-structure of the process. Thus, they are basically inconsistent with all of the models specified above. If we consider the main dimensions in these theories, this is also borne out. The models specify alternatives in the sense that each county is treated as an alternative. But, none of them takes into account whether all alternatives were considered in order to find the best, or if only a few were seriously regarded, and if so in what order. The models do not take consequences of alternatives

211

and goals into account at all. If one of the models predicts the choices, these theories are weakened in this context. If none of our models predict the choices, these theories will be indirectly corroborated.

Legal-bureaucratic theories generally assume that the relevant factors are those of relatively obvious rules of "service". In our case, these can be interpreted as being related to the total population and student population dimensions of obvious clientele. With the two actual power models, (a) and (b), the rules implied may be acceptable for most people in college location decisions but that is probably dependent upon what results the models produce, i.e. which location pattern emerges from the models. The two weighted distance models, (b) and (c), are more clearly consistent with these theories. Here the neutrality (and also "service") requirement is secured by the introduction of distance as a variable. This ensures that the schools are somewhat dispersed, and it produces a pattern of locations that gives the total/student population as easy an access as possible to the schools. Thus, the models may be justified by references to equality and equity considerations, considerations that are generally accepted in Norwegian culture.

Table 10.0. The connections between the five theories and the eleven models

	Theories			
Models	Democratic	Interest	Decision process	Legal-bureaucratic
Power:				
a) Total population	+	—	—	+
b) Student population	—	—	—	+
c) Parliamentary representation	+	—	—	—
d) Total income	—	+	—	—
e) Per capita income	—	+	—	—
Weighted:				
a) Equal counties	—	—	—	—
b) Total population	+	—	—	+
c) Student population	—	—	—	+
d) Parliamentary representation	+	—	—	—
e) Total income	—	+	—	—
f) Per capita income	—	+	—	—

"+" = relative consistency
"—" = relative inconsistency

These general connections between the theories and the models outlined here can be represented as in Table 10.1. In the table we have

212

tried to reflect the general consistency between model and theory (using a "+" to indicate relative consistency and a "–" to indicate relative inconsistency).

By examining the relative success of the several models (in section 4), we assess the support this set of decisions and our analysis gives to the four types of theories.

10.4 Testing the Models

The performance of the different models is presented in summary form in Table 10.2. A more detailed presentation is found in Stava (1971). It appears that the weighted distance models[13] give better predictions than the "pure" power models. This is also brought out when we look at the number of correct predictions; the weighted distance models do consistently better than the corresponding power models. This should indicate that distance is an important dimension in this case. But the fact that distance alone is not a very powerful explanatory principle is seen from a weighted distance model with equal power (clientele) in each county. The model in which distance is the only explanatory principle does poorly, with between one and three correct predictions.

Distance is important then, but it has to be appropriately weighted. And the best weight to use is the number of artium candidates. This model is best, and it predicts five counties correctly. The probability of getting five correct predictions by chance is 0.016. The difference between models that predict five and four correctly is marked. There is approximately ten times as great a chance of predicting four counties correctly by chance as of predicting five. The probability of getting four correct is 0.140.

The two counties "interchanged" by the best model are Vestfold and Telemark. These are neighbouring counties. The distance between them (as measured in the model) is only 35 km. This may make the false prediction less "serious" than it would have been if it had predicted a county distant from the actually chosen.

There is another sense of distance that may be used to evaluate the severity of the error also. This may be called "model distance". It is the addition in total weighted distance resulting from choosing another alternative than the best one (in the model's terms). In the case of Vestfold/Telemark: The greater the addition in weighted distance resulting from choosing Telemark "instead of" Vestfold, the more "serious" the incorrect prediction of Vestfold is.

In terms of this "distance" measure also, Telemark represents the second best alternative in terms of weighted distance. There is an

Table 10.1. The performance of the eleven models

Models	No. of correct predictions	Predicted but not chosen by the Storting	Not predicted but chosen by the Storting
Power:			
a) Total population	3	Hedmark, Östfold, Buskerud	Vest-Agder, Oppland, Telemark
b) Artium cand.	4	Östfold, Buskerud	Telemark or Oppland, Vest-Agder
c) M.P.s	3–4	Östfold, Hedmark, Buskerud, Vestfold	Vest-Agder, Telemark, Oppland
d) Total income	3	Östfold, Buskerud, Vestfold	Vest-Agder, Telemark, Oppland
e) Per capita income	3	Östfold, Buskerud, Vestfold	Møre og Romsdal, Nordland, Oppland
Weighted distance:			
f) Equal power	1–3	Aust-Agder, Sogn og Fjordane, Finnmark, Vestfold, Hedmark	Rogaland, Vest-Agder, Möre and Romsdal, Oppland, Telemark
g) Total population	4	Vestfold, Hedmark	Oppland, Telemark
h) Artium cand.	5	Vestfold	Telemark
i) M.P.s	4	Vestfold, Hedmark	Oppland, Telemark
j) Total income	4	Vestfold, Hedmark	Oppland, Telemark
k) Per capita income	4	Vestfold, Finnmark	Oppland, Telemark

increase of 3.4 percent in weighted distance by choosing Telemark instead of Vestfold.

10.5 An Historical Look at University Location Decisions

Does the distance model weighted with students explain the location of district colleges because of some peculiarity at the time of location? Or is the location rule expressed in the model a more permanent feature of Norwegian political culture? In order to get some tentative answers to these questions we have also used the model to examine Norwegian university locations.

For the location of the University of Oslo (1811) we lack data on the geographical distribution of students. As a substitute we used the distance model weighted with total population. According to the model, Oslo was the third best alternative (of 18). However, there is only a 1.3 percent addition in weighted distance when choosing Oslo instead of the "best" alternative (Oppland).

The location decision for Norway's second university was taken in 1946. Bergen was chosen. This also is the third best alternative in terms of the distance model weighted with students. Choosing Bergen represents 0.7 percent added weighted distance relative to best alternative (Sør-Trøndelag).

In 1968 the Storting decided to establish two more universities, one in Sør-Trøndelag (Trondheim) and one in Troms (Tromsø). The distance model weighted with students has Troms as second best alternative, with 7.0 percent added weighted distance relative to the model's "best" alternative. Treating Troms as Norway's third university, the model correctly locates the fourth to Sør-Trøndelag.

With the possible exceptions of Trondheim, the weighted distance models do not predict the historic location of universities. But it does appear that the places chosen were "good" alternatives in the models' terms. Although in a broad way the weighted distance model is consistent with university locations also, it does not usually predict the precise outcome.

We can also ask whether the best model reveals a pattern in the *timing* of locations. The summed weighted distance is now computed for a series of years. To begin with only the University of Oslo exists. New universities and district colleges are introduced in the years they are established. It is still assumed that students go to the nearest university or district college.[14] The idea is that the weighted distance may represent some form of "stress", and that if the "stress" surpasses an upper tolerable limit, or changes too fast, the political system will intervene to check it by creating new educational institutions.

The development of weighted distance is shown on Figure 10.0.

Figure 10.0. The Development of Weighted Distance, 1890–1985

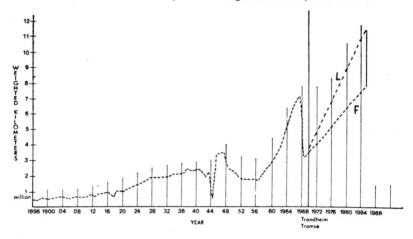

The figure makes it evident that there has not been a constant level of "stress" which has triggered off new university establishments. Rather, it appears that linear increases in stress is tolerated, while the system reacts to exponential increases. Possibly linear increases can be absorbed by various social and technical efficiencies (better communication, efficiencies of scale, etc.); but exponential changes cannot.

The sharp rise in "stress" makes reasonable the establishment of two new universities in 1968. The "stress" is brought down to a level approximating what would have resulted from a linear growth. A look at the projected student numbers makes it evident, however, that the "stress" would soon rise again. Thus, new universities would have to be established not long after those of Trondheim and Tromsø to prevent a new sharp increase in stress. One of the main candidates for a fifth university would be Stavanger. A fifth university in this town in 1969 would have reduced the stress from 3.6 million to 3.2 million weighted kilometers. Thus, this new university would have had a rather small effect in terms of stress. Against this background, the introduction of a new type of educational institution, the district colleges may be viewed as an appropriate answer.

Although the political system is too complicated to be captured in detail by such a simple model, the weighted distance model, and thus legal-bureaucratic theories, seem in a broad way to be consistent with the timing and number of university and colleges as well as their locations.

What will the effect of the district colleges be? According to current student projections, the estimated "stress" will be reduced from 11.7 million weighted kilometers (line L on graph) to 7.9 million weighted kilometers in 1985 (line F on graph). Although this reduction

216

is greater than the one a new university would produce, it does not prevent the "stress" from increasing relatively sharply. If we have confidence in the model, we would expect that it will not be possible to stick to the policy of having only four universities (until 1990), and at the same time keeping the district colleges from growing beyond the current intention, unless other alternatives to schooling are developed.

10.6 Discussion

The distance model weighted with artium candidates is consistent only with legal-bureaucratic theories. As a result, and subject to some of the qualifications noted above, our analysis supports legal-bureaucratic theories of political choice. It is, from many viewpoints, a surprising outcome. Not power, not interest groups, not voters, but some simple, even sensible, rules come to dominate – without explicit computation. Choice is apparently restricted by rules or norms too broadly shared to be noted but more restrictive then realized.

These rules seem to define sets of possible outcomes. The sets are generated by accepting minor deviations from a choice dictated by a strict application of the rule. Processual variations (e.g., in decision-process) may help determine which specific set is actually chosen. If only a few of the technically possible sets are normatively acceptable, as seems to be the case for college locations, the processes can explain only minor variations. The main patterns of the choices are better explained by focusing on how choice is restricted by norms.

In this case it would appear to be true that the system pursues a political solution within highly restrictive normative rules of equity. Although, as far as we know, no one in the system calculated anything approximating our weighted-distance criterion, the process constrained itself to solutions consistent with such a conception of fairness and need. In terms of distinction argued at the outset of the paper, our analysis indicates a case for treating decisions as explainable in terms of stable, structural elements in the situation, rather than in actions defining the apparent process of decision.

Use of the same apparent location rules over time indicates that the normative structure has remained relatively stable. The fact that the model performs relatively well over a period ranging from 1811 to 1970 suggests that the Norwegian normative context has remained remarkably stable. This stability is especially noteworthy when decisions are highly politicized. As the introduction indicates, this was the case for the district college decisions.

Democratic theories, interest-group theories, and decision-process theories focus attention primarily upon processes and procedures. Democratic theories stress voting or analogous procedures. Interest-group theories stress the dynamic interaction of groups in society and their use of resources to influence choices. Decision process theories stress the "micro" processes connected with the making of decisions. The elements in these classes of theories which are of primary importance for the substantial content of choice-preferences, interests, and goals do not constrain choice as norms do, rather they are motivations, pushes and drives. How and to what degree they will influence choice one cannot say until one has examined the way in which they are present in the process, i.e., examined the actions of the involved parties.

Theories focusing on actions and processes have gained currency in connection with the advent of behavioral and "realist" orientations. Without suggesting that we should abandon the obviously useful contributions to understanding of politics that has come from the "realist" and behavioral efforts of the past forty years, we argue the need for another perspective. The inherent ambiguity in interpretation of social and political events we suggest, is now being used, at least in Norway, to produce a systematic underestimation of the impact of concepts of equity and justice on the operation of the political system.[15]

NOTES:

* A slightly different version of this article appeared in European Journal of Political Research, 1, (1973), pp. 249—264.

1 District colleges are a new kind of educational institution in Norway. They offer instruction at a university level, but give shorter courses (2—3 years), and are not oriented toward research.

2 *Historisk statistikk, 1968* (Oslo: Statistisk Sentralbyrå, 1969) p. 611. *Statistisk årbok 1970* (Oslo: Statistisk Sentralbyrå, 1970) p. 301.

3 Innst. S. nr. 308 (1968—69), p. 594.

4 Per Karstensen, reported in *Stortingets forhandlinger 1969*, p. 4235.

5 It is the explanatory force of the theories that is of interest here, not their normative value. Thus, we do not intend to say that only democratic theories are "democratic".

6 This presentation primarily builds on Dahl (1956).

7 This presentation builds primarily on Truman (1960).

8 This presentation primarily builds on Feldman and Kanter (1965), and Cyert and March (1963), and Rosenau (1967).

9 This presentation builds primarily on Weber (1968), Peltason (1968), and Eckhoff and Jacobsen (1960).

10 The calculation proceeds as follows:

    (1) We identify the locations of existing colleges and universities.

    (2) We specify a single possible new location (any one).

    (3) We compute the weighted distance of a geographical unit from its *nearest* college (from among the set specified in 1 and 2). This is simply the product of the distance times the weight assigned to the unit.

    (4) We compute the total weighted distance of all geographical units from a *system* of college location (i.e., that specified by 1 and 2). This is simply the sum of step 3 over all geographical units.

(5) We replace the possible new location in step 2 with another possible location and repeat steps 2 and 4. We do this for *all* possible locations.

(6) We identify the *minimum weighted distance system* and select the new location that it includes.

(7) Steps 1 through 6 are repeated until the desired number of colleges have been located. The new college locations of the previous computation sequences are then located as existing (in step 1) in the subsequent sequences.

11 Two important points need some elaboration, however: Is the models' assignment of preferences reasonable, and do they predict according to the Rule. Regarding preferences, all four models assume that preferences are determined by geographical attachment, i.e., every individual prefers a district college in his own county. Considering the activities and expressed wishes of counties preceding the location decisions, these assignments of preferences do look reasonable. A drawback with fixing preferences in this way is, however, that we do not allow for coalitions.

The second requirement, that the models predict according to the procedure stated in the Rule, is satisfied for both power models. The two weighted distance models are more "dubious" in relation to this requirement, because the majority principle is modified by introducing distance. As this weighting precludes having all district colleges in the most densely populated parts of the country, it may be a way of securing the minorities' rights, an idea consistent with reasoning in democratic theories. With some assumptions that do not seem too unreasonable, these four models may be said to be consistent with democratic theories.

12 It seems reasonable to treat the counties as interest groups in this context, and their interests were clearly to get a district college for their own county. Most counties made claims upon the government in the connection.

The four models account for one of the clusters of variables (internal group characteristics) mentioned in the discussion of these theories, and in this cluster only one variable, financial resources. In this context it seems reasonable, because the counties look relatively equal with respect to those other characteristics, while with respect to financial resources, there are marked differences, however.

In the two weighted distance models, resources alone do not explain locations. The introduction of distance is, however, consistent with these theories. It may, in the perspective of these theories, be interpreted as a way of securing outcomes in accordance with the "rules of the game". Making these presumptions about other relevant factors, the four models are consistent with interest group theories.

13 We measure the distance between any two counties as the air distance between their most populous towns, and we assume the whole weight (of the different weighting schemes) are located in these towns.

14 The program used to compute weighted distance is shown in Appendix II. The measure of distance used here is road distance. We have run the program both with road and air distance without any significant differences. Because we lack data for several years on how many students each county has, it was necessary to make an estimate. We made this for each year by: (1) assuming that the same proportion of the total population in each county was students; and, (2) distributing the total number of students at universities and colleges between the counties according to (1). As we have data on total populations in the counties and the number of students at universities and colleges, the program could assign a specific number of students to each

county. For the period 1970–1990 we have projected student data (see *Innstilling om videreutdanning* I, Oslo 1966) p. 13.

15 For a Norwegian discussion of justice, see Eckhoff (1971); for an American, see Rawls (1971).

16 This program and the one presented in Appendix III were made by James G. March in collaboration with Michael D. Cohen.

Appendix I. Map of Norway

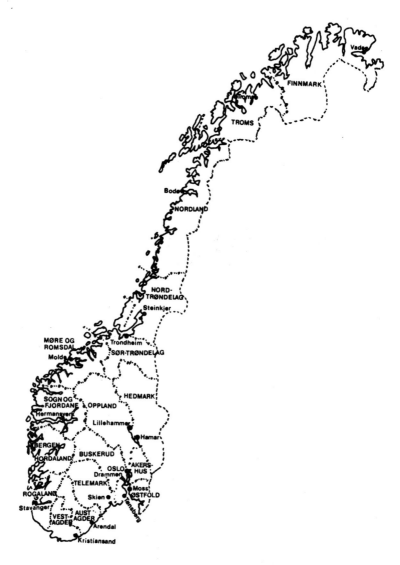

```
            *JOB   SOSIJK,RUN=FREE,KP=29,PAGES=100
 1                 DIMENSION IP(20),IAL(20),IDI(20,20),JTR(20,20),
                   BJWT(20,20),KTR(20,20),A(20),S(20),T(20),C(20)
 2     1000  FORMAT(20I1)
 3     1001  FORMAT(2(I2,1X))
 4     1002  FORMAT(10(I4,1X))
 5     1003  FORMAT(5(I7,1X))
 6                 READ (5,1001) N,M
 7                 READ (5,1000) (IAL(I),I=1,N)
 8                 DO 20 I=1,N
 9        20  READ (5,1002) (IDI(I,J),J=1,N)
10                 READ (5,1003) (IP(I),I=1,N)
11                 DO 999 IM=1,M
12                 DO 30 K=1,N
13                 DO 40 I=1,N
14                 IF (IAL(I).EQ.1) GO TO 50
15                 KTR(K,I)=1000000
16                 GO TO 40
17        50  KTR(K,I)=IDI(K,I)
18        40  CONTINUE
19        30  CONTINUE
20                 DO 35 I=1,N
21                 S(I)=1000000
22                 DO 45 K=1,N
23                 IF (KTR(I,K).GE.S(I)) GO TO 45
24                 S(I)=KTR(I,K)
25        45  CONTINUE
26        35  CONTINUE
27                 DO 37 I=1,N
28                 DO 39 K=1,N
29        39  JTR(I,K)=S(K)
30        37  CONTINUE
31                 DO 70 I=1,N
32                 DO 60 K=1,N
33                 IF(IAL(I).EQ.1) GO TO 70
34                 IF(IDI(I,K).GE.JTR(I,K)) GO TO 60
35                 JTR(I,K)=IDI(I,K)
36        60  CONTINUE
37        70  CONTINUE
38                 DO 80 I=/N
39                 DO 90 J=1,N
40        90  JWT(I,J)=JTR(I,J)*IP(J)
41        80  CONTINUE
42                 DO 100 I=1,N
43                 T(I)=0
44                 DO 110 J=1,N
45       110  T(I)=T(I)+JWT(I,J)
46       100  CONTINUE
47                 V=1000000000
48                 DO 120 J=1,N
49                 1F(T(J).GE.V) GO TO 120
50                 V=T(J)
```

221

```
51              IB=J
52         120  CONTINUE
53        1200  FORMAT(1H1,2X,19HNEW LOCATION NUMBER,2X,I2/)
54        1210  FORMAT(////2X,26HTOTAL NUMBER OF REGIONS IS,2X,I2/)
55        1220  FORMAT(//8X,6HREGION,2X,I2,2X,17HIS ALREADY FIXED/)
56        1230  FORMAT(//8X,11HALTERNATIVE,6X,23HSUM OF
                WEIGHTED TRAVEL /)
57        1240  FORMAT( 23X,I2,18X F10.0 )
58        1250  FORMAT(///2X,31HTUS THE NEW LOCATION IS
                REGION,2X,I2/)
59        1260  FORMAT(///8X,6HSCHOOL,6X,14HRELATIVE SIZE /)

60        1270  FORMAT( 10X,I2,15X,F4.2 )
61              WRITE(6,1200) IM
62              WRITE(6,1210) N
63              DO 200 I=1,N
64              IF(IAL(I).EQ.0) GO TO 200
65              WRITE(6,1220)J
66         200  CONTINUE
67              WRITE(6,1230)
68              DO 210 J=1,N
69         210  WRITE(6,1240) J,T(J)

70              WRITE(6,1250)IB
71              IAL(IB)=1
72              DO 214 I=1,N
73              V=1000000
74              DO212 J=1,N
75              IF(IAL(J).EQ.0) GO TO 212
76              IF(IDI(I,J).GE.V) GO TO 212
77              V=IDI(I,J)
78              A(I)=J
79         212  CONTINUE

80         214  CONTINUE
81              IF(IM.EQ.1.) GO TO 999
82              WRITE(6,1260)
83              DO 220 I=1,N
84              C(I)=0
85              DO 230 J=1,N
86              IF(A(J).NE.I) GO TO 230
87              C(I)=C(J)+IP(J)
88         230  CONTINUE
89         220  CONTINUE

90              W=0
91              DO 240 I=1,N
92         240  W=W+C(I)
93              DO 250 I=1,N
94              C(I)=C(I)/W
95         250  WRITE(6,1270)I,C(I)
96         999  CONTINUE
97              STOP
98              END
```

Symbols

N	= geographical units (alternatives). M = new locations.
IP (I)	= weight assigned to alternative I.
IAL (I) is	0 if alternative I does not have college, 1 if it has.
IDI (I,J)	= distance between alternatives I and J.

Appendix III. Program used under "Stress" assumption of weighted distance

```
        *JOB  SOSIJK,RUN=FREE,KP=29
1             DIMENSION KTP(20), LTP(20), IAL(20), A(20), S(20), B(20),
              BC(20), IP(20,75), IPS (20,75), IDI(20,20), IQ(20)
2             INTEGER A
3       1000  FORMAT(2(I3,1X))
4       1001  FORMAT(10(I4,1X))
5       1002  FORMAT(5(I7,1X))
6       1003  FORMAT (20I1)
7       1005  FORMAT(20(I2,1X))
8             READ(5,1000) KKL,N
9             READ(5,1005)(IQ(M),M=1,KKL)
10            READ (5,1001) (KTP(KK),KK=1,KKL)
11            READ(5,1001)(LTP(KK),KK=1,KKL)
12            LTPD=LTP(KKL)
13            KTPD=KTP(1)
14            LUT=LTPD—KTPD+1
15            DO 20 I=1,N
16        20  READ(5,1002)(IP(I,IT),IT=1,LUT)
17            DO 30 I=1,KKL
18        30  READ(5,1002)(IPS(IQ(I),IT),IT=1,LUT)
19            DO 40 I=1,N
20        40  READ(5,1001)(IDI(I,J), J=1,N)
21            DO 950 KK=1,KKL
22            READ(5,1003)(IAL(I),I=1,N)
23            DO 100 I=1,N
24            S(I)=1000000
25            DO 110 J=1,N
26            IF(IAL(J).EQ.O) GO TO 110
27            IF(IDI(I,J).GE.S(I)) GO TO 110
28            A(I)=J
29            S(I)=IDI(I,J)
30       110  CONTINUE
31       100  CONTINUE
32            KD1=KTP(KK)
33            KD2=LTP(KK)
34            IT=KD1—1896
35            DO 900 KT=KD1,KD2
36            IT=IT+1
37            XPST=0.0
38            XPT=0.0
39            DO 200 I=1,N
40            DO 210 J=1,KKL
```

```
41        210   IF(I.EQ.IQ.J)) GO TO 201
42              GO TO 200
43        201   XPST=XPST+IPS(I,IT)
44        200   XPI=XPT+IP(I,IT)
45              ST=O.
46              DO 300 I=1,N
47              XR=XPST/XPT
48        300   ST=ST+(S(I)*IP(I,IT)*XR)
49              DO 400 I=1,N
50              IF(IAL(I).EQ.O) GO TO 400
51              B(I)=IPS(I,IT)/XPST
52        400   CONTINUE
53              DO 500 I=1,N
54              IF (IAL(I).EQ.O) GO TO 500
55              C(I)=O.
56              DO 510 J=1,N
57              IF(A(J).NE.I) GO TO 510
58              C(I)=C(I)+IP(J,IT)
59        510   CONTINUE
60        500   CONTINUE
61              DO 600 I=1,N
62              IF (IAL(I).EQ.O) GO TO 600
63              C(I)=C(I)/XPT
64        600   CONTINUE
65        1100  FORMAT(6X,5HYEAR:,2X,I4,6X,7HSTRESS:,F10.0,
                B3X,5HUNIV.,3X,5HPRED.,3X,6HACTUAL)
66        1101  FORMAT(44X,I2,6X,F4.2,5X,F4.2)
67              WRITE(6,110) KT,ST
68              DO 700 I=1,N
69        700   IF (IAL(I).EQ.1) WRITE(6,1101) I,C(I),B(I)
70        900   CONTINUE
71        950   CONTINUE
72              STOP
73              END
```

Symbols

KKL	= colleges in last time period.
N	= alternatives (i.e., counties).
IQ (M),	identifies in which county(ies) the colleges are.
KTP,	starting year.
LTP,	stop in this year.
IP(I,IT)	= population in county I in time period IT.
IPS(IQ(I),IT)	= students at college in county I in time period IT.
IDI(I,J)	= distance between counties I and F.
IAL(I)	= 0 if county does not have college, 1 if it has.

11. Participation, Deadlines, and Choice

STEPHEN S. WEINER

Stanford University

11.0 Introduction

Organizational life within urban school districts in the United States is currently characterized by a heavy flow of problems and insistent demands that problems be resolved. In response to these conditions, conventional administrative theory tends to emphasize the identification of clear and consistent organizational goals and the creation of long-range plans as major ingredients in the remedy for the managerial woes of urban school districts. Above all, we are often informed, "management by crisis" must be avoided.

Yet, attempts to establish goals for urban school districts inevitably arrive at one of two destinations. On the one hand, goals may be highly abstract and vague and, thus, yield no guidance for implementation. On the other hand, goals may turn out to be specific but yet be ripped asunder and made inoperable by contending factions within the organization's political process. Similarly, efforts in such districts to create long term plans either are never initiated or, if begun, are likely to be ignored. If goal setting and long-range planning are impossible within some organizations, then the presence of crises may be an unavoidable aspect of decision making.

Urban school districts exhibit the basic characteristics of organized anarchy – vague and inconsistent goals, unclear technology, and fluid participation. Therefore, we will view decisions in such a context as a result of the confluence of four streams: choice opportunities, solutions, problems and participant energies (Cohen, March, and Olsen, 1972). In particular, our aim is to detect how these streams interact under crisis or deadline conditions.

A keener understanding of organizational response to deadlines should prove useful not only in providing retrospective explanations of the nature of decisions reached under deadline conditions, but also in providing guidance to individuals who are interested in the creative use of deadlines to affect participation in organizational choices and, hopefully to affect decisions themselves.

There can be no question that life in a school district prone to crisis is likely to erode seriously the energy of even the most dedicated leader. However, it may also be true that leadership within such organizations is possible. The very existence of crisis, and their accompanying deadlines, can create useful opportunities to move an organization in a direction deemed desirable by its leaders.

The existing theory of organized anarchies does not require that decisions be reached or problems solved by a specified time. By implication, the theory holds that such requirements are neither generated within the organization nor imposed by the organization's environment. The organization simply works on decisions until they are made.

However, when one observes the actual operation of organizations it becomes evident that organizational environments are not always indifferent as to whether organizations reach a given decision or resolve certain problems. Environmental impatience, at least some-times, results in deadlines being imposed upon the organization. Such deadlines serve as a cue to direct attention to those choices and problems subject to a deadline and divert attention away from choices and problems unaffected by deadlines.

Where an organization's goals are ambiguous, the nature of its processes in transforming inputs into outputs are unclear, and the probable reactions of its environment to a given decision are difficult to anticipate, it becomes difficult to determine which choices are "important" and which are "unimportant". In such organizational settings deadlines for decisions may provide a convenient substitute set of signals that enable decision makers to select current choice opportunities and problems that "deserve" immediate attention.

Like the choice opportunities to which they are applied, deadlines may be ambiguous for two reasons:

(1) Deadlines may be ambiguous with regard to the problems that must be considered in connection with a given choice.
(2) Deadlines may be ambiguous with regard to the date of the deadline. The effectiveness of deadlines as a cue for attracting the attention of organizational participants is drastically reduced by uncertainties associated with the date of the deadline, or the firmness of the date.

To be maximally effective as an attention cue the deadline must not only be certain, it must also be coercive. That is, compliance with a deadline is based upon incentives or sanctions involved in the deadline situation. The incentive may be a grant of resources and the sanctions may include denial of resources, public harassment for failure to comply, or the threat of imposing a decision in which the affected organization has not been consulted.

Deadlines are not an unusual feature of organizational life. Some deadlines are imposed by elements of the organization's environment; others may be created within the organization. Some deadlines are familiar and the organization's response to them may become quite routine. Other deadlines may be unanticipated by most, if not all, of the participants in a given organization. In this chapter we are concerned with the effects of deadlines that are both non-routine and are imposed externally.

11.1 The Case Study

We wish to inquire into the impact of a deadline upon participation rate and the flow of problems and solutions in an organizational decision-making situation. The inquiry is conducted within the context of the decision-making process within the San Francisco Unified School District concerning racial desegregation of the city's elementary schools. The history of this decision-making process permits us to examine the flow of problems, solutions and participant energy both before and after a deadline was imposed on the choice process.

11.1.0 *The Organizational Setting*

The San Francisco Unified School District was founded more than 100 years ago. It is currently responsible for the schooling of more than 80,000 children, between kindergarten and the twelfth grade, within the city of San Francisco.

The highest policy making body within the District is the Board of Education. At the time of the study described in this chapter, the Board was composed of seven members appointed by the Mayor of San Francisco.[1] The Superintendent of Schools is the chief executive officer of the District and is hired by the Board of Education. Three Associate Superintendents (Business, Administration, and Instruction) report to the Superintendent. In turn, eight Assistant Superintendents report to one of the Associate Superintendents. The twelve individuals who occupy the positions of Superintendent, Associate Superintendent, and Assistant Superintendent comprise the "top" decision-making group within the District's administrative hierarchy.

The District is a highly labor intensive enterprise. During the 1971–72 fiscal year personnel costs represented approximately 85 percent of the organization's $ 116 million operating budget.

In recent years the ethnic composition of the District's student body has been undergoing a significant change.

Table 11.0. Ethnic composition of San Francisco Public school enrollment

	1966 percent	1970* percent	1971* percent	Change 1966–71 percent
Black	26.3	28.3	30.0	+ 3.7
Spanish surname	12.1	13.3	13.8	+ 1.7
Chinese	13.6	14.9	13.9	+ 0.3
Filipino	2.2	4.1	5.9	+ 3.7
Japanese	1.7	1.8	1.8	+ 0.1
Korean	0.1	0.3	0.3	+ 0.2
American Indian	0.2	0.3	0.3	+ 0.1
Other non-white	1.3	1.9	2.2	+ 0.9
Other white	42.4	35.1	31.9	— 10.5
Total enrollment	91,359	87,363	80,896	— 11.4

*1970 statistics reflect enrollment before city-wide desegregation of elementary schools. 1971 statistics reflect enrollment after city-wide desegregation of elementary schools.

During the five year period between 1966 and 1971 the single most dramatic change in student enrollment was the decline of white enrollment from 42.4 percent to 31.9 percent. The declining proportion of enrollment represented by whites and the shrinking total enrollment means that the nuber of white students in the District, which stood at 38,774 in 1966, had declined to 25,805 in 1971 for an overall reduction of 33 percent in white enrollment in only five years.

As we shall see, the "flight" of white students from the San Francisco public schools, both through enrollment of children in private and parochial schools and the movement of families with school age children out of the city, proved to be a factor which influenced the nature of the desegregation plan which was ultimately adopted.

Changes in the ethnic composition of the District's administrative and teaching staff have failed to keep pace with changes in student enrollment. As of 1971, approximately 80 percent of the administrative and teaching staff was white, 10 percent was black and the other 10 percent were drawn from other minority groups.

11.1.1 Conflict Over Desegration

Throughout the decade of the 1960's desegregation of the District's student body represented the most controversial issue confronting the organization.

Although the District maintained no official policy requiring segregation of the races, the nature of residential patterns within the city meant that black students were largely concentrated in the Western Addition, Hunters Point, and Ocean View-Merced Heights-Ingleside areas; Latin or Spanish surname students largely attended schools in the Mission district and Chinese students were to be found primarily in schools serving the Chinatown area.

In 1961, several civil rights groups initiated demands that the District conduct a count of the students of various racial and ethnic groups in the schools so that the precise extent of segregation could be determined. In addition, these groups, including the National Association for the Advancement of Colored People (NAACP), asked that a citizen's committee be established by the Board of Education to consider steps that might be taken to desegregate the schools. These suggestions were largely ignored by the Board and the Superintendent, Dr. Harold Spears.

Under growing pressure the Board finally released a racial census of the schools in 1965. In 1966 the Board asked the Stanford Research Institute to examine alternative means of desegregating the schools.

Stanford Research Institute completed its work in 1967 and suggested twelve alternative desegregation plans. Among the alternatives were plans that provided for the "cross-town bussing" of white students in Western San Francisco into black ghetto areas in Eastern San Francisco. Stanford Research Institute also released the results of a survey of the San Francisco teaching staff that showed 51 percent of the teachers favoring retention of the neighborhood school system regardless of that system's implications for racial balance. Only 17 percent of the teachers favored bussing as a means of relieving racial imbalance.

In 1967 and 1968 civil rights advocates succeeded in persuading the Mayor of San Francisco, John Shelley, to appoint several new members of the Board of Education who favored racial desegregation. During this period Dr. Spears retired and the Board appointed Dr. Robert Jenkins, an educator well known for his previous efforts on behalf of school integration in other districts.

Early in 1968 Dr. Jenkins submitted recommendations on desegregation which were based, in part, on the Stanford Research Institute's proposals. Jenkins advocated the desegregation of some schools along with a simultaneous increase in resources and special programs for integrated schools, a concept he termed "educational equality-quality".

These proposals were submitted to a series of public forums in the District in early 1968. These forums were the most heavily attended meetings in the history of the District with attendance exceeding 1,000 in several cases. The meetings produced a tumultuous outpouring of sentiment opposed to any plan involving "cross-town" bussing. Chastened by the public opposition, the Board and Jenkins decided to create a citizens committee in the hope that a more acceptable plan could be devised.

During a year of deliberation the resulting Citizens Committee decided to propose a modified plan to create two elementary school "Complexes" in the northwest portion of the city. The Complex plan involved the enlargement of neighborhood school attendance areas and the initiation of localized bussing to integrate the schools in two sub-areas of the city, the Richmond and the Park-South. Only 20 percent of the city's elementary school students were to be involved. In order to make the plan more attractive, the expenditure of additional money on the affected schools was also proposed. Neither the all-white Sunset district, the center of opposition to bussing, nor the poorest ghetto area, Hunters Point, were involved.

The Board of Education withstood an onslaught of anti-bussing sentiment and authorized the initiation of the Richmond Complex for September, 1971. However, the gradual approach to integration angered the NAACP and, in the summer of 1970, that organization filed suit in the United States District Court asking for the immediate desegregation of all 102 elementary schools in San Francisco.

11.1.2 The Judge's Warning and District Response

In September, 1970 United States District Judge Stanley Weigel announced that the NAACP had submitted sufficient evidence to persuade him that the District had committed official acts that helped to maintain the segregation of black children in the elementary schools of the city. However, he added that unresolved cases then before the United States Supreme Court raised questions as to whether bussing was a permissible tool available to the courts to remedy school segregation. Weigel concluded that he would issue no order on behalf of desegregation until the Supreme Court acted on the pending cases. He added a warning that if the Supreme Court authorized the use of bussing he would require the desegregation of all elementary schools in San Francisco by September, 1971. Weigel urged the District to commence planning at once so that such an order could be implemented.

The District failed to respond to the Judge's request for an immediate beginning of desegregation planning. Four factors contributed to this lack of response:

First, although the District's steps toward desegregation had won the plaudits of some, they had also brought the wrath of many. Planning for additional desegregation held little promise of increasing public support for the schools.

Second, the District had initiated the Richmond Complex in the same month that Judge Weigel had issued his warning. The energies of the small corps of District staff that was both supportive of integration and skilled in the processes necessary to implement it were already fully absorbed in the Complex and the daily problems inherent in its first weeks of operation. Similarly, the energy of citizens who had worked for integration were devoted to the Complex.

Third, the District, which in past years had benefitted from healthy annual increases in property tax revenue, now found that increases in costs were outrunning increases in revenue. For the first time since the depression the District faced a very tight budget. Money could not be easily diverted into desegregation planning, especially since the fiscal year had already begun.

Fourth, Superintendent Robert Jenkins had resigned in the summer of 1970 and had been replaced by Dr. Thomas A. Shaheen. Shaheen had been in office for less than 60 days when Weigel made his announcement. Although personally committed to desegregation, Shaheen was busy with the myriad tasks inherent in assuming leadership in a large and complex organization.

In December, 1970 civil rights groups began to direct their attention to the District's lack of response to Weigel's warning. At a December Board meeting representatives of 13 civil rights groups demanded the immediate creation of a new citizen's committe to plan district wide desegregation. The Board directed Shaheen to prepare recommendations for action in January.

Unknown to the integration advocates the District's Business Office had begun to respond to at least one requirement for desegregation planning. The District did not have any data that linked the residence of students to their ethnic group. Nor did the District have the experience within their Data Processing office to exploit their computer facilities in a desegregation planning process. Anxious to use desegregation planning as a means to strengthen their capability to collect and analyze diverse types of data for a variety of planning purposes, the District hired a computer and planning consultant, David Bradwell. But the response of the Business Office was an exception. Elsewhere in the District the Judge's statement had failed to produce new activity.

The Superintendent's reply to the Board's December directive was constrained by three important factors. The District's Human Relations Office, created in 1963 as a concession to integration demands, did not have a reputation as an aggressive advocate for desegregation. There was considerable doubt that this existing entity could be used to mount a city wide integration plan. The only alternative was the creation of a new office. At the same time, experience in the Richmond Complex had demonstrated the need to involve central office staff, school site staff and citizens in the planning effort. There was no simple blueprint indicating how this might be accomplished. Finally, as already noted, the District had little slack in the budget and the money for planning effort had to be taken from the carefully husbanded Undistributed Reserve fund.

In late December, after informal consultation with the Board, Shaheen decided to appoint Donald Johnson, Planning Officer for the Richmond Complex, as Director of Desegregation, a new position. Throughout the balance of the fiscal year Johnson's only full time staff support was one secretary. Aside from office expenses, all of the other money in Johnson's new budget went to defray expenses in the separate Data Processing office where new student files had to be created and new computer programs written, and to pay for Bradwell's services.

Shaheen also recommended the creation of three committees to work with Johnson. The first, the Staff Committee, was appointed by the various divisions of the central office.

Examination of the minutes of the Staff Committee's meetings reveals that this committee fully expected to be the key architect of the desegregation plan. Such an expectation was consistent with past practice in the District where major policy recommendations were brought to the Board as a result of consultation in the central office with little or no input from school site administrators, teachers, parents, or community groups.

Although each member of the Staff Committee was ostensibly appointed to work on desegregation on a full time basis, in fact each staff member was not relieved of his other duties. Partly because of the press of other duties, the Staff Committee proved to be a group that merely met periodically to hear reports from the Data Processing Office and Bradwell. Due to its inactivity it had no discernible impact on the outcome of the planning process.

The second group, the Certificated Staff Committee, was composed of teachers and school site administrators. Money was provided to pay for substitutes for these individuals only on one afternoon per week.

Members of the Certificated Staff Committee were not well known to one another before appointment to this group. They were selected from different schools in the District. The geographical separation of the members and the lack of pre-existing ties among the membership led to an absence of informal consultation between their regularly scheduled meetings. After an initial spurt of weekly meetings, the Certificated Staff Committee met less and less frequently until shortly before the deadline. This Committee proved to be even more peripheral to the planning process than did the Staff Committee.

The lack of effective participation from the Certificated Committee may have been due in part to a policy adopted by the Citizens Advisory Committee (see below). The Citizens Advisory Committee (CAC) invited members of the Certificated Staff Committee to become active on CAC committees. Thus, the handful of Certificates Staff members with time and energy to expend were diverted into CAC meetings and had correspondingly less time for meetings of the Certificated Staff.

The third group, the Citizens Advisory Committee, became the prime instrument in the decision making process. Composed of 67 citizens appointed by members of the Board of Education, the CAC began its formal meetings later than either of the other two committees. A further delay occurred when the CAC voted during its second meeting to dissolve itself on the grounds that its ethnic composition did not reflect the ethnic composition of the District's student enrollment in that whites were "over-represented" on the committee.

In mid-March of 1971 the CAC was able to elect officers and to establish subcommittees.

11.1.3 Deadline and Response

On April 28, 1971 Judge Weigel ordered both the District and the NAACP to prepare separate plans for the desegregation of elementary school students in San Francisco. The Judge's order came one week after the United States Supreme Court had approved bussing as one means to remedy officials acts of discrimination against children from racial minority groups. The Judge set June 10, 1971 as the deadline for submission of both plans.[2]

In his order the Judge also required that the plans to be submitted to him must also outline steps to relieve segregation in the school staffs.

However, the Judge declined to set forth a numerical formula that would define desegregation of the schools.

Thus, as often is the case in governmental organizations, the District was directed to "do something" about segregation in the absence of any clear definition of what would constitute a satisfactory solution. The ambiguous order from the Judge left a good deal of flexibility to the District's internal decision making processes both in terms of defining the problems to be considered and in constructing a solution to those problems.

Prior to the judicially imposed deadline the response of the District and its three committees had been largely one of delay and indecision. The one exception to this characterization was the initial data collection efforts of the Data Processing office.

The response to the deadline included substantial changes in the flow of participation, the generation of solutions and the flow of problems.

11.1.4 *Flow of Participation*

The imposition of the deadline caused an immediate increase in the amount of time that an active participant in decision making had to expend on the choice process.

One measure of the increase in time expenditure is the fact that between February 16, 1971, the date of the first meeting of the Citizens Advisory Committee, and April 28, 1971, the date that the deadline was set, there were 25 meetings of the full committee or its subcommittees. In the pre-deadline period the Citizens Committee and its subcommittees thus averaged a meeting every third day. Between April 28 and June 2, the day that the Citizens Committee completed work on the plan, there was a total of 45 committee or subcommittee meetings for an average of more than one meeting per day.

A major feature of participant reaction to the deadline was that the participation rate of a small group increased dramatically whereas the participation rate of most members either remained stable or declined.

Table 11.1. Rates of participation by CAC members (Hours/month) before and after imposition of the deadline

Month	Participants				
	Less than 20 hrs./mo.	20–40 hrs./mo.	40–60 hrs./mo.	60–80 hrs./mo.	More than 80 hrs./mo.
March (pre-deadline)	64	0	2	1	0
April (pre-deadline)	57	3	1	5	1
May (post-deadline)	52	5	1	2	7

The data in Table 11.1 indicates that one effect of the deadline was to widen the gap in participation rates between the highly active minority and the largely passive majority within the Citizens Advisory Committee.

As noted earlier, the Citizens Committee had voluntarily disbanded in February so that the Board of Education might appoint additional minority members to eliminate "over-representation" by whites on the Committee. The imposition of the deadline, however, foreclosed full participation in the decision making by those who where unable because of work or other commitments to expand their rate of participation. Thus, the deadline led to a domination of the decision making process by middle and upper class white women, who had available time during the day because they were not employed and could arrange care for their children, and by other participants whose employers permitted them to devote daytime hours to the decision making process.[3] Table 11.2 compares the ethnic composition of the Citizens Advisory Committee, the 39 CAC members present when the final plan was adopted on June 1, 1971 and the ethnic composition of the most active twelve members of the Committee, as judged by a sample of Committee members and measured by meeting attendance data:

Table 11.2. Ethnic composition of the Citizens committee and the most active twelve members of the committee

	Percentage		
	Full Committee	June 1 vote	Active Members
White	37.0	51.2	66.7
Black	25.5	17.9	0.0
Chinese	10.5	12.8	8.3
Latin	13.5	5.2	16.6
Japanese	3.0	5.2	0.0
Filipino	6.0	5.2	8.3
Korean	1.5	2.6	0.0
Samoan	1.5	0.0	0.0
American Indian	1.5	0.0	0.0
	100.0	100.1	99.9

Interviews with members of the Committee, representing a cross section of activity levels, indicates that the expansion of energy expenditures was governed by the time available to the individual participant (and hence the nature of competing demands upon the participant's time); whether the individual participant possessed knowledge necessary to participate in the complex mapping process inherent in desegregation planning; and by the participant's attitude toward desegregation and bussing.

Interviews with black members of the Committee who were not active participants revealed that their lack of participation was due primarily to competing demands for their time. Black CAC members were in sympathy with the objective of desegregating the schools, including bussing. Some black members who were not active declared that it was not necessary for them to participate because the CAC "was in good (white integrationist) hands". Some black interviewees also expressed a measure of discomfort at participating because members of CAC had a detailed grasp of desegregation planning, and thus were far more knowledgeable or because the blacks were not familiar with parliamentary procedure.

235

On the other hand, interviews with Latin members of the Committee who were not active participants indicated that their lack of participation was due both to competing demands for their time as well as a basic hostility to the idea of bussing children to desegregate the schools.

Several Latin interviewees said that they sensed that the CAC was dominated by advocates of bussing and that the needs of Latin children, especially the need for bilingual instruction, would not be addressed by the CAC.[4] Thus, inactivity by Latins on the CAC was due, in part, to a desire to deprive the pro-bussing CAC of the "legitimacy" it might have gained had Latins participated more vigorously.[5] Similarly, the two inactive Chinese members of the CAC were individuals who actively participated in anti-bussing protests.

The theory of organized anarchies predicts that participation will be affected by the time requirements of a particular choice opportunity and by the relative attractiveness of other choice opportunities for individual participants. However, the theory does not call attention to the impact upon participation rates that arises from individual attitudes concerning the legitimacy of the decision that may emerge from the choice process.

Interviews with members of the Board, the Superintendent, Associate Superintendents, Assistant Superintendents and members of CAC, and examination of internal memoranda written by top District officials during the period September 1970–June 1971 indicate that none of the District's top officials devoted any significant amount of time to directing or influencing the planning for desegregation during this period.

Based upon the organization's experience of the prior ten years it was obvious that the nature of the final plan for district wide desegregation of 50,000 elementary school children would have a profound impact upon the future of the District. How do we account for the lack of attention by top decision makers to this supremely important decision making process?

We speculate that three elements contributed to this surprising inattention to desegregation.

First, as already noted, desegregation was a policy question fraught with complexity and in which the possibility of adverse public reaction existed at every step. It was not an arena into which a prudent District official would voluntarily cast himself.

Second, although the Judge's warning was clear, the final issuance of a desegregation order was contingent upon future decisions of the Supreme Court. Those decisions were not rendered until the latter part of April, 1971. Until that time it was entirely possible that energy devoted to district-wide desegregation planning could be obviated by a stroke of the Supreme Court's pen.

Third, and we believe this reason is central, the District was beset by a veritable nightmare of other crises and catastrophes beween September, 1970 and June, 1971. No sketch of these events can adequately portray the turmoil they caused. Here, however, are the major troubles and decisions which the District faced between September, 1970 and June, 1971:

A. In September, 1970 teachers and parents boycotted the Sir Francis Drake school in Hunters Point because the school was in an acute state of disrepair. The boycott lasted ten days and ended after the Superintendent agreed that a male, black principal would be hired at the school.

B. In October over 600 teachers appeared at a meeting of the Board of Education to protest the District's alleged failure to implement "quality" educational programs in the Richmond Complex. This protest followed a petition, signed by 1700 teachers and administrators, which condemned "large class sizes" and other ills in the schools.

C. In October students and teachers boycotted classes at Woodrow Wilson High School after a Samoan student had been shot at the predominantly black school.

D. In November the District's bond issue designed to finance the rebuilding of schools in Hunters Point was defeated by the voters.

E. An anti-bussing group initiated a school boycott in the Richmond Complex in November.

F. In December the major Latin-American organization in the city, the Mission Coalition, sued the District for "short-changing" 13 schools in the Mission District.

G. In the same month 200 angry teachers walked out of a Board meeting after the Board had refused to promise to rehire 64 of the teachers for the next semester.

H. In December the Board was informed that it would have to cancel plans to build either the Diamond Heights High School or Cabrillo Elementary School unless it could appropriate an additional $1.5 million for construction. These schools had been part of a 1964 bond issue and it had taken six years to get the projects out to bid. In the interim construction costs had inflated tremendously.

I. In January, 1971 100 members of the Elementary School Administrators Association attended a meeting to discuss affiliation with the Teamsters Union. This meeting was held in the aftermath of debate over state legislation to deprive San Francisco school administrators of tenure in their jobs. San Francisco is the only school district in California that provides tenure for school administrators.

J. In January the Board learned they faced a $6.7 million deficit in their budget for the next fiscal year. This constituted the most severe financial crisis since the Depression.

K. In the same month hundreds of students picketed and boycotted at several schools to protest the transfer of popular administrators due to the operation of the tenure system.

L. In February the Superintendent presented a plan to decentralize the District into three administrative areas. The Board refused to adopt the plan.

M. In February the Black Student Union began a protest at Balboa High School. Investigators reported no toilet paper, towels or soap in the boy's restrooms; absence of hot water in the girl's showers; leakage of water from the showers on to cafeteria tables; and replacement of windows with plywood. Rehabilitation costs were estimated at $3.8 million.

N. In the same month State Supreme Court Justice Mosk charged that 40 percent of the Chinese speaking students in San Francisco weren't receiving instruction in the English language in San Francisco schools.

O. In March the Superintendent proposed the demotion of more than half of the school administrators in the District. The Board voted to demote only white administrators, exempting racial minorities from the plan.

P. In March the American Federation of Teachers began a strike affecting all schools in the city. The local chapter of the California Teachers Association later joined in the strike. The walk out extended into April.

Q. In April the Superintendent presented his budget. Due to the lack of new revenue the budget proposed that 340 teaching positions be left vacant as a result of attrition and urged the elimination of 120 "relief" teachers currently employed so that other teachers could have a preparation period during the school day. As a result of the strike settlement a 5 percent increase in school taxes was proposed.

R. In the same month a leading structural engineer reported that a major earthquake would lead to disaster in the schools. An Associate Superintendent announced that he would recommend immediate closing of five of 63 unsafe schools.

S. In late April Federal Judge Weigel ruled that the District had less than 50 days to submit a plan for the complete desegregation of 102 elementary schools.

T. In May school administrators sued to retain their jobs and state hearings on the demotions were begun.

U. In late May a petition drive was opened to replace the appointed school board with an elected body.

Thus, before the imposition of the deadline Board members and top administrative officials were occupied with a heavy flow of other problems and choices. And, as noted above, before the imposition of the deadline some uncertainty existed as to the necessity for devising a city-wide desegregation plan.

Once the deadline was established the flow of competing problems persisted. In addition, a top administrative official who wished to inject himself into the desegregation planning process would have found himself in the midst of a complex and time-consuming decision making process that was already the subject of attention by highly active members of the CAC who had developed a sense of ownership concerning the desegregation planning process.[6]

The experience in San Francisco of federal consultants on desegregation is instructive in terms of the difficulty of gaining entrance to the decision making process under deadline conditions. In response to the San Francisco Superintendent's request to the United States Office of Education for assistance with desegregation, USOE dispatched a team consultants in late May, 1971. These consultants attempted to become involved in the planning process but were ignored by the local school staff and the CAC. Apparently, the federal consultants failed to gain entrance because of the shortness of the time deadline and the time commitments of the existing participants did not permit diversion of energy to brief the consultants on prior developments. In addition, the past experience of the federal consultants in the South disposed them to advocate a desegregation plan that required the bussing of children across the city. Such an approach was deemed unacceptable by the active CAC members. The experience of the federal consultants was a duplicate of the fate met by a consultant from the California Department of Education who had been dispatched to San Francisco earlier in May.

11.1.5 Generation of Solutions

Imposition of the deadline led to the generation of more than two dozen different plans to desegregate the schools. These plans were generated in May, 1971 by a self-selected group of participants termed the "Round the Clock" group. This group was present during the day and evening at the school district headquarters during May. Although some members of the District staff were a part of this group, the majority of members were drawn from the Citizens Committee. Again, the active citizens who dominated this process were largely drawn from the ranks of white women on the full Committee. Several of these women brought long experience in the politics of desegregation planning to their task in May. In addition, their intensive participation in the Round the Clock group sharpened their knowledge of the distribution of various ethnic groups throughout the city and afforded them detailed knowledge of the subtle differences among the many plans then being suggested. The overwhelming competence of these women in the planning process discouraged participation by others, particularly from minority groups, who felt themselves at a severe relative disadvantage in their knowledge of the complexities of planning for desegregation.

Unlike the professional planners on the District staff who were immobilized by lack of data and formal criteria for a plan, the white women were able to devise zonal maps for desegregation based upon their impressionistic grasp of ethnic composition and attitudes toward bussing in various San Francisco neighborhoods.

The generation of alternative plans was guided by only one formal criteria for desegregation adopted by the Citizens Committee five days after the deadline was imposed. This standard, originally suggested by the State Department of Education, defined a school as desegregated if the proportion of any ethnic group within that school was within 15 percent of the proportion of that ethnic group within the school enrollment of the entire district.[7] This criterion for planning was adopted before its full implications for a student assignment plan were understood. Adoption of the state guideline was later to be regretted by some members of the Committee because it foreclosed the possibility of adopting a plan that might have been met with greater acceptance among vocal opponents of bussing in the Chinatown area.

In addition to the state guidelines the other major premises that shaped the planning process resulted from the "lessons" of the recent history of desegregation conflict as perceived by the active white women on CAC.

The first "lesson" was that a Citizens Committee was an effective device for formulating desegregation plans. Belief in the effectiveness of using citizens committees was based largely on the success of the earlier citizens committee in promoting "school complexes".

The second "lesson" was that a desegregation plan that appeared to require "cross-town" bussing would prove to be politically unacceptable and would only stimulate additional white flight from the schools. This lesson was accepted by most of the active white women on the CAC as a result of their experience at the 1968 public forums. As noted earlier, thousands of San Franciscans attended these emotional rallies of resistance to "cross-town" bussing. Several individuals had been subjected to physical harassment and assault at these meetings and the result was the intimidation of integration advocates at the forums. Thereafter, integrationists in San Francisco were convinced that advocacy of "cross-town" bussing could only aggrevate racial tensions and defeat any form of desegregation.

As a result, of the 15 percent guidelines and avoidance of "cross-town bussing" the final "Horseshoe" plan adopted by the Committee on June 1, 1971, emphasized the creation of seven zones in the city in an effort to minimize "cross-town bussing" and to give the public the impression that the integration plan was merely enlarging the boundaries of neighborhood school attendance areas. In addition, the Horseshoe plan made only token alternations in the two Complex areas that had already been established. Protection of the Complexes was a product both of strong representation on the Committee by residents of the Complexes and a persistent lobbying campaign by parents and staff members within the Complexes. Thus, the Horseshoe plan strongly reflected the lessons of experience learned by desegregation advocates in the prior ten years.

Bradwell, the state and federal consultants, and several members of the District's professional staff advanced an alternative plan that would have subdivided the city into only three zones. The alternative, called "Tri-Star" violated the "lessons of experience" by appearing to require longer bus rides and by requiring the mixture of children from the centers of opposition to bussing, the Sunset and Chinatown, with students from the black ghetto in Hunters Point. The professional planners urged adoption of "Tri-Star" because it assured more thorough racial and socio-economic integration of the schools while permitting better utilization of the school's physical capacities. Until the end of the planning process the professionals refused to accede to the arguments raised by white members of the Round the Clock group that the Tri-Star plan involved unacceptable political risks. The Citizens Committee turned the Tri-Star plan aside and adopted Horseshoe instead.[8]

The dispute over "Horseshoe" and "Tri-Star" is but one example of the conflict that existed between the "professionals" and the "citizens". We now turn to that conflict and its relation to the process of generating solutions.

In the latter part of 1970 and the early months of 1971 David Bradwell, members of the District's Data Processing staff, and desegregation consultants from the California Department of Education ("the professionals") proposed and pursued a rational model for decision making concerning desegregation in San Francisco.

These planners proposed the following sequence of steps:

1) all relevant data bearing upon desegregation to be collected,
2) clear, consistent, operational criteria for a "best" plan be established,
3) that all feasible alternatives for a plan be examined,
4) finally, that a choice among the alternatives be guided by the state criteria.

The professionals were frustrated and angered by the CAC's failure to cooperate in the implementation of the rational model. Part of the failure to implement the rational model is attributable to a lack of data.[9] But, more fundamentally, the rational model proved to be inconsistent with the nature of the decision making process that the professionals sought to affect.

The rational model required a stable definition of the choice to be resolved. But the decision making process produced a fluctuating number of problems accociated with the choice. Participants in the ACA brought the issues of bilingual instruction, new techniques of innovative education, secondary school desegregation and integration with suburban school districts to the choice process. The instability of the definition of the choice to be resolved is further elaborated in our subsequent discussion of problem flow.

The rational model also required clear and consistent criteria; but the process did not provide them. CAC members unwilling to state criteria for plan selection unless and until the implications of those criteria for specific neighborhoods became clear. The complex nature of the process of drawing zonal boundaries in a desegregation plan meant those implications were far from obvious. In the one instance where the CAC adopted a clear criterion, the 15 percent rule, the committee later found, that this critenon interferred with their ability to draw a plan that would have helped reduce opposition to bussing expressed by representatives of Chinatown. Representatives of other school communities, such as the West Portal area, who served on CAC were unwilling to consent to abstract criteria until the details of a plan adhering to those criteria were established.

In addition, some of the criteria considered crucial by some white participants would have created tension in the CAC had they been publically announced. White members of CAC did not feel they were in a position to publicly announce their desire that the desegreation plan not embrace "cross-town" bussing or involve other features that would spur white flight from the schools. Such sentiments might have been viewed as "anti-black" by black members of CAC. The whites who were concerned about white backlash also considered themselves to be friends of the black community and did not wish to be the target for black criticism.

242

Finally, the rational model required the derivation of a solution from the criteria. Contrary to the expectations of the professionals, solutions existed before the criteria and data were available. In particular, white women on the CAC produced a number of plans before either criteria or extensive data were available.

Frustrated by a decision making process that they viewed as irrational and parochial, the professionals sought at the last moment, in late May, to advance the "Tri-Star" plan. This plan, although it met technical criteria important to the planners, also opened the possibility for extensive "cross-town" bussing. Tri-Star was defeated in the final vote taken by the Committee. Each of the outside consultants ultimately came to view the CAC process with both bewilderment and bitterness.[10]

11.1.6 *The Flow of Problems*

The theory of organized anarchy views the stream of problems entering or leaving an organization as a flow that is independent of the other streams of choices, solutions and energy. Thus, the flow of problems are seen as "disembodied"-problems move in a fashion that is unaffected by the movement of people.

The theory holds, further, that problems move autonomously among choice opportunities in a search for a choice process in which the problem can be resolved.

Analysis of the case study suggests several modifications of the theory:

Problem movement can be seen as intertwined with the movement of people. That is, problems are carried to and from choice opportunities by participants. However, within the context of a given choice, a problem may be exercised or activated by participants other than its original carrier.

Problems may move of their volition but they are also subject to ejection from a choice opportunity. Under deadline conditions the movement of a problem away from a choice opportunity may occur in one of two ways:

(1) The problem leaves with its carrier. As noted earlier, the time requirements of participating in a decision under deadline constraints may become substantially greater than the time requirement under non-deadline conditions. If a specific problem carrier cannot meet these higher time demands then he may choose to withdraw entirely from the choice process. Unless other participants share his concern with a given problem, then the problem will depart with its carrier.

(2) The problem departs followed by its carrier. Under deadline

conditions a participant who is busy elsewhere may not choose to withdraw entirely but to participate in a given choice on a part-time basis – he or she is present part of the time and absent part of the time. The possibility then arises that a problem of concern to the part-time participant is activated when its carrier is absent. In such instances other participants may decide to exclude the problem from further consideration because none of those present are willing to expend energy in resolving it. Its carrier will subsequently discover exclusion of his or her problem and, therefore, may withdraw entirely from the choice because it is no longer dealing with a problem of interest to the participant. Alternatively, a problem may be excluded by some formal decision (e.g., through voting), or given such low priority that the carrier leaves the choice.

The foregoing view of the interaction between problems and participation relies on an assumption that participants may be attracted to a choice both of desires to complete choices and by desires to raise and solve problems. This contrasts with the assumption used in the theory wherein participants are only attracted to a choice because of a desire to complete a choice.

These aspects of the theory may be illustrated by specific reference to the San Francisco study. The flow of problems with respect to the choice opportunity can be characterized as follows:

Table 11.3. Flow of problems with respect to the desegregation choice opportunity

Problem	Problem carrier	Date at which problem became intertwined or disengaged from desegregation
Socio-economic integration of schools	Superintendent Shaheen	February, 1971
Administrative decentralization of district	Superintendent Shaheen	Plan proposed in February. Killed by the school board in the same month.
Integration with suburban school districts	One member of the school board and one member of the Citizens Committee	February, 1971
Including school "innovations" in desegregation plan	Several members of the Citizens Committee	March and April
Strengthening bi-lingual programs in the District	Chinese and Latin members of the Citizens Committee	March
Desegregating secondary schools	Citizens Committee	April

244

Forecasting student migration and future enrollment	David Bradwell	December, 1970
Developing bussing policy and setting up bussing office	Member of CAC and Desegregation Office	April
Setting guidelines for minority hiring	Minority members of CAC	April

Eight of the above problems were still interwined with the desegregation planning process when the deadline was set by Judge Weigel. Consideration of five of the problems, socio-economic integration, integration with suburban schools, school innovations, desegregating secondary schools, and forecasting future enrollment, ceased shortly after the deadline was imposed. The first four problems had been brought to the choice opportunity by individuals who were expending only small amounts of energy on desegregation planning. In the fifth case, forecasting student enrollment, Bradwell's energy was absorbed elsewhere during the month of May.

Three of the eight problems, bilingual education, minority hiring, and setting bussing guidelines, had all been brought to the choice opportunity by individuals who expended a great deal of energy after the deadline was set.

Thus, the nature of the problems considered as part of the final desegregation plan appears to have been more dependent upon the energy expended upon them by interested participants rather than upon any rational definition of the problems that "should" have been considered in the planning process.

11.2 Summary of Theoretical Implications

The theory of organized anarchies suggests a choice opportunity is a passive receptacle for solutions, problems and participant energy; that a choice has permeable boundaries such that solutions, problems and participants may move into and away from the choice at their own volition; and that a choice will benefit from the energy of participants not already absorbed by other choices.

The San Francisco study stimulates a view of the flows of problems, solutions, and energy, when the choice is subject to a deadline, that varies from the theoretical predictions. Problems and solutions, on the one hand, and participants, on the other hand, are intertwined. Problems and solutions are carried by participants. Deadline conditions erect a barrier (due to time requirements and the relative competence of active participants in the deadline choice) around the choice that resists the entrance of new problems and participants. Deadline conditions cause a dramatic increase in the energy that must be devoted to the choice by active participants. Participants are forced to either withdraw from other obligations to stay "on top" of the deadline choice or become partially or totally inactive in the deadline choice. Thus, for active deadline participants, time contributed to the choice is not freely given but is largely coerced. As a result of the partial or total withdrawal of some participants, some problems will be ejected from the choice.

This altered view of the behavior within a choice process under deadline may be seen as the consequence of three effects: A garbage ejection effect; an energy conservation effect; and a competence multiplier.

A choice opportunity, before a deadline is imposed, can be viewed as a garbage can into which various kinds of problems and solutions are dumped as they are generated. The choice opportunity behaves as a passive receptacle. However, once a deadline is imposed certain problems and solutions are ejected from the garbage can.

It appears that the *garbage ejection process* is initiated as the result of a comparison by participants between the amount of energy that would be required to solve all the problems they have accepted and the amount of energy it then appears they will be able to apply to the choice opportunity before the deadline. If such a comparison leads to a conclusion by participants that they have accepted more problems than they can handle, then the participants actively undertake to eject some of the problems they had previously accepted. Thus, energy deficit calculations appear to be essential elements of the garbage ejection process under deadline conditions.

Under deadline conditions, where problem "overload" exists, choice opportunities change from a passive mode of receiving problems into an active mode of excluding some problems from consideration, thus setting the excluded problems adrift either to be considered elsewhere in the organization or to flow out of the organization entirely.

The garbage ejection process proceeds in a manner that *conserves energy*. It retains those problems that have attracted participants who are willing and able to spend substantial energy on the choice opportunity. In the case study none of the "garbage" ejected from the decision making process was associated with participants who evinced high participation rates. Each of the problems ejected from the garbage can under deadline conditions had received lip service but no substantial energy expenditure by a participant.

Thus, it would appear that the garbage ejection process functions in a fashion independent of any rational definition of the problems that must be resolved by the choice, but rather in a way that conserves high energy expenditures on the choice. Participants in the choice process are content to allow certain problems to remain after a deadline is imposed if such problems can "pay their own way" through attracting participants with time to spend on them.

Before the imposition of the deadline modest variations appear in the energy contributions of participants. These modest variations in participation rates are associated with differences in levels of competence, with those participants having competency in current problems and solutions tending to be somewhat more active than other participants.

The effect of the deadline is not only to eject some "garbage" from the garbage can but also to concentrate attention upon the problems that remain for consideration. Those participants who are able to expand their participation rates do so and dramatic differences quickly appear between those who are most actively involved and the balance of participants.

The tendency for the most active participants to spend greater energy on the choice is reinforced by two things. The first is the fact that they are relatively free of other obligations and thus are able to spend large amounts of time on decision making. The second is the fact that as high participation rates continue the most active members become a relatively small group possessing a near monopoly position concerning the competencies required in decision making.

The joint operation of these factors constitutes a positive feedback loop where activity causes greater competence and greater competence leads to increased activity. The total effect of this feedback process quickly cumulates along both dimensions of activity and competence leading to what we describe as the *competence multiplier*.

Thus, one effect associated with the sharply increased participation rates by some participants in the choice is that the most active participants gain a much higher share of the competence and experience necessary to deal with the remaining problems. As they become substantially more competent it becomes more difficult for other potential participants to gain access to the decision making process.

11.3 Conclusion

Our study of decision making on desegregation within the San Francisco Unified School District illustrates several key respects in which traditional models of organizational decisions fail to describe accurately the processes within an organized anarchy: Operational criteria for a "good" decision either do not exist or are not widely shared among participants in the decision making process. Data essential to even a rudimentary understanding of the impact of various decision alternatives is often missing or garbled. The definition of the problems to be solved within the context of the decision is not stable; problems flow to the choice opportunity and flow away from it largely in response to concerns that are being generated within and without the organization; as a function of the relative attractiveness of other choices; and as a function of the time constraints imposed upon a given choice. Deadline conditions lead to the emergence of several distinctive alternations in the flow of problems and participation: garbage ejection, energy conservation and the multiplication of competence.

What tactical advice to participants in organized anarchies can be distilled from these observations? We believe that these major rules for administrative leadership present themselves:[11]

(1) Distract the opposition. Participants within an organization have limited attention and energy. Therefore, rational actors should seek to assign their opponents on a given issue to work on competing issues. If other issues are not under debate, then create some as an alternative object for the energy of your enemies.

(2) Be selective in your ambitions. A participant in an organized anarchy must be modest in the number of decisions he seeks to mold at any given time. There are limitations on the energy of your opponents, but there are limitations on the time of your allies as well.

(3) Impose deadlines judiciously. The legitimacy of decisions, and thus their prospects for implementation, depend upon perceptions that "all sides" have been heard and represented in the decision making process. Therefore, committees and task forces should ordinarily contain both allies and opponents. But the ability of committee members actually to participate in a given decision depends upon the time each individual must spend on alternative choices and time requirements of the choice you wish to shape. Impose an unexpected and short deadline when your allies on a given committee have time available and your opponents are hard pressed elsewhere. Extend and relax deadlines when your allies are busy elsewhere and your opponents have the luxury of concentrating on the choice that is vital for you. When you are unable to impose deadlines, seek the cooperation of others (courts, the press, pressure groups) in creating them. Thus, from your perspective, some decisions may be "better" if they can benefit from more planning, others will be better if they are deprived of planning time.

(4) Use your friends in the environment as a resource. In low

technology organizations outsiders may possess, as much expertice as insiders. This means that advisory committees composed, either in part or in total, of outsiders can be used to expand the ranks of your allies within the decision making process. In an organized anarchy that is over-loaded with problems, the significance of formal position for the outcome of decisions is depressed and the significance of time availability is accentuated. If your friends on the outside have time available, use it.

If our description of the process of decision in an organized anarchy is correct, such rules may have some modest validity. Certainly, the course of events leading to the desegregation procedure in the San Francisco schools suggests that organizational leadership involves the careful management of scarce attention and energy as much as it does the exercise of decision skills.

NOTES:
1 In November 1971 the voters in San Francisco approved an amendment to the City Charter creating an elective school board. The new Board was elected in June 1972 and took office in August 1972.
2 Johan Olsen has pointed out that Judge Weigel was a unique participant in the planning process inasmuch as he was able to substantially affect the decision merely by issuing written orders. The Judge did not have to attend any meetings during the choice process nor did he have to expend substantial energy as did other participants who affected the final outcome.

The Judge's influential position depended upon the acceptance of his authority by the other participants. With the exception of Chinatown residents, none of the groups opposed to bussing even suggested that the Judge's order be disobeyed.

Acceptance of the Judge's order was dependent upon socialization of the citizenry into the American system of law. Residents of Chinatown, many of them recent immigrants from Hong Kong, did not accept the Judge's authority and openly demanded that Weigel simply be ignored.

The order came as a welcome relief to long time advocates of school desegregation in San Francisco. After a decade of controversy, these advocates finally had the strong shield of the federal judiciary behind which they could plan a city-wide integration plan.

It is interesting to note that the Judge himself became a victim of the deadline he set. When the District and NAACP plans were submitted to the Court in June 1971 the Judge admitted that he was overwhelmed by the details and complexity of the plans. However, the Judge did not have the time to carefully review each plan in detail because of the self-imposed necessity to implement the plans in September.
3 Interviews with the white women who dominated the planning process indicate that their participation was motivated not only by a desire to participate in decisions that affected the future school assignment of their own children and by an ideological commitment to civil rights but also by a desire to exercise untapped organizational skills. For many of these women,

participation in school district affairs became an outlet for existing personal competencies that ranged beyond the skills required of a homemaker and wife.

4 In fact, CAC had established an active Bilingual Subcommittee that made strong recommendations for the expansion of the school district's bilingual program, including added services for Latin students. Of the total Latin delegation of nine members on CAC only two Puerto Rican women were active. Both of these women supported desegregation.

5 Dahl (1964) discusses this legitimacy aspect at some length. However, while a participant may express his negative feelings by leaving the choice, he may also remain and use the choice as an opportunity for expressing his negative feelings. That is, he may know that he cannot affect the immediate, substantive outcome, but assume that, through expressive behavior, he may affect the conditions under which future choices will be made (Olsen, 1972).

6 Administrative participation may have also been discouraged by the fact that CAC members had been appointed by the Board. "Undue interference" with the citizens by top administrators might have led to citizen complaints to individual Board members. Generally speaking, however, members of CAC expressed disappointment that they saw so little of the top administrators during the planning process.

7 This state "guideline" was devised for use in school districts with two ethnic groups — white and black. It proved to be poorly suited to the multi-ethnic character of school enrollment in San Francisco. For example, using this guideline, a San Francisco elementary school with 40 percent black enrollment was considered desegregated while a school with 40 percent Chinese enrollment was considered to be segregated.

8 The Citizens Committee approved the Horseshoe Plan on the evening of June 1, 1971. It was submitted to an all-night meeting of the Board of Education on June 3rd. Faced with a court deadline only one week away, the Board members had little choice but to accept the recommendation of the Citizens Committee they had appointed. The Horseshoe Plan, in a slightly revised form, was deemed acceptable by Judge Weigel and was implemented in September, 1971.

9 The District lacked data concerning the residence and ethnicity of its student body; data on utilization of its classrooms; data on the socio-economic status of its students; data on migration patterns of families with school age children within the city; and information on feasible bus routes within the District. The professionals insisted that this data was required before decisions could be reached.

10 Undoubtedly the presence of a deadline exacerbated this situation. Given a much longer planning period the professionals might have been able to present detailed plans prepared in conformance to a number of different criteria. This elaboration of various alternatives might also have reduced the relative advantage (over other CAC members) enjoyed by the Round the Clock group inasmuch as members of this group were able to devise plans without the assistance of the professionals.

11 For a related set of rules for college presidents see Cohen and March (1974), Chapter 9.

12. Position and Presence in the Drift of Decisions

JAMES G. MARCH
Stanford University

PIERRE J. ROMELAER
Stanford University

12.0 Introduction

Most of the events in organizational life are not heroic. Minor actions, minor decisions, and minor changes fill ordinary days. Organizational history is an interpretation of minor things. Studies of decision making in organizations often reflect a bias. We seek to understand events in a way that satisfies our taste for drama. We tend to assume that great consequences must have had great causes, that decisions were necessary events, and that the explanation of organizational choice lies within the choice.

Much of this book is devoted to an alternative view. We have argued in a number of ways that decisions are streams rather than events, that choices are contextual, and that understanding alternative pasts is as significant as understanding alternative futures. The present chapter is in that tradition. We seek to use the study of four non-heroic decisions in a university as the basis for elaborating our understanding of behavior in choice situations. In particular, we examine the interaction of formal position (and the associated power) with the allocation of attention in ordinary, consequential, but not grand, decisions.

Although the variation with the literature on organizational decision making is large, four ideas with respect to decision process are typical:

1. *Temporal bounding.* A decision process is characteristically seen as having a reasonable well-defined beginning and ending. The beginning is a recognition of the "problem"; the ending is the choice made by the organization. Subparts of the process are similarly bounded in time.
2. *Participant bounding.* It is ordinarily assumed that a decision process attracts a relatively well-defined and relatively stable list of actors. These actors come to the decision because of the nature of the problem; they leave when the choice is made.
3. *Intention bounding.* We usually imagine that the actors in a

decision process can be characterized by some *a priori* and well-defined intentions. The decision outcome is produced through the interaction of those intentions within a power structure.

4. *Importance bounding.* We typically endow the decision we study with importance. It is to be understood as attracting from the actors the same sort of significance that we as observers give it. Indeed, we tend to focus most of our research attention on choices that are critical.

Within this broad structure, there are differences and disagreements. Allison (1969, 1971) has shown, for example, the alternative perspectives afforded by rational, political, and organizational conceptions of decision when applied to a critical case of public decision making. There has been substantial borrowings of ideas developed for the study of economic organizations into the study of public organizations and vice-versa.

In addition, there have been persistent indications that a conception of decision making as having strict temporal, participant, intention, and importance bounding may not fit some significant instances of organizational choice. Recent work on university decision making has characterized universities as being organized anarchies and university decision making as being describable in terms of a garbage can decision process. In these conceptions an organized anarchy is an organization typified by unclear goals, poorly understood technology, and variable participation. A garbage can decision process is one that produces outcomes more or less as a by-product of a process for exercising (rather than solving) problems. The importance of any particular situation is limited by the varieties of alternative situations available for organizational participants.

The frequency with which such observations occur suggests some possible reasons for our difficulty in interpreting the role of official position, (formal) power, and participation in the decision events in organizations. While it seems likely that official position confers an advantage in influencing the course of events, that advantage is constrained by the structure of decision making, the obligations of position, and the limitations of time (Cohen and March, 1973). We need, however, a better understanding of the trade-offs between (formal) power and presence in organizational choice.

The present studies are an attempt to understand some major features of four instances of organizational choice against the background of such theoretical concerns. They report case studies carried out by different individuals, with somewhat different perspectives. Nevertheless, we believe the major implications of the case studies are fairly clear. As we will indicate below, they are generally consistent with the ideas of organized anarchy; they suggest some important qualifications; they lead to some speculations.

12.1 The Sample of Case Studies

The four case studies were carried out in a single medium-size American university in the period from January to May, 1972. The university has a full collection of undergraduate, graduate, and professional programs; and it is committed to a substantial program of research in all fields. At the time of the studies, the university faced a general situation similar to that of most of American higher education. It had recently passed through a period of considerable student unrest, including significant instances of violence on the campus. It was now facing a period of slower growth and financial stringencies. According to most observers, the university had experienced a recent history of more than usual stress and more rapid than ordinary change.

We wished to examine some example of decisions promulgated within the university during the 1970–1971 school year. Our choice procedures were simple. Each year the university publishes a catalogue detailing the academic program at the university. That catalogue represents one part of the fundamental statutes of the institution. The statements of curricula and other program features published there are treated by students and faculty as official. The catalogue for 1971–1972 was (as one would expect) substantially the same as the catalogue for 1970–1971. It was not, however, exactly the same. The statutes had been changed in a variety of ways.

The changes from 1970–1971 to 1971–1972 ranged from minor changes in grammar, to changes in course offerings, to changes in program requirements and regulations, to changes in the organizational structure of the university. The total amount of change in the catalogue was modest; the changes that were made were mostly minor.

We have selected four instances of change observed in the 1971–1972 catalogue. The selection was neither random nor particularly precise. We exhibited a bias toward cases of relatively substantial change, but we did not seek the four "most important" changes. The cases vary considerably in importance, three being fairly high-level decisions, one being quite local. None would qualify as historic in a grand sense. Specifically, they include:

1) The change of the Department of Speech and Drama to a Department of Drama.
2) The elimination of architecture from the Department of Art and Architecture and the transfer of the architecture faculty to the College of Engineering.

253

3) A change in the grading system, eliminating the computation of grade point averages, eliminating university limitations on the use of "pass/no credit" grading, eliminating the suggested distribution of grades, and decreasing the number of alternative grades that are used by faculty.
4) The addition of a new field for doctoral students in the Department of Economics.

Each of these changes occurred in the 1971–1972 catalogue. We report investigations of the four processes that led to the changes and attempt to relate the results of those investigations to the literature on organizational choice. Each of the case studies involved a systematic effort to exhaust three types of available traces of events: The memories of participants, official files, and contemporaneous reports. None of the traces are clear. Memories are spotty and biased. Records are often almost non-existent. Relatively few of the events are important enough to secure public attention. Nevertheless, we have some confidence that the studies are reasonably, if not impressively, complete.

The report of the cases here is short. In part, this is dictated by the desire to focus the paper on general implications of the reports rather than on their detail. In part, it is dictated by the scarcity of detail in the record. But we think it is also a property of the process. Though the time span is often relatively long, the course relatively tortuous, and the outcomes sometimes uncertain, the decision process itself is rather sparse.

12.2 The Elimination of the Program in Speech

12.2.0 *The Change*

The catalogue for 1970–1971 contains a section discussing the faculty and program for the Department of Speech and Drama. Twenty faculty members are listed and 117 courses. In 1971–1972, the catalogue was changed. There was now a Department of Drama with a faculty of fifteen members and 100 courses. There was no longer any mention of speech as a program or division, although three courses taught by an associate professor of speech were still listed within the Department of Drama.

12.2.1 *The Sequence of Events*

The action reflected by the catalogue change in 1971 was the end of a long process. In 1946 the Department of Speech and Drama (a part of the College of Liberal Arts) listed 76 courses in the catalogue and a faculty of ten. About 45 percent of the courses (and 60 percent of the faculty) were in drama and theater arts; the remainder were in public speaking (35 percent), speech correction and psychology, teacher training, radio broadcasting, and English for foreign students. The department grew during the next decade. By 1954, the catalogue listed some 126 courses. Forty percent of the courses were in drama, 20 percent in speech correction, psychology, and audiology, 20 percent in rhetoric, public speaking, and oral interpretation, and the remainder scattered among radio, television, teacher training, and general subjects.

The faculty also grew. By 1954 the faculty was divided into five groups. The first was a group concerned with speech correction, speech science, and audiology; the second was a group concerned with radio and television broadcasting; the third was a group (five faculty members) concerned with rhetoric and public speaking; the fourth was a single faculty member concerned with English for foreign students; the fifth was a group concerned with drama and theater arts. The department offered baccalaureate, masters, and doctorate degrees in several areas, including speech. In addition to teaching courses, the department was heavily involved in a number of non-courses responsibilities, most notably the provision of dramatic performances on the campus, some consulting on speech and hearing problems, and coaching of an intercollegiate debate and forensic team. The chairman of the department was a professor of drama.

The 1954–55 period was the high point for speech (as a part of the Department of Speech and Drama) at the university. Over the following fifteen years it underwent a series of transformations. In a general sense, it was reorganized. Most of the components found new homes in the university; rhetoric and public speaking did not. The result appears to stem from a series of related episodes starting in 1956.

In 1956 a new dean was appointed to head the College of Liberal Arts. The dean came to the university with the expressed intention to make the university into one of the best in the country. Departments were encouraged to seek national reputations through new appointments. A series of events affecting the speech program followed the arrival of the new dean. Although he was not responsible for initiating all of them, there is no question that he contributed to the climate that produced them:

(1) One of the full professors in rhetoric and public speaking retired in 1956 and was not replaced at that level.
(2) In 1957 the faculty involved in speech correction, psychology,

and audiology left the department to form a new section in the College of Medicine at the university.

(3) In 1958 the undergraduate major in speech was eliminated (though not undergraduate courses or the graduate programs).

(4) Also in 1958 the most highly regarded young professor in the speech program was allowed to resign his assistant professorship to accept an appointment at a competing major university.

In a period when most programs at the university were expanding and improving, the speech program was contracting and allowing its best faculty to leave.

In December 1961 a new dean, with similar attitudes, became Dean of the College of Liberal Arts. Within the next two years, there was a new spurt of activity. By this time the faculty in rhetoric and public speaking consisted of one full professor, one assistant professor who had been there for several years, and three instructors or acting assistant professors who had only recently been appointed. One of the latter served as coach of debating. The associate dean of the College initiated a series of contacts with members of the speech faculty concerning the future of the program in speech.

The conversations between the associate dean and the speech faculty appear to have been conducted with relatively little notice to, or concern by, the chairman of the Department of Speech and Drama. The latter position was held then, as it was throughout the period, by a professor of drama.

According to the associate dean (in a memorandum to a faculty member teaching in the radio and television part of the program):

"Art Jensen [the only remaining full professor in rhetoric and public speaking] indicated concern about the future of the speech program and the speech faculty. I suggested that he and his group address a memorandum to me outlining their needs and plans. At his request I have agreed to meet with his group on the afternoon of Thursday, February 22, just to get acquainted with them and their interests."

A few weeks later, Professor Jensen died, leaving the program in rhetoric and public speaking without any tenured faculty members. The associate dean met on November 19, 1962, with the untenured faculty members in the program. This meeting, as well as others about the same time, are recalled differently by the different participants. The associate dean was to say 15 months later, in recalling the meeting, that he had informed the faculty that "the situation obtaining in the Speech program was unprecedented in University practice —

namely, that work on the graduate level was being directed by a group of faculty members not one of whom had been carrying on an active program of research and publication such as is usually involved in graduate teaching and one of whom had not yet completed the work for his Ph.D. degree." This interpretation is supported, though not conclusively, by a memorandum written by the associate dean to the chairman of the Department of Speech and Drama indicating procedures for phasing out the doctoral program. This memorandum, however, was not seen by the speech faculty.

The speech professors involved interpreted the message of the meeting to be that the Ph.D. program in speech should be reorganized. Toward that end, they undertook a series of meetings among themselves about the program. The debating coach, an assistant professor, became spokesman for the group. In May 1963 he sought a meeting about "our doctoral program" and the difficulty the faculty was having shaping a program to meet the associate dean's requests. His memorandum gained a penned comment from the dean of the College directed to the associate dean: "What doctoral program? There is to be none."

At the same time, the deans were moving toward establishing a new Department of Communication Science as a modern, academically respectable form of "journalism" program. The idea was to develop a new program based on three components:

(1) The television and radio parts of the speech faculty.
(2) The stronger faculty in an existing journalism program.
(3) New behavioral science faculty to be recruited.

In 1963 the new department was formally created and the second exodus of program and faculty occurred from the Department of Speech and Drama.

In February 1964, the associate dean and the debating coach engaged in a last exchange over the matter. The associate dean complimented the professor on his work as debate coach and for his devotion to his subject, but noted that the coach had "let that very devotion blind you to the meaning of events." The associate dean also indicated that he expected that the debate coach would probably be denied tenure. The coach left the university the following summer, and a new assistant professor was hired to continue the coaching responsibilities.

Although all graduate seminars were eliminated, courses continued to be provided by four non-tenured members until 1968. In that year, two events occurred. The program in English for foreign students was transferred (along with the relevant faculty member) to the Department of Linguistics; and the senior assistant professor in speech was promoted to a tenure position as an Associate Professor of Speech and Education, in effect moving to the College of Education.

By this time, there was a new associate dean in the College of Liberal Arts. He was faced with the question of the renewal of contracts in speech for non-tenured faculty. On the basis of a brief review of other speech departments in the country and of the scholarly work of the faculty in this program, the associate dean recommended that the program in speech be discontinued. The recommendation came at the same time as pressures grew to find ways of saving money in the university budget and was accepted quickly by the dean and the provost of the university.

During the whole process, three groups were involved slightly but neither continuously nor effectively. The leadership of the Department of Speech and Drama was not active. During the period, the chairmanship changed several times. It was however, always a professor of drama. They were actively concerned with securing foundation support for the drama programs. As one of the chairmen said, "We never knew what was going on. Things were decided elsewhere, not here." Speech professors did not feel that the chairman represented them. Discussions about the future of speech were carried out between speech faculty and outsiders without involving the chairman of the department.

Second, the students were not involved to any appreciable extent. Student enrollment in speech courses was persistently high. Indeed, high course loads were at one point cited by an administrator as a problem in the program. A student referendum supporting a continuation of the program in speech resulted in a favorable vote, but it did not become a significant student issue.

Third, the alumni were not activated. Although there was some support expressed for the debating program, there was never a clear alumni position in support of the speech program as a whole. Nor was there any effort to organize such a position.

12.3 The Transfer of Architecture

12.3.0 *The Change*

The catalogue for 1970–1971 lists the departments in the College of Liberal Arts. One of the departments listed is the Department of Art and Architecture. In the 1971–1972 catalogue there is a Department of Art. Architecture had been moved from the College of Liberal Arts to the College of Engineering. The change reflect a series of actions that include the elimination of the degree of Master of Architecture and the creation of the degree of Master of Science in Urban Design.

258

12.3.1 *The Sequence of Events*
Courses in architecture had been taught at the university since 1926. Originally, they were given by a Department of Graphic Arts; more recently by the Department of Art and Architecture. The Division of Architecture was small. About 50 students were taught by one or two full-time faculty assisted by local architects serving as lecturers. Although the program was not accredited by the American Institute of Architects; students were relatively successful (as compared with national experience) in obtaining licenses to practice.

The action recorded in the 1971–1972 catalogue had a long history. For most purposes the critical series of episodes began in 1961. At that time, there were two regular faculty in the Division of Architecture. One, John David Brown, was a tenured. full professor and director of the program. He had joined the university faculty in 1948. The other faculty was an assistant professor who had been on the staff since 1960. These faculty members were joined by 26 visiting lecturers, local architects who worked part-time for small honoraria. According to Brown, the budget for the entire program was $23,350 of which $19,600 was salaries. The program offered a Bachelor of Architecture degree, and a non-degree professional program.

In 1961 the university was in the midst of a period of growth and improvement. The dean of the College of Liberal Arts had been brought to the university in 1956 with an apparant mandate to strengthen the university's national position. He was generally seen as having been successful. Early in 1961, the dean sent letters to the responsible individuals in several weak programs indicating that they should indicate plans for their future. His announced intention was to bring programs to a level of excellence or eliminate them.

One such letter was sent to Professor Brown about the status of the program in architecture. Brown's response was a memorandum (June 1961) to the Department of Art and Architecture suggesting five things:
(1) That the architecture program should have a separate identity.
(2) That faculty, staff, and facility resources should be improved.
(3) That the curriculum should be enlarged. (4) That a Master's degree program in Architecture should be instituted. (5) That accreditation should be secured.

The Brown reply to the dean was discussed in the department faculty meeting in November 1961. In the meantime, however, the dean had resigned and gone on sabbatical; Brown was in Europe, not expected back until April 1962; and the Department of Art and Architecture was operating under an acting chairman.

A new dean took office in December 1961. He identified Art and Architecture as one of his problem areas and indicated in an exchange with the acting chairman early in 1962 that the department was in trouble. He had similar feelings about several other departments, most notably music, drama, speech, and modern languages. While looking for new appointments to lead reorganizations of these departments, the dean sought short-run adjustments.

In February 1963 the dean and the acting chairman were reported by Brown (in a memorandum to his part-time lecturers) to have decided to "eliminate the professional program in Architecture and the Bachelor of Architecture degree while continuing to offer a four year pre-professional program leading to the degree B.A. in pre-architecture." These decisions were apparently made in December 1962. Adverse administrative feelings were further communicated in February 1963 when the dean authorized Professor Brown to open discussions with the dean of the College of Engineering about common interests; and the Provost of the university questioned the appropriateness of an architecture program. One month later the dean rejected the appointment of a new faculty member in architecture, noted the need for a strong leader in architecture to supervise its development, and again indicated an intention to phase out the Bachelor of Architecture degree.

The pressures from administrative officials led Brown to seek support from the architecture profession. He gained letters of support or assurances from the part-time faculty, alumni, students, the A.I.A., and friendly figures in academic architecture elsewhere. A committee was established. Letters were dispatched to the dean. The dean's response (May 1963) was to argue that it would be unwise to expand the program in architecture until a vigorous new leader could be found.

In the fall of 1963 a new permanent chairman (an art historian) of the Department of Art and Architecture assumed office. He had a number of concerns; architecture was not one of the prime ones; but he did request a summary of plans for the future of architecture at the university.

The next eighteen months were a period of proposal generation within the Division of Architecture. Plans were formulated to shift emphasis in the architecture program; to initiate a professional master's degree program; to authorize increases in students, faculty, and budget; to secure accreditation; and to create a separate Department of Architecture. None of the plans indicated where the resources for expansion would be found, nor did they indicate the name of a new major appointment. For the most part, the proposals were able to secure formal support in the Department, some enthusiasm among architects, and little or no support from the administration.

The vigor of the 1963 administrative pressure on the program was replaced, however, by passivity. Other concerns attracted most of the

260

attention of the dean and the provost. Without active support from the dean, however, few of the proposals from the Division of Architecture could be implemented. A rough equilibrium continued.

There was an exception, however. In 1965 the proposal that the degree of Master of Architecture be approved was transmitted from the Department of Art and Architecture. The Dean of the College of Liberal Arts wrote to the Dean of the Graduate Division recommending that the degree not be opproved. He said, "My concern is rather that the decisions regarding the future of architecture should involve a developing and comprehensive plan in terms of which specific programs such as the one here considered can be evaluated and supported at the required level." Nevertheless, the degree was approved and the Master of Architecture program was instituted.

The dean maintained a low intensity concern. He sought outside evaluation of the program from the Dean of the School of Architecture at a major institution. This consultant helped develop an idea of the money requirements for establishing a first-rate program: $1,000,000 for a building and an annual commitment of $300,000. Such a commitment was not in sight. At this point, Brown was the only remaining regular faculty member in architecture; he was on tenure and not scheduled to retire until 1978.

There was a new series of unsuccessful proposals. In March 1967, a professor in the Department of Mechanical Engineering proposed a merger of architecture and design studies in the School of Engineering. Involved was a proposed Division of Architecture and Urban Design. A possible donor who might provide financial resources was courted without success.

In December 1967 a new provost asked the Dean of the College of Liberal Arts to chair a committee to consider the future of architecture at the university. The committee was to include the Dean of the College of Engineering, the Chairman of the Department of Art and Architecture, the Associate Provost, and a senior faculty member from the Department of English. With the possible exception of the art and architecture chairman, none of the members of the committee was particularly favorable to the continuation of the arrangements as they existed. The memorandum from the provost raised the possibility of discontinuing existing architecture degree programs.

In 1968 (while the Dean of the College of Liberal Arts was on leave) another proposal was made, this time by Professor Brown, the Dean of the College of Engineering, and the Chairman of the Department of Civil Engineering. The proposal was for a Center for Environmental Design in the College of Engineering. A year later (just before the dean returned), Brown proposed the same program again, this time suggesting that the architecture program report directly to the provost.

This second proposal was followed by a request from the acting dean to the provost that the five-man committee be reconstituted so that a "decision on the fate of architecture can be determined".

When the dean returned in the fall of 1969 the financial position in the school was much different from what it had been during most of the previous 20 years. The university faced serious budget problems. Although Brown continued to make proposals for modification or expansion of the program in architecture, they were not considered viable. Increasingly, the administrative problems was a personnel problem – what to do with a tenured faculty member without a program. In November 1969, the chairman of the Department of Civil Engineering met with his faculty and Professor Brown. Subsequently, the chairman proposed that Brown join his faculty. On January 26, 1970, the chairman wrote to the provost:

"Our plan is not to continue the graduate professional architecture program, but to gradually divert the resources now existing in graduate architecture into environmental design . . . Specifically, we request the transfer of John David Brown into the Department of Civil Engineering . . . In addition, all funds and accountrements for the architecture program would be transferred at the same time."

This proposal was approved by the two deans involved and by Professor Brown. On February 9 it was formally approved by the vicepresident of the university on behalf of the president and provost.

The announcement of the action precipitated a response. The chairman of the Department of Art and Architecture reported that he was completely taken by surprise. In an article in the student newspaper, he was reported as saying, "I've been shafted from behind without hearing anything new about it in several months." A group of students protested the move to the president of the university. They proposed the creation of a Department of Environmental Arts and expressed considerable concern that the program would be devoured by the College of Engineering. The local architect-lecturers expressed a feeling that the university was moving toward an engineering rather than humanistic view of environmental design.

The protests led to some consideration by the deans that the change might be delayed for a year, but by March 1970 the protests had died down. The transfer was affected.

In June 1975 the provost of the university announced that the architecture program would be phased out as soon as practicable, probably after 1976–1977.

262

12.4 A Change in the Grading System

12.4.0 *The Change*

The following statement appeared in the 1970–1971 catalogue:

"The degree of Bachelor of Arts (B.A.) or the degree of Bachelor of Science (B.S.) is conferred upon the candidates who: 1. Have attained at least a 2.0 Grade Point Average for all registered units . . ."

No such statement appeared in the catalogue the following year. The change in the catalogue reflected a change in the grading system within the university. In particular, the university shifted from a system that provided grades of A, B, C, D, and F, with some options for Pass/No Credit grading to a system that provided grades of A, B, C, and No Credit, with minimal limitations on the use of Pass/No Credit grading. These changes were accompanied by some changes in the requirements for maintaining good standing in the university and by the elimination of a standing suggestion with respect to the distribution of grades.

12.4.1 *The Sequence of Events*

Formal action to make the change in the grading system was taken by the Academic Assembly on May 14 and 21, 1970. That action was one step in an essentially continuous process of grade system modification and debate. The last sequence of events in that process began with a 1966 decision to offer a limited form of Pass/No Credit grading on an experimental basis. The move, like similar moves throughout the country, was associated with student pressure and was explicitly intended to encourage students to take courses in subject areas outside their major fields.

The 1966 action was one of a series of early efforts at reform in university education. In 1967, the president of the university appointed a commission charged with considering all aspects of education at the university – the Education Study Commission (ESC). The ESC involved a large group of faculty, students, administrators, and consultants, as well as full-time staff. It was organized into a number of major subcommittees with particular concern for some broad area of educational matters.

Over the course of several months, ESC issued reports and recommendations covering a wide range of issues. Included in the volume entitled *Undergraduate Education* were some recommendations in grading procedures. ESC recommended the adoption of an A-B-C-Pass-No Credit system of grading. The recommendation was accompanied by a rationale that included a critique of the alleged misleading degree of precision in the existing system, a comment on the lack of relationship between grades and adult achievement, and the de facto upward drift in undergraduate grades. The recommendations included a statement that "some of us would have preferred a simple two grade system of 'honors' and 'pass'."

The recommendations for changes in grading fell into the purview of the Academic Assembly. The Assemly included some 50 members. It was a new representative group elected by the faculty. It had been established in 1968 in the context of student protest. At that time it appeared to be difficult for the faculty as a whole to conduct legislative business with much decorum or consistency. The Assembly was in the first years of its existence; it was still developing procedures; it was also attempting to cope with the peak period of unrest on the campus. The period covered by our report was one of considerable stress. The university was deeply involved with Viet Nam, Cambodia, Kent State; there were occupations of university buildings, strikes, and major confrontations over the continuation of ROTC on the campus. Windows were broken; meetings of students, administrators, and faculty were almost continuous; there were tear gas and police arrests on the campus.

It was within this context that the Assembly established procedures to consider the recommendations of the ESC. The process was aided by the fact that the Chairman of the Assembly had also been a principal in the ESC. Under his guidance, it was decided to establish a group of small, *ad hoc* floor management teams to guide the ESC recommendations through the Assembly. The first two of these teams were appointed on January 9, 1969; but neither was concerned with the issue of grading.

The Assembly consideration of ESC recommendations was complicated by continuing events on the campus and by the problems of establishing joint deliberations with a student organization (the Student Education Committee). Progress was slower than had originally been hoped. As a result, the Steering Committee of the Assembly decided on May 30 to create two new floor management teams. One was to consider the issues of university governance, including the creation of a new dean to have general responsibility for undergraduate education; the other was to consider the university grading structure. At the same time, the Steering Committee decided that a new standing committee of the Assembly should be created to deal with undergraduate education.

These decisions were reported to the Assembly on June 5. Staffing of the two new floor management teams was completed by June 16. Only the team concerned with governance went to work immediately, however. The team on the grading structure was, by agreement with its chairman, delayed until later in the summer.

In fact, the fourth team never operated. On August 7, the Assembly adopted the recommendations of the governance management team that a single Committee on Undergraduate Studies (CUS) be charged with "general responsibility for undergraduate academic matters". On September 11, the newly elected Assembly, noting the overlap in the responsibilities, discharged the grading floor management team in favor of the Committee on Undergraduate Studies.

The Committee took time. On September 25, the Assembly adopted a formal charge to the Committee. On September 30, the Committee on Committees appointed seven faculty members to the CUS. Two of the members, including the new chairman, had been active in formulating the ESC recommendations. Indeed, they were chosen partly for that reason. The Committee met for the first time on October 15 and noted that the first item of business was the work on grading. The three student members of the Committee were appointed on November 5.

The CUS discussed the proposed changes in the grading structure in meetings on February 4, February 18, February 25, and March 11. The Registrar of the university participated with the Committee during the last three meetings. He was particularly active in identifying the detailed implications of alternative plans and in showing how to translate educational philosophy into concrete institutional procedures. As one member of the Committee observed, the Registrar "helped us touch base. There were a number of areas of difficulty we had not considered which he brought to our attention."

The prime figures in the discussion, however, were three faculty members, two of whom had also been active in formulating the ESC recommendations. The Committee discussion rather quickly accepted the general feelings reflected by the ESC; and the major issue was whether to recommend a change to a three step (honors, pass, and no credit) or a four step (A-B-C-Pass-No Credit) system.

The organization of the options around the three-step and four-step alternatives appeared to be a function of the continuity from the ESC provided by the chairman and one other member. No other serious alternative was presented. A February 25 straw vote on the alternatives (including the alternative of no change) indicated strong support within the Committee for change. No one supperted the "no change" option as a first or second choice. Support for the three-step and four-step options was about equal.

After the relatively even division of opinion of the Committee became apparent, there was an informal effort to have the Committee members discuss the issues with their constituencies. This led to the feeling on the part of the Committee that it would be hard to obtain faculty approval of the more radical, three-step proposal. The feeling was not based on much evidence. Indeed, there is little sign that any serious effort to influence the Committee was initiated from outside the Committee (except by the Registrar) or that the issues being discussed by the Committee impinged significantly on the consciousness of any appreciable number of students or faculty. Attention was overwhelmingly elsewhere.

At the March 11 meeting, the Chairman (who personally favored the three-step system) recommended that the Committee support the four-step proposal. He argued, and the Committee agreed, that such a proposal was more likely to secure support and could become a transition to the more radical system.

On April 16 the CUS reported its recommendations to the Assembly. Other items before the Assembly required that the report be delayed as an agenda item until April 30 (the second meeting after the report had been transmitted by the Committee). On April 30, however, the Assembly was embroiled in a debate of ROTC, the bombing in Cambodia, and related matters. Consideration was delayed until May 7, and then again until May 14.

On May 14 the recommendations were again on the agenda under "unfinished business". The discussion was taken in a Committee under the chairmanship of the professor who was chairman of the CUS (who had also been active in the ECS). Although there was relatively little debate, the consideration came so late in the meeting that final consideration of some items had to be delayed until May 21, at which time the Assembly finally adopted the entire list of CUS recommendations.

Members of the CUS had anticipated a fair amount of controversy in the Assembly. They had expected considerable resistance to the proposals and were surprised that the proposals passed with considerable ease. They probably overestimated the importance of what must have appeared to be a minor item on the agenda and its symbolic significance within the context of the day. As one observer commented, "It was the feeling of the day that change was good and to resist change was subversive."

12.5 A New Doctoral Field in Economics

12.5.0 *The Change*

The 1971–1972 catalogue contained a list of fields of study for doctoral candidates in the department of Economics. One of the fields listed was the "Theory of Choice". That field did not appear in similar lists in prior catalogues. It was an addition to the list in 1971–1972; none of the fields listed in 1970–1971 were eliminated.

12.5.1 *The Sequence of Events*

The Department of Economics was relatively small in 1971. Only a distinct minority of the economists on the faculty of the university held full-time appointments in the Department of Economics. The department was in the College of Liberal Arts. There were professorial appointments of economists also in the College of Business, the College of Education, the College of Engineering, and the Institute of Agricultural Research. The economists who were not in the Department of Economics were, on the average, more likely to have applied interests. The department was widely viewed as having a commitment to "pure" economics.

The Department of Economics had had a long history of concern for mathematical economics and various aspects of decision making under uncertainty. During the 1950's, the department participated in discussions about the possibility of establishing a program in applied mathematics. In 1965 an unsuccessful proposal for such a program was made. About the same time one of the leading professors in the department involved in the proposal left to join the faculty at another university. In fact, over a period of a few years at this time, several senior faculty left. They included some of the faculty members who had been most important in building the reputation of the department in mathematical economics and economic theory.

In 1967 a new senior appointment in mathematical economics, Professor Smith, was made in the department. In 1968, a new assistant professor, Professor Jones, was hired. Jones' speciality was in the economics of uncertainty, but he taught no courses in that area during the 1968–1969 school year. In 1969 another specialist in uncertainty, Professor Larson was appointed as an assistant professor in the department. His appointment was a joint one with a research institute at the university.

In 1969–1970 Jones taught a course in the theory of uncertainty. During the same year, Professor Watkins, an economist in the College of Business, was teaching a two-course sequence in choice theory and social decisions. Neither course experience was entirely satisfactory. Jones felt that the attendance in his course (5 students) was small because students were interested in fulfilling the course requirements imposed by the formal fields of study recognized by the department. Watkins felt that his attempt to appeal to both M.B.A. and Ph.D. students was not entirely successful.

Partly as a result of these experiences and partly as the natural outgrowth of a sharing of interests, Jones, Watkins, and Larson began talking about a three-course sequence (one course taught by each) they might jointly offer. Late in 1969 Jones approached the chairman of the department about the idea. Conversations between Jones and the chairman, joined on at least one occasion by Larson, continued through the early Spring of 1970. The chairman reported to interviewers that he thought the idea was reasonable, citing as one reason the fact that Professor Jones' course had been "well-attended". During the early part of these discussions, Professor Smith was away from the campus; he was not active in them after his return, but supported the idea. A faculty meeting in the Spring of 1970 approved the creation of the sequence as a new field for doctoral students. Discussion was minimal, and no serious objections were raised.

The faculty approval was followed by negotiations among administrators about the funding of the several courses. There was quick agreement that the department would fund Jones' course and that the College of Business would fund Watkins'. Professor Larson's support was in dispute. The discussions were complicated by Larson's position. Although he held a half-time appointment in the department, the remainder of his salary was provided by a research institute from grant money. Moreover, he had closer ties – both in terms of intellectual interest and in terms of probable career prospects – with the College of Business. Finally, it was agreed that the department would pay for the course for the 1970–1971 year.

Although these decisions were too late to be included in the 1970–1971 catalogue, students were informed by the faculty involved and by a notice posted on the department bulletin board. The three course sequence was taught in 1970–1971. Student enrollment averaged about 12 students per course of whom about three or four were from the Department of Economics. Students from the College of Business and the College of Engineering made up most of the rest.

A new department chairman assumed office in the Fall of 1970. He and Professor Smith had a series of disagreements over the value of the new field of study. Over Smith's objection, the chairman decided that the department would not provide funds for the Larson course in 1971–1972 and directed that the course be deleted from the draft of the 1971–1972 catalogue, replacing it with a course on welfare economics. Theory of Choice was left on the list of doctoral fields, but identification of actual course offerings within the sequence was omitted.

12.6 Some Features of the Process

There are three major themes that run through these reports. They have some significance for understanding organizational choice in organizations like a modern American university. The first theme is the relatively small number of active participants. A few of these were active in more than one of the cases. They were entirely senior administrative officials. Most of the participants appeared in only one of the stories. Most potential participants did not appear at all. The second theme is the interaction of position in a decision structure (see Chapter 3) and activation. There was clearly a trade-off between having a position of authority and having the time and commitment to spend. The nature of the trade-off was complicated by the combinations of attention claims at any point in time (see Chapter 3; Weiner, Chapter 11). The third theme is one of orderly drift. Although the process was confused and not determined uniquely by the external context, neither was it surprising. The events that were produced were consistent with what was happening throughout American higher education at the time.

12.6.0 *The Importance of Unimportance*

Probably the one most conspicuous feature of the processes we have described was the low salience of the decisions to most potential participants. If we can judge from these decisions, most of the decisions that produced changes in the university catalogue at this time were relatively unimportant to most individuals who might have had access to the process. The participants were few in number. Most of them most of the time had other important things on their minds. Many of the people who might conceivably have been involved were either not involved at all or were involved very sporadically.

This low saliency was signalled not only by the rather small number of individuals actively concerned in the decisions, but by the frequent difficulty that participants in the decisions had in recalling the events involved. Memory, as well as attention, was brief. These were rather highly decentralized decisions of rather fleeting significance.

The decision with respect to architecture involved very few people. Those directly concerned, particularly Professor Brown, were devoting a considerable amount of time. No one else was. Key administrators had this problem on their agenda, but it did not stay persistently at the top. Moreover, leaves of absence and changes in positions resulted in an erratic flow of attention. There were periods of relatively intense attention followed by months of neglect.

A similar situation existed with the speech decision. Over the fifteen years of this decision process only a handful of people were involved. On the administrative side, almost all of the activity involved a dean and an associate dean with their immediate staffs. The only faculty members with any significant involvement at all were faculty members immediately concerned. No one else was activated. Moreover, the active actors attended only sporadically. Administrators were stimulated to action when they came into office or when some specific action had to be taken. Most faculty members similarly. Concern was highly variable. There were many other things to do.

Very few people were active in the grading decision. Two or three figures in the story are persistently prominent. They participated in the ESC deliberations; they were active in managing the approval in the Assembly. They waited patiently as the Assembly argued the merits of various responses to public atrocities in Viet Nam, Ohio, and Cambodia. Most faculty, most students, and most administrators were not visible in the process. Most of those who were visible participated only briefly.

Most people were not there because they were somewhere else. They were on strike, dealing with demonstrations, debating the future of the country. Or they were carrying on their teaching, administering, learning, and research. When the recommendations finally made their way to the floor of the Assembly, participants were weary with strife over other things. The grading issue might have become a garbage can for all of the other concerns before the Assembly, but there was no need for one. This was not a situation in which major problems needed good arenas for airing (Christensen, Chapter 16). There were lots of attractive choice opportunities for the great debates. In garbage can terms, the decision was made in a classic oversight/flight manner (Cohen, March, and Olsen, 1972).

Involvement in the decision in economics was local. The three faculty members for whom the program was designed (and by whom it was designed) secured the support of the chairman of the department and the associate dean of the College of Business. It was not significantly opposed by anyone; the primary problem was one of funding and the long-term implications for the departmental appointment of one professor (Larson). Students were mostly not interested and certainly not active. They did not appear to know about the decision until after the faculty action. Most faculty were unconcerned and hardly aware.

The observation that only a few people were involved in these decisions should not be misunderstood. The processes that produced the decisions took time, over a decade in two cases. They were not secret. A number of people were involved overtly; others knew the changes were under consideration. Very few people were active, however. For the most part, most participants were some other place. To observe the most obvious thing, all four of the decisions we have considered overlapped in time. The participants in one were, for the most part, not the participants in the others. Most people played no part in any of them.

Low salience in decisions does not necessarily mean that the process will be calm or free of conflict. Quite the contrary. Although many people do not participate, those who do are often inclined to feel strongly about the issues. The strength of their feelings is frustrated by the inclination to small changes and the passivity of others. The combination may produce decision performances of considerable tension and eloquent orchestration; it may produce an inclination toward bizarre machination on the part of active participants; but the noisiness of the process should not be confused with its general subjective relevance. In this kind of situation, decision conflict, decision inertia, and general decision indifference are mutually reinforcing.

Low saliency seems to us endemic to academic organizations. There are two conspicuous reasons. First, the decisions taken within academe are rarely heroic. Even those that might have some fundamental effect on the academic establishment or life within it are unlikely to seem particularly important relative to the kinds of problems in which university community members participate, actually or vicariously, in the broader community. For most participants either Washington politics or family crises seem significantly more critical than general academic policy. What seems to attract participants generally is of much more immediate implication for their own lives. The threatened faculty members in architecture and speech were active. In the case of the economics program, the most active participants were three junior faculty members. They needed students; they needed solid academic appointments; they needed mutual intellectual reinforcement. The proposed program seemed to offer all three. It did not arise from student demand or from general faculty consideration of the needs of economic education. The generation and orientation was local.

Second, the relative unimportance of academic decisions is reinforced by the twin principles of consensus governance and policy gradualism. The university has a tradition of proceeding through rules of consensus. Serious efforts are made to persuade the community to move together. Such efforts predispose the system to compromise and to modest changes in existing procedures. Changes occur gradually. But this incrementalism, in turn, reduces the average saliency of decisions to participants. Small changes are, in general, less likely to appear important than large changes.

The positive feedback is strong. The inclination to small changes reduces the salience of the individual changes. At the same time, the general sense of low saliency in decisions increases the attractiveness of consensus as a procedure. Why coerce people over unimportant matters? Consensus rules lead to incrementalism, which reinforces low saliency. The process is strong. It is not pathological. It is, in fact, the core of the basis for effective social governance and the system of trust on which such governance lies. The critical point here, however, is not whether low saliency is normatively attractive, but to understand that it is a characteristic and consistent feature of university decision making.

Low saliency of decisions results in a kind of decision process that is rather distant from the classic conceptions of temporal, participant, and intention bounding. It is somewhat closer to some descriptions of organized anarchy. Neither the beginning nor the end of the process is well-defined. A decision that has been made may be unmade. It is not quite clear when things are finally settled. Neither is it clear when things start, except possibly retrospectively. Certainly many things seem to start and go nowhere or go somewhere rather distant from where they were expected to go by the participants at the birth.

In fact, our procedure for marking decisions by a comparison of catalogues concedes more clarity to the process than it has. The change in economics was already somewhat problematic by the time the catalogue was published. The new chairman had acted to eliminate part of the course sequence. The demise of architecture precipitated efforts to develop a program in urban planning. Speech was eliminated but was alive in three different places on the campus. The new grading system, by reinstating " + " and "–" signs on grades, appears to have "reduced" a five-point grading scale to a ten-point one.

In general, actors are part-time and changing. As the process develops individuals wander in and out. The persons filling the relevant administrative positions change more rapidly than the issues are resolved. At each stage a different group is involved (perhaps overlapping to some degree with some previous stages). The "stages" themselves are not predetermined.

On the whole, it appears that the decision outcomes are produced by a sequence of locally understandable steps heavily dependent on some special features of the moment in which they occur and the specific combination of problems and people involved at that moment. The chaining of these locally understandable steps produces the long process. Since the sequence is heavily dependent on some of the branches, the history wanders.

12.6.1 *Position and Presence*

Participants were not equal in their impact on the process. At least in these cases, influence over the flow of events appeared to depend on two things: The first was presence. Since few people were involved and those who were involved wandered in and out, someone who was willing to spend time being present could often become influential. The second factor was position. Per unit of time spent, deans, chairmen, and provosts had more impact than individual faculty members or others.

The discussion above has detailed the way in which being present made a difference. In every case, the willingness and ability to be present made individuals important to the flow of events. Memoranda that were written normally had to be answered. Issues that were raised normally had to be acknowledged. Individuals willing to work were granted considerable latitude in determining what garbage was left in the can (see Weiner, Chapter 11). Long delays were achieved by formally-weak people.

The impact of position was also clear. Consistently, a chairman or a dean exercised discretion and thwarted initiative. Action often required a positive approval from an administrative officer. This could be delayed or denied. Authority to pursue senior appointments, make judgments on tenure, or spend extra resources was important enough to provide leverage over action. The ability to fix agendas and specify alternatives in the grading case; the ability to encourage desertions in the speech case; the ability to do nothing in the architecture case were all important aspects of the position of dean. The department chairman was crucial to the economics decision. Initially, his approval seemed to make faculty approval relatively routine. Later, a new chairmen's resistance prevented full implementation.

Position and presence were related. Relative to most potential participants, major office holders – deans, chairmen, provosts, and the like – devoted more time to these decisions than almost anyone else. It was their job, and they were generally energetic about it. However, they were busy. Their attention was divided among a variety of concerns and a large multitude of decision situations. In every case, there were some other people who were spending more time than the key administrative figures. In some cases, other figures were spending considerably more time.

As a result, we need to consider the trade-off between position and presence in the kind of process we have described. The issue is best illustrated by examining the events in the speech and architecture cases. They were quite similar. In the case of architecture, the power and position of individuals involved varied greatly. The two deans of the College of Liberal Arts who were active during this period were both considered strong academic leaders, noted for their vigor and strongmindedness. The two provosts were similarly highly respected academic administrators. The dean of the College of Engineering controlled the resources of a major engineering program. They were all heavyweights. Professor Brown did not have a significant position in the university. He was a tenured faculty member, valued by those colleagues who knew him; but his position was tangential to the interests of most faculty, and he had never been a faculty leader. Brown's supporters among local architects were not among the more

273

important financial or political supporters of the university. Despite this imbalance of power and position, Brown delayed the elimination of his program for ten years. The apparent difference was in the amount of time and effort he was willing to devote to the problem relative to the time and energy available to others.

Neither in the architecture nor in the speech case did we have the complication of countervailing position clearly defending the lower status groups. We have relatively clear situations in which commitment and energy hold off strong opposition over a long period of time. A similar argument, though less compelling, can be made in the other two cases. The activists in both cases had allies with position; but it nevertheless appears true that the simple ability to be present when an occasion for decision occurred and the willingness to persist over a relatively long period of not particularly decisive action were significant factors.

Observations on the trade-off between position and presence are familiar to students of political processes. What was distinctive about the functioning of this university was two things: First, the very low level of general activation. As a result, the chance was substantial that variations in presence would be large. Second, the heavy load on persons holding high position. As a result, the amount of attention any dean or chairman could devote to any one question was likely to be small. The joint consequence of the two things was to make the trade-off between position and presence particularly important.

12.6.2 *The Slope of the Field*

Low salience produced a wandering history. This wandering was, however, not random. We believe that the studies described above suggest some significant implications of the ideas of anarchy and decisions as artifacts. The process drifted. The drift was conspicuous. It was dependent in detail on almost chancelike occurrences and the combinations of substantially exogenous flows of people, problems, and solutions. But the drift occurred within a context of belief structures, social norms, resource distribution, and interpretive themes that produced systematic bias in the drift. Moreover, the differential participation rates assured that the norms reflected by relatively frequent participants normally directed the wanderings more than the norms of others.

The cultural and organizational context of decision drift is well illustrated by our four cases. Although each of them had some specific features that depended on the details of the process at this time in this university, none of them produced a result that would have been surprising at any other similar American university. The outcomes were normatively conservative. Speech departments had become uncommon at major universities; architecture was rarely connected to art; pass/fail grading had spread rapidly through American universities as a response to student unrest; the theory of choice was a recognized new field in economics. No one proposed eliminating the Department of Physics, or shifting law to political science.

Consider the grading change. This university, like others, had a history of cycling on grading procedures. The enthusiasm throughout American higher education was strongly in support of pass/fail grading. The university was not a leader in the movement; its action came relatively late. Even those members of the community who thought the change ill-advised had to concede that the innovation was common among good schools and had not seemed to result in a violent wrench with traditions of quality education. As the school drifted, it drifted in company with other universities with which it was accustomed to compare itself.

Or consider the attitudes about speech. Many of the actions of the deans reflected a widely-held belief that speech was not a proper scholarly field. Speech was characterized by one key participant as "intellectually shallow". The basic attitudes were shared by most actors, other than those who were on the speech faculty. They were biases of the general academic culture that were independent of, and not particularly attentive to, the particular facts of the particular case.

Because of these features of the cultural values, the decision performances in each case were partly educational reinforcement of cultural values. The prolonged exercises in speech and architecture were reminders to participants and observers of the dominant cultural values of academe. The debate over the grading change was an opportunity for affirming publicly a normatively appropriate concern for students.

The stability in values also produced a stability in outcomes despite the flow of participants. In several of the cases, the time span was considerably longer than the tenure of a particular office-holder. The administrative hierarchy of the university exhibited the usual rate of turnover. During the period covered by the report on the architecture "decision", the university had three presidents (one of them "acting") and two provosts; the College of Liberal Arts had three deans (one of them "acting"); the Department of Art and Architecture had five chairmen (three of them "acting"). Administrative actors moved on and off the stage rapidly relative to the flow of events. The turnover was not unusual; the period of time covered was ten years. Each turnover, however, produced a possibility for a shift in direction. Brown's success in delaying the outcome might have had a different implication for the ultimate result if it were not true that the turnover of administrators produced no significant variation in their policies. Whether the stability stemmed from the necessary logic of the situation, or from a common cultural bias, or from the dependence of administrators on the permanent staff, policies were more stable than people.

Taken in broad perspective, the four case studies we have examined suggest the following possible metaphor for decision making within a university. Consider a round, sloped, multi-goal soccer field on which individuals play soccer. Many different people (but not everyone) can join the game (or leave it) at different times. Some people can throw balls into the game or remove them. Individuals while they are in the game try to kick whatever ball comes near them in the direction of goals they like and away from goals that they wish to avoid. The slope of the field produces a bias in how the balls fall and what goals are reached, but the course of a specific decision and the actual outcomes are not easily anticipated. After the fact, they may look rather obvious; and usually normatively reassuring.

13. University Governance: Non-participation as Exclusion or Choice

JOHAN P. OLSEN
University of Bergen

13.0 Introduction

Individuals vary in their participation in organizational decision making. The variation is easily observable and can be related to differences among individuals, among organizations, among decisions, and among points in time. It forms a major focus for modern organization theory, as well as classical political philosophy.

Within organization theory, two primary questions have been asked: First, what are, or ought to be, the constitutional arrangements with respect to participation? Who should have the right to participate? What justifies a particular distribution of participation rights? Second, how do, or should, participants allocate their time within the constitutional rules? When is the right to participate not exercised? What justifies a particular pattern of attention to participation opportunities?

In recent years the discussion of participation has often assumed that individuals who participate (i.e., those in power) seek systematically to exclude others from participation if they can; and that individuals who do not participate (i.e., those out of power) seek to obtain participation rights. We have grown accustomed to the idea of a power struggle between those who take part in making decisions and those who do not. Groups that do not take part in governance are, in this perspective, absent by exclusion rather than by choice.

Suppose that instead of assuming that non-leaders always demand leadership and participation (in the absence of manipulation or threat), and that leaders always resist new demands, we treat participation and leadership as activities people *seek* under some circumstances and *avoid* under other circumstances. Such a focus supplements the concern for the representativeness of government and the demands for participation with a concern for the difficulties of getting people to take interest in participation. Unwillingness to accept leadership and responsibility, the tendency to look at participation as a sacrifice, has often been a reality, both in specific organization and in the political system at large. Dicta emphasizing the duty to participate, as well as the social sanctions for not participating, seem to suggest a problem that recent concerns about participation rights seem to ignore.

Consider the situation in a university. Academic man often wants to influence events. Traditionally, however, he has not been very willing to allocate time and energy to administrative or participatory activities. Active involvement in university governance is to a very limited extent consistent with the time-demands of a scientific career, and not very attractive to many faculty. Time is scarce, and the problem of allocating attention and energy among competing claims on available time is a real one. It is especially important in organizations where the major individual rewards are connected to activities other than participation in the governance of the organization. Major universities are a classic example.

We examine two questions: (1) Under what conditions will non-leaders demand (or not demand) participation? (2) Under what conditions will leaders resist (or not resist) giving new groups participation? These questions will be approached within a framework of individual rational choice. By relating rewards and costs to different types of participation, we show the conditions under which it is rational for non-leaders to demand (or ignore) organizational participation. Likewise, we show the conditions for some leaders to resist (or not resist) such demands.

Such an approach is of little relevance for organizations in which participation is a function of stable prerogatives and duties, or where many participants operate on purely altruistic motives, obligations or loyalties. For instance Rousseau's ideal citizen, not calculating individual costs, but only taking into consideration what is best for the society at large, would be an *alternative* model (Rousseau, 1966). While the citizen in a society founded on the Social Contract will participate even if this is perceived as an individual sacrifice, in our model of individual rational choice a potential participant would *not*. We acknowledge that most people both historically and currently, do not think of themselves exclusively as isolated individuals with values and interests of their own, but also as group-members. Moreover, we are impressed by the importance of the role of duty in organizational behavior. We simply wish to examine the possible clarification provided by a model in which participation is viewed as a choice rather than as automatic.

13.1 The Basic Ideas

The ideas presented here were developed in the context of some empirical studies of the University of Oslo (Olsen 1968, 1971). The primary concern was the participation of faculty at the department level. Three sets of observations were used: (1) Historical data on how the classical institute with all formal power in the hands of the chair-

278

man, developed during the 19th Century. (2) A case-study of the first important break with this classical pattern – the reorganization of the Departments of physics and chemistry in the 1960's. (3) A survey (1968) of faculty attitudes towards departmental governance. In this chapter, we focus upon elaborating the theoretical concerns, and illustrating them by means of the survey data. The case study data are reported (in part) in Chapter 14 of this volume; the historical data are not discussed here, but generally they support the conclusions presented.

We can describe *non-leader behavior* as falling along a continuum from strong efforts to obtain participation to strong efforts to avoid participation. Similarly, we can describe *leader behavior* as falling along a continuum from strong efforts to resist non-leader participation to strong efforts to solicit non-leader participation. The resulting combination of non-leader and leader behaviors defines the state of the organization (from the present point of view).

For purposes of exposition, we consider a simple partitioning of such a space (Table 13.0). We assume that the demand for participation by non-leaders is either "high" or "low". "Low" demand includes situations where non-leaders are indifferent to participation and situations where they resist it strongly. Similarly, we assume that leader resistance to participation by non-leaders is either "high" or "low". "Low" resistance includes both situations where leaders are indifferent to letting new people in and situations where they are very eager to have them. The result of proceeding in this way is Table 13.0, which defines four basic conditions:

I: *High demand, high resistance.* A power struggle.
II: *High demand, low resistance.* Circulation of elites.
III: *Low demand, high resistance.* Stable leadership structure.
IV: *Low demand, low resistance.* Leadership as a burden.

Table 13.0. Found combinations of the level of demand for participation and the level of resistance to such demands:

		Leaders' resistance to participation by non-leaders	
		HIGH	LOW
	HIGH	I	II
Non-leaders' demand for participation			
	LOW	III	V

In order to understand both the level of demand and the level of resistance as consequences of rational considerations, we will focus on three major clusters of variables:

279

(a) Factors affecting the importance of the decision-making unit in terms of the rewards provided or the utility-structure of potential participants. The range of rewards and burdens distributed through organizational choices varies. We will look at the distribution of possible outcomes, the probable ways in which decision-makers will allocate available resources and burdens. This distribution is affected particularly by the degree to which rewards are divisible and by more stable rules about how rewards should be divided.
(b) Factors affecting the *alternatives to formal participation*. We study the effectiveness of formal participation relative to other ways of affecting personal rewards. We consider the importance of "exit". That is, how participants may be able to control the effects on themselves of organizational choices by leaving the organization or by substituting outside rewards for the rewards distributed through the organization.
(c) Factors affecting *the prospects for future leadership*. A rational actor does not try to maximize his rewards and minimize his costs at a given point in time, but has a more long run perspective. Given an organization with different positions and different degrees of participation and power connected to each (which is assumed to be relatively stable), we consider how the probability of moving from one position to another affects the decision to demand participatory rights. Specifically, we study how the probability of leaving a non-leader group and going to a leader group affects demands for participation by non-leaders.

Given some understanding of these three clusters of variables, we can examine the circumstances under which an organization will find itself in one or the other of the four cells in Table 13.0 under the assumption of substantially rational behavior on the part of the participants. At the same time, we can consider the probable organizational consequences of being in one cell or the other, and the alternative strategies for moving the organization from one cell to another. We turn to such concerns in Section 13,2, after a more detailed look at the three clusters of variables affecting participant behavior.

13.2 Three Clusters of Variables

13.2.0 *The Importance of Organizational Decisions*

A necessary, but not sufficient, condition for desiring participation in organizational decision-making is simply that something of value for the individual is distributed through the choices made by the organization.

What are the prizes and burdens distributed through organizational choices? To what degree are things of value affected through these processes? We include both "rewards" in terms of material benefits (substantive rewards) and rewards related to the process itself (e.g., development of personal abilities, psychological needs for importance, status, acceptance etc., or simply relaxation and fun).

Consider the following questions related to a university-situation. To what degree are hiring, firing, salary and promotion decisions made by the department, and to what degree are they settled elsewhere (at the school-level, in committees, in the Ministry of Education, in the "academic market")? Does the department control student admissions? Does the department collectively decide teaching loads and course content? If not, are these (a) personal decisions (each faculty-member decides his own activity); (b) non-decisions (e.g., formalized through stable rules or given by outside units); (c) arranged through bilateral negotiations between certain individuals? Does the department collectively decide which people are going to do what research? Is research money channeled through the decision-making units of the department? Do department-decisions affect the feelings of self-esteem, status and acceptance among the potential participants?

We also need some assumptions about the subjective values of the individuals. What are the things they desire? What do they want to avoid? Research money will be much more important to participants in some fields than in others (e.g., physics and theology). Here, as elsewhere, there will be differences between locals and cosmopolitans; or between rich and poor.

In order to induce a rational person to use time in an organization, (a) this organization must be perceived as an important provider of important satisfactions, and (b) it must be possible for the individual to affect the allocation of rewards and burdens through participation in organizational decision-making. Thus the more resources are regulated via norms, rules and "programs" or decisions external to the organization, the less interest there will be in participation. The desire to change such stable norms certainly may be a major reason for action. Here, however, we are concerned with rules, norms, and choices which cannot easily be changed from within the organization. The greater the range of rewards accessible to decision-making the greater the interest in one's own participation – and the greater the resistance to participation by others.

However we need to ask not only about the range of rewards controlled by the organization, but also about the possible ways these rewards may be distributed. Rewards are divisible to different degrees

281

(Dahl, 1964, Olson, 1968). Divisibility may be an aspect inherent in the reward itself, or may be enforced through laws and rules, which are difficult to change in the short run and often have to be changed via units external to the organization.

To give some examples from a university context the general prestige and reputation of a department is a "public good" for all its members, and to a very low degree divisible (even if exceptional members may have their reputations separated from that of the institution). Money and social acceptance are very divisible rewards. A certain type of experimental equipment (e.g., a reactor) is only partly divisible. A reactor may be used only by some research-groups, but on the other hand it may be used by all within a relevant group.

Highly divisible rewards may, however, via administrative rules be made less divisible or selective. In Norway, as an example, external rules related to position and seniority are used to prescribe salaries, eliminating questions of wages as department decisions. At some American universities, on the other hand, a department receives a certain amount of money for departmental salaries and may allocate it among its members as the decision-making bodies wish. Or we may observe situations which are hybrids, e.g., where the department allocates some money, where all people in a certain category have to receive the same amount, but where the department has to decide how to allocate the resources among the different groups. If such rules are part of a larger system, they can only be changed through activities external to the department, and would in the short run have to be taken as fixed.

How, then does divisibility affect the pattern of (internal) activation? We suggest that the less divisible the rewards, the less interest in participation. The tendency will be that each participant hopes that others will assume the costs of providing the "public" or indivisible good. Where rewards are divisible between groups, but indivisible within a group, we may find strong demands that the group as such should be represented in the organization's decision-making units, emphasizing its *right* of participation. But at the same time it may be difficult to find anyone to represent the group and an emphasis on the *duty* to take one's term among the group-members. As long as there are no divisible or selective rewards, one may have a group-feeling, but have problems finding someone to take leadership.[1]

The *way* rewards are divisible also becomes important. Consider an organization where rewards (e.g., salaries) are divisible between hierarchical groups (e.g., professors and assistants), but not within each group. Here we expect (as stated above) each group to demand representatives. However, if the rewards are divisible only *across* hierarchical groups (e.g., the reactor example above) we expect non-

282

leaders to take less interest in having their (hierarchical) group represented as long as those representing the field prove competent. If this reasoning is basically correct, different patterns of demands for participation will be found as a consequence of the technology in the fields. For instance, in fields where the same equipment is shared by many hierarchical groups but cannot be shared over different fields, groups lower in the hierarchical structure will be less interested as groups, in formal participation than in fields where rewards are more divisible, or divisible only along hierarchical lines. Also, under the former conditions leadership-groups will be more willing to let new groups, lower in the hierarchy, take part in organizational choices.

Within most organizations, and clearly within Norwegian universities, there are important differences among sub-units, both with respect to what rewards they are allocating and with respect to how these possibly may be divided. We will use the importance of organizational decisions to describe the sum of these two aspects, expecting different degrees of importance to affect the patterns of demands for participation and resistance to participation. The more important the organizational choices, the stronger the demands for participation. The less important the decision-making processes, the more participation will be perceived as unattractive and not made an organizational issue by non-leaders. Demands for reorganization in such cases will come from the leaders themselves.

13.2.1 *Alternatives to formal participation*

Given some degree of importance of organizational choices, a potential participant first has to estimate whether he will be able to affect the outcomes at all through participation. Then he has to consider two alternatives: (a) other ways of affecting the outcome of organizational choices than through formal participation, and (b) "exit"-possibilities, that is the possibility of controling the effects of organizational choices on himself. Each of these alternatives is viewed as a sufficient, but not necessary, condition for not demanding formal participation.

Among alternative ways of affecting organizational choices, most formal procedures for collective decision-making are relatively cumbersome and time-consuming. These procedures (e.g., studies and discussions in order to find alternatives, distribution of information, clarification of different preferences, coalition-building and voting, and discussions of the procedures themselves) try to take into account all values and beliefs, and pay for this by making decision-making somewhat slow and often undramatic in results. Thus, as long as individual, informal action is effective in serving a person's interests, it will be preferable to formalized, decision-making behavior. We assume non-leaders will try to get what they want via ad hoc and specific action on an individual or small group-basis more than through collective organization of the "non-leader-group" demanding collective representation. This, of course assumes that there are no positive pleasures in the process of participation. Where such pleasures exist, the predictions would have to be modified.

If organizational decisions are made by means of relatively clear and stable criteria (e.g., positions are always allocated according to professional competence as measured in the academic market-place), the individual has another way of affecting the content of choices. We expect him to have some tendency to try to affect his position on the criteria (e.g. through scientific activity) rather than engage in organizational activities. In situations where time is a scarce resource we also expect that the more specific one's interest, compared to the range of decisions made in the organization, the less will be the tendency to demand formal participation, since this means that one will have to take part in many decisions which are viewed as irrelevant.[2] Our model in general suggests that the most "rational" strategy for a potential participant is to find someone who shares his bias and is good in defending it, but otherwise to keep out of the decision-making processes.

A situation in which rational decision-makers do not participate if they can get what they want without the costs of participation or if their participation does not affect the distributions of rewards, produces some problems for very rich and very poor organizations and for consensus-dominated organizations. In a very rich organization, and in an expanding organization there will be a tendency towards giving most potential participants an acceptable share. Most demands can be met easily. It is not necessary to participate. In the extremly poor organization, there is not that much to fight about.

In the organization with consensus about what to do and how to do it, participation will be defined as a burden and as a sacrifice if the organization cannot provide selective rewards to leaders. The more similar potential participants are in terms of their values and beliefs, the more often we expect to find rotation-arrangements for leadership, so that each has to take his turn. Also the more widespread the consensus, the more often we expect to find an ideology emphasizing the duty of participation. Since decision-making in a consensus-organization can make little substantive difference, consensus-dominated organizations will tend to be led by people who rank process-oriented rewards relatively high, or who particularly identify with the organization and therefore accept the obligations imposed by the norms.

So far we have considered only formal authority, that is where the legitimacy of leaders and their policies is derived from the positions they hold and the rewards and sanctions inherent in these positions. In a university it is also important to look at the effects of different degrees of consensus on professional competence and authority, particularly perceptions of competence related to organizational decisions. We ask to what degree there is consensus on the distribution of expertise and skill in the organization and how that consensus matches the leadership structure. The more leaders derive their legitimacy from non-leaders' agreement that leaders should make decisions because of special skill, the less "legitimate" leaders need to be formal leaders in order to confirm themselves as leaders.

In organizations with a strong emphasis on professional competency and agreement on what that means, formal participation will not be perceived as an alternative for people without such competence.[3] We expect demands for participation to be stronger in fields where what is accepted as knowledge changes rapidly. Also, the less the consensus on a single paradigm (Kuhn, 1965), and the more different schools within the same department, the stronger the demands for formal representation of these groups. The more the recruitment and socialization-processes recruit people with similar values and beliefs, the less the demands for participation, and the less the resistance against letting others have participation.

The pure dominance of professional criteria as the basis for leadership and decision-making will be challenged the more expensive the research, the clearer the socio-political relevance of the field, and the more the department itself increases in size[4] and complexity. In the last case "competence" will not be restricted to purely professional quality, and scholarly competence, but will also have a clear "managerial" aspect.

As we have seen, formal participation is only one of several ways of affecting the allocation of rewards and burdens through organization. Other ways will often be preferred. Moreover, an individual may control the effects of organizational choices on himself, without necessarily affecting the outcomes of the choices. He may under some conditions, remove himself from the control of the organization.

He may leave. The more and the better the alternatives outside the organization, the less the interest in formal participation. Torgersen (1967, 1970) has observed that in "boom" periods internal control mechanisms become less important. There is less conformity, more relaxation of professional standards, more experimentation. Also there may be a relationship between exit opportunities and the possibility of affecting organizational choices (as discussed above). The better the external alternatives for an individual, and the more dependent the organization is on him, the more he may get his premises included in organizational choices without formal participation. Thus, while a group with external options takes less and less active part in the formal decision-making system of the organization, their values and beliefs become more and more important for those (formally) running the organization. Moreover, such groups will be less "bounded" by organizational decisions, to conform less to its demands. At a time in which organizational success is defined in terms of the quality of the faculty and the quality of the faculty is determined by the strength of outside demand for their services, we have a prototypic situation in which power and participation will be separated.

Sometimes the individual can remain in the organization without depending on it for resources (e.g. financing his research through the research councils, foundations etc.). The easier the access to such external sources of rewards, the less the involvement in the formal government of the organization.

In many university organizations the perquisites of individuals do not depend on participation. In cases where the major rewards are linked directly to employment status, a high security of employment is likely to increase the feasibility of a low-cost withdrawel from participation while not formally leaving it. High status people may simply deactivate themselves. Low status people will focus upon activities that may change their status. In situations where the major rewards are *not* linked to employment status, high job security is more likely to increase the participation demands from all groups.

There are important differences across institutions and across individuals with respect to the availability of alternative ways of affecting organizational choices and opportunities for "exit". We summarize these two aspects by talking about alternatives to formal participation. We expect variations in alternatives to have important effects on both demands for participation and resistance against participation.

13.2.2 Prospect for Future Organizational Leadership

A rational actor not only wants to maximize his rewards and minimize his costs at a given point in time, but also to do this for longer time periods.[5] He considers his prospects for benefiting or suffering from the existing system at some future date.

What are the prospects for social mobility in the organization? To what degree can a non-leader expect participation in the future via normal circulation of elites? To what degree can the potential participant affect his own chances for future leadership through the use of current time and energy?

The potential participant confronts the "classical" problem, whether he as a non-leader should ask for participation through his (non-leader) group, or whether he should try to get participation by trying to leave his group. The answers to these questions are (among other things) dependent upon the size of each group, and the number of years the actor expects to stay in each group.

Let us call the number of leaders, n, the number of non-leaders, m, the expected number of years as a leader, y, the expected number of years as a non-leader, x, the current power of leaders, P_l, and the current power of non-leaders, P_n. We want to know the conditions under which a non-leader will prefer a shift in power, k, from leaders to non-leaders. We assume that all leaders have the same amount of power, that all non-leaders have the same amount of power, and that the number of leaders and non-leaders is stable over time. Assuming no discounting of future returns, a non-leader will seek a shift of power of amount k, if:

$$x\left(\frac{P_n}{m}\right) + y\left(\frac{P_l}{n}\right) < x\left(\frac{P_n + k}{m}\right) + y\left(\frac{P_l - k}{n}\right)$$

$$\frac{y}{n} < \frac{x}{m}$$

From this we see that a non-leader is more likely to prefer a transfer of power (which is assumed to summarize the benefits and costs of participation) from leaders to non-leaders,

(a) the smaller the number of non-leaders
(b) the larger the number of years he expects to be a non-leader
(c) the larger the number of leaders
(d) the fewer the number of years he expects to be a leader

The more an organization is stratified, with few chances of internal, upward mobility, the greater the chances that non-leaders will demand participation (given some degree of decision importance and a not too rich mix of alternatives to formal participation). The better the chances for rapid mobility, the more difficult to produce collective action among non-leaders. Each individual will tend to focus on (informal) individual or small-group action, and this will be particularly characteristic of informal professional leaders (because they are more likely to expect promotion). The mechanism will be more "efficient" the more legitimate the rules and procedures for promotion among non-leaders, and the more the criteria for success are related to other time and energy-consuming activities than participation in the procedures of governance (e.g., research work).

We can use the same set of ideas to consider the leader's actions.

Using the equation above we assume that (a) the smaller the number of leaders, (b) the fewer the number of years a leader expects to stay as a leader, (c) the smaller the number of non-leaders, and (d) the larger the number of years a leader expects to be a non-leader, the less resistance against demands for participation from non-leaders. Organizations with a high probability of downward mobility for leaders (from a leader-position, to a non-leader position), tend to move towards Cell II or Cell IV (if the expected leadership-period becomes so short that it is not really worth fighting for).

In Norwegian universities the prospects for internal mobility have varied over time, and today there are significant variations across departments. Also there are variations in perceived possibilities for mobility across persons. These variations in prospects would be expected to have some significant effect on participation behavior.

13.3 An Examination of the Four Cells

How do our three variables (importance of organizational choices, alternatives to formal participation, and prospects for future leadership) affect the patterns of demands for participation from non-leaders, and the patterns of resistance against such demands from leaders? With what effects (if any) on the distribution of formal authority? As a preliminary assumption we treat "importance" as a necessary, but not sufficient, condition for demanding participation or resisting such demands. The two other variables are treated as sufficient, but not necessary alternatives to demanding or resisting formal participation.

The extreme conditions leading to the situation of Cell I is one in which:

(a) Both leaders and non-leaders perceive organizational choices as important to them.

(b) Neither of the groups has easy alternatives to formal participation.

(c) There is little likelihood of moving from the position of non-leader to a leader-position, or from the position of leader to non-leader.

This is the situation closest to the classic "power struggle" model, with strong "they-versus-us"-feelings. Changes in the distribution of formal authority are slow. It is a situation with substantial strain within the organization. Some aspects of the distribution of resources (including which groups each part can activate on their side) decide who will be the leaders. This is the most "visible" state of an organization, a fact which probably has contributed to giving it disproportionate attention. Under such circumstances the formal distribution of authority, power and status become more and more visible and important (March and

Simon, 1958). Leaders emphasize their formal rights to decide (together with using other resources and threats).

The high tension situation of Cell I will not often be perceived as attractive by any of the major groups (e.g., in a university) if it endures over a long period. There are several possible strategies available for leaders and non-leaders to escape the strains of Cell I. Leaders may try to weaken the pressure for leadership (so that the organization moves in the direction of Cell III). One well known strategy is to try to change the perceptions of the prospects for future leadership and participation among the most active of the non-leaders, or simply to try to coopt some of them (Selznick, 1949). Another possibility is to provide easier exit-possibilities for non-leaders, or to try to force some of this group to exit. Likewise, leaders may try to improve the exit-possibilities of leaders as a class, so that the organization moves in the direction of Cell II.

Cooptation of specific non-leaders, or providing exits for them, will work as a solution when only a few non-leaders are "activists" and their demands are not representative of the non-leader group as a whole. However, in high stress situations like that of Cell I we expect the "activists" to be fairly representative for their respective groups. The exit or cooptation will be ineffective unless they apply to the group as a whole. The exit-solution will be prefered to cooptation in organizations where the ideological element is important (e.g., in organizations based on some set of ideas and where the founders or first-generation leaders are still in charge). Cooptation is more likely in bureaucratized organizations with little emphasis on "ideology".

The non-leaders may try to force the leaders to exit. Likewise they may search for attractive exits for the leaders or themselves (and move the organization towards Cell II). A well known strategy is also to demand an increased number of leader-positions, and thus a potential expansion of the organization. This strategy is least likely to be used in organizations where there are important differences in ideology between leaders and non-leaders. In such situations forcing leaders away, or leaving in order to form a new organization, are likely solutions. Obviously, the more everybody view the organization as "unique", the more likely that the power struggle will go on until one group is able to force the other away (or the organization has its resources cut off because its reputation and its ability to provide certain outputs are destroyed).

Situations leading to *Cell II include the following:*

(a) Leaders and non-leaders judge the importance of organizational choices differently; specifically, non-leaders consider them more

289

important than do leaders. Suppose the types of choices facing an organization change over time. Each time a change takes place, a new group, for which the new choices are relevant, activates itself. At the same time, the leaders, for whom the new choices have no particular great relevance, are glad to deactivate themselves. This certainly is the perfect coalition-situation and particularly likely if new demands are consistent with old, if resources are fairly large, or if demands are time-specific.

Another possibility, and probably a more common one, is related to a tendency to believe that one's closest superiors have more "power" than they really have. Subordinates do not easily see all the constraints superiors are working under but their "decisions" are very visible. Thus, non-leaders will activate themselves. Over time the leaders discover more and more of the constraints. We observe a "disappointment"-effect making the new leaders happy to leave what they believed was a powerful position, when a new group of non-leaders demand participation.

(b) Even if both groups perceive organizational decisions as important, we may end up in Cell II if the alternatives to formal participation are easy for leaders but not for non-leaders. In this situation the new leaders will be those without external options. Old leaders will either stay in the organization and get the rewards they want from other sources or leave the organization. In order to stay in Cell II, the situation must be one in which each wave of new leaders discovers alternatives to participation after becoming leaders; each wave of non-leaders has few alternatives.

(c) Finally there is a situation where both groups judge organizational choice as important; none has good alternatives to formal participation; but the chances that leaders will become non-leaders and vice versa, are fairly large. If the probability for a (random) leader becoming a non-leader is much higher than the reverse – a very common situation as long as the number of non-leaders is stable and larger than the number of leaders – the tendency of Cell II is self-reinforcing. However, (as mentioned) if the probability of going from a leader to a non-leader-position increases strongly, we move toward Cell IV. That is non-leaders will not take much interest in becoming leaders for a very short period.

In Cell II reorganization of the (real) power-structure is a continous process, with steady, incremental changes. Tension and criticism tend to be low compared to the situation of Cell I. Reorganization is unlikely to become a "big issue". Often reorganization under these conditions will take place informally, without any changes of the formal organization. If the organization decides to formalize changes taking place over some time, this decision will be observed by the outsider as an important break with the past. The organization-members themselves, however, will probably perceive it as a formalization of what has already taken place. This type of reorganization may also change the image of legitimacy of the organization in some part of its environment without changing any of the day-to-day-operations. A well-known example would be to change the name of the organization. Since the situation of Cell II assumes a steady circulation of leadership, it demands that new leaders by becoming leaders acquire some of the characteristics of the old leadership, (e.g., good alternatives to formal participation, or down shifting perceptions of the importance of the decisions after taking leadership). When this does *not* happen, the organization moves toward Cell I. Alternatively, if the new leaders experience disappointment concerning the importance of the organizational decision, this "discovery" may spread to the rest of the organization, and the organization moves toward Cell IV.

Situations leading to Cell III include those in which:

(a) Organizational decisions are viewed as important by leaders, but not by non-leaders.
(b) Both groups view the decisions as important, but the non-leaders have better alternatives to participation than the leaders. One such situation will be a good external market for non-leaders; allowing them to leave the organization easily, as when a university is looked upon by non-leaders as a training place for future careers in other organizations. Another possibility is that non-leaders (but not leaders) have external sources of resources. We may for instance imagine a situation in which non-leaders are the most qualified professionals, which may often be true in fields with a rapidly changing body of knowledge and a clear external validation of "quality".
(c) Both groups perceive decisions as important and have few good alternatives to formal participation, but non-leaders can easily anticipate becoming leaders soon through "normal" organizational promotion and leaders expect to stay leaders.

The better the possibilities for upward mobility within the university, and the more such mobility is speeded by means of activities *other* than university governance (e.g., research activities), the less non-leaders will choose to use their time on participation, and the more they will channel their time and energy to other activities qualifying for leadership-positions. We have earlier argued that the better the prospect for future leadership through natural processes among non-leaders, the less likely that leaders will resist demands for participation.

However, the situation of Cell III may be one where there are very clear criteria for professional competence, and consensus that nobody without a certain level of competence should participate. At the same time non-leaders have very good prospects for reaching this level in a relatively short time.

The situation of Cell III probably is the most stable one so long as the relative sizes of the leader and non-leader groups can be maintained. The chances for reorganization are small or non-existent, and the organization-map tends to reflect the real distribution of authority in the organization. If we (as here) assume that the passivity of non-leaders primarily reflects a choice of their own, the emotional "climate" in the organization will be good. If, however, the non-activity is·a result of anticipated sanctions, there will be a high level of dissatisfaction in the organization.

Our model suggests that if non-leaders (in Cell III) start perceiving organizational choices as more important, perceive their alternatives as less good, or their prospects for future leadership as declining, we move towards Cell I. Likewise, if leaders start viewing organizational decisions as less important or are getting better alternatives to formal participation, we move towards Cell IV. In order to get to Cell II, these two trends would have to come simultaneously. That is, perceived importance, alternatives and prospects would change in opposite directions for the two groups. This probably is the least likely situation.

Finally, the situations leading to Cell IV include those in which:

(a) Both leaders and non-leaders judge the choices made by the organization as relatively unimportant. The organization does not allocate anything of real importance to either group.
(b) Decisions may be perceived as important, but both groups have good alternatives to formal participation.
(c) Decisions are perceived as important, no one has good alternatives, and while non-leaders have good prospects for future leadership, leaders do not.

The Cell IV situation is closest to one in which leadership is perceived primarily as a burden by everyone. Each person tries to avoid the costs of participation. We expect to find rotation-arrangements for administrative positions, but the rationale is not to provide power-sharing but cost sharing. This may be a situation where leaders are least representative of their constituencies, e.g., people for whom there is little demand even in periods where nearly all groups have good market-situations may become leaders. Traditional "elite" groups will not be in charge. In Cell IV ideosyncratic and random factors may also have an important effect on who takes leadership.

Consistent with the traditional emphasis on demands for participation, and the assumption about high motivation, Cell IV is the situation which has received least attention. This is unfortunate since such studies may throw some light on sides of leadership-problems and techniques which often are not considered (e.g., the relative effectiveness of "negative" and "positive" means for inducing certain activities in the organization, and the conditions under which the former is of little value).

13.4 Participation at the University of Oslo

For a rational decision-maker attempting to maximize his self-interest participation under some conditions will be attractive, making the right to participate the central matter. Under other conditions participation will be unattractive, a sacrifice accepted as an obligation. Three clusters of variables affecting the conditions have been presented above. Within a framework of rational choice, we have discussed some conditions under which there will be demands for and resistance against participation of new groups. Especially we have focused on four possible combinations, and discussed the conditions under which they will develop and the effects they will have on reorganization of the distribution of formal authority in an organization. We now proceed by illustrating some of these theoretical concerns by means of data from the University of Oslo.

The University of Oslo is the major university in Norway. Founded in 1811, it had only 5,600 students in 1960. By 1968 there were 13,900 students, and by 1972 the number had passed 20,000. In 1968 there were 2,244 full time appointments, of these 1,118 were faculty positions. The budget was 289,2 million Norwegian kroner (a little more than 50 million dollars). The university is allowed a certain amount of self government. However, several major issues are not internal choices of the university. With the exception of the fields of medicine and dental medicine the university has until recently been open for all students completing secondary education. Student admission is a "non-decision". All salaries for a particular rank are the same and are decided outside the university; the work load is related to the formal positions. The criterion for promotion has (in this century) basically been scholarly merit. Job security has been extremely high. Norwegian full time appointments are for life. This security together with a comparatively high status of university jobs has made mobility between the academic and non-academic sphere rather low.

The formal right to participate in university governance has been closely related to formal position. The highest governing body of the university is the Collegium. In 1968 its members were the Rector and

Vice Rector (both elected directly by an assembly where the full professors and the associate professors have a very strong majority), the deans of the seven schools (Fakultet) and one representative elected by the assistant professors and one by the students. The director of the university and the assistant director were members, but without the formal right to vote. The central administration of the university has been weakly developed.

The first director was appointed in 1962 on the initiative of the Ministry of Education and after long resistance from the university itself. As late as 1960 there were less than 10 administrators with a university degree or other higher education.

In 1968 the intermediate levels, or the schools (Fakultet), were each governed by a Dean, a Board and a Council, with a School Secretary leading the administration. In the Council all full professors and associate professors met, while the other groups (including the students) sent only a very limited number of representatives.

The third level – and the one we will be focussing on here – is the department. In 1968 there were 110 departments. It is very difficult to discover any general, underlying principle for the way in which the departments were divided. The sizes varied from 134 full time employees (research fellows not included) in the Department of chemistry and 120 in physics, to small "departments" with one or two people. The Department of chemistry had more than seven times the faculty of the smallest school (Theology).

Until 1963 all the departments were formally run by a department chairman. He was appointed by the Collegium and most often he had life-time tenure. However, actual practice within this frame, was quite heterogenous. In departments with more than one full professor there were usually subdepartments with a fair amount of independence. The leaders of the subdepartments would often be department chairman for 3-year periods. In some place we find "sections", units formally a part of the schools, and discussing and making decisions concerning teaching and exams, but (formally) having no authority over the research-policy and the department budget. In the section all faculty could meet. The division of labor between the departments and the schools varied in important ways. In the "professional schools" (theology, law, medicine, and dental medicine) the school would be the most important unit coordinating teaching and exams. In the other schools the departments would be more autonomous.

Studying a Norwegian university, one very soon realizes that the people governing the organization have not cared much about producing "data" about what they have done and why. We have used the written materials and statistics available. This has been supplemented by a case study of the department reorganization starting in 1963–64.

In the spring of 1968 we administered a questionnaire to all faculty-members asking about their perceptions of how the department were governed and their attitudes towards the governance. The questions were especially related to the differences between the "classical insti-tute" model and the new "physics model" – the latter introducing elected, representative decision-making units, changing completely the formal role of the chairman, and assuming a strong office organization led by a department secretary. 757 persons answered the question-naire, 6 of them were such that they could not be used in our analysis. 751 answers give us a total response of 87 % of the people present during the term (excluding people abroad, with long term leave due to sickness, unfilled positions etc.). There are some variation in the response rate from different categories of faculty, but in general the material should give a good basis for evaluating the perceptions of and attitudes towards different ways of distributing formal authority. (For a further discussion, see Olsen, 1968, 1971).

Consider the following three questions related to (a) the powers of the department chairman, (b) the procedure for appointing the chairman, and (c) the way of defining the problems of the non-tenured faculty.

(a) The respondents were confronted with the following statement: "It follows from the position as chairman of a department that he has the responsibility for all decisions, and therefore that he has to have all final authority in all decisions, for instance budget proposals, how to spend resources, working-plans and allocation of work".

Although the respondents were not so informed, this quotation came from the unanimous recommendation from the university on the law given in 1955 and still governing the institution. 17.4 % of the respondents agreed completely with the statement. 38.2 % agreed partly. 39.0 % disagreed completely. 3.3 % did not have any opinion or did not answer, and 2.1 % gave other answers. (N = 751).

(b) On the question: What would your attitude be towards a proposal stating that the department chairman should be elected for a limited timeperiod by all faculty in full time, permanent positions?

46.6 % agreed completely, 22.2 % agreed partly. Only 19.7 % disagreed completely, while 8.7 % did not have any opinion or did not answer and 2.8 % gave other answers.

(c) The third question tried to capture two different ways of defining the problem of the non-tenured people: In your opinion, what is most important for the non-tenured faculty – to get information about the decisions of the department leaders (6.1 %), to have an opportunity to inform the department leader(s) about their points of view (18.2 %), to have a limited number of representatives in the department leadership (28.2 %), that all faculty in full-time, permanent positions should participate in the same way (22.4 %), that also the recruit group (fellows and assistants) should participate in the same way as other faculty (22.6 %). 1.8 % did not respond or did not have any opinion, 0.7 % gave other answers. While approximately 1/4 perceived the problem as one of giving and getting information, 3/4 viewed it as a question of formal representation.

The three questions are focused more upon the participation of hierarchical groups than the respondents as individuals. Probably they will therefore indicate more general attitudes towards the participation of groups, rather than necessarily reflecting an individual choice as to whether to use one's own time on participation or not. As a result we would expect our questions to show a somewhat more positive attitude towards participation than we would observe in the real choices of individuals deciding whether to spend their own time on administrative work.

Together the three indicators give a picture of fairly little support for the "classical" model with no formal rights of participation to non-tenured faculty. There is a tendency to be willing to give the chairman the right to make decisions throughout the year, but with the option to remove him. Thus one possible interpretation of these numbers is that the respondents want participation, but the least costly one, in terms of time and energy.

The general idea of non-participation as *exclusion* make us expect that the tenured faculty will seek to keep the powers of the department chairman, not having him elected, and defining the problem of the non-tenured faculty as one of information while the non-tenured faculty will seek the opposite. Table 13.1. does not support this prediction. On the contrary, there is *no* correlation between the status of the respondents and their attitudes towards increased participation in the governance of the departments. Considering the University of Oslo as a whole, the absence of any relationship between formal position and attitude towards participation, combined with a desire for an expansion of the participation of the faculty-groups traditionally not taking part in department governance, provide us with a situation close to that of Cell II (Table 13.0). We now proceed by trying to explain this *general* situation, before turning to the explanation of the *differences* between departments.

Table 13.1. Attitudes towards participation, by formal position

(a) Attitudes towards giving the chairman all formal authority	Tenured faculty	Non-tenured faculty	Assistants and fellows
Agree completely	21.5	18.4	14.9
Agree partly	37.7	38.4	47.8
Disagree completely	40.8	43.2	37.3
Total	100.0%	100.0%	100.0%
(N)	(191)	(359)	(161)

gamma-coefficient : 0.01

(b) Attitudes towards electing the chairman			
Agree completely	49.1	53.7	54.4
Agree partly	26.9	24.9	23.5
Disagree completely	24.0	21.4	22.1
Total	100.0%	100.0%	100.0%
(N)	(175)	(341)	(149)

gamma-coefficient : 0.05

(c) Definition of the problem of the non-tenured faculty:			
A question of information	24.0	24.0	28.1
A question of representation	76.0	76.0	71.9
Total	100.0%	100.0%	100.0%
(N)	(196)	(366)	(171)

gamma-coefficient : 0.03

The similarities in attitudes are not a result of a perceived equality in influence. There are important differences in how the different groups perceive their own influence upon the teaching and research-policies of the department. The higher the status, the more perceived influence (Table 13.2). When, however, we ask the degree to which respondents are generally satisfied with available possibilities for having an impact upon decisions they find important for themselves, the differences are very small. Given four categories (very satisfied/fairly satisfied/fairly unsatisfied/very unsatisfied), 28.1 % use one of the two negative categories (only 8.6 % are very unsatisfied). 26.9 % of the non-tenured, and 32.9 % of the assistants and fellows declare themselves unsatisfied.

The combination of (a) perceived large differences in influence, (b) much smaller differences in satisfaction, and (c) great similarities in attitudes towards increasing the participation of non-leader groups,

297

Table 13.2. Perceived own impact on teaching and research policy of the department during the last three years, by formal position.
Q.: To what degree have you the last three years been able to have any impact upon the teaching/research-policy of this department?

Own impact has been	Teaching				Research			
	Tenured faculty	Non-tenured faculty	Assistants and fellows	All combined	Tenured faculty	Non-tenured faculty	Assistants and fellows	All combined
Very great	34.6	12.8	3.4	17.5	33.3	14.1	5.4	17.9
Fairly great	45.2	39.6	15.3	36.7	35.9	29.7	11.7	27.7
Fairly small	14.9	29.0	37.2	26.3	19.0	23.7	35.1	24.8
Very small	5.3	18.6	44.1	19.5	11.8	32.5	47.8	29.6
Total	100.0%	100.0%	100.0%	100.0%	100.0%	100.0%	100.0%	100.0%
(N)	(188)	(321)	(118)	(627)	(153)	(249)	(111)	(513)

This question was asked only those who had taken part in teaching/research in the department the last three years.

may provide us with a starting point for understanding better what "government" means in a university organization. It becomes important to analyze more closely the substantive side of the decision-making process in the departments; what the rewards and burdens allocated are, along what lines rewards and burdens may be divided, whether faculty fight, and what they eventually fight about.

Consider the following questions: To what degree are there different opinions about what kind of teaching and research the department should give priority? Do the faculty in a department make joint decisions about teaching and research which may reflect these differences in opinions?

The similarities in attitudes cannot be explained by assuming a high level of consensus. Close to half of the respondents reported that there were different opinions about both the teaching and the research policy of the department (with a fairly strong tendency towards tenured faculty "seeing" less conflict than the two other groups).

The differences, however, are not made the basis for joint decisions. Less than half of our respondents (43.8 %) had participated in any formal meeting about the teaching policies of the department, 32.3 % had formal discussions and 23.9 % had done neither. The larger the department, the clearer the tendency to coordinate teaching through formal meetings. This is not true concerning research policies. Only 13.4 % had participated in any formal meeting. 34.4 % had participated in informal discussions and 52.2 % had not taken part in either formal meetings or informal discussions about the research policy of the department. Add to this, that between 40 % and 50 % of those who had taken part in any formal or informal discussion of the research policy had done this *outside* the department (at the school level, meetings arranged by students, professional associations etc.) Although our questionnaire was clearly biased towards assuming that a departmental teaching and research policy existed, 6 % (N = 751) explicitly answered that the department did not have any "policy" for teaching. 21 % gave the same answer for research. Probably some others being of the same opinion, have responded that they had not taken part in any meetings or just not answered the question[6]. There is a clear pattern in who claims that there is no joint policy and that each faculty-member does the research he wants: 42 % in the humanities and 34 % in theology gave this answer, compared to 11–13 % in medicine and dental medicine and 16 % in the sciences.

So far our data have indicated (and more evidence will be presented later) that the traditional model of the scholar who does the research he himself chooses, and teaches what he wants, still was fairly strong in (parts of) the university, though it was much less frequent for teaching than for research. "What the scholar himself chooses" refers to the absence of hierarchical decisions and coordination, not a general absence of coordination. One important set of constraints is related to the norms of the academic disciplines, and to the training and socialization taking place. Where the working habits are derived from a professional or academic culture, there is less need for the explicit rule or command. The decentralization of research decisions and the lack of formal coordination of research activities in the departments should, according to our model, reduce the interest in formal participation on the department level. Furthermore, while 2/3 of our respondents say that their main interest is research, less than 1/3 say that research is their main activity.[7] To understand demands for participation, we have to recognize that the coordination going on more is related to *teaching* than to *research* activities.

The perceived lines of conflict make it even less likely that disputes over representation of different *hierarchical* groups should be significant in most departments. Among faculty who perceive intradepartmental differences in opinions concerning research and teaching policies, only 3–4 % say that these differences are between members of the different hierarchical groups (Table 13.3). The potential conflicts are found between different subspecialties, especially with respect to research matters.

Table 13.3. Perceptions of the lines of conflict in the department:

The differences in opinions are found:	Teaching	Research
Between holders of different positions	4.1	3.1
Between sub-specialities	47.4	74.0
Between both these lines	22.2	15.5
No stable lines	26.3	7.4
Total	100.0%	100.0%
(N)	(266)	(257)

This question is responded to only by those who answer that the differences in opinions are very great or somewhat great.

What are the *effects* of (perceived) conflicts upon the attitudes towards participation? If there are no differences in opinions, there is not much to fight about, and we should expect little interest in formal participation. In addition, we assume that different conflicts compete for the attention of potential decision-makers (Schattschneider, 1960). If there are strong conflicts along *other* lines, hierarchical representation will become less relevant. However, the issue is confounded somewhat by organizational tactics. If for example, one sub-discipline will benefit from involving non-tenured faculty in decision-making processes, we may have proposals for change. Such attempts may well

300

be launched in the name of expanding the rights of participation of new groups or democratization even though their motivation lies elsewhere. While it in general is important to recognize this possibility, it does not seem to be intervening in the case at hand.

As expected, those who do not see any potential conflict are least interested in expanding the formal participation by reducing the formal authority of the chairman[8] (Table 13.4). The faculty who emphasizes *other* conflicts than the hierarchical ones constitute a middle group, and the faculty who mentions hierarchical conflict is least willing to agree that the chairman should have all formal authority. As predicted, differences in opinion about teaching-policy affect attitudes towards participation more than differences in opinions about research-policy.

Table 13.4. Attitudes towards participation, by respondents' perceptions of differences in opinions concerning the teaching, and research-policy of the department

Perceived differences in opinion about teaching-policy:

Attitudes towards giving the chairman all formal authority:	No differences	Other differences than hierarchical	Hierarchical differences mentioned
Agree completely	22.9	13.8	6.1
Agree partly	41.0	38.1	39.4
Disagree completely	36.1	48.1	54.5
Total	100.0%	100.0%	100.0%
(N)	(415)	(189)	(66)

Perceived differences in opinion about research-policy:

Attitudes towards giving the chairman all formal authority:	No differences	Other differences than hierarchical	Hierarchical differences mentioned
Agree completely	19.9	15.9	10.5
Agree partly	41.8	37.1	47.4
Disagree completely	38.3	47.0	42.1
Total	100.0%	100.0%	100.0%
(N)	(452)	(232)	(19)

Hierarchical differences[9] include both those who mention only such differences, and those who mention both hierarchical differences and differences along the sub-disciplines.

Other differences include those who answer that the differences are found between the sub-disciplines or that there are no stable lines.

If it is correct that coordination of teaching-activities are the most important decisions in most departments, we should expect to find significant differences in the attitudes towards participation between those departments where teaching is coordinated on the school-level, and those where teaching is coordinated at the department level. This expectation is strongly supported by the data in Tables 13.5 and 13.6. There are significant differences in attitudes also when we control for size (measured by the numbers of faculty-members) and for differences between hierarchical groups. The interpretation of these findings, however, is problematic.

The four schools coordinating teaching at the school-level are the four professional schools: Theology, Law, Medicine and Dental Medicine. There are two different "explanations" of the differences;

(a) We can use the rational choice model of participation, recognize that the most important decisions are those about teaching affairs, and predict that the interest in participation at the department-level (dependent on the degree to which the decision-making unit allocates anything of interest to the potential participant) will be higher in the three schools where the departments decide on teaching programs.

(b) Alternatively, we can assume there exist some important "cultural" differences between the professional schools and the other parts of the university.[10] These differences are such that we would predict the same differences in attitudes as the choice-model does. The "cultural" differences would be related to differences in recruitment, in differences inherent in the disciplines and in the close connections between the professional schools and certain other parts of society (e.g., the church, the hospital, the courts), and the values and beliefs dominating these institutions. Members of the professional schools in general are assumed to be more negative towards academic self-government, academic freedom, etc. (e.g., Lewis, 1966).

We do not have a "crucial experiment" to decide between the two explanations. However, a few points may be worth noting. The non-tenured faculty of the four professional schools have not been less interested than their colleagues in the three other schools in participation at the school level, in the Collegium, or in the Association of non-tenured faculty. In 1968 both the representative of the non-tenured faculty in the Collegium, and the chairman of the Association came from the professional schools. Further, there is no doubt that the faculty in the two clusters of schools perceive large differences in the relative importance of the departments and the schools as decision-making units. Listing 8 decision-units (from the Collegium to the sub-departments), we asked the faculty to indicate which was most important for them in their daily work at the university. We can rank the schools in terms of the percentage of the faculty who mention the school as most important:

	School mentioned as the most important of the 8 units by
1. Theology	92%
2. Law	59%
3. Medicine	33%
4. Dental Medicine	27%
5. Humanities	21%
6. Sciences	9%
7. Social sciences	7%

There are large differences in the perceptions of the relative importance of the different units between tenured and non-tenured faculty. The tenured faculty emphasizes the importance of the school, the non-tenured faculty finds the departments and sub-departments most important. However, the relative importance attributed to the school varies across the seven schools in the same way for all categories of faculty (Olsen, 1968, Table 5.1., page 100).

The choice model predicts that interest in participation at the school-level will vary as the importance of the school as a decision-making unit varies. The "cultural" model does not. We look at the participation in the meetings in the *school* councils in 1970. The councils met from 7 to 10 times during that year. Computing the median absence rate from these meetings, and ranking the schools from low absence to high absence, we have the following list:

1. Theology	0%
2. Dental Medicine	20%
3. Law	26%
4. Medicine	29%
5. Humanities	35%
6. Sciences	38%
7. Social Sciences	40%

These findings support the choice model. The four schools having the lowest rate of absence are the four schools ranked as relatively most important. Combining this with the much lower interest in participation in department governance among the faculty in the four professional schools compared to the faculty of the three other schools, the results are quite consistent with the model of participation as an individual, rational choice, but do not support a "cultural" explanation of the differences as clearly.

Our model of individual, rational choice treats "importance" as a necessary condition for activation. The analysis of the two aspects of "importance», (a) the range and utility of the rewards and the burdens distributed through the decision-making units, and (b) the possible

Table 13.5. The attitudes towards participation, by school and formal position

(a) Attitude toward giving the chairman all formal authority:	Humanities, Sciences and Social Sciences		Theology, Law, Medicine and Dental Medicine	
	Tenured faculty	Non-tenured faculty	Tenured faculty	Non-tenured faculty
Agree completely	18.4	14.4	27.3	26.2
Agree partly	29.6	36.6	53.0	55.3
Disagree completely	52.0	49.0	19.7	18.5
Total	100.0%	100.0%	100.0%	100.0%
(N)	(125)	(390)	(66)	(130)
(b) Attitude toward electing the chairman:				
Agree completely	59.0	62.2	29.3	28.6
Agree partly	22.2	22.4	36.2	31.1
Disagree completely	18.8	15.4	34.5	40.3
Total	100.0%	100.0%	100.0%	100.0%
(N)	(117)	(370)	(68)	(119)
(c) Definition of the problem of the non-tenured faculty:				
A question of information	16.4	19.3	38.2	43.5
A question of representation	83.6	80.7	61.8	56.5
Total	100.0%	100.0%	100.0%	100.0%
(N)	(128)	(405)	(68)	(131)

Non-tenured faculty includes here the assistants and fellows.

ways of dividing these rewards and burdens, has been consistent with the basic, theoretical ideas of this study. *First,* the findings that the faculty in general has not perceived participation as a very important issue and that participation has not been an issue producing much hierarchical conflicts, has been related both to the fact that most departments do not make many important decisions, and to the observation that rewards most often have to be divided between the sub-disciplines, more seldom between the hierarchical groups. *Second,* differences in the relative importance of decision-making units have been shown to have strong explanatory power concerning differences in attitude towards participation.

304

Table 13.6. Attitudes towards participation by size of the department and by school

NUMBER OF FACULTY MEMBERS:

	Less than 5		5–10 faculty		11–20 faculty		More than 20 faculty	
	T/L/M DM	H/S/SS	T/L/M DM	H/S/SS	T/L/M DM	H/S/SS	T/L/M DM	H/S/SS
(a) Attitude toward giving the chairman all formal authority.								
Agree completely	42.4	30.6	24.7	31.5	23.4	17.5	–	8.6
Agree partly	45.5	47.2	59.7	39.7	52.3	34.2	–	32.5
Disagree completely	12.1	22.2	15.6	28.8	23.4	48.2	–	58.9
Total	100.0%	100.0%	100.0%	100.0%	100.1%	100.0%	–	100.0%
(N)	(33)	(36)	(77)	(73)	(77)	(114)	–	(292)
(b) Attitude toward electing the chairman:								
Agree completely	25.0	57.1	26.8	47.8	28.8	58.7	–	66.0
Agree partly	20.8	28.6	40.8	20.9	31.5	22.1	–	22.2
Disagree completely	54.2	14.3	32.4	31.3	39.7	19.2	–	11.8
Total	100.0%	100.0%	100.0%	100.0%	100.0%	100.0%	–	100.0%
(N)	(24)	(28)	(71)	(67)	(73)	(104)	–	(285)
Definition of the problem of the non-tenured faculty:								
Question of information	56.3	25.0	39.2	24.7	39.2	24.1	–	14.3
Question of representation	43.8	75.0	60.8	75.3	60.8	75.9	–	85.7
Total	100.0%	100.0%	100.0%	100.0%	100.0%	100.0	–	100.0
(N)	(32)	(36)	(79)	(73)	(79)	(116)	–	(308)

T = Theology, L = Law, M = Medicine, DM = Dental Medicine, H = Humanities, S = Sciences and SS = Social Sciences. The numbers of respondents in the category: Departments with more than 20 faculty members within the schools of theology/law/medicine have too few cases for computing of percentages.

We now turn to the effects of differences in "alternatives" and "prospects". The low level of coordination and joint decision-making in many departments, combined with a high level of socio-economic security for all full-time faculty, probably make staying in the organization but investing little time in the "decision-making-processes" an attractive alternative to formal participation. In the following we analyze "alternatives", or the relative effectiveness of formal participation compared to other ways of affecting decisions or controlling the effects of such decision upon oneself; and of "prospects", or how the level of demands for participation at a given point in time is affected by perceptions of future mobility.

Our model predicts that demands for participation (and resistance towards such demands) will be less frequent in periods with considerable "slack" in the system. During expansion, most people will get some resources without activating themselves; the need for making joint decisions will be reduced; and it will be less difficult for sub-disciplines with different perspectives to split and develop their own departments. Most parts of the University of Oslo have been expanding strongly the last decade. The expansion was also (1968) expected to continue.[11]

What then are the effects of differences in perceived expansion upon attitude toward participation? While differences in expansion the last 10 years do not correlate with attitude towards participation, there is a (not very strong) relationship between attitude and expected future expansion. While 23 % and 18 % of those expecting strong expansion or some expansion are willing to give the department chairman all formal authority, only 7 % of those expecting status quo or scaling down give this answer. Further 62 % of the latter category agree completely that the chairman should be elected, against 51 % of the two other categories. There is no correlation between expected expansion and the way the problem of non-tenured faculty is defined.

The explanatory power of expansion is probably reduced by the fact that most parts of the university have expanded, and that the university leadership has shown a tendency toward "giving everybody something". (Wetlesen, 1967). Even departments which have not expanded in terms of new positions, have their budgets increased. The lack of coordination also should be expected to reduce the relevance of expansion, i.e. we should expect the degree of expansion to have a larger effect in strongly coordinated departments than in very loosely coupled departments, where expansion simply means adding more people who do their own thing, without any joint decisions. Our data do not permit a good test of these predictions.[12]

The general expansion affect both the chances for promotion and for getting resources. Thus, alternatives in terms of leaving the system should be expected to be of less importance, (strengthening the general tendency towards low mobility for full time faculty between academe and other sectors of Norwegian society). Less than 1/5 of our respondents feel their chances are very good of getting an equally good job outside the university-sector (18.5 %) or at a foreign university (17.6 %). Furthermore most of these have not been thinking about leaving the university. Their chances for success (in their own terms) are fairly great also *within* the university. There is no correlation between (perceived) exit-possibilities and attitude towards participation.

If it is correct that the most important decisions in the system are those related to teaching affairs, it will be difficult to "exit" by getting resources from outside while staying in the organization. If, however, decisions on research-money were the most important, it is easy to see how faculty could control the effects of department decisions on themselves by "compensating" by external resources. In the latter case we would expect, (a) the more a department gets from outside, given a certain level of costs in the field, i.e. controlling for research technology, the less the interest in participation in department governance, and (b) the differences in attitudes between those who get much and those who get little from outside would be larger the more expensive the research. None of these predictions are given any support in the data (Olsen, 1971, Table 19). This observation adds support to the argument above that one should not focus upon research-activities when trying to understand the demands for participation in the university studied.

We look at the effects on attitude towards participation of different degrees of perceived informal influence upon important decisions. In the university studied, there are different opinions about both teaching and research. The more these differences are transformed to joint choices and related to the allocation of important burdens and rewards, the more we would expect those who are not satisfied with their formal participation to express a strong desire for an expansion of the formal participation. All the three indicators of attitude towards participation show that those unsatisfied with own informal influence more than those satisfied want an expansion. However, the differences are fairly small. Of those satisfied with own influence 20 % agree completely that the chairman should be given all formal authority, 42 % agree partly and 38 % disagree completely, as against 16 %, 34 %, and 50 % of those unsatisfied. Of those satisfied with own influence 50 % agree completely that the chairman should be elected, 24 % agree partly and 26 % disagree completely. This against 58 %, 29 %, and 13 % of those dissatisfied. Further, the differences are even smaller concerning the definition of the problem of the non-tenured, where 74 % of the satisfied and 78 % of those unsatisfied with own influence say the problem is one of representation. These patters of moderate differences are what we would expect to find in an organization not making too many joint choices, i.e. where the well-being of the person is not completely dependent upon the outcome of departmental decisions and where the lack of influence is not too important for the "loosers".

The size of department is another indicator of the chances for *informal* influence. So far the reorganizations have taken place in the largest departments. In the survey data there is a very clear and nearly linear relationship between size of department and attitude towards participation. 37 % of the respondents at the smallest departments (less than 5 faculty members) agree completely to give the chairman all formal authority. As size increases, this percentage decreases to 28 %, (in departments with 5–10 faculty members), 20 % (11–20 faculty members) and 9 % in the largest departments with more than 20 faculty members. Likewise only 17 % in the smallest departments disagree completely with giving the chairman all formal authority, increasing to 22 %, 38 %, and 58 %.

The same clear pattern is found in the two other indicators. In the smallest departments only 42 % agree completely with the statement that the chairman should be elected (33 % are completely against it). These percentages change to 66 % agreeing completely and only 13 % disagreeing completely in the largest departments. In the smallest departments 40 % define the problem of the non-tenured as a question of information, a number decreasing to 15 % in the largest departments.

However, we know that the largest departments are disproportionally found outside the four professional schools, and in Table 13.6 we read the effects of size when controlled for the two groups of schools (the four professional schools vs. the three others). In spite of very small numbers of respondents in many of the categories, the effect of size is still clear. In the professional schools, however, the main difference is found between the departments with less than 5 faculty members and the others. In the other schools the most important difference is found between the largest department (more than 20 faculty members) and the others. The only case inconsistent with the expected trends is the very smallest departments in Humanities/ Sciences/Social Sciences, which very strongly want the director elected. The total number of these respondents are 28, and given the consistency in the other patterns, we assume some specific factors to be operating.

The problem is how to interpret these differences. Increasing size often is assumed to change behavior in organizations because face- to-face relationships become difficult, and the organization has to be governed in formal ways. As people become dissatisfied with their relations with one another, they tend to ask for representation (e.g., Dill, 1964). On the other hand political apathy is often correlated with size. As size increases the complexity also often increases, and many potential participants feel "lost". It may also be expected that the larger the department, the more likely that more than one sub-discipline and more than one "paradigm" will be present and the more likely that conflict will occur. Further, the larger the departments, the larger the chances that duplication of courses will take place. In the Norwegian system this most of the time means that several faculty members have to agree on the content of one course. Thus the more duplication, the more joint decisions. However, we should not forget that the responses may simply reflect the attitude that given the larger size, the chairmanship becomes a very "costly" position, and that one man should not be burdened with it. With the present data we will not be able to say anything more specific about the relative effects of these and other factors.

Finally, in this section we analyze the effects of different prospects for future leadership through upward mobility. Two indicators of prospects for future leadership through social (hierarchical) mobility in the organization are used;

(a) The respondents' own perceptions of their prospects for advancement within the organization (excluding all the full professors), and (b) the actual ratios between tenured and non-tenured positions in each department. The expected tendency can be seen in both sets of data (Tables 13.7 and 13.8). The less good the prospects for advancement, the less the respondents are willing to give the director all formal authority. Among those with the "best" ratio between tenured and non-tenured faculty only 30.9 % disagree completely with giving the chairman all formal authority, while half of the respondents in departments with the least good ratio disagree completely. The same tendency – but somewhat weaker – is found in the perception-data.[13] Together, these two data-sets give some support for the hypothesis that reduced possibilities for hierarchical mobility within the organization, makes it less likely that the participants will support an arrangement giving all formal authority to one person.

The analysis of "alternatives" and "prospects" has given some support to both the value of the rational choice model for understanding participation, and to the basic picture that has been drawn of the university. It is not possible in this study to be very precise about the relative explanatory power of the different variables upon desires for participation. The indicators used are often too imprecise for such purposes. They have, however, been precise enough for studying the potential value of the rational choice model. They have also lead us to some basic properties of universities in general, and especially of the importance of explicit decision-making in organizations such as a university.

Table 13.7. The attitudes towards the formal authority of the department director, by department-ratio of tenured to non-tenured faculty:

Attitude toward giving the chairman all formal authority:	The ratio of tenured to non-tenured faculty is:		
	LOW	MIDDLE	HIGH
Agree completely	14.8	17.2	19:5
Agree partly	34.8	39.8	49.6
Disagree completely	50.4	43.0	30.9
Total	100.0%	100.0%	100.0%
(N)	(135)	(407)	(139)

LOW   = The ratio is .2 or lower
MIDDLE = The ratio is between .2 and .4.
HIGH   = The ratio is higher than .4.

Table 13.8. The attitudes towards the formal authority of the director, by respondents' perceptions of own prospects for advancement

Attitude toward giving the chairman all formal authority:	Prospects for advancement:	
	Very/fairly good	Not very good
Agree completely	24.4	18.5
Agree partly	48.7	45.7
Disagree completely	26.9	35.8
Total	100.0%	100.0%
(N)	(134)	(381)

13.5 Conclusion

The main aim of this chapter was to examine the possible clarification provided by a model in which participation is viewed as a choice rather than automatic. The study has underlined the need to supplement the view of participation as something attractive to be fought for, with a view taking into account a "cost"-side analyzing participation as a sacrifice. The findings cannot easily be understood in a framework stressing hierarchical conflicts between tenured and non-tenured faculty. A major observation is that hierarchical position do not explain any of the variation in the attitudes towards increased participation in department governance. The analysis clearly indicated the complexity of processes of influence in a university.

Our explanations of the patterns of demands for and resistance to increased participation have been related to how the specific situation of the University of Oslo affected the *importance* of departmental choices, the *alternatives* to formal participation, and the *prospects* for future leadership. We have considered (a) general factors like that many decisions are removed from the university, the strong expansion, the high socio-economic security of faculty etc., and (b) factors varying across departments like whether the coordination of teaching affairs was located at the school or department level, the size of departments, the ratio of tenured to non-tenured faculty etc.

More important, however, our analysis has been related to some basic aspect of the university as an organization dominated by professionals primarily focusing upon creating, transmitting and storing knowledge. Two factors have been considered. *First,* the moderate importance of explicit decision-making. *Second,* the divisibility of rewards and burdens, which more often seems to follow the lines of sub-disciplines than any other lines, including the hierarchical ones.

Models of hierarchical command or of power-struggle miss important aspects of governance of a university. The university is a large, complex organization in terms of the number of employees, budgets, the complexity of tasks etc. However, it is "run" without the level of organization, coordination and joint decision-making that many make a major part of their definition of "organization".[14] We have been studying an organization without any ultimate center of authority, issuing orders down the hierarchy in a clear line of command. Since most people define an organization as something close to a Weberian ideal bureaucracy, it is important to stress that the university is much more loosely coupled. The level of coordination, governance and joint decision-making certainly will affect the interest in participation.

The lack of coordination through formal decision-making does not mean that each faculty-member is "autonomous", or that processes of influence do not operate. It only means that hierarchical command, supervision and control, as known from traditional bureaucracies, play a more moderate role in the governance of this type of organization. The university should be looked upon as *biased* in the way that it emphasizes some values and beliefs more than others, takes more interest in some problems than others etc. But at the same time we should be aware of the difficulties of changing these biases through formal decision-making. The values and beliefs emphasized are related more to the general "academic marketplace" than to any specific organization. By defining the criteria for expertice, prestige, rewards and acceptance, the academic marketplace constrain the degree of discretion for organizational decision-makers, and influence the day-to-day behavior of most participants in the university. They reduce the importance of "decision-making", they strongly affect the divisibility of rewards, they increase the importance of "socialization", and they make the organizational blueprints – including the formal rules about participation – less important.

NOTES:

1 An underlying assumption is that both the importance of what is distributed through organizational choices, and the perception of individual efficacy is held constant. An important debate on participation in situations of collective or individual goods was initiated by Olson (1968) who argued that class-oriented action will never occur if the individuals that make up the class act rationally. The larger the class, the larger the problem of activating rational actors. Each want to get the rewards, but want others to pay the costs or participation. For a criticism of this view see Rogowski (1969) and Frohlich and Oppenheimer (1970). The latter argue that Olson's conclusions cannot be derived as a logical consequence of rational self-interested behavior. A main point is that the potential participant must decide whether to activate himself or not through estimating the probabilities that his contributions will be efficacious or not. To do this, he must estimate the probabilities associated with the possible levels of donations by others. By making a larger donation the individual increases the probability that he will receive the good for any given set of probabilities he attaches to the behavior of others. Without knowing something about the mechanisms whereby potential participants can coordinate their expectations regarding the probable actions of others, we cannot give an answer of effects of increasing size.

2 In Coleman's model of rational choice (1964, 1966) an actor with such specific interests would be very powerful within the system. An important difference between our predictions and those of Coleman, is that ours are strongly related to assumptions about time as a scarce resource, while Coleman does not take into consideration (time and energy) costs related to search, coalition-building etc.

3 This argument was strongly illustrated when we tried to explain the lack of demands for formal participation at the University of Oslo by the technical and administrative staff (Olsen, 1968).

4 Size is a variable that often gives clear correlations with other variables within a study, but often gives less consistent patterns across different studies. This is related to the fact that size is often treated without the possibility of correcting for all the other intercorrelated variables. Size is often related to the growth of a bureaucracy, that is with specialization and delegation to fulltime employees. Bidwell, however, argues that there is no firm empirical evidence for the linkage of size and bureaucratization in school systems. (Bidwell, 1964, p. 1001).

5 A certain discount-rate may operate, making immediate power relatively more attractive than future power. This factor becomes more important the longer the time-perspective. In organizations where it is very difficult to predict future events, we would expect demands for participation immediately to be stronger.

6 This tendency can be read out of several tables. In Table 13.2 the low number of respondents (n $=$ 513 for research) is partly reflecting the fact that this question was asked only those who had been in the department three years or more. The *differences* in the number of respondents on the questions of teaching and research policies, have to be understood in terms of several people perceiving some coordination of teaching, but not of research-affairs.

7 There are no differences in attitudes towards participation following from what the main interest of the respondents were, e.g. interest in research, teaching etc. which might give different "utility-structures". These differences in interest were measured both by the direct answer in the questionnaire and the writing of research-reports, attendances to research-conferences etc.

8 In order to reduce the number of tables, we report the answers on all three indicators only for the most important variables. Where we limit ourself to attitudes towards giving the chairman all formal authority, the general patterns are the same for the two other questions. Also, these distributions can be found in Olsen, 1971.

9 Since the number of respondents who perceive *only* hierarchical conflicts is very small, we have to merge the categories in this way. Both the theoretical ideas presented above, and the trends in the empirical data (prior to the combination of the categories) justify these reductions. However, the differences will be smaller since the majority of those mentioning hierarchical conflicts also "see" conflict between the sub-disciplines.

10 With culture we simply mean the shared beliefs and orientations that unite the members of a collectivity and guide their conduct. (Blau and Scott, 1966, pp. 2−8). More than 50 years ago Veblen argued that the professional and technical schools have more in common among themselves as a class, than this class have with the academic aims and methods of the university proper (Veblen, 1957, p. 29).

11 More than 90 % of our respondents described their discipline as having strong or some expansion the last 10 years, 7.3 % answered that it had been status quo, and 1.1 % described the tendency as one of scaling down the discipline. 26.6 % expected a very strong expansion the next 10 years, 60.6 % some expansion, while only 8.5 % expected status quo and 0.5 % a scaling down of their discipline in the next 10 years. (3.8 % did not answer the question or did not have any opinion).

12 It is also likely that the relationship between attitude toward participation and expansion is curvelinear, i.e., that no expansion and very strong expansion produces little interest in having participation while the middle categories (some expansion) produces demands for access to department governance. The categories used in the questionnaire are not adequate for testing such points of view.

13 Evaluating the perception data we should take into consideration that 21.7 % did not respond (after we have excluded the full professors who should not respond to this question). Only 6.1 % of the rest (N $=$ 477) perceive their own chances as very good. This stands in strong contrast with their perceptions of future expansion in the field, and clearly a "norm of modesty" is working, making the data less reliable.

14 We primarily consider processes related to research and teaching. In universities like in most other organizations we expect the traditional bureaucratic model to be most relevant for understanding processes like monthly payment of salaries, cleaning of the buildings etc. Thus, we may think about different models as describing some processes in organizations but not others.

14. Reorganization as a Garbage Can

JOHAN P. OLSEN

University of Bergen

14.0. Introduction

Organization implies intention. Although we recognize that any particular organization is also a collection of history and a relatively complex set of activities, relations, and symbols, we ordinarily interpret organizations as social instruments. They are intendend to facilitate the accomplishment of objectives. They are intended to exhibit elements of efficiency and effectiveness.

Reorganization similarly suggests intention. Reorganizations have been proposed, implemented, and understood mainly as solutions to problems. Organizations are changed deliberately in order to achieve greater efficiency, more human satisfaction, or some new type of substantive policy (Mosher, 1967). The idea is a familiar one (see Chapter 1): Problems arise; analysis suggests that the problem lies in the organization; a reorganization is adopted; the problem is solved (or sometimes not if the analysis is faulty). As we have noted earlier (see Chapter 6), an organizational decision can sometimes be viewed as a result of a process in which decision makers, or some winning coalition, solve their problems or resolve their conflicts. A similar interpretation of reorganization may often capture important elements of the phenomenon.

Often, however, reorganization is a garbage can. It is a choice opportunity that collects an assortment of loosely-connected problems, solutions, and participants. The collection may include a variety of substantive concerns; different participants may graft onto a reorganization decision solution to almost any current problem. Thus, reorganizations have become simultaneous vehicles for discussing efficiency of communication, firing managers, concealing unfortunate budgetary comparisons, and changing the standard operating procedures. Reorganization is a choice opportunity that provides relatively open access for problems of almost any type.

Because it is a choice opportunity with relatively free access for problems and solutions, discussions of reorganization are likely to attract not only any number of independent practical problems but

314

also a disproportionate number of symbolic issues. As a result, a reorganization sometimes may be most adequtely described as a process through which an organization arrives at an interpretation of what it has become or what it has been doing, what it is becoming or what it is doing, what it is going to become or what it is going to be doing. Such a perspective emphasizes the expressive, symbolic, and image-exercising aspects of a reorganization. It underlines the need for examining reorganizations as occasions for discovering or accepting new organizational values, or occasions for confirming and giving reassurance about old ones.

In this chapter we consider the interplay of practical problems and image-exercising in the reorganization garbage can. The base is a case study of a major reorganization in a Norwegian university. The study combined the examination of archival materials, interviews, and a general questionnaire. It is reported in greater detail elsewhere (Olsen 1968, 1971).

The institute directorship of the university has been described as the last stronghold of feudalism in Europe (e.g., Consolazio, 1961). As late as 1963–64 the department chairman of a Norwegian university was an autocrat, in the sense that he had all *formal* authority and responsibility in his hands. In the middle of the 1960's a major reorganization took place in some departments. The "classical" (German) model with small, one professor-ruled institutes, without any administrative staff was abandoned. The role of the full professor and chairman was dramatically changed. The idea was to construct large departments, governed thorugh a system of collective decision-making. A council, a board, and a chairman were to be elected. Non-tenured faculty, technical and administrative staff, and students were for the first time formally allowed to take part in departmental governance. At the same time, the role of a department secretary was introduced as an attempt to strengthen the office organization. This new departmental organization became known as the "physics model", and has played a major role in Norwegian discussions of university governance over recent years.

The new departmental organization was developed for the Department of Physics at the University of Oslo.[1] The present study began as an attempt to understand why the reorganization took place, and why it came first in the physics department. As the study developed, it exposed several counter-intuitive features to this "victory for democracy".[1] Instead of being a bloody battle around the last stronghold of feudalism, the reorganization took place without many people attending to it, and with very little conflict. As a matter of fact, the autocrats themselves (full professors and administrative leaders) were the most active in changing the system. Although those without any formal power seldom showed much interest, they ended up with substantially increased representation in the new decision-making units.

While in retrospect celebrated as a crusade for democracy and participation, the reorganization did not begin as an issue of power and influence. On the contrary, it started as an attempt to solve a classic practical problem for the department leaders. They wanted to be relieved from routine work. As time went by, reorganization became a "garbage can", a meeting place for participants, solutions, and problems. Many of the issues ultimately related to the choice were distant from the day-to-day-life of the Department of Physics. They became elements of the definition of reorganization as the reorganization accumulated extensive symbolic meaning.

The exercising of issues, problems, solutions, and images cannot easily be understood as attempts to affect the immediate, substantive (material) outcome of the choice at stake. The symbolic-expressive exercises seemed to be ways of testing and changing conceptions of the "ideal" department. They were related to the character, the mission, the goals, and the beliefs that different participants wished to have dominate a university department. Partly these exercises need to be understood in terms of their potential impact in other choice arenas. Physics was the arena, but not the only object.

The process is an extended garbage can. As a result, we analyze it by considering the streams of problems, solutions, and participants. We look at how different groups defined the situation in 1963–64: What problems they brought, what had caused the problems, and how the problems could be solved. Further, the patterns of activation are described: How some groups took strong initiatives and became heavily involved; how others more or less ignored the reorganization. We then turn to the solutions chosen by the organization. The process is divided into two phases. The *first* was primarily focused on making the organizations more "rational and efficient", and on reducing the costs of participation for leaders. In the *second* phase the demands for participation among non-leaders became more important, and the new representation system was developed.

14.1 The First Phase

The first phase of the reorganization discussion covers the period from May, 1963 to April, 1964. During this period the choice opportunity (reorganization) collected an assortment of problems, solutions, and a little participation energy. It was a minor set of issues for most people, a moderate concern for a few, a major concern for almost no one.

14.1.0 Problems, Solutions, and Participants

At the beginning, and through the first phase, most potential participants had completely empty models of the situation. They did not formulate their points of view. They were unconcerned and uninvolved. This was true for a majority of the faculty, the students, the research assistants, and the technical-administrative staff. The chief body of university governance (the Collegium) did not involve itself. The faculty in other departments seems to have barely noticed what was going on. Relative to all the other claims on their attention, reorganization of the Department of Physics was insignificant and distant.

Amidst this extensive sense of irrelevance, there were two groups who saw reorganization initially as an opportunity for exercising (and perhaps solving) some problems. The groups defined the problems somewhat differently. The *first* group was a group of full professors who were, or recently had been, department chairman. Their problems were the pragmatic concerns of academic lower management:

(a) The administrative burdens had become too heavy for the department leaders because of the growth in the department. The leaders had to be relieved of some routine work.

(b) The growth had also made the "section" unfit as an administrative unit.[2] Too many people were involved. The section was difficult to handle and very time-consuming.

(c) The department had a strong need for making joint decisions. Projects had become very expensive. When one group got money, all the others were affected. Thus, the department needed an organizational structure that could establish priorities.

(d) The department had grown unevenly. There were only a few new full professorships or associate professorships, but many assistant professorships. Several of the latter had become highly qualified professionally. It was difficult to give any professional rationale why they should not participate in department governance.[3]

(e) There existed a large discrepancy between the way the department actually was run and its formal constitution. It was of some importance to legalize and formalize the changes which had already taken place. The department for a decade had had a council which had no formal standing, but which was accepted as binding internally. The section (in which all participated) had been very active. Nobody had tried to limit the discussions and decisions to pure teaching matters. The chairmanship had rotated among the senior professors.

(f) One of the secretaries had assumed considerable informal responsibility. It seemed necessary, in order to keep her in the department, to find a position which better reflected the work she was actually doing. The administrative leaders of the department considered it very important to keep this secretary in the department.

The *second* group of participants were the administrators on the school and university level. They clearly perceived the existing department-structure of the university as "inefficient". They wanted to make the system less costly to run, and they wanted to reduce the "chaos". They saw the Department of Physics as only one instance of some general problems. They believed:

(a) The general growth in the activity of the university had made existing channels of communication and control inadequate.
(b) The large number of small departments governed by professors with little interest in administration and little information about the increasingly complex web of laws and rules produced a stream of questions from the departments to the school and university administration. It also produced some incorrect handling of issues, which the administration had to correct.
(c) As the university was asking for more and more money, it was important to develop better documentation for the budget proposals. (Wetlesen, 1967, pp. 52–53.)

The early ideas about reorganization grew out of these simple concerns for solving ordinary problems. Both groups (though for somewhat different reasons) saw a need for eliminating the sections, consolidating the structure into a smaller number of larger units, strengthening the position of the secretary, and introducing a more formalized decision making system. For the department chairman this provided a justification for enlarging the job of the secretary (and thus retaining her), getting rid of the sections, and providing a formal justification of the existing departmental council. For the university administrators the proposed reorganization introduced a useful arm of the administration (the secretary) into the department and reduced the span of control. On both sides, the values that were emphasized explicitly were those of administrative efficiency and the improvement of professional quality.

These proposals for solutions, in combination with the ambiguity of the issues of efficiency and the ease of access to the reorganization garbage can, stimulated two other groups of participants. The first were the defenders of the classical institute. Their thinking was made explicit in letters from the Head of Theoretical Physics, a subdepartment of the Department of Physics. The basic argument was that nothing had happened which made changes in the organization-structure necessary.

(a) Professional authority was still seen as the only basis for department government. The way full professors were appointed was the guarantee that they were the best qualified people. Using a voting procedure was unfitting to decision-making within academe. Such a procedure would be working against the authority and responsibility of having a university chair. It would be natural for the full professor (chairman) to consult his colleagues before he made decisions, but *whom* he should consult, *when,* and *about what,* were the decision and responsibility of the professor.

(b) The need for professional, administrative help was also denied. The general development of a stronger university administration was perceived as a burden, not as a help to the professor. What he primarily needed was more help in typing his manuscripts, etc.

(c) The recent changes in curricula toward a course system, with credit connected to each course (and not as earlier with exams only after two or more semesters), had weakened the students' ability to think independently, had made the university more school-like, and had given each professor less control over his subject. The new reorganizations were viewed as unfortunate extensions of these tendencies.

(d) As long as all parts of a department were not gathered in one building, a joint decision-making system and administration would be costly and inefficient.

The organizational solution suggested was to keep an arrangement with smaller departments with full authority and responsibility over a limited area for each full professor. The demand for more coordination was met with a strong demand for autonomy. Each institute should be allowed to arrange its own affairs as it wanted. This would both increase the professional quality and be more efficient. A modified version was to accept that the professors had to be relieved of routine-work, but to deny the importance of coordination of different sub-departments. Each sub-department should make all the important decisions and be governed by the full professor in the field.

The second group of new participants in the discussion of reorganization were the leaders of the university association of junior faculty, representing junior faculty throughout the university. While the chairman of the association was an assistant professor in physics, those most concerned with the rights, power, and status of junior faculty on the department level in this period mainly came from other departments, where these issues in general were perceived as more important and more problematic than in the physics department. The activity of junior faculty in the Department of Physics was rather modest. The reorganization of their department became a garbage can with respect to the rights, power, and status-issues. However, these concerns were clearly not created by the activities in the physics department.

Three months before the events in the Department of Physics (February 1963), representatives from the junior faculty discussed the relative emphasis they should put on demanding participation at the department, school, and collegium level. The participants realized that both the actual arrangements and the wishes for participation at the department level varied across the schools. The minutes from the meeting in the association state that the discussants talked little about *how*, (if at all), the non-tenured personnel should go about to increase its influence in the sections and in the departments. One possible solution mentioned was that the department was to be organized by establishing a board for the chairman which would be under some control from the section. A committee was appointed to work on the issue.

The events in the physics department provided an opportunity for discussing participation rights. Leaders of the association of junior faculty protested that the new arrangements gave the junior faculty less influence and was less democratic than the existing arrangements. At the same time, the existing organization, and its distribution of formal authority in general were attacked. The protesting letter stated that: "It is not seldom that decisions with great importance for the non-tenured faculty members' work are made without being submitted to organs where this group has a real possibility to influence the decision." The department chairman should not be allowed (the letter said) to decide if junior faculty members should participate.[4] It was emphasized that junior faculty should be involved in the decision-making process as early as possible in all important decisions (i.e., budgets, allocation of resources, and personnel-policy). The demand concerning stronger influence for the junior faculty was related both to the well-being of this group, and to professional quality. It was argued that the new organizational arrangement would work against these values. The group suggested that the Collegium appoint a committee to analyze the situation in the different schools and propose a new administrative arrangement for the university as a whole.

Thus at the outset, the discussion involved problems ranging from the highly specific and localized problem of reclassifying a valued secretary, to issues of general university policy with respect to administrative coordination and faculty governance. Only a few people were involved; this was only one of several arenas for them; for most of them the problems of the Department of Physics, *per se,* were incidental to the relevance of those problems for the symbolic battles for administrative efficiency, participatory democracy, and professional competence.

14.1.1 *The Flow of Events and Activity*

Table 14.0 shows the time line of the more important events in the reorganization process. The plans for reorganization were initiated by the upper levels in the organization. They came from some full professors who had had administrative responsibilities, and some full-time administrators. The committee proposing the new department rules was appointed by the dean, a former chairman of the Department of Physics who also took an active part in its work. It consisted of four full professors, one junior faculty and the secretary who later became department-secretary in the physics department.

Other groups either reacted, trying to delay the decisions and win time, or they ignored the choice. The junior faculty association and the defender of the "classical institute"-model both (but on very different premises) tried to get the decision postponed. However, not even the decision in the Collegium (June 19, 1963) to postpone the decision had any significant effect on the process. When it was discovered that in spite of the decision in the Collegium the School had continued working out the plans for the new department-organization, the highest governing body of the university did not try to force its will (February 27, 1964). The Council of the School of the Sciences did not even discuss the final proposal.

Junior faculty was represented in all units handling the decision. They never dissented, even when the participation issue did not become important. We observe an increasing interest in the participation question but solutions and strategies were still very unclear. The reorganization initiative worked as a "spark", leading the junior faculty to take points of view they did not express earlier. The letter on behalf of the Association of junior faculty (June 19, 1963) attempted to make the participation question a university-wide decision, but the events in the Department of Physics took place so rapidly that all problems were "solved" on the department level. In the Department of Physics junior faculty took less interest in the participation-issue.

The strongest defender of the "classical institute"-model also tried to stop or postpone the decision. When he did not succeed, he simply declared that he did not intend to participate in the new arrangement with "his sub-department". Nobody tried to force him. The decision in the School of the Sciences was made unanimous with the exception of a paragraph on uniting small departments into larger ones. Here two voted against. In general the faculty in other departments remained passive. The students, assistants, and the technical and administrative staff never became activated.

It should be added that the *absolute* level of activity was low. In terms of the number of meetings held, the number of people involved, and the degree of writing, the level of activity was much lower than one might expect in an apparently important decision. The process was characterized by a very limited search for alternative organization models. There was very little data or argumentation. No studies were made. The reports from the Administrative Board and the departmental committee were extremely short papers. Few participants tried to clarify the consistency in their values and beliefs. Few attempts were made to build coalitions against the proposal.

14.1.2 *The Solution in the First Phase*

The Administrative Board of the School stated as its task the development of an administrative arrangement adapted to the large size of the departments, which, as much as possible, would relieve the scientists of administrative burdens if they were willing to delegate responsibilty and authority over routine functions. The administrative unit which should be the point of departure for the future organization of the departments had to be the large department like Pharmacy, Physics, Chemistry, and Mathematics. These units were to be "administered as any other large firm by (a) a board, (b) an administrative director (chairman) and (c) a strong office organization, the department secretariat. The latter was perceived as the most important element in relieving the professors of administrative responsibilities and burdens and providing close contact to the administration at the school and university level. The Administrative Board proposed to dissolve the sections as administrative units and to dissolve the positions of section-chairman and secretary. It was proposed to merge smaller departments into larger units as soon as "the external conditions made this appropriate".

The new department board would "be responsible for the great lines in the department's policies, internally and externally". It would consist of all the leaders of the sub-departments, and a number (to be specified later) of the professors, associate professors, assistant professors and students. It is not clear from the document whether administrative and technical personnel would be represented. The chairman would be elected from among the full professors or associate

Table 14.0. Time line of events

Dates	Events
May 15, 1963	The Council of the School of the Sciences discusses the proposition of reorganization of the departments from the Administrative Board of the School and decides to support it.
May 22, 1963	The Association of non-tenured faculty at the university sends a letter to the Collegium demanding that the question of the participation of non-tenured faculty at the department-level has to be considered. The Collegium postpones the decision.
November 2, 1963	The Administrative Board of the School of the Sciences asks the Departments of Physics and Chemistry to make an outline for an administrative arrangement for the two departments built on the decision in the Council of the School. The committee is asked to work quickly.
December 21, 1963	After some consultation, two meetings are arranged. The committee proposed a department Council (in addition to the chairman, board, and administrative staff). This proposal is discussed informally in the two departments.
January 3, 1964	The committee proposal is ready.
February 24, 1964	The Administrative Board of the School accepts the proposal (with some smaller changes). The Council of the School does not discuss it.
February 27, 1964	A letter is sent from the assistant university director (earlier secretary of the School and a signer of the initial proposal from the administrative board about reorganization) to the School, saying that since the school has already decided to try out the new arrangement, it is better that the Collegium accepts this formally.
March 3, 1964	The School asks the Collegium to accept the arrangement.
March 13, 1964	The Collegium accepts the arrangement, temporarily for one year.
March 21, 1964	In a letter to the Collegium the leader of the sub-department for theoretical physics says that he will not take part in the new arrangement.
November 29, 1965	The Department of Physics in a letter to the School proposes a permanent arrangement which accepts the reorganization made, but introduces (a) a stronger representation of the non-tenured faculty members, (b) states that all the members of the Council and the Board should be elected, (c) introduces permanent committees for teaching policy and personnel-policy, and finally, (d) eliminates the sub-departments. All the research areas should be represented in the Council and the tenured faculty members should not necessarily any longer be in a majority.
December 14, 1965	Collegium accepts this arrangement for one year.

professors for a one year term. He would decide whether decisions had general interest and therefore should be presented for the board. The sub-departments would be kept, but only as working units, not administrative units.

The committee from the departments of physics and chemistry, which was appointed to work out the new rules in more detail, proposed one important change: the introduction of a council.[5] The Council was supposed to work out the long range policies, but at the same time the committee stated that they wanted to try out these arrangements before the division of labor between Council, Board, Chairman, and Secretary was decided. The stated dilemma was to find a balance between, on the one hand, keeping the number of participants so low that the units could work, and on the other hand, letting all interests in the department have access to the governing organs. The interests of the leaders of the sub-departments were especially taken care of: The chairman was not allowed to make decisions in any important issues without discussing it with them. Discussing the committee-proposal and whether the students would be represented in the Board of the departments, the conclusion in the Administrative Board was that, "it was agreed that such representation was not appropriate in an executive unit as this".

The new *Council* consisted of the following: (a) All leaders of sub-departments, all full professors and associate professors, (b) the department leaders for teaching affairs, (c) two representatives from the junior faculty (besides those otherwise included), (d) one representative from the technical staff, (e) the chairman of the (department) student body.

In the *Board* all sub-departments would be represented, and in general all interests in the departments would be taken care of. The members were: (a) the department chairman, (b) one full professor or associate professor from all the sub-departments not having the chairman, (c) one junior faculty member, and (d) one of the department-leaders for teaching affairs (who should participate only in pure teaching matters). The chairman would be elected from among the full professors or associate professors by the Council, and the department secretary should function as secretary both in the Council and the Board.

The discussion of reorganization exercised two broad kinds of concerns: On the one hand, there were the concerns with the everyday organization of the Department of Physics. How should things be done in the department? On the other hand, there were the concerns with the major symbolic issues of efficiency, professional quality, and participation. Whose definition of the issues before the university would be accepted and what precedents would be set? As might be expected in such a situation, discussion and decision tended to become relatively independent.

Very little was written during the process, and the written documents by and large were of modest relevance for the situation in the physics department. The size aspect emphasized in the Administrative Board, was completely irrelevant. Even if theoretical physics were separated, both departments were larger than the new norm proposed. The new Council did not operate very differently from the section, and the real governance of the departments were still dominated by consultation among a few leaders. The felt need for a new bureaucrat was very real, but it should be remembered that one of the secretaries was already doing this job. In order to understand the process observed we have to look for potential relevance of this process for events *outside* the immediate arena.

The department leaders, being concerned with their own load of routine-matters, tried to secure a better position, in terms of status and salary, for the person already working as secretary.[6] To get a new position, the image of the department held by the governmental "0 and M" – bureau had to be changed. They had to believe that the new department-organization would be more efficient.[7] By and large this could be done through formalizing the system as it was operating already.

Neither was the university administration primarily concerned with changing the physics department. The reorganization provided an opportunity to create a formal position (department secretary) which might be useful as an incentive in future bargaining with other departments. At the same time the administration through the reorganization got a definition of the "ideal"-department, which could be used as a model for other (smaller, non-bureaucratized) departments in the future. For the university administration the reorganization became a garbage can into which they dropped the problems they had in their relations with these other departments. These issues were closely related to the long run problem of the administration: reducing the amount of administrative chaos and building more "efficient" routines.

The reorganization also became a choice opportunity into which the leader of theoretical physics could throw the problems he perceived relating to the general development of the Department of Physics, (e.g., a trend toward a more "school-like" institution and the changes in the role of the full professor). The defender of the classical institute model did not succed in having his definition of the situation accepted. The new constitution represented a break with important elements in his model. But he claimed his price: It was accepted that he (and thus others like him)[8] could withdraw from the new arrangement. The passivity of the professors in some other departments has (at least partly) to be understood on the basis of this understanding that no full professor should be forced into the new arrangement.

The leaders of the junior faculty in the university at large tried to have the problem of junior faculty participation related to the choice. They perceived it as easier to have a formal representation of junior faculty accepted in the Department of Physics than in most other places. In this way it would be important to provide a model which could be used in future bargaining in other departments. However, the garbage can moved too fast in the first period. The participation issue never became central. For the first time, junior faculty, students, and the technical/administrative staff became formally represented in department government; but compared to the arrangements that had operated informally, they gained little in the physics department.

During this first phase the different participants by and large stressed the same general (and non-operational) values, but they had different opinions about what was going on, and about the effects of the possible alternatives. The choice-process became a dumping place for problems and issues which were primarily related to definitions, problems and images outside the Department of Physics. Several groups did not attempt to change anything in the physics department, but found the process of reorganization fitted for exercising their general problems. There was no conflict, leadership by the full professors with administrative responsibilities, a steady expansion of participation rights, and a continuation of informal professional authority exercised by physicists of recognized professional stature. Although the symbolism of participation became a frequent theme, there was almost no overt conflict in which the lines of cleavage divided senior and junior faculty.

14.2 The Second Phase

14.2.0 *The Flow of Events and Activities*

The new rules (November 1965) of the Department of Physics stated as the two most important principles: (1) To introduce a stronger representation of the junior faculty; (2) All seats should now be filled through elections, to eliminate all ex-officio-memberships in the Council and the Board. The new rules deemphasized hierarchical groups as the basis for representation, and focused on the research-groups. Senior people were given 50 percent of the seats in the Council. If, however, a junior faculty member was elected as representative of a research-group, he should count within these 50 percent. Thus, the senior faculty for the first time could become a minority in the Council. In 1968 the Council had 11 professors/associate professors, 8 assistant professors, 1 student, and 1 representative from the technical administrative staff.

Another important change was the introduction of standing committees, first for teaching and personnel policies, then for research. Formally these had only a recommanding role vis-a-vis the Council. Informally it was agreed to give them the real decision-making power. In none of these committees did the rules automatically give the senior faculty a majority. At the same time the new committees weakened the position of the sub-departments. The committee for research policy was recruited from the different research-projects active in the department. Thus, representation became dependent on the activities going on, not the hierarchical positions of the different participants.

The importance of the sub-departments was deemphasized in many different ways. The department chairman in general praised the new organizational arrangement because it made possible the formulation of better priorities from a joint organizational point of view (rather than being based on the special interests of the sub-departments). The dean of the School of the Sciences stated very strongly that:

"The sub-departments are subordinated to the department. The authority and responsibility of the single professor or sub-department leader is limited to activity within the constraints the department sets for his activity."

These changes represented another step away from the "classical institute" model. In 1968 the attack was made even more explicit. The dean, in particular, was attacking the one-professor dominated department. The large, "democratic" department was described as superior both in relieving the scientist of administrative burdens, getting a better overview and coordination of the whole organization, (which certainly was in opposition to the principle of "non-intervention"), "educating" people, and providing well-being in the organization.[9]

While there is a relationship between increased activity by junior faculty and changes giving them stronger formal participation, it is much more difficult to find any connection between demands from assistants, students, and technical-administrative staff and the fact that these groups received a stronger representation. In the physics department the participation-problem never became a strong issue among students, assistants, and technical-administrative staff. Moreover, in the second phase, the university administration, and other groups external to the department, have been less involved. The university administration first tried to "sell" the physics-model to other departments. Their desire for larger departments was met, but not through the uniting of smaller departments. A general growth process in the university increased the size of many departments. Several of these growing departments wanted secretaries. The administration did not have to campaign in order to sell the idea. Soon the demand was larger than the supply of such positions. External events then made the participation and governance issues more central and reorganization became a choice opportunity in several departments. The university administration, and the leaders of the association of junior faculty could meet again over the same issues of the rights, power, and status of junior faculty. The most visible of these meetings took place in departments in the humanities and the social sciences. Here students and sometimes junior faculty activism seemed to threaten the values of efficiency (and thus attracting the university administration). The general interest in the symbols of participation, power, and status was higher, and at the same time these issues were to a lesser degree than in physics solved in informal ways (attracting the students and junior faculty leaders). Furthermore, in 1967 the University of Oslo appointed a committee with the mandate to give a recommendation about the general organization of the university. This committee attracted much of the time and attention of faculty interested in the issues of participation and organization. Thus the attractiveness of the relatively quiet physics arena dropped dramatically. While the outside participants faced each other in new arenas, the most active participants in physics were some of the traditional leaders (full professors with administrative responsibilities), and the key issues have not been hierarchical but professional.

There was no dramatic break with "feudalism". The process observed has been one of continuous, incremental increases in the formal rights of new groups. The reorganization worked as a spark for this issue, by first getting acceptance for the representation in department governace of faculty fully qualified professionally, but without chances of getting full professorships for budgetary reasons. Then the issue became participation for other reasons than professional qualification. The general drift of the process has been away from the "classical" institute-model, but this drift is a long process – starting before the reorganization became a choice opportunity in the Department of Physics, and still under way. In the period observed it resulted in the elimination of most differences in formal authority between senior and junior faculty. With a minor exception all decisions were unanimous. The reorganization has not been a process where different alternatives have clashed; there never was a major confrontation with traditional leaders on one side and non-leaders on the other.

14.2.1 The Context of Events

In order to understand the development of reorganization in the Department of Physics and the way in which the expansion of participation rights to junior faculty in the department took place without seriously posing the issue of hierarchical conflict, we need to attend to the other things of potential relevance that were going on before and during the process of reorganization. The fact that the new organizational arrangement was made temporary, made it necessary to return to it each year. It became a choice opportunity and "garbage can" open during a period where a lot of things relevant for the physics department took place. Reorganization took place in a specific economic and professional context.

In Norway, as in most other industrialized countries, the decade from 1958–1968 was an exciting one for people in physics. A stream of students and money flowed into the field. The Norwegian situation is summarized in Table 14.1. We attend to the growth in new positions since most other resources in the Norwegian university system are closely related to the number of positions.

While the physics department as late as 1958 was very small – employing only 29 persons, in 1968 the number was 115 (in addition to this there were several fellows and assistants paid through outside sources, especially research councils). Although the number was still increasing, the growth had clearly started to level off by 1968. In 1967–68 the budget was 12–13 million Norwegian kroner (approximately 2.3 million dollars) per year. Close to 100 percent was public money. While some parts of the budget clearly were "bounded" (e.g., in salaries which the department could not affect), the department was allocating resources that interested most of the employees. The extension of participation rights came, not when the department was static, not when it was growing very rapidly, but about the time growth leveled off.

Physics was the first academic discipline in Norway which had to make decisions connected to the question of survival of whole sub-fields. During the period studied it became clear that a small country like Norway could not develop all branches of physics. Much of the discussion and decision-making became focused upon whether, and where, a particular field of physics should exist in Norway. Should Norway participate in large international projects? How large a percent of the total grants should be used outside the country? (Riste og Spangen, 1968, «Grunnforskning i fysikk i Norge», The Central Committee of Norwegian Research, 1968.)

Attitudes on these major choices were not likely to follow hierarchical status lines. On the contrary, they must have worked toward uniting different status-groups within each field. Full professors, junior faculty, students, and technical-administrative staff within each project all had a common interest in getting equipment, or fighting the proposals. We assume that different types of conflicts compete for the attention of decision-makers (Schattscheider, 1960). Hence, the emphasis on non-hierarchical conflicts has made it more difficult for hierarchical issues, like the participation-issue, to get much attention. If this is true, the technology of the field, making team-work necessary and producing a common interest in certain types of (expensive) equipment, can be expected to produce a tendency toward making non-leaders less interested in demanding formal participation, and leaders less interested in resisting such demands. The groups demanding formal participation would primarily be those which were not established already and thus were not represented by a full professor, the fields in which the full professors were not viewed as very competent in defending the field, and fields that may gain by extending participation to junior faculty.

The lines of cleavages produced by the technology also became very relevant to the distribution of other resources, for instance new positions. After the leveling off-period had started, each project had to compete with each other in order to expand. These trends are consistent with the fact that after 1965 it became clear that representation would be based on the research activities going on. Under such circumstances potential participants will perceive the *right* to participate important in the discussion *between groups,* but may have problems finding people willing to represent the groups (viewing participation as a duty within the group). This expectation has been supported by the development in the Department of Physics. After the representation of the research groups had been solved through the reorganization, we find a tendency toward increasing difficulties in finding people willing to represent the groups and in general to take leadership.

The description of the context of the choice so far helps us understand why the issue of the representation of the hierarchical groups did not produce a high level of activation and conflict. Why then, was the question of participation attended to at all – if it was not related to demands for a redistribution of the resources and burdens allocated through the department? We have suggested one reason why leaders might have pressed the participation issue: They expected help with the burden of administration and with the issues dividing the fields. In a similar fashion, we can observe that junior faculty may have become somewhat more interested in participation during the latter part of this period because of changes in their position. During the latter part of the decade of the 1960's, both the alternatives to formal participation and the prospects for assuming leadership roles in the future were shifting for junior members of the physics department.

Consider some alternatives to formal participation. We find considerable consensus on the view that the Department of Physics, long

Table 14.1. The growth in different categories of faculty and in technical/administrative staff in the department of physics, University of Oslo 1950–1970

Position	1950	'51	'52	'53	'54	'55	'56	'57	'58	'59	'60	'61	'62	'63	'64	'65	'66	'67	'68	'69	70
Professor	3	3	3	3	3	3	3	3	3	3	5	7	7	7	7	7	7	8	8	8	8
Associate professor	2	2	2	2	2	2	2	2	2	2	2	2	5	6	6	6	6	6	6	11	11
Assistant professor	6	6	6	6	6	6	6	6	9	18	23	31	33	36	37	39	41	42	42	42	43
University scholars and assistants*	5	5	6	5	5	4	4	4	4	9	12	17	22	27	29	29	29	23	26	27	28
Faculty (total)	16	16	17	16	16	15	15	15	18	32	42	57	67	76	79	81	77	79	82	88	89
Technical/administrative staff	5	5	6	6	6	8	9	10	11	17	18	22	25	27	27	29	35	36	44	45	45
TOTAL	21	21	23	22	22	24	24	25	29	49	60	79	92	103	106	110	112	115	126	133	134

*Scholars and assistants paid through research councils and other grants excluded.

331

before the reorganization started, had allowed non-leader groups to participate informally. Until 1958 the size of the department was very moderate, making informal participation much easier. The rapid growth in the next 5–6 years clearly reduced the chances of informal influence.

Exit was also easy. The expansion and the "richness" in the period 1958–1963, where the faculty-positions increased from 18 to 76, made it easy for most potential academic entrepreneurs to get the new positions they wanted to their fields. The problem in these years was to find people to hire. The policy was to hire only new graduates, and up to 60 percent of the graduates were recruited for university-position some years (Lindbekk, 1967, p. 220). The tendency toward greater interest in participation came when it became clear that the growth had stagnated. The possibility of staying in the department[10] and compen--sating non-participation in department governance through being financed from outside had been present, but this alternative had clearly been of declining importance since 1965 (Olsen, 1971, Table 5 and note 24). Most important – the Research Council for Scientific and Industrial research from 1970 had withdraw its support to nuclear physics and high energy physics. We should expect increasing size, low mobility, decreasing richness and the reduction in outside sources to increase the interest in formal participation to the degree which such participation was viewed attractive.

Finally, we look upon the prospects for future leadership, assuming that a potential participant may view gaining participation through his group, and through *leaving* his group in the future, as competing alternatives.

In 1957 the ratio between, on the one hand, full professorships/ associate professorships and, on the other, assistant professorships were 5:6 (.83). The heavy inflow of students, however, changed this ratio very strongly. The number of assistant professors with the highest teaching load (lektor) increased from 2 in 1957 to 29 in 1965. During the first half of the 1960's the ratio of full professors/associate professors to assistant professors was .3. The prospects for getting leadership through the usual channels (scientific merit) decreased in the beginning of the 1960's. The prospects became even worse because the department had recruited only among new graduates, producing a cohort-problem of a whole age-group reaching the level of profes- sional qualification for full professorships at the same time. This happened around 1965. The department was not able to get new top- positions, and the people filling the full professorships were still relatively young. In situations where participation in the government of the department are viewed as attractive, we should expect these tendencies to generate a demand for influence and participation.

In general we could expect these tendencies to produce an increasing interest in formal participation. Clearly the organization has been distributing rewards attractive for both leaders and non-leaders. However, we suggest that the technology in the field has made hierarchical conflicts – with strong demands for participation from non-leaders and strong resistance against these demands from leaders less likely. The ways in which the main rewards could be divided have not followed the hierarchical lines. On the contrary, they have followed the sub-disciplines and made it more difficult for hierarchical conflicts to attract attention. The emphasis on the research groups reflects this tendency. Junior faculty will increase demands for participation but *not* as representatives of the *class* of junior faculty. There is no evidence indicating that the priorities of the department became changed after junior faculty, the technical-administrative staff, and the students were given participation rights.

So far this interpretation has been built upon the assumption that the technology of the field and the equipment used, produced decisions where the potential outcomes had to be divided *across* more than *along* hierarchical groups. This view may now be expanded: Even where the technology of the field is not reflected in any material structure, the sub-disciplines will strongly affect the ways decision-outcomes can be divided, and thus provide the most likely lines of cleavages and conflicts. Also the impact of professional authority, the social inertia following a long training and socialization period, etc. will modify the effects and the importance of any change of organizational blueprints.

Some data on the differences between the departments that accepted the new organizational arrangements, and those who keep the classical model, supports such an interpretation. In a university-wide survey (1968) there were no differences in attitudes toward formal participation in the two types of departments. Neither did the faculty in the "new" departments feel more influential or more satisfied than their colleagues in other departments (Olsen, 1971, Tables 21–23). All the fellows and assistants in the reorganized chemistry department with *one* exception, answered that the leader of the sub-department took the most important decisions. The same answer was given by 50 percent of the other non-tenured faculty. Only 26 percent of the total faculty viewed the department council (which in the new "constitution" was made the highest governing body of the department) as the place where the most important decisions were made (Olsen, 1968, p. 114). In the physics department 1/3 of the fellows and assistants perceived the leader of the sub-department as the single most important decision-making unit. That was more than four years after the sub-departments had been formally abolished.

Finally, it should be obvious to anyone who has lived through the period of the 1960's in higher education that a part of the symbolic importance of participation rights came from considerations far beyond the confines of the University of Oslo and the Department of Physics. The external critique of university governance found the reorganization garbage can attractive here, as it did in many universities around the world.

First, the criticism raised through several publications of the Organization for Economic Co-Operation and Development (OECD). Here the European institute-organization dominated by one professor was attacked as outdated. The American department-organization was described as more efficient, more able to innovate, and more able to make decisions and state priorities (e.g., Ben David, 1966). The argumentation, for instance, of the dean closely followed these lines. *Second,* the criticism raised through the international wave of students' demand for participation, both in Norway and more strongly in other countries. These demands were, by the students, closely related to central values in the Norwegian community, as democracy and equality. In the physics department the values of being "progressive", "democratic", "egalitarian", etc. could easily be accepted and the "problems" related to them "solved". A major argument of this study is that these values could be applauded, and the symbolic-expressive rewards collected, with very little effect upon the basic priorities of the department.[11] This is not to deny the importance of the symbolic commitment thas was reflected. It was real. We have simply rediscovered the ancient observation that it is easier to be virtuous when there is some incentive.

14.3 Conclusion

The reorganization arrived as a choice opportunity at a point in time when an overwhelming majority in the physics department did not view organizational arrangements as problematic. Reorganization was stimulated by full professors who were administrative leaders, together with full time administrators at the school and university level. In the first period they could move the process at a rapid pace. They did not have to search for or create a solution. The Department of Physics had become large, the office organization had been strengthened, and informal participation had been increased. The "solution" suggested by those taking the initiative was to acknowledge these changes, making them an ideal for arranging other departments. The two groups of administrators had different reasons for doing it, and they perceived different consequences following their initiative.

A key to the understanding of the process is the fact that physics was the first department at University of Oslo to open the question of reorganization as a choice opportunity. For some time this was the only garbage can available for such general issues as participation, power, and university governance. Because of this, it attracted participants who had little direct interest in the physics department. Physics was the only arena available for expressing their concerns. Major features of the process, such as the drop in outside participants during the second phase of the process, is related to the increase in the number of available garbage cans. In this period several departments considered the reorganization question as a choice opportunity. A university-wide committee on reorganization also became attractive for participants interested in the issues of participation and governance. The relative attractiveness of reorganization in the physics department as a garbage can clearly declined.

The new position of department secretary was a means for coping with a management and cost problem. Management costs were an issue throughout the period studied. They still are. The big department was celebrated at the same time as the leader of theoretical physics was allowed to break away (and reduce the size of the Department of Physics). The university administration had its desire for larger departments fulfilled. However, this took place through a general growth process, not through the uniting of smaller departments. As a consequence of the growth, the traditional opposition against "bureaucrats" in the departments disappeared from most parts of the university (Olsen, 1968). There was no need for convincing departments of the advantages of having department secretaries.

While we find aspects of problem solving, problems were "solved" in unexpected ways. Furthermore, the reorganization initiative in both unintended and unexpected ways activated new groups. The leaders of the Association of Junior Faculty arrived too late to have their problems connected decisively to the reorganization garbage can. The reorganization of physics, however, became a catalyst for a debate where important differences in the situation of junior faculty across different departments, were clarified. Especially, it became evident that status, power, and participation issues were less salient in the Department of Physiscs than in many other departments. When new choice opportunities arrived, these issues and these participants shifted their attention away from physics.

A debate was started also inside the Department of Physics. Since the new organizational arrangements were announced as preliminary, the garbage can was kept open for several years. The context of the department changed. In particular, as alternatives for junior faculty declined, they became more interested in participation. The change from rapid growth to leveling off also changed the senior faculty's focus of attention from problems of efficiency to problems of stating priorities. This shift was not related to a change in the dominant coalition of the department. The process was managed by the same leaders during the whole period. The most important aspect of the process was, however, that both senior and junior faculty came to the conclusion that the dominant cleavage in interests divided different research groups, not different status groups. This recognition produced a decision making system with representation based on the research groups.

The reorganization process in physics also helped encourage the highest governing body of the university (The Collegium) to attend to these issues. The immediate impact of this body was insignificant, except for the (important) fact that they made the new arrangements tentative and therefore kept the garbage can open. But in the Collegium, as elsewhere in the university, a process of interpretation was started. It culminated in the establishment of a general reorganization committee, which in the next turn provided an area for the senior faculty in physics to interpret what had taken part in the physics department.

While our data indicate that the rewriting of the constitution had only moderate effects upon the everyday life of the Department of Physics, the results were presented publicly in terms of a victory for increased participation and "democracy". This interpretation has to be related to the definitions of problems and solutions presented from outside, especially the OECD-discussion and the general student-movement. Thus, in keeping with ancient tradition the interpretations construed the past in terms of the virtues of the present.

NOTES:

1 The first part of the process went on in both the Department of Physics and the Department of Chemistry. Later some other departments introduced a version of the new organizational arrangement. In order not to overload this version with too many details, the story is focused upon the physics department, which also was driving the process.

2 The section is a unit discussing teaching affairs but not research matters. Its formal status most places is as a school — not a department unit, but the heterogeneity of its way of functioning was (and is) very great across the university. The Collegium is the highest governing unit of the university. The basic structure of University of Oslo is described briefly in Chapter 13 of this volume.

3 It is impossible to say *how important* this argument was in the beginning (1963—1964). In the written material it seems to be of little importance. There may be two reasons. First, that it simply was not important. Second, that it was not stressed for tactical reasons. Full professors in other departments, for instance, were perceived as relatively negative to increased participation of junior faculty.

4 In 1968 only 9.4 percent of our respondents in a university-wide survey (N = 752) agreed completely to a statement saying that many decisions of great importance and interest for the non-tenured faculty was (today) made without any consultation of any representatives of the non-tenured faculty.

5 The reasons for this change was not made clear. However, the new proposal was closer to the existing organizational arrangements. Also the change could be viewed as a concession to the claim that the proposal from the administrative board would decrease the level of participation for junior faculty.

6 There may also be some more subtle effects. Demands for being relieved from administrative burdens reminded everybody that the most important activity in the organization was research, and that the administrative leaders, while using most of their time on administration still perceived themselves as scientists.

7 In the Norwegian system the creation of a new *type* of position like department secretaries first has to be accepted by the governmental "0 and M" bureau. The central value of this bureau clearly was "efficiency", and the modern firm was viewed as being the most efficient type of organization. Thus, the argumentation has to be understood as an attempt to get a new position by affecting the image of a "university department" held by the "0 and M" people.

8 The reorganization provided an opportunity for exercising the principle of non-intervention on issues where one full professor had strong opinions. At this point in the process full professors in other departments who were ambivalent to the new plans or against them, probably stayed inactive because they believed they would not be forced to introduce the new arrangements in their own departments.

9 The trend toward stronger emphasis on the participation-aspect has continued since 1968. In the Department of Physics the difference between senior and junior faculty in department governance has been eliminated, and both the students and the technical-administrative staff have stronger representation. In 1970 the department Council had 30 representatives, 17 faculty members, 5 from the technical-administrative staff and 8 students. In the fall term a junior faculty member was elected chairman (the senior faculty argued that some of the junior faculty "had to take their term"). The department has also introduced an open assembly as an advisory body in all department affairs.

10 The possibility of leaving the university has not been viewed as very attractive by the faculty in physics. Most basic research takes place in the university context. The communication between scientists inside and outside the university has been modest, and the mobility between top-positions inside and outside academe has been near non-existing (Riste and Spangen, 1968, Skoie, 1969).

11 In a study of the technical university in Copenhagen, Christensen (1971) shows that the senior and junior faculty have the same preferences concerning what the university should do and not do across a wide range of options.

15. The Process of Interpreting Organizational History

University of Bergen

15.0 Introduction

Individuals in organizations try to make sense of their experience even when the experience is ambiguous. They impose order, attribute meaning, and provide explanations. One set of theoretical ideas for understanding the ways in which ambiguous events are interpreted, and thus how people come to believe what they believe, can be found in various notions of consistency or balance in beliefs and perceptions. The basic assumptions about interdependencies between cognitive organization and attitudinal organization, as set forward by Heider (1958) and Newcomb (1959) predict that individuals who are in "balanced states" will not change their attitudes and beliefs. Those who are out of balance will move toward greater consistency from less consistency. Heider suggests a structural view of this process. The various parts of the beliefs and attitude-structure are connected by binary-valued links (e.g., like-dislike, aprove-disapprove, etc.). If a structure is out of balance, it will be brought into balance by a series of changes in the links. Our observations suggest the possibility of an alternative view, i.e., a continuous shift-process. The individual moves toward balance by shifting everything a little bit simultaneously. Whether balance is actually achieved depends on the rate of shifting relative to the rate of change in exogenous factors affecting beliefs.

This change process is the major focus of this chapter. An attempt is made to examine the structural view and the continuous shift view of the process in terms of a case study of how a school within a major American university tried to find a new dean. The basic story is reported in Chapter 6.[1] The situation was one with high relevance and a strong "learning potential". The decision was considered an important one. The usual decision procedures were not used. The experience with collective decisions was small. The participants had few shared, unambiguous "facts" about what was going on and why.[2]

For each of eight major events in the history of the decision, we consider the belief structure of the organization and how it changed. We attend to who changed in what ways, and relate the changes to the

338

organizational conditions under which each event took place. In particular, we consider the contact patterns, the trust, and the integration in the organization, together with the relevance of each event.

15.1 The Events

When the search process started the school was fairly well integrated. No major groups perceived themselves as alienate. The general level of trust was high. There was no evident "opposition" and "establishment" defining the patterns of interaction. The less positive relationships between the dean and the director for one of the programs, were generally defined as a personal conflict and as a problem of personalities.

15.1.0 *The Resignation of the Dean*

The resignation was a surprise for the faculty, and the dean did not give many clues as to why he was leaving the position. The local newspaper found the event newsworthy, indicating that it was strange that a dean "stepped down" from a deanship to become an "ordinary professor" again. Internally, neither of the classic interpretations –new job or a bureaucratic disagreement with superiors – was announced or hinted.

What were the immediate interpretations of this event? Basically none. Nobody provided any public interpretation. In interviews faculty members indicated that they were confused and bewildered, and that they wanted to wait and see. To the degree that explanations were suggested they focused on the "costs" of being a dean in terms of time and energy. We relate this silence to the fact that most faculty members were in an inbalanced situation. They did not like the resignation. They viewed it as a product of the dean. They trusted the dean, and felt integrated in the organization. They perceived the resignation as important.

In such a situation the balance hypothesis suggests several possible changes. *First,* the faculty could start to perceive the event as less important. The resignation could be perceived not as a resignation, but as an attempt to rally support and reassurance. Or the faculty could start perceiving the position of the deanship and the role of the departing dean as less important. Given the history of the school and the behavior of the dean no one seemed to entertain any of these "solutions" in the early days. *Second,* the faculty could "loosen" the causal relationship between the dean and the resignation. However, nothing seemed to indicate that there were external factors forcing the dean to resign (e.g. the administration, his health, etc.). *Third,* the faculty could start liking the event. The dean could have a plan with his resignation. For example, it might come to be believed he did it in order to provide a new leader who could make great contributions to the mission of the school. The faculty at this time, however, perceived the dean and the school as strongly linked. Nobody found such an explanation very likely. *Finally,* balance could have been reestablished through a change in the "liking" of the dean. It could have been suggested that the dean had changed, that he had lost his faith in the school, that he could not any more be trusted. Again – in the short run at least, this seemed to be a too dramatic break with the history of the school. The somewhat milder version – that the dean had got an outside job offer which he found better – was highly inconsistent with the strong belief in the uniqueness and greatness of the school.

The most important observation – the reluctance to interpret and explain the event in public or in interviews – indicates postponement or non-attention to events as an alternative to bringing back a balanced situation immediately. The processes of change appeared to start with withdrawal. Failing to find a clearly consistent explanation, most individuals seemed to treat the event as an anomaly and to give it less public attention than a comparably important explicable event would have secured.

15.1.1 *The Failure of the Search Committee to find an Acceptable Dean Candidate*

As late as the end of the search committee-centered phase there were no clear changes in the patterns of contact, the degree of trust, the degree of integration, or the perceived relevance of the choice of a new dean (and thus of a failure to find an acceptable candidate). What were then the immediate reactions on the committee's failure? Again we observe a reluctance to provide interpretations. The committee made some moves which indicated that they had reduced their level of aspiration. Candidates were approached personally and not via telephone; they were not attended to sequentially; and the committee moved from the class of "super-stars" to the class of "stars", without going outside the group of scientists with a strong, established professional reputation. But as a unit the committee did not interpret their experiences for the faculty. The activity slowly faded away. The committee died without publicizing its memoirs or its will.

The dean's reaction could be interpreted as a reduction in the level of aspiration. However, it could also be interpreted as an emphasis on choice criteria different from those used by the committee. The dean himself did not elaborate his view, and he did very little to convince others.

In interviews three "movements" were observed. No firm explanations were generally accepted, but a set of questions were becoming clear. The first was related to the quality of the school: Had the quality of the school (and the university at large), its students and its faculty, its library, its computer facilities, and its locality been overrated? The second question was related to the importance of the deanship: Should the powers of the (new) dean be modified to accommodate changes in the powers of the research-teaching groups and growth? The third question was related to what had really taken place in the committee: had the committee done its job well? The trends seemed to indicate some subtle and not easily observable changes in the individuals, changes that nobody yet was prepared to offer in public discussions, or as explicit explanations in the interviews.

The observations may again be related to what basically was an unbalanced situation. The failure to find an outstanding candidate was disliked. The search committee had been trusted, and yet it could not provide an acceptable outcome. The adjustments of the level of aspirations were attempts to redefine "liking", or what should be perceived as an acceptable outcome. However, the faculty did not appear to try to restore balance by changing one dimension. On the contrary, we observe that both the trust of the committee, the relevance or importance of the deanship, the linking of the outcome and the behavior of the committee (e.g., the reference to market factors) were simultaneously opened up for questions. There were questions, but few conclusions.

In the period before the next event the situation was more labile in terms of contact, trust, integration, and relevance. Differences among the members of the faculty began to develop more clearly. Still there were no easily observable major changes in basic beliefs.

15.1.2 *The Proposal that the School should Introduce Traditional Departments*

There was a proposal that the school should abandon its organization in favor of a more traditional form. The proposal was made by a full professor, member of program B and the search committee, who was in the school for his first year. It was supported by a group of tenured faculty in program B. They stressed the fact that the programs did not have names reflecting the disciplines, and that this made recruiting of faculty and students more difficult.[3] Only a few months earlier the faculty had affirmed, by a unanimous vote, that it did not want departments. Now the reaction was strong, public and negative. The main points of view were summarized in a memorandum one month later. Of equal importance – the dean rejected the proposal.

There was no ambiguity concerning who had caused the proposal, or who supported or was against it. The tendency toward balance is seen in the fact that those behind the proposal expressed some degree of distrust toward the dean, the author of the memorandum against departments, and other defenders of the "anarchy"-ideology of the school. They were accused of not being willing to let others do their thing, and of acting against their own permissive ideology. The defenders of the anarchy, on their side, strongly disliked the proposal. We see a change in the expressed trust and liking of those behind the proposal.[4] For the first time there was a fairly clear development of subgroup allegiance and outgroup distrust.

The next events took place within short intervals. Their context was a beginning polarization of contact, a reduction of trust, a beginning feeling of alienation on the part of program B-leaders, and a feeling of high relevance.

15.1.3 The three outside Candidates invited to the School

Three possible dean candidates were invited to visit the campus. This initiative was taken by the dean, the associate dean, and the chairman of the search committee. The faculty was informed about it in a memorandum signed by the dean. The process by which the three candidates was singled out was ambiguous to most faculty.

The dominant interpretation was that the three candidates were unacceptable. The tenured members of program B now were in a state of "balance". They viewed the dean as taking the initiative, and running the process. They expressed their distrust in the dean, and questioned whether he any longer believed in making the school a high quality institution. They accused "the establishment" of trying to get around external tests of quality by simply defining as good whatever they themselves did.

How did it happen that the supporters of the dean also came to the conclusion that the three candidates were unacceptable? Here it is crucial to look at the contact patterns. While program B in the period held regular meetings and provided channels for communication, and interpretation, the other programs did not. None of the leaders of the "establishment" offered their followers any theories about the candidates (for different reasons, discussed in Chapter 6). The silence of the dean was interpreted (wrongly) by his followers as lack of support for any of the candidates. Now they got into a balanced state through deemphasizing the causal connection between the dean and the three candidates. They also perceived the dean as much less active than did the "opposition".

15.1.4 The "Memorandum-crises"

In the midst of the process, the dean and the director of program B exchanged highly emotional memoranda regarding rumors about rumors. Another senior faculty member added a third memorandum stating that he was shocked by the events. The events took place in the same period and under the same conditions as the one described above. The demand for information was clearly not met, or it was not met from trusted sources. *Rumors* (i.e., statements and opinions widely disseminated but without any discernable source and without any known authority) became a surrogate – providing some "understanding". This was the case of the rumor suggesting that the chairman of the search committee had been inactive in order to become dean himself. It also was the case of the rumor, or the rumor about a rumor, suggesting that the dean and the chairman of the search committee were playing games, inviting unacceptable candidates in order to pave the way for a named inside candidate.

The change in the "climate" of the school can be seen in the words used in the memoranda. The dean talked about "an extraordinarily destructive rumor", and called it a lie. The director of program B generalized the strong reaction of the dean. The dean was characterized as a person who behaved strongly and directly, but providing little evidence others could use to form explanatory constructs. The director also made it quite clear that he was not a great admirer of either the dean or the candidate suggested in the rumor. While this was a statement presenting the act of the dean as an incident *confirming* the director's definition of the school and of the dean, the other faculty member writing a memorandum stressed the *changes* that had taken place. Especially he was distressed with "the power politics that had engulfed the school". His emphasis on power politics,[5] the description of the search committee as inactive and his own participation in it as unrewarding, represented the first public interpretation of the search process as a whole.

The memoranda-crises can be viewed as an explosion of feelings, emotions, and beliefs building up through the process, but not tied together in any coherent interpretation, and never stated publicly. What then was the reaction in the school to this emotional outburst among some of the leaders? Generally the episode was disliked. In interviews the memoranda were described as "childish" or as "over-reactions". The whole thing should be forgotten as soon as possible.

The response was more one of embarrassment and withdrawal than involvement.

Again the situation was one where it was very difficult to present any balanced "explanations". As a result, most people avoided making strong interpretation. While a certain polarization had taken place among the leaders in the school, this was not the case for the inactive part of the faculty. An effect of the memoranda-crises, however, was that the lines of conflict were more clearly recognized by more people, and that some of the latent inhibitions against acknowledging the presence of different interests and opposing groupings were weakened.

The next event therefore, took place in a situation where the contact patterns were rather polarized, where the distrust between the leaders were recognized explicitly, where the "opposition" expressed their alienation, and where the relevance of the events still was considered high.

15.1.5 The internal Candidate proposed by Program B

The candidate behind which program B gathered was a member of this program, he was perceived by many as having a somewhat rough personal style, he was a former student of the dean, the dean's first appointment in the school, and its first associate dean. The faculty in the two other programs found themselves in a cross-pressure situation. The candidate was linked both to the "opposition" and to the dean.

The major reaction was one of expressed confusion and a demand for interpretation. This demand was not met. Given the degree of ambiguity it is not surprising that the faculty in program A and program B ended up with different conclusions. Some showed their doubt by not attending the final faculty meeting (March 17), some voted against the candidate. But most found the candidate acceptable, and the majority of those present voted for him.

These people came into a balanced state by modifying both their evaluation of the candidate (e.g., his style) and the causal connections (e.g., who took the initiative). Some of the strongest followers of the dean loosened the causal links between the candidate and program B, and stated that they independently had come to the conclusion that he was the best candidate available. A member of program C, a strong supporter of the dean, made the formal presentation of the candidate in the faculty meeting. He argued, without giving much evidence, that the candidate had changed his style fairly lately. An important assumption for the group in programs A and C who agreed with this view, was that the dean supported the candidate. Up to this time, the dean had refused to state his preferences.

15.1.6 *The Dean's Statement that He did not Support the Candidate*

The first expression of position by the dean was a statement to the vice-chancellor. In reporting the faculty recommendation, the dean said he did not support it. The faculty heard about the statement indirectly. There was no ambiguity about it. It was, however, a surprise.

Nobody came out with any clear explanation of *why* the dean had acted as he did. The reactions may be divided in three classes. First, the leaders of the "opposition" easily came into a balanced explanation, viewing the dean as the cause, disliking and distrusting him, and disliking his act. Second, the "non-leaders" in program B, together with some of the tenured faculty in the two other programs, had come to the conclusion that they wanted the dean to continue in his position; but they did not want to change their opinions about other candidates simply because they knew that the dean was against the candidate. This indicates that they had reached a differentiated view on the dean – trusting him in some respects but not in others. The third response was from the majority of faculty in program A and C. They reported that they would change their opinions on any candidate if they knew the dean was against this candidate.

Consider the interplay between contact and trust. The first group now had little contact with the dean, and distrusted him. The second group started out with trusting both the leaders in program B and the dean. During the process they were exposed to information only from the leaders of program B. They developed a differentiated view of the trustworthiness of the dean. The majority of the faculty in programs A and C did not interact much with the leaders in program B. Neither did they receive any interpretations from the dean. However, the trust of the dean was stronger than their independent judgment of the qualities of the candidate. Said the program C member presenting the candidate, "Over time I have experienced several situations where I did not understand why the dean acted as he did. However, I have been pleased with the final outcomes".

Here the school's handling of the choice process ended. We observe polarization in interaction, and changes in the trust and integration-aspects. The learning in terms of a reduced level of aspiration is more questionable. Some indications of such a reduction have been presented. However, both the initiative of the chairman of the search committee (the questionnaire asking for the preferences of the faculty, March 7), and our questionnaire data indicate that outside candidates had a chance to be accepted only if they had a very strong, professional reputation.

15.1.7 *The Vice-chancellor's Decision*

The vice-chancellor decided to appoint the chairman of the search committee as the new dean. The vice-chancellor, (himself a faculty member in the school) at the time he took over, had a positive trust relationship to most participants. He was perceived as a friend by people who did not like each other. His decision not to support the program B candidate produced a strong negative, and public, reaction from the program B leaders (threat of resignations, statements of distrust and dislike). They related his decision directly to the dean's refusal to support the candidate. The dean, the chairman of the search committee and the other leaders of "the establishment" did not state their theories about the actions of the vice-chancellor publicly. In interviews most of their followers tended to stress both that the program B candidate was needed in other parts of the university, and that the dean had not supported him. There were no serious efforts to confront the different explanations with each other.

The polarization aspect was underlined when program B as a unit boycotted the faculty meeting in May where the perspectives for the future were to be discussed. Furthermore, both groups indicated that they had been reinforced in terms of what organizational arrangements were best for their purposes; program B stating that they wanted to keep their program fairly structured, program A stating that they found the anarchy model best. The residual group (C) did not operate as a program and did not have any meeting discussing these issues.

15.2 An Interpretation

We want to call attention to three conspicious features of the process:

First, the sparsity of interpretations. We observe (a) that some important events were never accounted for, (b) that some events were interpreted or "explained" through rumors, or in the form of tentative questions, more than through explicit, public statements, (c) that some events were attended to only in retrospect. Often there was a considerable time lag between events and the interpretation of them. These interpretations of old events were colored by the experiences of new ones. In an otherwise ambiguous world clearcut events (like not getting a desired department) had strong effects not only on future events and interpretations, but also on the past – through reinterpretations or through filling in interpretations of events not attended to so far.

Second, the "opposition", more than the "establishment" or those loosely related to the school, provided explanations and theories. We observe that the faculty members active in the process "learned" more than the passive ones,[6] but also that among the active ones those in opposition, feeling alienated, were most willing to state their interpretations of events. The public discussion was differentially a discussion by those who found the various crises confirmatory of their beliefs.

Third, the interpretations presented were dominated by standard models of choice. They emphasized the impact on events of organizational factors, organizational choices and the will, motives, and abilities of organizational decision-makers. There was little inclination to link them to external forces or to luck. The dominant idea was that somebody was running the process.

The data do not support a structural view of the change from imbalanced to balanced states. We find only one case where the change took the form of an immediate change in the binary couples linking the attitude and belief-structures. This was when the tenured people in program B changed their liking of the vice-chancellor to disliking as a result of his decision not to accept their dean-candidate. In all the other cases we find a somewhat slow change. Many things were modified simultaneously and slightly. Interpretations and explanations were postponed, especially in the first part of the process. Only after a social base (an opposition) had started to form, did the latent inhibitions against admitting the presence of conflicting interests and points of view start to break down. The changes in "liking" and "seeing", in attitudes and perceptions appeared to take place simultaneously.

The data also indicate that this situation was one in which the "opposition" was more active than the "establishment" in providing explanations, and where the acts and motives of internal decision-makers were emphasized. This result is closely related to some common situational factors. Especially, we would expect to find this pattern in an organization where the process experiences of the participants are ambiguous, but where the outcomes are clearly less good than expected. In our case the very high aspirations and expectations dominating the organization were *not* confirmed by the environment. This pattern will be found in "bad times". Under such conditions it will be easier for the opposition than for established leaders to find balanced explanations. The latter are caught in a dilemma. Balanced explanations are difficult to provide. However, if they remain silent, their inactivity will be used as a cue by their followers, with the possibilty of false conclusions. The traditional strategy for the establishment obviously is to locate the reasons for the lack of success in the environment or in special and unlucky circumstances. To the degree that this possibility is blocked, the opposition will dominate the learning process. Likewise, in good times we may expect established leaders to do the interpretations and explanations, emphasizing the impact of their own decisions and acts. Now the opposition will either remain silent or try to get attention to external factors providing or contributing to the organizational success.

In both cases, other members of the organization are likely to be substantially less active. We have noted how imbalance produces a short-run tendency to withdraw from the interpretation arena. The result is that during times that are unambiguously bad from the point of view of generally shared organizational goals public interpretations are differentially influenced by persons for whom that result is no surprise – those who are most alienated from the existing system.[7] Conversely, during times that are generally perceived as good public explanations will be differentially influenced by persons for whom that result is no surprise – those who are most integrated into the existing system.

These effects combine to produce a possible reason why most people come to see outcomes as a consequence of intention. The opposition differentially influences the interpretation of bad times. It prefers to attribute failure to the actions of the establishment. Failure is a product of incompetence or evil. The establishment differentially influences the interpretation of good times. It prefers to attribute success to its own behavior. Success is a product of virtue and ability. As the world goes up and down, the relatively inactive audience is exposed to a steady flow of interpretations that predominately emphasize human intent as an explanation of events.

Variation in the dominant sources of interpretation, however, is dependent on free access to the instruments of public interpretation (mass media, memoranda). Where dissident groups are inhibited from such access, we would expect both a greater tendency toward confusion in bad times and a reduced long-run tendency to attribute failure to human intervention. Organizations, or societies, that have a long history of authoritarian restriction of legitimate public explanations will be more likely to develop ideologies and theologies that emphasize non-human factors in man's fate than will organizations, and societies, that permit relatively free access to communication. Organizations and societies with strong and organized oppositions will tend to exaggerate the importance of human action for human destiny; other societies will tend to exaggerate both man's responsibility for success and God's responsibility for failure.

NOTES:

1 This chapter builds on theoretical ideas presented in Chapters 1—4 and on empirical data presented in Chapter 6. The timing of the eight events attended to was:

September 27, 1968: The dean announces his intention to resign.

End of December 1968: The failure of the search committee to find an acceptable dean candidate becomes clear in the school.

February 9, 1969: A decision is made to invite three outside candidates to visit the school.

February 228, 1969: An exchange of highly emotional memoranda in the school.

March 12, 1969: One of the Programs in the school gathers behind an internal candidate.

March 18, 1969: The dean reports to the Vice-chancellor that he does not agree with the majority of the faculty meeting (March 17) which voted for the internal candidate.

May 1—31, 1969: Informally, the faculty come to know that vice-chancellor has proposed the chairman of the search committee as the new dean.

2 The degree of ambiguity and uncertainty was increased by the fact that there was no presidence for the choice. The emphasis on the uniqueness of the organization made external referents (i.e., other schools trying to find a dean, and the results they got) less relevant. Also, some of the key concepts used in the organization for judging outcomes (e.g., ability to innovate) were discovered to be rather obscure. Furthermore, the degree of ambiguity was related to more stable aspects of the organization and to properties of the choice process itself. Few people were exposed to the ongoing events. There was a fair amount of "uncertainty absorption" (March and Simon, 1958). Most often the definition of the situation could not be decisively challenged by anyone with a motivation to do that. The lack of subunits in the organization produced a situation where the channels for distributing interpretations and explanations were not clear and established from the beginning. Finally, the process was set up without any effective collective "memory" and retrieval system. Very little was written during the process, and the written part never played any important role for the theories developed post hoc.

3 Thus, while the proposal was formulated in "efficiency" terms, we may speculate that both the proposals about departments and about a special committee in the field represented by this group in program B, had a "political" or control aspect. Such an organizational arrangement would reduce the importance of the dean.

4 As time went by the proposal came by this group to be identified with *all* members of program B. According to our data this was an overgeneralization.

5 The resignation was basically an expressive act. The committee had stopped functioning a month ago. Nothing indicated that it would be working again. The use of the term "power politics" had strong symbolic connotations related to conflict and distrust. Its most likely empirical referent was the bargaining between the tenured members of program B and the dean, initiated by the professor now resigning. In retrospect (and given the "negative outcome") this was described as power politics.

6 Those active held opinions and gave interpretation of more events than those passive. Also, they perceived more consequences of the process. In the questionnaire each faculty member was asked to indicate the probability of his being in the school three years afterwards and to what degree this probability had changed in the last couple of weeks (during which the

memorandum crises and the open conflict took place). Among the seven most active participants, four said that the probability of staying had decreased, among the next eight on the activity scale only one gave the same answer, and among the rest of the faculty the crises had not changed at all the probability of being in the school for the next three years. Actual behavior afterwards indicate that these verbal expressions were very realistic. The tendency is clearly that the more active in the process, the more likely to leave the school. Two of the major opponents both left to the same university. However, we should be careful to take the choice process as the cause for these people leaving. In general these were the people with the best outside offers and they might have left in any case. Our judgment, however, is that the process had an independent effect.

7 The argument that imbalance will result in a (short run) tendency to withdraw from the interpretation arena is consistent with the way cross pressure has been treated in voting research (e.g., Lazarsfeld, Berelson, and Gaudet, 1960; Berelson, Lazarsfeld, and McPhee, 1954; Campbell, Gurin, and Miller, 1954). Other students have seen a cross-pressure situation or a (intra-personal) conflict situation as a source of increased activity and innovation (Simmel, 1955; March and Simon, 1958). Our argument is related to situations which are generally accepted as "bad" so that the possibilities for innovation is blocked in the short run. Obviously short-run withdrawal may be combined with long-run innovation.

An important conclusion drawn from the cross-pressure hypothesis in the voting studies has been that cross-pressure tends to reduce social tension and to stabilize political systems. As used here there is clearly no necessary connection between cross-pressure or imbalance and system stabilization.

16. Decision Making and Socialization

SØREN CHRISTENSEN
Copenhagen School of Economics

16.0 Introduction

The idea of decision is a theory. It assumes a connection between activities called the decision process, pronouncements called decisions, and actions called decision implementations. The decision process brings together people, problems, and solutions and produces a decision. The process may involve problem-solving; it may involve bargaining, it may involve some system of power. Whatever the mechanism, the process generates an outcome. That decision, in turn, is converted into specific actions through some variation of a bureaucratic system.

The presumptions involved in such a theory are the focus of this report. We wish to consider some complications in assuming that the prime concern of a decision process is a decision. The data reported cover decision making in a Danish alternative school over a period of about six months. An effort was made to trace the development of problems into joint decisions and then into implementation. Our findings suggest that not all problems are translated into joint decision making efforts; that choice opportunities sometimes have to be created in order for problems to be aired; that choice opportunities can become garbage cans for many problems and solutions; that not all decisions are implemented; that for many purposes it is misleading to think of decisions as the primary output of decision processes; and that changes occur without decisions. Although each of these phenomena creates some problems for conventional thinking about decision making in organizations, the observations appear to be understandable by considering some critical properties of the alternative school that was studied and relating those properties to what we know about other organizations.

The alternative school studied is explicitly counter-cultural. The school was founded, in part, as a rejection of conventional schools. It emphasizes non-intellectual and political aspects of child development. The parents and teachers share a common commitment to democratic, socialist, egalitarian institutions and life styles. As a result, the form of decision process is a matter of considerable ideological significance; and the discussions and decisions about educational policy are not casual.

The garbage can model of organizational choice (Cohen, March, and Olsen, 1972) is used as a general framework for our observations. We try to elaborate the viewpoint of that model by looking explicitly at the perspectives of the various participants and the function of decision processes within the organization. The orientation is contextual. Why are participants here rather than somewhere else? What are the consequences of linking different problems in the same choice opportunity?

In particular, we will explore the ways in which choice situations are opportunities for discovering meaning in organizational events. How does the meaning of a decision change over time? What are the symbolic components in decision? What are the consequences of characterizing the process of decision as an occasion for education in social norms and for the development of legitimate interpretations of events? In an organization in which technology is unclear, how do participants come to believe in a particular model of the world?

Although the ideological nature of this organization probably has emphasized some of the phenomena we have observed, we think that their existence is not limited to what is usually considered ideological organizations. On the contrary. We think that they occur in most organizations, most of the time: Ideology means a commitment to a set of ideas; a theory of the world. Using this definition of ideology, most organizations qualify as ideological organizations, although to a varying degree. Business firms and universities have ideologies that play a part in decision making in these organizations. For example, organizational wisdom about rational behavior in the business firm is often referred to and used in argumentation although the external conditions for making rational decisions are often not met.

16.1 The Organization

This study was made in an alternative school situated in a suburban area outside Copenhagen. The school is a private elementary school that, in accordance with Danish free school laws, is refunded for some 75 percent of its operating costs by the government. It was founded by a group of parents in 1967 and started operating in August of that year with about 30 children and two teachers. When the school was founded, the Danish movement to establish alternative schools had existed for some years. During the decade starting in 1960, about 25 alternative schools were founded, primarily in the Copenhagen area.

Three things were stressed by the founders:

1) The school should be small in order to allow for all parents, children and teachers to know each other.
2) The school should be governed in a democratic way and the parents should be able to influence all decisions.
3) The curriculum should deemphasize the intellectual aspects of education and promote manual, productive activities as well as social abilities.

The school planned to grow to eight grades (covering the compulsary education period in Denmark) by adding a group of about 15 children every year. In 1971 the school had some 110 children ranging in age from 6 to 12 years and covering grades one to seven. There were ten full time teachers and a few part time teachers. At the start of the school year in 1971–72, the class structure of the school was still rather traditional. The school was divided into grades according to the age of the children. This class organization was reflected in *the parents meetings,* one for each grade that met with the teachers of the grade 5–8 times a year.

Originally, a school board consisting of parents was elected on a yearly basis by the general assembly of all parents. Although the position was not filled immediately because of the small size of the initial school, the original plans also included a school principal. This structure was changed in 1969. The change was not a consequence of specific adverse experience with the original organizational arrangements. Rather it was a reflection of the ideals of democracy that play an important role in the organization.

Since 1969 the highest decision making body for the school is *the house meeting,* which meets at least once a month. All parents, teachers and children have access to the house meeting and decisions are made on a one-person-one-vote basis. The daily management of the school is in the hands of *the teachers meeting* and *the school committee* (the former school board). The teachers' meeting (with collective leadership) is responsible for carrying out educational management, the school committee for financial and administrative management. Permanent working groups are organized to deal with buildings and finance.

Although this way of organizing has subsequently become rather fashionable in Denmark, in 1969 it was considered "avant garde". The members of the school still consider it a very important feature of the school[1] in spite of practical experience showing that many of the parents are not able to influence the decisions.[2] The decision structure of the school is important as a reflection of part of the ideology of the school.

Participation is fluid. The ideal of the organization is equal, substantial, and continuous participation for all members. Parents serve as substitute teachers five to eight days a year while teachers are having planning days; each member of the school contributes approximately 50 hours of construction work during the summer holidays; maintenance of the school is carried out by parents in teams of ten persons each week; all members of the organization are urged to participate in the various meetings. Despite this, participation varies considerably. Most parents have only limited connections with the school. Some members are very active. Teachers are particularly active. They participate through teachers meetings and house meetings in many of the management activities. Some parents are much more active than others.

The variation in participation produces problems. On the one hand, it runs against the democratic ideals of the organization. There is a feeling that more people should feel free to involve themselves. The school committee has often been in the situation of trying to find exciting topics for the house meeting agenda in order to induce parents to come to the meetings. There is a persistent sense of unease with the inequalities in participation rates among parents. At the same time, the difference between parents and teachers is also a problem. Teachers are involved more. In fact, the relations between teachers and parents are often a complication for the democratic ideals of the organization. Egalitarian norms seem to be potentially at odds with differential participation rates, with the employer-employee relationship, and with the layman-expert relationship.

The technology of the organization is unclear and not well understood. As in other educational organizations it is difficult to spell out the cause/effect relationship by which children learn. In this organization, where the emphasis is as much on social and productive abilities of the children as on intellectual abilities, the importance of the persons actually doing the teaching is probably even stronger. This has important consequences, especially in an organization with democratic ideals. How can the parents influence activities if the only technology is the persons actually doing the teaching? Decisions on hiring and firing of teachers, on resource allocations, and on finance can be made on a majority basis, but it is very hard to imagine how decisions concerning actual teaching can have any effects without the consent of the teachers.

The goals of the school are unclear. In 1967 when the school was founded it was stressed that productive, manual activities and social abilities should be given more weight than in the public schools; intellectual abilities should be deemphasized. The ambiguity of these terms is obvious. When it comes to deciding specific activities for the school, these goals do not provide a set of criteria for decision. This does not mean that they are irrelevant in the decision making in the organization, or that the participants fail to perceive them as important and relevant. On the contrary. They are often used in discussions, but they are used as arguments to support specific proposals rather than as a set of preferences to evaluate alternatives.

During the last few years discussions at the school have further been heavily influenced by political issues. In 1967 the child and his individual needs were stressed; recently the political importance of education has taken an important role. Some of the members argue that politics is an underlying issue in all education. The school should be conscious of this issue and train children in a democratic, socialistic way. The school is perceived as an alternative organization that through its structure and decision making process can provide its members with an opportunity to have real influence on the organization. It is also seen as an arena for discussions of important political questions in society and their relation to the curriculum of the school.

16.2 The Decisions

16.2.0 *The Events*

Between August 27, 1971, and January 7, 1972, the House Meeting made three specific decisions by vote of the members:

August 27: By a unanimous vote, the House Meeting decided to establish a "Society of Friends of the School" with the purpose of facilitating the construction of a new classroom.

November 5: By a vote of 69 to 6, the House Meeting decided to change the school from a traditional grade-divided school to an open, free-choice school with no grades.

January 7: By a vote of 26 to 20, the House Meeting decided to rehire a teacher who had been fired by the group of teachers.

Although these decisions were decided by vote after considerable discussion, none of them were implemented. The school did not proceed to build a new classroom; it did not change the overall structure of the school, the teacher did not return. In a literal sense, the decision process was ineffective.

Nevertheless, some things happened. If we look at the school when the school year started in August 1971 and again in January 1972, we observe a change in the educational structure of the school. In August 1971 the school was structured into classes very much like most traditional schools. In January 1972 the children of the grades (3, 4, and 5) had a free choice of subjects with the exception of one hour in the morning. One teacher had left the school; two members of the School Committee had resigned; some parents were actively considering leaving the organization.

It is difficult to explain what happened to the decisions, or how the changes occurred, without a relatively detailed look at the sequence of activities within the major arenas within the school: The house meetings, the teachers group meetings, the meeting of the School Committee, and the meetings of one of the parent groups (3rd grade). Initially, those groups were functioning relatively independently, although there was considerable overlap of membership. Over time they became considerably interrelated.

16.2.1 *The Data*

The data presented in this section were collected primarily through participant observation of the meetings held in the school during a six month period from August 1971 to January 1972.[3] All written material such as discussion papers, proposals and official minutes of the meetings were also available to us. A series of interviews with some members of the school in October and questionnaires to all members of the school in the Spring of 1972 served as background material for the data reported here.

Our primary intention is to present the decision making process of the highest decision making body of the organization: the house meeting. In August a "Society of Friends of the School" was established. In November it was decided to restructure the school. In January it was decided to "re-hire" a teacher who had been excluded in the end of November by the teacher group.

In order to understand the decision making at the house meetings, we also considered other significant groups in the organization to see what they did during the same period. We found that most of the activities of the school committee, the teacher group and the parents' meeting in third grade either were related to or helped us to understand the house meetings.

The data are voluminous. In order to make the presentation here manageable, we report only a small portion of the data; but we have tried to report it in a neutral way, imposing as little theoretical structure on the report as possible. We note events as they occurred in the terms in which they occurred. In subsequent discussions (Sections 16.3; 16.4; 16.5) we try to identify the major phenomena and to indicate their significance for a theory of organizational decision making.

16.2.2 The House Meetings

August 27.   The only important issue on the agenda for this meeting is a proposal to establish a "Society of Friends of the School". The idea behind this proposal it to create a liaison between the school and the public authorities. The school needs more space. In order to build, approval from the Ministry of Education is required. This takes time. If some other body could negotiate with the ministry, the building can be erected and sublet to the school. Later the school could apply to the ministry to buy the building. The case is presented as a purely technical matter. It is suggested that all members of the school should also be members of the society and that a small building of 50 square meters should be built. This is approved unanimously.

A member of the school suggested that a discussion of the goals of the school should be started. It is decided that the school committee should arrange for tickets to a theatre play "Do you remember our school-time" that might serve as a stimulus to later discussions.

October 8.   The agenda for the house meeting says "the school – what do we want". The basis for the discussion is the theatre play and a written paper from one of the parents. In this paper he discusses the present educational structure and different alternatives. He is himself an architect and claims that the coming construction of school building requires a decision on educational structure.

In the discussion the present educational structure is criticized. It is too rigid and the possibilities for the children are too small. The teachers are criticized for not saying what they want. The teachers, on their part, criticize the parents for the same thing. A parent suggests that the house meeting make a decision on the priority of the educational goals of the school. He suggests the following list of priorities: 1. Social abilities, 2. Productive abilities, and 3. Intellectual abilities. This theme is discussed for some time, but there is an apparent confusion about the meaning of the labels and whether it is possible to separate the different abilities. Finally a vote is taken to determine whether this theme should be further discussed and the result is that the house meeting refuses to accept this list of priorities (31 votes to 19 votes).

October 29.   The school committee has produced a proposal for a new educational structure which is more flexible than the present one. The main point in the proposal is to break up the present class structure and make it an "open" free choice structure. In the debate there are two parties. The teachers report that they are presently debating the goals of the school and that they have problems of cooperation in the teacher group. Several parents claim that it is necessary to clarify the goals before making decisions on the structure. The majority of the participants at the meeing, however, judge the school committee proposal to be an improvement on the present system. A vote shows a clear majority to go on with the restructuring proposal and make the final decision on this issue in a week.

November 5.   There has been intense activity in the school during the last week. A number of meetings have been held and these are reflected in the numerous discussion papers that have been sent out with the agenda for the meeting today. In the agenda it is stated that a principal vote on the educational structure is going to be taken today. During the discussion the teachers declare that they are willing to vote for the school committee proposal and stop the discussion of goals for some time. The general impression of the meeting today is that a dominant issue from the last house meeting – the goals of the school – is considerably less salient. The vote taken at the end of the meeting shows that the school committee proposal for a new structure is passed with 59 votes for, 6 votes against, and 4 abstaining. It is also decided that several working groups be formed to let the parents participate in the implementation of the new structure.

December 3.   During a teacher's planning session (18.–23. Nov.) held outside the school the teachers had decided to exclude (i.e., fire) one of the teachers. The teacher in question left the session and did not show up at the school subsequently. This meeting is called in to discuss the problems around the excluded teacher. Strong criticism

358

is directed at the teachers by the parents. The teachers are blamed for having gone against the rules of the school. Under the rules, hiring and firing of teachers is a house meeting question. This means that the school committee on the agenda of the meeting has left the question of firing the excluded teacher open. The teachers are also blamed on moral ground for having shown so little tolerance toward the excluded teacher. It is argued that the ideals of the school require tolerance. It is decided to form a mediating committee with three representatives from the teachers and three representatives from the school committee. The task of this committee is to try to establish a compromise and present this at a house meeting.

January 7. There is some confusion about the situation. The mediating committee has not given any specific proposals. In the discussion many participants show concern about the case because all energy has been concentrated on this problem. One of the teachers then proposes that the excluded teacher is invited to come back to the school. A parent suggests that the firing be considered a reality that nothing can be done about. A vote is taken and 26 participants vote for the proposal to invite the excluded teacher to come back. There are 20 votes for the other proposal. The likelihood that the excluded teacher will decide to come back is not high. (In fact, the teacher does not come back.)

16.2.3 *The Teachers' Meetings*

August 25. Only two weeks after the start of the new school year a personal conflict between two of the new teachers (they do the teaching in the "difficult" 3rd grade) is announced at the teachers' meeting. They propose that 5 of the 17 children in 3rd grade be moved to 2nd grade. The other teachers (except the 2nd grade teacher who has accepted and apparently also welcomed the decision) go into a discussion of other possibilities. The more experienced teachers particularly hesitate to accept this solution as they anticipate a reaction from the parents. Some parents have already, through personal contacts with the old teachers, reported that some of the children of 3rd grade are not too happy with the climate in 3rd grade. There is a parents' meeting in 3rd grade tomorrow and as there are no immediate solutions to the problem. The teachers agree that the two 3rd grade teachers shall not inform the parents tomorrow. The meeting with the parents of 3rd grade on August 26th goes on without any mention of the conflict. By September 1 a de facto decision has been made. The former 3rd grade teacher moves to 2nd grade. The decision has actually been taken by the two teachers involved.

September 15. In the middle of September teachers are involved in three meetings: There will be an official welcome from the school committee on the 13th; the remaining 3rd grade teacher is going to explain the 3rd grade situation to a parents' meeting on the 14th; and there is a regular teachers' meeting scheduled on the 15th. At the meeting with the school committee the new teachers are welcomed to the school. The school committee suggests that the teachers come forward with their problems. There is no reaction on part of the teachers.

The message to the parents from the 3rd grade teacher that the other former 3rd grade teacher is now teaching in 2nd grade receives a strong negative response from parents. The parents send a resolution to the teachers asking them to revise once again the distribution of teachers to classes as it is clear that the 3rd grade now is being treated unfairly.

At the teacher's meeting the following day the resolution from the parents leads teachers to look into the number of teacher hours per class. Some changes are made so that one of the old teachers will take over some lessons in the 3rd grade. One of the old teachers at this point mentions "that now that the problem with 3rd grade is solved we should not forget that there is a personal conflict between two of the teachers and this ought to be treated soon".

September 22. At the regular teachers' meeting there is a request from the school committee that the teachers describe the present educational structure of the school. The school committee is interested in putting the question "what do we want of this school" on the agenda of the house meeting, and as a starting point they would like the teachers' description of the present situation. The

360

teachers are a little confused about this question, but agree to ask one of the parents – who is an architect – to help them formulate an answer to the school committee.

October 5.   The architect and his wife – who have children in 3rd grade – come to the meeting with the teachers with a paper sketching out possible ways of structuring the school. A structure with no classes is a dominant possibility in the paper. There is also a letter written by the wife connecting the problems in the 3rd grade with the present class structure. In this letter the teachers are accused of not having solved the problems in the 3rd grade, and of following an individualistic teaching practice instead of collective leadership. She goes through the history of the 3rd grade pointing that this has always been the case and that there are good reasons for the current bad situation in the school. She claims that the experimental school has become nothing more than a private school on public school premises. She also identifies a solution to the problems: a complete restructuring of the school, abandoning the classes, and a general discussion of the goals of the school.

The point of departure in this letter is the problem in the 3rd grade; but this problem is generalized so that it becomes the problem of the whole school. The cause of this problem is imputed to be the teachers' lack of cooperation and interest for each other's problems. An emphasis on intellectual abilities rather than social and productive abilities is charged. As solutions to these problems the writer points to a complete restructuring of the school (no classes) and a general discussion of goals (deemphasize intellectual abilities).

The teachers are clearly taken by surprise. In the discussions that follow, there is sharp conflict between the former 3rd grade teacher (now in the 2nd grade) and his present colleague in the 2nd grade on one side and the other teachers on the other side. "You have solved your problems, but you don't care about the rest of the school". "You two are always so critical toward the rest of the group, but what is actually your own program?"

361

October 13.   For the teachers' meeting today the former 3rd grade teacher has written a paper around the problem of educational priorities for the school. He is sure that the priority should be: social abilities, productive abilities, intellectual abilities, and claims that until the teachers have decided on this ("which is actually a discussion of the goals of the school") it is meaningless to talk of means to implement the goals (e.g., structure). The conflict in the teachers' group in this way is generalized. It is not a question of two teachers against the rest of the group. It is a question of educational goals. This becomes the theme of the teachers' group for a long period of time. The problems around the structure are not taken up in spite of the pressure that is put on the teachers. It is clear that the parents of the 3rd grade want more changes to improve the climate, but this is refused by the teachers as just "patching up". On October 21 the architect (author of the restructuring paper) called in a selected number of parents (primarily 3rd grade parents) and the teachers to what was later referred to as an extra-parliamentary meeting. The specific purpose of this meeting was to discuss what could immediately be done to improve the climate in the school. The teachers refused to do anything. "The problem is to find out what we want to do with the school. When this is clear it is no problem to make specific changes in the structure".

October 26.   The school committee has sent out a proposal for a new structure that is going to be discussed at the house meeting on October 29. In the agenda for the meeting it is announced that it can be expected that proposals may be put up for decision. One item on the agenda says: "The teachers tell how far they have come in their clarification of the problems". The teachers now have meetings for three consecutive days (26th, 27th, and 28th). The main problem discussed is the goals of the school. Not until the last meeting do the teachers consider how to react to the school committee proposal for a restructuring of the school. They agree to play a tactical game, and to announce that they are willing to accept the new structure. They believe that they are the real decision makers when it comes to implementation of any new structure.

November 3. The final decision at the house meeting on the structure was postponed for a week. This means that the teachers can expect a final decision at the house meeting on November 5. The teachers discuss how they should react to the restructuring proposal. It is clear that it is the problem of goals and the problem of cooperation in the teacher group that are the main focus of the teacher group. They realize on the other hand that the parents have put pressure on them to accept changes in the structure. They decide that they are willing to vote for the proposal put forward by the school committee, but they hope that so many proposals will be put forward at the meeting that no final decision can be made.

November 10. On November 8 there was a meeting between the teachers and the teachers of a highly admired experimental school. During the discussions the teachers from the other experimental school explained that they did not pay any attention to goals or ideologies. They just "did things". They also explained their structure with no classes. This apparently made a great impression on the teachers. Two days later at the teachers' meeting, it is proposed that the teachers jump out into a new structure without any transition period as decided at the house meeting.

November 18–23. At the planning session which is being extended because of a snow storm the main topics are new structure and ideology. The point of departure for the new structure is not the house meeting decision and plan for implementation of a new structure, but the model from the other experimental school. The discussion of ideology is justified as a necessary wrapping of the new structure. "Otherwise the parents are not likely to accept it". The main event on the planning session, however, is the firing of one of the teachers. She participates in the week-end, but has to go home on the evening of the 19th. In the course of the evening it is decided by the remaining teachers that she does not fit the group and that two of the teachers the following morning shall go down to her with her things. The decision to fire the teacher has consequences. It provides the teacher group with a feeling of having solved the

363

problem of cooperation in the group. It generates a very practical problem of reallocation of teaching resources. It provokes a confrontation with the parents.

Having excluded the teacher, the discussion in the group only touches the reactions from the parents. They do expect some reactions from the 3rd grade parents who may have come to like the teacher, but they do not foresee the massive reaction from the parents and the house meeting on the procedure.

November 25. Since the planning week-end the teachers have been engaged in meetings with 3rd grade parents, and with the school committee. They have been strongly reproached for their action. They start formulating an ultimatum asserting that if the excluded teacher were re-hired, all the teachers will leave.

December 1. After receiving reactions on part of the parents, it is decided to withdraw the ultimatum. The discussion also touches the new structure. They talk about it as if it is a fully developed plan that they are now prevented from executing because of the firing-case. They decide that the 3rd and 4th grades be merged to take care of the staffing problem created by the firing of the 3rd grade teacher. They agree, however, that this step has nothing to do with the new structure.

January 3. The pressure that is put on the teachers because of the firing-case creates a strong group solidarity in the teacher group. But also their behavior toward the parents changes. They engage in discussions with the school committee, they try to predict the reactions of the parents at house meetings. The teachers formulate a proposal to give the excluded teacher an offer to come back.

January 5. In the beginning of January the teacher group decides to merge the 5th grade with 3/4th grade. The immediate trigger for the action is the fact that the 5th grade teacher is going to take a leave of absence from the school for 3 weeks. The teachers point out to each other that this has nothing to do with the new structure. (In fact, this merging is in line with the restructuring proposal and in fact becomes permanent.)

16.2.4 *The School Committee Meetings*

August 30.   Two teachers show up for the school committee meeting. One of the teachers in the 3rd grade suggests that he moves to the 2nd grade, and the second teacher seconds this proposal. There is some discussion about the proposal. The school committee gets assurance that the other 3rd grade teacher approves of it, but no decision actually comes out of the meeting.

September 13. The school committee is welcoming the new teachers. After the welcome they propose that the .teachers come forward with their problems, but the teachers do not respond to this proposal. The school committee discusses the house meeting agenda for the meeting on October 8. They are trying to build "an exciting agenda". "Otherwise only a few parents will show up".

October 11.   One of the teachers is present at the school committee meeting today and the school committee members complain about the lack of contact between the teachers and the school committee. That especially is a problem with respect to the problems that are being discussed at the house meeting. The teacher reports that the group is discussing ideology and refuses to involve the school committee in this discussion. "We have to finish our discussion first".

October 25.   On October 17 the school committee received a letter from a parent in the 3rd grade. He has earlier in the month discussed the structure of the school with the teachers. In the letter he proposes not to take a new class into the school next year and to give up the building of a new class room which was decided on the house meeting in August. The school committee is rather confused. The architect is chairman of the board "Friends of the School" that has taken initiative in building the new classroom. Now he is proposing to stop the project. In his answers to the many questions from the school committee members about his proposals he says "In all that I am doing for the time being I put great emphasize in assuring that a program decision for the school is made." The building of the new classroom is, in fact, given up; but the school committee refuses to cancel next year's class: "That will create too much trouble among the parents who have counted on this class for their children".

The house meeting agenda (for the meeting on October 29) is planned. One of the school committee members (who is also a parent in the 3rd grade) has made a proposal for a new structure. This proposal is accepted by the school committee and sent out to the parents and teachers as a school committee proposal.

November 1. The school committee is very disappointed over the house meeting. They feel that the parents are very confused and that this is primarily caused by the teachers' silence at the house meeting. The two representatives from the teacher group who are present at the school meeting claim that the teacher group is not prepared to take a stand in this question. "We are discussing goals."

November 8. At the house meeting yesterday the proposal from the school committee for a new structure was passed. It was decided that a number of working groups would be established to implement the new structure. The school committee now is eager to see that the teachers become members of these groups. "Otherwise the groups will get no real influence on the system". The school committee is surprised that so many of the parents at the house meeting "feel alienated" and agree that this is caused by the lack of information from, and contact with, the teachers. The school committee realizes its dependence on the teachers. As one of the members comments: "The problem is that we cannot work without the cooperation of the teachers, whereas they can create a school without us". Possible reasons for the lack of interest in these problems on part of the teachers is discussed. The conflicts in the teacher group are mentioned as one possibility.

November 12. The problem of cooperation with the teachers is the main topic for discussion at this meeting with the teachers. The teachers are not too happy about the house meeting decision. After some discussions of the proposal, the teachers and the school committee agree to interpret the house meeting decision as a "vote of confidence in the teachers". The teachers propose to "outline a whole new school" on the forthcoming planning week-end on November 20–23. The school committee asks to be part of this planning, but the teachers are not willing to involve the school committee.

November 25. A meeting between the school committee and the teachers is arranged because of the firing of one of the teachers by the teacher group. The teachers formulate an ultimatum: If the excluded teacher is re-hired, the other teachers will leave the school. They admit after some discussion that the teacher group has no formal power to fire a teacher. That is a house meeting decision. But the teachers present the problem as a fait accompli.

November 26. The school committee has arranged a meeting with the fired teacher. Her version of the case is somewhat different from the other teachers'. In a discussion in the school committee after she has left the meeting the members again talk about the relation between the teachers and the parents as a "credibility gap". Now they hope the teachers will start cooperating with the school committee. They feel, however, that there is no acceptable alternative but to ratify the firing decision.

December 2. The agenda of the meeting is again the firing case. Two of the committee members have now decided not to accept the firing. They define the problems as a moral issue and are not willing to give in. Still the school committee wants to give some protection to the teachers. As they plan the house meeting tomorrow, they decide to choose a chairman "who has always been loyal to the teachers and who can see to it that the house meeting does not lynch the teachers".

December 13. The house meeting on December 3 brought no solution to the firing case. A mediating committee with representatives from the teachers and the school committee was established. It becomes clear that there is a wide disagreement in the school committee about the problem.

January 10.   The house meeting on January 7 brought a final solution to the firing case. It was decided to invite the fired teacher back, but none in the school committee or the teacher group seriously believed that the teacher would come back. The relations between the teacher group and the school committee have improved considerably. The teachers are now more willing to involve the school committee in their decisions. But as a consequence of disagreement over the firing-case two members leave the school committee.

16.2.5 *The 3rd Grade Parents' Meeting*

September 14. It is a shock to the parents when one of the teachers informs them that the other 3rd grade teacher is going to teach in the 2nd grade instead of the 3rd grade. The parents have had many problems with teachers in this particular class. In 1970 there was a conflict between the two teachers who had the class at that time. In 1971 the class got a new teacher, who, however, left the school after only one year due to problems with the other teachers. Thus, for the third consequtive year the parents experience problems with teachers.

The teacher reports that disagreement over the educational program in the class is the reason for the decision of the other teacher to go to the 2nd grade. The teacher assures the parents that it is no great problem; but the parents are worried. They discuss what can be done about it; and although there is a great deal of scepticism about the ability and willingness of the teacher group to do something about the problem, it is decided to formulate a resolution from the parents' meeting to the teacher group asking the teachers to reconsider the distribution of teacher hours among the classes. During the discussion it is also mentioned that a real solution to the problem would be to restructure the school so that it became an open school instead of a class-divided school. This suggestion is, however, not discussed further at this meeting.

October 9.   There is a meeting of parents, children, and teacher of the 3rd grade. The idea of the meeting is to let the children evaluate the present school system and if possible give suggestions for change. The parents are surprised to see how well the children formulate the problems and especially they are impressed with the many proposals made by the children.

October 15. The restructuring of the school to solve the problems of the 3rd grade is discussed. The teachers present refuse to enter into a discussion of a possible merger of the 3rd and 4th grades, asserting that the teacher group is having general discussions about the problems.

November 29. The remaining 3rd grade teacher has been fired by the teacher group. Heavy criticism is directed toward the teacher group. The lack of tolerance toward the fired teacher, the way she was fired, the lack of responsibility toward the 3rd grade, and the problems in this class are discussed. A suggestion to merge the 3rd and 4th grades or the 2nd and 3rd grades is considered; but the final decision is to keep the 3rd grade separate and through a reallocation of teachers to classes assure that the 3rd grade is not slighted.

16.2.6 *The Intermeshing of Participants, Problems, and Arenas*

Table 16.0 provides a consolidated summary of the flow of events we have described. It reveals something of the way in which relatively independent flows were tied together, partly by their timing and partly by the complications of finding choice opportunities and solutions for problems. The longer problems lingered, the more they became connected to issues. Relatively routine concerns became enmeshed with more complicated concerns. All of the actions occurred against a background of the ideological nature of the organization. From an early stage in which the groups functioned relatively autonomously and considered different problems, the process continued until the groups were heavily intertwined and all problems looked the same. From an early stage in which relatively few participants were active, the process continued until many participants were involved. From an early stage in which the ideological purity of the organization was not publicly identified as a problem, the process continued until much of the energy in the system was devoted to reasserting fundamental principles.

The general process has three properties of special interest to a student of organization decisions:

(1) Although important problems, and some solutions looking for problems, were identifiable by August, there were no choice opportunities to which those problems and solutions could attach themselves. Some of the important activities related to the decision involved the

369

Table 16.0. The combined chronology of events, August 25–January 10

Date	Arena	Problem	Initiated by	Attempted solution
August 25	Teacher group	Conflict between the two 3rd grade teachers.	Teachers	Accepting the conflict and letting one of the teachers switch to the 2nd grade.
August 27	House meeting	Enlarge building capacity.	School committee	Establish Society of Friends to secure building.
August 30	School committee	Conflict between the two 3rd grade teachers.	Teachers	Letting one of the teachers switch to the 2nd grade.
September 13	School committee	How to get parents to house meeting.	School committee	Build exciting agenda.
September 14	Parent meeting	Loss of one of the 3rd grade teachers.	Teachers	Ask teacher group to reconsider allocation of teaching.
September 15	Teacher group	Parent dissatisfaction.	Parents	One of the "old" teachers will take some extra hours in the 3rd grade.
September 22	Teacher group	Request from school committee that teachers describe present structure.	School committee	Call in a "professional" (i.e., the architect).
October 5	Teacher group	Letter from 3rd grade parent saying that 3rd grade problem is only a symptom of bad cooperation among teachers.	3rd grade parent	Discussion of goals and ideology.
October 8	House meeting	Long range plans for buildings.	Chairman of "Friends" (who is also a 3rd grade parent)	Proposal to set priorities of education goals (defeated). Continue discussion of school.
October 9	Parent meeting	Problems in the 3rd grade.	Parents	Proposals from children to improve the situation.

Date		Subject		Action
October 11	School committee	How to involve teachers in talks with committee.	School committee	Request to teachers (no result).
October 15	Parent meeting	Problems in the 3rd grade.	Parents	Possible merger of 3rd and 4th grades.
October 25	School committee	Proposal to cancel building plans and new class next year.	Chairman of "Friends"	Class room building canceled; class plans reconfirmed.
October 25	School committee	Educational structure.	School committee	Put proposal before house meeting.
October 28	Teacher group	Proposal for new educational structure.	School committee	Discussion of goals and ideology.
November 1	Teacher group	Conflict between two 2nd grade teachers and rest of group triggered by parental letter.	Teachers	Discussion of priorities of educational goals.
November 1	School committee	How to involve teachers in talks about the new educational structure.	School committee	Request to teachers (no result).
November 3	Teacher group	Proposed new educational structure and vote in house meeting.	School committee and others	Agree to vote for proposal but hope it is not accepted or managed in implementation. Further discussion of goals and ideology.
November 5	House meeting	New Structure for school.	School committee	Proposal from School Committee is accepted. Groups are to be established to implement new structure.
November 8	School committee	How to form groups to implement new structure.	House meeting decision	Seek to get teachers involved in groups (no result).
November 8	Teacher group	Advice from other experimental school that action is more important than goals.	Meeting with teachers at another school	Proposal to jump immediately to new structure.
November 20	Teacher group	Bad social climate in teacher group.	Teachers	Exclusion of teacher from 3rd grade.

Table 16.0. (contd.)

Date	Arena	Problem	Initiated by	Attempted solution
November 25	School committee	Exclusion of teacher by other teachers.	Teachers	Put the problem before the house meeting.
November 25	Teacher group	Reaction to exclusion.	School committee	Threaten ultimatum: if teacher is re-hired, other teachers leave.
November 29	Parent meeting	Problems in the 3rd grade; action to exclude teacher.	Parents	Possible mergers of grades or re-allocation of teacher time.
December 1	Teacher group	Reactions to exclusion.	Parents and school committee	Withdraw ultimatum.
December 1	Teacher group	Problems in the 3rd grade.	Parents	Merge 3rd and 4th grades.
December 2	School committee	How to protect teachers from "lynching".	School committee	Find chairman to conduct the house meeting.
December 3	House meeting	Exclusion of 3rd grade teacher by teacher group.	School committee	Mediating group of 3 teachers and 3 school committee members formed.
December 13	School committee	Mediation between conflicting teachers	School committee	Mediation give up.
January 3	Teacher group	House meeting vote upcoming on teacher.	School committee	Propose rehiring of teacher with-out commitment on consequences.
January 5	Teacher group	Leave of absence for teacher.	Teachers	Merge 5th grade with combined 3rd/4th grade.
January 7	House meeting	Firing case.	School committee	Vote (26–20) to rehire teacher.
January 10	School committee	Conflict over firing case.	Events of recent past	Two members of the School committee resign.

creation of choice opportunities within which the problems could be exercised and (possibly) solved.

(2) All of the formal house meeting decisions were considered very important to the organization, attracted an unprecedented number of participants to house meetings during the period, and were decided through a formal voting procedure. Yet none of the decisions were ever implemented.

(3) There is a separation of process and outcome. Many of the things going on within the decision process have relatively little to do with the outcomes. The separation is particularly conspicuous when the process becomes a mechanism for developing belief and mutual socialization into the beliefs of the group.

16.3 The Creation of Choice Opportunities

One of the conspicuous things about the process we have described is the extent to which choice opportunities had to be created in order to exercise the problems perceived by participants. These opportunities did not appear at a rate fast enough to accommodate the problems and solutions presented to the organization. From the point of view of the garbage can model, this suggests some limitations on viewing the four streams – problems, choice opportunities, solutions, and participation – as independent. We need to consider more carefully how choice opportunities arise.

According to Cohen, March, and Olsen (1972), choice opportunities are "occasions when an organization is expected to produce behavior that can be called a decision. Opportunities arise regularly and any organization has ways of declaring an occasion for choice. Contracts must be signed; people hired, promoted or fired; money spent and responsibilities allocated".

The garbage can process may, however, depend on the way choice opportunities arise. We suggest the following broad classes:

1) *Institutionalized* choice opportunities (e.g., the annual general house meeting where the school committee is elected) routinely accepted as a choice.
2) Choice opportunities triggered by *external effects* (e.g., firing or resignations) and immediately accepted as requiring action.
3) Choice opportunities created through a *social process* (i.e., the choice opportunity does not automatically arise but is created through a process by which it is decided that the organization should solve some problems or attend to some solutions).

Organizations will differ widely with respect to the mix of choice opportunities. If we view an organization not simply as a vehicle for solving well defined problems but as a collection of problems looking for decision situations in which they might be aired and solutions looking for issues to which they might be an answer, we expect the question of choice opportunties to be an important one for participants. In particular, participants will have ways of promoting their problems and solutions through the social process of creating a choice opportunity. Thus, the creation of choice opportunities is heavily influenced by the participation patterns and by the way individual concerns by participating members are translated into collective agenda items.[4]

Participation patterns reflect implicit decisions by members of the organization about the allocation of energy. Those decisions are bounded by the ideology of the organization and the press of competing claims on time. An important part of the ideology is that everyone should participate in decision making. The formal structure of the organization (e.g., the house meeting) is designed to facilitate full participation. There are social pressures toward involvement by the parents. Nevertheless, participation cannot be taken for granted. Low participation at house meetings has often concerned the school committee. Not everyone participates, and rates of talking vary widely among those who come to meetings.

In general, we suggest that participants try to have their own problems solved and their own solutions adopted; that they attempt to minimize the energy expended in doing so; and that this way of allocating time and energy will be reflected in the activation pattern in the organization. In allocating energy, participants meet competing claims on their time. These claims come both from different activities within the school and from outside activities (e.g., family, work, politics).[5] Participants are not all the same. They have different problems and solutions. They have different external commitments. Consequently, we will expect participation to vary both over time and among different decision arenas. Moreover, resources to solve problems and have solutions adopted (e.g., expertise, command over technology) are not equally distributed among the participants; and participants vary in their dependence on different decision arenas and on each other.

The activation of participants depends on the distribution of alternative claims on their time, on the distribution of their concerns, and on the distribution of their resources for dealing with those concerns. As activated participants appear in decision arenas, they bring along a variety of problems and solutions seeking a choice opportunity within which they might be considered. In the original garbage can formulation, it was assumed that there was always a stream of choice oportunities that formed garbage cans for the active problems and solutions. The free school did not routinely generate many choices. As

Table 16.1. The flow of problems, solutions, participation, and choice opportunities to the house meetings: August 27–November 5

Meetings	Problems	Solutions	Participants	Routine choice opportunities	Created choice opportunities
August 27	Lack of space	Establish Friends of the School. Construct new building.	A few	None	Establish Friends of the School.
October 8	Present situation in school is unsatisfactory. Conflict among teachers. 3rd grade.	Reinstate primary goals of the school.	Many	None	Vote on goal priorities. Long range building plans.
October 29	Present educational structure is unsatisfactory. Conflict among teachers. 3rd grade.	Eliminate grades. Merge 3rd and 4th grades.	Many	None	None
November 5	Present educational structure is unsatisfactory. Conflict among teachers. 3rd grade.	Establish "free choice" system. Defer details.	Many	None	New educational structure.

375

a result, it was possible for a sizable inventory of problems and solutions to occur. The inventory, in turn, stimulated attempts to create choice opportunities.

This process stems from the more or less rational concerns of participants, but the changing meanings that different groups of actors attach to the choice give the decision process a dynamic of its own. At any point in time a choice will be interpreted by different groups of actors in the light of their own problems. The participants will simultaneously engage in actions and reactions that they find appropriate in the light of their own definition.[6] As Norton Long (1958) has observed: "conscious rationality is far more characteristic of the parts (the actors) than of the whole (the community)".

The events approximated a problem-solving mode of behavior, subject to ambiguity about what the problems were and what solutions might be appropriate. Choices were invented in order to deal with problems. The social acceptance of a choice required social acceptance and definition of the problem. The definition of problems and solutions changed through the process.

Consider the house meetings. We can review the activation of participants for the house meeting during the period from August to January and the activities of other groups in the organization in the light of the problem of creating a choice opportunity. At the heart of this review is the fact that the steady flow of problems and solutions between August and November was not accommodated by a flow of routine choice opportunities. This difficulty is illustrated in Table 16.1.

The organization was simultaneously attempting to organize feelings into a relatively articulate position, trying to satisfy a variety of quite disparate sentiments by relating them to each other in a way that would permit the organization to act, and seeking an arena in which the sentiments might plausibly be exercised. The only choice opportunity that had been routinely generated was one having to do with space planning and buildings. If that opportunity had been a little more developed, it might well have become the garbage can for the concerns. Since it was not, the organization struggled to provide an exercise ground for problems and solutions. It hit finally on the restructuring of the class organization and was able to use that newly created choice opportunity as an arena.

The outcome is suggestive of the kind of choice opportunity that will be developed when an organization has developed an excessive inventory of problems and solutions. Under such conditions the most "efficient" garbage can will be a choice opportunity with relatively unsegmented access (so almost any problem or solution can be associated with it) and relatively unsegmented decision structure (so almost any participant can involve himself). In this organization, the house meeting provides a relatively unsegmented decision structure; the problem was to invent a choice opportunity relevant to almost any problem.

From a pure garbage can perspective, it is matter of indifference what choice opportunity is created so long as it offers relatively open access for a wide variety of problems. Two classic garbage can choices were proposed: The first was a discussion of the goals of the organization; the second was a discussion of the structure of the organization. Both are excellent alternatives. Organizations regularly develop reorganization as a choice alternative when the inventory of problems grows large. Almost any organizational or individual problem can be discussed in the context of reorganization and can be made to appear relevant to it. Similarly, the determination of long-term, general objectives is a regularly introduced choice opportunity to accommodate general, diffuse sentiments of problems (Cohen and March, 1974).

What is distinctive about the process in the house assembly is the conflict over which of the two garbage cans would be accepted. Should the organization focus on a discussion of the educational structure or on a discussion of long-run objectives? For the most part, the teachers preferred to have the locus of discussion be the problem of goals, while the bulk of the third-grade parents preferred to focus on restructuring. The dispute had both symbolic and immediate substantive significance. The immediate substantive impact of a restructuring decision (if it were implemented) would be on the daily work of the teachers and their pupils. The symbolic significance of the choice of a garbage can was probably more significant, however. Discussions of the pedagogical structure were implicit criticisms of the teachers; discussions of long-run objectives were implicit criticisms of parental backsliding on the goals of the free school.

16.4 The Failure to Implement Choices

The house meeting decisions to restructure the school came after an extended and vigorous debate climaxed by a strongly positive vote. Most people were involved; most points of view were heard; most people supported the decision. Yet, it was never implemented, and in a short time it was almost forgotten. In fact, none of the three decisions made during the six months of our observations (establishment of the "Friends of the School", restructuring of the school, re-hiring of the teacher) was ever implemented. How do we account for this curiosity of the process?

We believe there are four features of a garbage can decision process, as exemplified by the case we have detailed, that tend to produce decisions that are not necessarily implemented. The features are general. We do not believe they are limited to this particular organization or this particular decision. On the contrary, we believe them to be characteristic features of life in most organizations and particularly in organized anarchies.

First, the explicit outcome of a decision process is often substantially less important than the process. (See also Enderud, Chapter 17.) During the process some important things happen. Values are expressed and tested against the beliefs of others. Social status is established. Sentiments are exposed. Signals about beliefs and intensions are transmitted. Ideological, political, and personal victories and defeats are experienced. Individual roles are executed. In the Free School all of these are important. To focus on the overt decision is to miss many of the phenomena associated with the choice situation. Once the process has ended, there is little reason to presume that the apparent result of the process will have much meaning. In the present case, the decision to restructure the educational program at the school was, to a considerable extent, simply a vehicle for the ideological and interpersonal conflict in the organization. Similarly, in the case of the re-hiring decision we found that bringing the excluded teacher back was not important. At the point in time when the decision was made many of the members knew that the excluded teacher had already accepted another job. The decision served primarily to tell the teachers that the school was a parent-governed school and that the firing of teachers (like other important matters) was house meeting business.

Second, implementation of a collective decision often involves the active collaboration of a group of "bureaucrats". In most cases, the distribution of attitudes within the group charged with implementation will be different from the distribution in the decision body. As a result, it is quite possible that implementation will be controlled by individuals or groups who disagree with the decision. Stein Rokkan wrote about national politics: "Votes count but resources decide." (Rokkan, 1968.) The problems with democratic control of bureaucracies occupies a large part of the literature on politics and administration. It is an old problem; but still a problem. In the Free School, the teachers were vital to an implementation of a restructuring decision which they had considerably resisted. Their ultimate willingness to acquiesce in the house meeting decision was based, in part, on an explicit awareness on their part that they would play a critical role in any implementation.

Third, the particular combination of participant energy and attention that permits a decision to be taken is unlikely to be sustained. In this case, the level of attention was unusually high during the decision. Almost all members of the school were involved. A total of 12 papers, reports and resolutions totaling some 28 typewritten pages were presented at the November 5 house meeting. Compared with normal house meeting activity, this was quite high. The level of activity stemmed from two things. Some participants were trying to solve immediate practical problems that they had been unable to solve in other arenas. Other participants were there because the discussion had become socially defined as important rather than because of the explicit content of the decisions. There is no reason to expect that such a pattern of activity will be sustained. Other arenas will claim attention. The perceived importance of the implementation will probably be less than the perceived importance of the grand debate. Interest in the issue will change as people return to other places. As a result, some of the pressure is gone by the time of implementation.

Fourth, other problems and other solutions come to absorb the attention of the organization. New crises arise. In this case, only two weeks after the restructuring decision was made, the teacher group precipitated a new crisis by firing the third grade teacher. Most of the decision energy in the school was directed toward this new crisis. As a result, the implementation of decision is compromised by the instability of the flows that originally permitted it. A decision is made because of a particular combination of problems, solutions, and participant energy. The combination is due to a variety of external factors (as well as some internal ones). It is unlikely to persist after the decision. Old participants drift away; new participants drift in. Old problems and solutions drift away; new problems and solutions arrive. The instability is endemic to a garbage can process. It is accentuated by the event of a decision, since that event triggers a reconsideration of attention allocation.

Any one of these factors alone will produce some kinds of disparities between decision and implementation. The frequency with which decisions are made but not implemented is not a freakish result of careless administration; it is a property of the organizational system for decision. Nor should it be viewed as a necessary defect. Garbage can decision processes are highly contextual. The decisions they generate are not necessarily better than the implementations that follow them. Indeed, it is probably better to view the whole process of decision as a much more continuous one in which actors interpret their earlier "decisions" by reviewing the subsequent interpretations and modifications of them. The intellectual distinction between decision and implementation fails to recognize the flow of participants, problems, and solutions that produce and interpret both, and significantly underestimates the educational and symbolic importance of decision.

379

16.5 The Separation of Process and Outcome

The usual presumption about a decision process is that the primary *raison d'etre* for a decision process is the decision it generates. The process we have observed in the Free School seems to have a different logic. The overall impression of decision making in the school is that whereas the decision process is sometimes quite important (measured by the number of participants activated and their activities in connection with the meetings) it is difficult to establish a clear connection between the process and the outcome. The problems that exist in the organization seem not to be important determinants of the decision process and the decisions that are made are often "forgotten".

We believe this pattern stems in large part from the fact that the Free School acts within a special situation characterized by three complications:

(1) It is culturally deviant. The school was founded on the premise that the public schools were deficient in important ways. As a result, it does not accept the broader culture as a source of beliefs about education. It is a deviant sect.

(2) It is committed to direct democracy and collective leadership. By a strong ideological bias, members of the organization are resistant to efforts that might be interpreted as providing specialized leadership for special purposes or other forms of decentralization.

(3) It is a way of life. The commitment demanded from parents, teachers, and children makes the school a more nearly total institution than most schools. It commands a good deal of emotional and intellectual loyalty; it serves a wider range of personal needs than the typical public school.

These features of the Free School as an organization are conspicuous. They are features that make the school attractive to its members and to observers. They are intended to produce behavioral consequences, and they do.

The Free School uses joint decision making as a form of socialization. The process is separated from the outcome because process has become a procedure through which the organization interprets and reinterprets what it is doing and what it has done; a procedure through which members of the organization develop a set of ideas about the technology of education; a procedure through which individuals construct and communicate theories of themselves and seek reinforcement for their beliefs; and a procedure for providing mutual protection from the inroads of an alien environment.

Such uses of decision processes are common to all organizations (Edelman, 1964; Olsen, 1970a). They become particularly overpowering when the organization is culturally deviant, committed to collective decision making, and emotionally important in the lives of its members.

Consider first the cultural deviance. Beliefs about the cause and effect relationships in education constitute the technology of a school. The technology is in the garbage can model described as: "Although the organization manages to survive and even produce, its own processes are not understood by its members. It operates on a basis of simple trial-and-error procedures, the residue of learning from the accidents of past experience, and pragmatic inventions of necessity" (Cohen, March, and Olsen, 1972). However, many educational organizations manage to operate *as if* the technology were clear. The participants share models of cause/effect relationships which are used in the assessment of the activities and in making decisions to change these. For example, general cultural norms and values, professional training, and an institutionalized public school system make it possible to define a socially shared technology in public elementary schools in Denmark. The assessment of activities is made through comparison with other elementary schools.

When an organization functions under conditions of no general cultural support of its activities – which is the case in this organization – there is no criteria for testing the activities because there is no shared belief about the cause/effect relationships. Under such conditions the activities in the organization will be dominated by efforts to develop an understanding of what is going on, in other words, of a technology that makes it possible to test the activities of the organization. This is reflected in the decision making of the organization. Rather than using the decision process as a vehicle for providing solutions to the problems that occur in the organization and to implement these solutions, the process itself becomes a social situation where the belief structure is developed and communicated. The inputs to the process (problems and solutions) do not determine the process, and the outcome of the process (the decisions) can be seen as more or less incidental.

A fundamental part of the belief structure in this alternative school is the commitment to direct democracy (which "secures" parent influence) and collective leadership (which gives all teachers an "equal influence"). Part of that commitment is based on an assumption of a cause/effect relationship between these arrangements and the educational results of the school. Thus, they form a part of the theory that school participants treat as sacred technology.

At the same time, these structural arrangements also have an important impact on the way in which decision making takes place. Cyert and March (1963) observed how business organizations managed to survive with conflicting goals by sequential attention to the goals. The segmentation of the organizations made local rationality possible. A similar sequential attention to problems would allow for a local or ad hoc rationality to develop in a school. In fact, that appears to be common. The unsegmented structure, however, channels all problems that cannot be solved at the parents meetings and teachers meetings to the house meeting. This arena becomes a recipient of all the problems as they are perceived by the different groups in the organization. Much the same argument can be made about collective leadership. The lack of a shared belief about any specialized leadership function in the organization prevents a version of local rationality and make all problems common problems.

Consider finally the extent to which the organization is a way of life. The organization is a school. But for the teachers it is also the way they earn an income, and the house meeting is their employer. For some of the members the organization is more than a school, it is a community. They are linked to the organization in many different ways, acting as substitute teachers and repair-workers (which is compulsory) and spending time every summer doing constructing work.[7] To many members of the school their attachment is very important and their relations with other members play an important role in their lives. This influences both the activation of participants and the decision process of the house meeting.

Where the organization operates as a prime social community, the decision process becomes an occasion for development of social values and the expression of sentiment. The house meeting is partly a religious ceremony in which public virtue is exhibited and reinforced. It is partly a social meeting in which good friends are greeted and given affection. It is partly a training center in which novices are given exposure to proper behavior and proper attitudes. It is partly a private opportunity for resolving doubts, developing argument, and testing ideas before returning to battle with outside forces. It is also partly an opportunity for making collective decisions; but that part of the obligation is easily lost in the others.

The three features of the organization interact to produce a predilection to separate process and outcome. The technology is unclear and cannot become a shared belief structure through comparison with other schools because the Free School is openly a deviant school. As a result, the decision process is used as an occasion for developing a set of believers about the technology of education. This tendency to use collective decision making as an opportunity for socialization is made stronger by the fact that decentralized development of local rationality is precluded by ideology and by the fact that the school occupies a comparatively large place in the lives of the participants.

16.6 Conclusions

We have examined the process of decision in a Danish free school. The school was created as an alternative to the public elementary school with a commitment to a clear ideology of education and organization.

We have identified three major features of the processes observed over a six month period in a Danish free school: First, it was necessary to create choice opportunities in order to exercise the problems in the school. These choice opportunities became large garbage cans for existing concerns. Second, there was a persistent failure to implement decisions. Even decisions that involved many individuals with a relatively high degree of activity over several weeks of discussion were somehow not translated directly into action. Third, the decision process was separated from decision outcomes. Rather it seemed to have such a major role in the development of belief that the outcomes were almost incidental.

The three features are, of course, interconnected. Where the decision process performs major symbolic functions (Edelman, 1964), there will be a tendency for process and outcome to become separated; there will be a tendency for outcomes to be relatively unimportant and less likely to be implemented; there will be a necessity for the invention of major choice opportunities to facilitate socialization. The separation of process and outcome has been observed in other studies of organizational decision making (Olsen, 1970, 1970a; Stava, 1971; Cohen and March, 1974), as well as in another analysis of this organization (Kreiner, 1972). What particularly distinguishes the Free School from the other studies mentioned is the position of the school vis-a-vis the dominant social and political culture.

Olsen in his study (1970) of the budgetary process in a Norwegian commune noticed how the budget had very little to do with the activities and arguments of the participants during the decision process. He concluded his study by pointing to the ritual aspects of decision making, arguing that to understand the activities of the decision makers during the budgeting procedure very little is gained by using traditional decision making models. Rather decision making should be looked upon as a ritual act. What Olsen saw as ritual acts are one form of what we have called a separation of process and outcome. The local politicians in Olsen's study acted to maintain the existing normative context of local budgeting, to give the voters an impression of rational policy making and competent leadership. The established organizational structure (the commune) has a general cultural support which acts as a substitute for the unclear technology[8] and which is nurished by the activities of the politicians leaving the voters with an impression of "meaning". In the school, on the other hand, the lack of a general cultural support, introduces a struggle for "meaning" of decision making.

The struggle for meaning is not easy. Like other deviant sects, the Free School teachers, parents, and students face an environment that is tolerant but not particularly supportive. The social reality perceived by members of the school is not perceived by large numbers of other individuals and institutions in the society. The threat of ideological weakening is real. During 1972–1973 a significant number of the parents left the school. Much of the activity in the house meeting is ritual; but there is a difference between the character and force of a ritual act that supports a stable political system and a ritual act that seeks to develop and sustain deviant social values.

Finally, we should make note of one thing that might easily be lost. During the ritual and struggle for meaning, the school went on. There was a program, and it changed from time to time. Students went to school and met teachers. The world neither collapsed nor stayed constant. If change is not a direct result of the decision process, how does it occur?

Our observations suggest that change occurs in response to specific problems that are kept out of large garbage cans, rather than as a product of heroic decision making. When the issue of restructuring the school became a major issue of social values, the decision was not implemented; later decisions to restructure the school (in a different way) were made rather routinely as responses to rather mundane considerations of teacher reallocation. The earlier discussions undoubtedly affected the later actions to some degree, but the most conspicuous conclusion to be drawn is that, within this organization at least, the context within which a problem or solution is discussed is more important than the specific problem or solution involved. We would expect the major changes within the Free School to take place in relatively "technical" contexts that are not seen as involving the grand issues of goals, long-run planning, or fundamental values. As numerous earlier students of revolutionary institutions have noted, revolutionary action should be informed by revolutionary consciousness but can easily be obstructed by the process of revolutionary rhetoric.

NOTES:

1 In a questionnaire administered to the members of the school (parents and teachers) in the spring of 1972 we asked: "an organization can be assessed by the quality of the decisions made or by the decision making system that it uses."

"A. How would you in general judge the quality of the decisions made during the last six months?"

Quality

High	Medium	Low	
24 %	27 %	51 %	(N = 78)

"B. How important do you — for ideological reasons — consider the decision making system in the organization (collective leadership, direct democracy)?"

Importance

High	Medium	Low	
62 %	9 %	29 %	(N = 81)

2 Some 48 percent of the parents report to have problems that they (for various reasons) were not able to relate to the joint decision making arena (the house meeting).

3 Most of the data collection in connection with this study was made by Bjarne Hallander and Kristian Kreiner who have reported other parts of the study: Hallander (1973), Kreiner (1972).

4 Bachrach and Baratz (1963) discuss the same phenomenon which they call "non-decisions" suggesting that non-decision-making is "the practice of limiting the scope of actual decision making to 'safe' issues by manipulating the dominant community values, myths, and political institutions and procedures".

5 Johan P. Olsen in his study of reorganization in a Norwegian University (see Chapter 13) shows how participation can be viewed as a rational choice. Participation in the formal governing bodies of the University thus depends on the possibilities that the participants have to solve their problems outside the formal bodies.

6 This perspective is what could be called a "member-perspective". David Silverman (1970) calls it "the action frame of reference".

7 To give an impression of the community nature of the organization we asked the members to indicate how many of the friends they had seen during the last six months who were also members of the school. Whereas 40 percent answered that none of their friends were also members of the school, 31 percent indicated that half or more of their friends are also members of the school. Out of the 15 members who by the members were rated as the most influential in the decision making, 13 answer that 50 percent or more of their friends were also members of that school (for 8 out of the 15 it was as high as 75 percent or more).

8 John W. Meyer in Scott (1970) discusses how what he calls "the charter" (the wider social definition of the product of the school) effects the students, which is in line with the argument made about the general cultural norms and values acting as substitutes for an unclear technology.

17. The Perception of Power

HARALD ENDERUD
Copenhagen School of Economics

17.0 Introduction

Social scientists who ask questions about power in organizations, local communities, or political systems, usually find people willing to answer them. Responses to questions about who has power or influence[1] have been interpreted in two different ways. On the one hand they have been viewed as saying something about the "real" power distribution or power structure (e.g., Hunter, 1953, 1959). On the other hand they have been viewed as images or beliefs which are interesting in their own right and regardless of their accuracy (e.g., Form and Sauer, 1960; Dye, 1962; Rose, 1967; Form and Rytina, 1969).

The later perspective is used in this chapter. We focus on beliefs about power in modern organizations. We are not interested here in the correctness, consistency, or meaningfulness of the beliefs. The primary task is to examine the differences in power assigned to various participants by themselves or by observers, and to identify the factors associated with variations in perceived power.

What are the cues participants use to form beliefs about power? Students of choice in organizations (as well as in local communities, and political systems at large) have experienced difficulties in drawing clear conclusions about power from their direct observations. Although much of the literature describes the difficulty as a problem in measurement, there are good reasons for not reducing the questions to the issues of getting access to the right data and inventing the right measurement techniques. We face a major problem of theory-building (March, 1966). An assessment of relative power held by various individuals and groups in the organization implies a complex theoretical analysis and presumes *a priori* questions about the meaningfulness of the concept. Nevertheless, individual participants in organizations are able to answer questions about their own power and the power of others.

In order to examine the formation of belief about power, we might consider whether the events of life in an organization provide the kind of information presumed in theories of power. A standard idea about power is that those who have power arrange things as they want them. As a result, it is argued that those who benefit most from the choices made in an organization have power. In this spirit, a major procedure for analyzing the distribution of power has been to isolate a set of key decisions in an organization; to observe who participates and what their preferences are; and to record the outcome of the process. Inferences about who is powerful are made by determining who "won".

The "ideal" conditions for forming inferences about power from a choice situation are close to those assumed in a standard interindividual or intergroup conflict model (March and Simon, 1958, ch. 5). There is a limited number of participants. They have clearcut preferences and beliefs. They understand the relevant means-end connections. There is not consensus. All participants cannot win at the same time. It is possible to relate the outcome to the preferences of the participating groups.

The identification of initial positions, the decision-making process, and the outcome of that process, assumes an observation capacity beyond that of most participants in modern organizations. Furthermore, everyday life in organizations frequently deviates considerably from the ideal conditions outlined above. There may be fluid participation, unclear technology, and a high degree of consensus. How do participants in organizations come to believe who has power under such conditions?

17.1 The Basic Ideas

An answer to the questions about power will partly be a statement about how, in general, beliefs are formed in organizations. Some such ideas are offered in Chapter 4 of this volume. The effort here is both less general and more empirical. We attend to two aspects of the bases of subjective assignment of power:

First, we consider the difference between the power attributed to an individual by himself and the power attributed to him by others. As a starting point we ask whether participants might be using the standard conflict model as a basis for their beliefs about power. According to the standard conflict model, participants are interested in making decision outcomes correspond to their *a priori* preferences. By such reasoning, we would expect power beliefs to be positively related to satisfaction with the outcomes of the process. Of course, even if this model is the one actually used by participants, this prediction may not turn out to be entirely correct. Satisfaction with outcomes (for others) is often difficult to observe and compute.

In such a case we might expect participants to use more visible measures to serve as substitutes for assessing power. Such indicators could very well be status and process criteria since such criteria are usually more readily visible and it is easy under most conditions to provide a rationale that such criteria actually are positively related to the "real" variables of preferences and outcome.

We think it is possible to explore the "indicator substitute" variant of the conflict model by considering the differences in the power attributed to an individual by himself and by others. It may for instance be argued that the indivdual will be "closer" to knowledge about his own preferences and interpretations of outcomes. We may expect this to be reflected in the patterns of self-rating and peer-rating.

The assumption that preferences and satisfaction with outcomes are more visible to ego than to alter, is based on three simple arguments: First, interindividual communication difficulties are larger than intra-individual differences. Second, participants avoid making early and clear statements in the tactical game which often is a part of joint decision making. Similarly, they may conceal preferences out of fear of having or expressing "wrong" or non-winning preferences. Third, participants may want to blur their own interpretation of outcomes vis-a-vis others (e.g., their constituency) in order to save face after a defeat. Or they blur outcome interpretations in order to reduce the magnitude of a victory, in order to avoid attacks on their newly acquired benefits (whether it be "goods" or "power").

At the same time, it should be observed that insofar as "power" is a relative concept, any statement of power involves an assessment of preferences and outcomes for all participants. In such a case, self-ratings are likely to be as difficult to make as peer-ratings. As we shall see, the issues are not easy to sort out, but there is some indication that the "power" concept in self-ratings is different from the "power" concept in peer-ratings.

Second, we consider the differences between "insiders" and "outsiders". The distinction between "insiders" and "outsiders" in an organization is not a simple one. We will be concerned with (a) the interaction or communication network of the organization (i.e., those who participate frequently compared with those who are on-lookers), and (b) the status-system of the organization (i.e., those with high formal status compared with those with low formal status).[2]

For the individuals in each of these groups we will be interested in the beliefs held about one's own power, and the power of others, and in other factors systematically related to the variations in such beliefs.

17.2 The Organization Studied and the Data

The decision-making system studied is the collection of collegial assemblies at the Technical University of Denmark (DTH). These included a Senate, 5 faculty councils, 4 study councils and 4 study boards. The 14 assemblies had 500 member positions during the observation period (1969–70). Due to a substantially overlapping membership, the actual number of participants was about 200. These assemblies were responsible for most collective decisions made at the university.

This system deviates in several ways from the "ideal" conditions for observing power. The decade of the 1960's had been one of relative affluence at the Technical University of Denmark, as far as financial resources were concerned. There was little conflict over scarce resources. There was considerable agreement about preferences across status groups. In all the major decision-arenas studied, there was high uncertainty about the consequences of taking different strategies. It often was difficult to pin down who had decided what. Many major choices were made outside the university (e.g., the Ministry of Education). There was a complex interplay between "recommending" assemblies and "deciding" assemblies. Thus, it was not always easy to determine what had become the result of joint decisions or who had actually "won". There were different interpretations, and most of the participants clearly had very limited knowledge about what had actually taken place (Agersnap and Gudnason, 1971; Andersen, 1971, 1972; Christensen, 1971; Enderud, 1971).

As a result of all these, there was a considerable degree of ambiguity in the decision making process (what had actually taken place), in outcomes, and in the relations among processes, outcomes, and initial preferences.

A questionnaire was administered to the holder of each position, (so that a person holding several positions would give more than one answer). 363 questionnaires (71 percent) were returned. There is a tendency toward high status people being less willing to respond. Among the full professors and the administration 67 percent (N = 223) answered, among the assistant professors 74 percent (N = 195), and among the students 81 percent (N = 93).

Self-rating of influence was measured by the response to the following question:

"How do you evaluate the possibilities of making your own influence effective on the final decisions in the above mentioned assembly?"

The peer-rating of influence was measured by the response to the question:

"Mention the names of three persons (or more) whom you consider to have the greatest influence on the final decisions in the above mentioned assembly."

Since there was no specification of decision arena, we assume that the answers reflect some kind of average assessment. Although respondents were asked to rank influentials according to importance, we will make a simple distinction between those mentioned at all, and those not mentioned. For the self-ratings a similar distinction is made between ratings of "very great", "fairly great", and "medium" on the one hand and "rather low" and "low" on the other. Unfortunately the formulation of the two questions is not identical. While the one on self-rating may suggest (perceived) *potential* influence, the one on peer-rating suggests (perceived) *exercised* influence. Our observations at DTH, however, have indicated that the distinction between potential and actual power is perceived as more important by social scientists than among those taking part in our study.

While 92 percent of those returning the questionnaire answered the question about their own influence, only 64 percent responded with respect to what power *other* participants had. This means that less than half of the total population answered this question. Two reasons were given by the respondents for not answering this question, (a) that such a question was too personal or "odious" and (b) that there were no stable patterns or that the question was too difficult to answer.

In total, 118 persons were mentioned at least once as being influential. Ninety-five of these answered the questionnaire. This group thus had a higher response rate than average for the population as a whole.

In addition to a peer-rating score and a self-rating score, each individual was characterized by twelve other items; as specified in Table 17.0.

Table 17.1 shows the intercorrelations (gamma) among the 14 variables involved in the study across all respondents. Correlations that are *not* significant at the .05 level are shown in parentheses.[3]

Inspection of this table indicates a few conspicuous things:

(1) The relation between peer-rating (13) and self-rating (14) is positive but modest. Persons who see themselves as powerful are more likely than not seen as powerful, but the relation is not strong.

(2) Both self- and peer-ratings are related to participation and status variables (i.e., variables 6–12), but the relations are stronger for peer-ratings. Individuals use cues of activity level

Table 17.0: Variables to be correlated with power ratings

Variable number	Variable name	Observational or questionnaire item	Response categories used in analysis
1	Centrality of information sources	Where do you get information about issues considered in the above assembly?	(a) Only from written sources or at most a minor part from either issue initiators or other people, but not both. (b) A minor part from both issue initiators and other people, or a fair part from one of those groups. (c) More than a minor part from both issue initiators and other people.
2	Information surprises at meetings	To what extent do you think that new information emerges during meetings, information that you should have been given at an earlier stage?	(a) Very often or fairly often (b) Seldom or never
3	Belief that decisions have been made before meetings	To what extent do you think that important issues actually have been decided by unofficial negotiations before being brought up in the assembly?	(a) Very often or fairly often (b) Seldom or never
4	Existence of unsolved problems	Are there problems or issues that you miss being dealt with in the assemblies	(a) Yes (b) No
5	Satisfaction with the way assembly reaches final decisions	How well do you think the above mentioned assembly functions with regard to reaching final decisions?	(a) Very well or fairly well (b) Less well or poorly
6	Number of assembly membership	(A person could belong to as few as one or as many as 14 assemblies.)	(a) One or two (b) More than two
7	Meeting attendance	(Number of meetings actually attended by the member during spring term 1970 as a percent of all meetings in that assembly)	(a) Less than 75% . (b) 75%–85% (c) More than 85%

Variable number	Variable name	Observational or questionnaire item	Response categories used in analysis
8	Speaking share in assembly	(Share of the speaking over meetings in spring term 1970 – – by direct observation.)	(a) 0% (b) Greater than 0%, no more than 4% (c) More than 4%
9	General activity	(An index constructed on the basis of the following question: When you – – outside of meetings – – speak with other members of the assemblies, how often do you speak about the following things: – Formulation of the issue – Drafting of solutions – Discussion of solutions – Strategies	Each of the four domains of discussion could be answered "very often", "fairly often", "seldom", or "never". In each domain the responses were scored (respectively) as 1, 2, 3, 4. Summing over the four domains yielded scores ranging from 4 to 16. For analysis the group was divided into two groups – – those with relatively high scores vs. those with relatively low scores.
10	Range of contact within university	How often do you – – outside of meetings – – speak to persons in the following groups about assembly matters? The groups mentioned were: The presidency, the administration, full professors, junior professors, and student members of the assemblies.	(a) With all but one of the groups, or all of the groups, more than a few times a year. (b) Less contact than that
11	Number of committee memberships	(Number of memberships on committees of the assemblies)	(a) 0 (b) 1 (c) More than 1
12	Formal status	(Participants in the assemblies were identified as being from the presidency, chief administrators, full professors, junior professors, or students.)	(a) Presidency, chief administrators, or full professors (b) Junior professors or students

392

Table 17.1. Inter-correlations (gamma) between all variables

Var.		1	2	3	4	5	6	7	8	9	10	11	12	13	14
1	Information directly from issue initiators and other members as main source ("often")	X	(−.09)	(−.13)	(.17)	(.18)	.41	.39	.38	.63	.65	.37	.03	.43	.45
2	"Surprise information" received during meetings (very often or quite often)		X	(.09)	(.19)	−.32	(−.24)	(.01)	(−.13)	(0.9)	−.29	−.27	−.43	−.40	−.60
3	Believing that decisions have actually been made before meetings (study matters)			X	.38	−.29	−.30	(.02)	−.11	(.03)	(−.10)	(.06)	−.29	(−.27)	−.38
4	Amount of unsolved problems				X	−.30	(.01)	(.14)	.20	(0.2)	(−.20)	.47	−.50	.24	(.06)
5	Satisfaction with assembly's ability to make final decisions					X	(.20)	(.00)	(.00)	(−.06)	(.04)	(.01)	(.18)	(.13)	(.30)
6	Overlapping assembly membership						X	(.14)	.47	.52	.78	.19	.43	.66	.27
7	Meeting attendance							X	.38	.29	.38	(.18)	−.10	.48	(.13)
8	Speaking share in assembly								X	.47	.65	.46	.59	.87	.48
9	General activity (speaking to other members)									X	.63	(.19)	(.00)	.62	.33
10	Contact range inside University (No. of groups)										X	.34	.62	.85	.35
11	Committee membership (No. of committees)											X	(.17)	.63	.43
12	Formal status												X	.73	.40
13	Peer rating													X	.47
14	Self rating														X

Note: N's vary. All are greater than 250. Correlations in parenthesis are not significant at the 0.05 level.

and formal status in making power judgments both about themselves and others, but the ratings of others are more tightly linked to such variables.

(3) Both self- and peer-ratings are related to perceived centrality in the process (i.e., variables 1, 2, 3), but the relation is stronger for self-ratings. An individual's sense of being central to the decision process is associated with both his self-rating of power and with the power rating made of him by peers, but it is more closely tied to the self-rating.

Taken collectively, these observations suggest that both peer- and self-ratings of power are connected to such directly observable process variables as participation rates, centrality, and formal status. The more conspicuous variables (e.g., formal status, speaking share) are differentially important for peer-ratings; the somewhat less conspicuous variables (e.g., centrality) are differentially important for self-ratings.

These aggregate results, however, need to be disaggregated into our groups of "insiders" and "outsiders". We have suggested two different dimensions of insiderhood: (1) Place in the contact network in the university, (2) Place in the status network in the university.

We can ask first whether an "insider" rates the power *of others* different from the way an "outsider" does. In this study, the answer is that he clearly does not. Using the peer-rating measures we have defined, peer-rating by insiders correlates very highly with peer-rating by outsiders (gamma = 0.96 for the contact network-dimension and 0.97 for the status-network dimension). Insiders and outsiders see the same pepole as powerful.

We ask second whether an "insider" rates his own power in a way different from the way an "outsider" rates his own power. Table 17.1 showed the overall correlation between self-rating (variable 14) and the 13 other variables. We can examine the extent to which these aggregate data conceal differences between "insiders" and "outsiders". Table 17.2 shows the gamma coefficients for the relation between self-rating of "insiders" and "outsiders" and the 12 variables for two different ways of defining "insiders" and "outsiders".

The data suggest two reasonably sharp differences between the way an "insider" evaluates his own power and the way an "outsider" does:

(1) The self-ratings of outsiders are more consistently tied to perceived centrality, participation, and status variables than are the self-ratings of insiders. Thus, the self-ratings of outsiders are more similar to peer-ratings than are the self-ratings of insiders.

(2) The self-ratings of outsiders are positively related to satisfaction variables (4 and 5); the self-ratings of insiders are either unrelated or negatively related to the same variables. Thus, out-

394

siders tie their own power more to "outcome" variables than do insiders.

Table 17.2. Relations between self-ratings by "Insiders" and "Outsiders" and 12 other variables

| Variable number | Insiders | | | | Outsiders | | | |
| | Contact network | | Status network | | Contact network | | Status network | |
	gamma	N	gamma	N	gamma	N	gamma	N
1	0.54	160	(0.33)	122	(0.16)	170	0.55	213
2	-0.43	169	(-0.28)	133	-0.70	170	-0.70	211
3	(-0.36)	129	(-0.35)	97	-0.43	131	-0.35	166
4	(0.24)	161	0.61	126	-0.64	166	(-0.18)	204
5	(-0.05)	169	(0.14)	131	0.61	167	0.34	210
6	-0.18	169	-0.40	133	0.48	173	0.59	213
7	(0.13)	146	(0.01)	110	(-0.06)	171	0.29	212
8	0.47	167	(0.09)	128	0.35	166	0.62	210
9	(0.16)	164	(0.10)	124	(0.28)	168	0.50	211
10	..		(-0.20)	131	..		0.49	210
11	0.57	169	0.54	133	(0.13)	171	0.32	212
12	(0.05)	169	..		0.66	172	..	

Note: Correlations in parentheses are not significant at the 0.05 level.

17.3 Discussion

The data presented here are subject to a number of alternative interpretations, and it is not easy to distinguish among them. On balance, however, the data seem to support three general notions: First, peer-ratings of power are closely associated with process signs of power and feelings of centrality. People who have formal status, talk a lot, belong to committees, and feel they are close to the action are generally rated by others as having power. Such peer-ratings are not associated with measures of satisfaction with either the process or the outcomes of decision making. Thus, there is no support in these data for the notion that persons rated as having power are those who, by their own reports, have been able to get what they want. If anything, it appears to be truer that those persons who are relatively dissatisfied tend to become active and, as a result, are viewed as having power.

Second, self-reports of power by persons (insiders) who are close to the centers of apparent power in the university are not closely associated with any of the major clusters of variables measured in this study. Self-reports of power by insiders seem to be considerably confounded by the problems of sorting out the elements of dissatisfaction, shifting aspirations and reference points, and the richer awareness that involvement brings. The fact that insider assessment of the power of other persons is much more regular suggests that the irregular pattern of insider self-reports stems more from variations in subjective states than from systematic improvement in power perception.

Third, self-reports of power by persons (outsiders) who are not close to the centers of apparent power in the university are associated with measures of participation, status, and centrality. In that sense, they are like peer-reports, and unlike self-reports of insiders. In addition, they differ from both peer-reports and insider self-reports by being positively related to satisfaction measures. For outsiders, self-reports of power appear to be a mix of felt participation and felt contentment.

In short, respondents in this study infer power in others from their participation and formal status, not from signs that the others are satisfied with the process or the outcomes of decisions. For the most part, people who are seen by others as having power see themselves as being relatively central and active; but they are somewhat less likely to see themselves as being powerful. People who see themselves as relative outsiders relate their own power both to the participation cues and their own satisfaction. They are the only ones who show a connection between power and satisfaction with the outcomes of the process.

Since the study does not attempt to assess what real resources were distributed to whom, it is not possible to say whether those people perceived as more powerful in fact got more of the scarce resources than those who did not. Such a thing is certainly possible despite the fact that they were, if anything, less satisfied with the outcomes than were those people perceived as less powerful.

With that caveat, however, the present data give general support to the idea that beliefs about power in others are better understood as stemming from observations of the process of decision rather than from observations of the outcomes; beliefs about self-power are better understood as resulting from an interaction between participation in the process and one's satisfaction with it and the outcomes from it.[4]

NOTES:

1 In this chapter power and influence will be used as synonyms.

2 As would be expected, the two distinctions are interrelated (gamma = 0.62).

3 Together with Goodman-Kruskal's gamma, we have used χ^2-tests. Where the significance level is below 95 percent the numbers are put in parenthesis. While all others are above the 95 percent level, most of the important relationships are also above the 99 percent significance level.

4 It should be noted that this lends some parenthetical clarification to the issue of whether "power" is zero-sum. It would appear that power in others is more likely to be seen as relative than is self-power. Thus, individual beliefs of own-power (or powerlessness) are partially indices of individual satisfaction and can rise or fall without reference to others; individual beliefs of other people's power are mostly relative — if someone gains, someone else loses.

Bibliography

Abelson, R. P. et.al. *Theories of cognitive consistency: A sourcebook*, Chicago, Rand McNally, 1968.

Agersnap, T., and Gudnason, C. H. Danmarks tekniske højskoles organisation og arbejdsformer, Copenhagen 1971 (mimeo).

Allison, G. T. "Conceptual Models and the Cuban Missile Crises", *The American Political Science Review*, Vol. LXIII, Sept. 1969, No. 3.

Allison, G. T. *Essence of decision*, Boston, Little, Brown and co., 1971.

Andersen, Ib. De faglige forsamlinger på Danmarks tekniske højskole, Copenhagen 1971 (mimeo).

Andersen, Ib. Beslutningssystem og magtstruktur i en akademisk organisation, Copenhagen 1972 (mimeo).

Axelrod, R. Schema theory: An information processing model of perception and cognition, *The American Political Science Review*, Vol. LXVII, December 1973.

Bachrach, P., and Baratz, M. S. "Decisions and Non-Decisions: An analytical framework", *American Political Science Review*, Vol. LVII, (Sept. 1963).

Becker, Gary S. "A Theory of the Allocation of Time", *The Economic Journal*, Vol. LXXV (September, 1965), pp. 493—517.

Bem, D. J. *Beliefs, Attitudes, and Human Affairs*, Brooks Cole Publishing Company, Belmont, 1970.

Ben-David, J. *Fundamental Research and the Universities*, Paris, (OECD), 1968.

Berelson, B., and Lazarsfeld, P. F., and McPhee, W. N. *Voting*, University of Chicago Press, 1954.

Berelson, B., and Steiner, G. A. *Human Behavior, An Inventory of Scientific Findings*, Harcourt, Brace and World, N. Y., 1964.

Bidwell, C. E. "The School as a Formal Organization" in March, James G.: *Handbook of Organizations*, Rand McNally, Chicago 1965.

Blau, P. M. and Scott, W. R. *Formal Organizations*, Routledge Paperback, London 1966.

Bolman, Frederick de W. *How College Presidents are Chosen*, Washington, D. C.: American Council on Education, 1965.

Campbell, A., Gurin, G., and Miller, W. E. *The Voter Decides*, Row, Peterson, Evanstone, Illinois, 1954.

Caplow, T. and McGee, R. J. *The Academic Marketplace*, N. Y., Basic Books, 1958.

Carnegie, Dale. *How to Win Friends and Influence People*, New York, Simon and Schuster, 1936.

397

Christensen, Søren. *Institut og laboratorieorganisation på Danmarks Tekniske Højskole*, København 1971 (mimeo).

Cohen, Michael D., March, James G., and Olsen, Johan P. "A Garbage Can Model of Organizational Choice", *Administrative Science Quarterly*, Vol. 17, No. 1, (March 1972), pp. 1—25.

Cohen, Michael D., and March, James G. *Leadership and Ambiguity: The American College President*, New York: McGraw-Hill, Carnegie Commission on the Future of Higher Education, 1974.

Coleman, J. S. *Community Conflict*, N. Y., The Free Press of Glencoe, 1957.

Coleman, J. S. Collective Decision, *Sociological Inquiry*, Spring, 1964.

Coleman, J. S. Foundations for a Theory of Collective Decisions, *The American Journal of Sociology*, Vol. LXXI, No. 3, May 1966.

Consolazio, W. V. "Dilemma of Academic Biology in Europe", *Science,* 1961.

Crecine, J. P. *Governmental problem solving: A computer simulation of municipal budgeting*, Chicago, Rand McNally, 1969.

Cyert, R. M., and March, J. G. *A Behavioral Theory of the Firm*, Englewood Cliffs, Prentice-Hall, 1963.

Dahl, A. *A Preface to Democratic Theory*, Phoenix Books, Chicago: University of Chicago Press, 1956.

Dahl, R. A. *Who Governs*, New Haven, Yale University Press, 1964 (5th printing).

Dill, W. R. "Business Organizations" in March, James G., *Handbook of Organizations*, Chicago, Rand McNally, 1965.

Dye, T. R. Popular Images of Decision-Making in Suburban Communities, *Sociology and Social Research*, 47, (October 1962) pp. 75—83.

Eckhoff, T. Vitenskaper, profesjoner og klienter, *Nordisk Forum*, Vol. 2, 1967.

Eckhoff, Torstein, *Rettferdighet*, Universitetsforlaget, Oslo 1971.

Eckhoff, T. and Jacobsen, K. D. *Rationality and Responsibility in Administrative and Judicial Decision-Making*, Copenhagen: Munksgaard, 1960.

Edelman, M. *The symbolic uses of politics*, University of Illinois Press, Urbana 1964.

Enderud, Harald. Rektoratet og den centrale administration på Danmarks tekniske Højskole, Copenhagen: Copenhagen School of Economics, 1971 (mimeo).

Enderud, H. G. Four faces of Leadership in an Academic Organization, Copenhagen 1973.

Feldman, J., and Kanter, H. E. Organizational Decision-Making, in March, J. G. (editor), *Handbook of Organizations*, Chicago, Rand McNally, 1965.

Ferrari, Michael R. *Profiles of American College Presidents*, East Lansing: Michigan State University Business School, 1971.

Festinger, L., Riecken, H., and Schachter, S. *When Prophecy Fails*, Minneapolis, 1956.

Form, W. H., and Rytina, R. Ideological Beliefs on the Distribution of Power in the United States, *American Sociological Review*, February 1969, Vol. 34, No. 1.

Form, W. H., and Sauer, W. L. Organized Labor's Image of Community Power Structure, *Social Forces*, 38 (May 1960), pp. 332—341.

Friedrich, C. J. *Constitutional Government and Politics*, Harper, New York, 1937.

Frohlich, N., and Oppenheimer, J. A. "I get by with a little Help of my Friends", *World Politics*, Vol. XXIII, No. 1, October 1970.

"Grunnforskning i fysikk i Norge", *Hovedkomiteen for norsk forskning*, melding nr. 3, Oslo 1968.

Gamson, W. A. Experimental studies in coalition formation, in Borgatta (ed.): *Social psychology: Readings and perspectives,* Chicago, Rand McNally, 1969.

Glenn, James R., Jr. Chief Executive Time: An empirial study of the time allocation of American college and university presidents, Unpublished Ph.D. thesis, Stanford University, Stanford, Calif. 1975.

Haas, E. and Collen, L. Administrative practices in university departments. *Administrative Science Quarterly,* 8, 1963–64, pp. 44–60.

Hallander, B. En Undersøgelse af magt og indflydelse i et direkte demokrati, Copenhagen 1973 (mimeo).

Heider, F. *The Psychology of Interpersonal Relations,* John Wiley, New York 1958.

Hernes, G. Interest, Influence, and Cooperation, Unpublished Ph.D. Dissertation, Johns Hopkins University, 1971.

Hernes, G. Some notes on multicollinearity in path analysis, Bergen, 1970, (mimeo).

Hill, Winfred F. *Learning. A survey of psychological interpretations.* (Revised edition), Scranton, Chandler Publishing Comp., 1971.

Hirschman, A. O. *Exit, Voice and Loyalty,* Harvard University Press, Massachusetts, 1970.

Hollander, E. P. Conformity, status and ideosyncracy credit, Psychol. Rev., 65, 1958, pp. 117–127.

Hunter, F. *Community Power Structure,* Chapel Hill, University of North Carolina Press, 1953.

Hunter, F. *Top Leadership, U.S.A.,* Chapel Hill, University of North Carolina Press, 1959.

Ibsen, H. *Peer Gynt,* Aldine Press, London, 1963.

Jacobsen, K. D. *Teknisk hjelp og politisk struktur,* Universitetsforlaget, Oslo 1964.

Jacobsen, K. D. Ekspertenes deltakelse i den offentlige forvaltning, Oslo, 1968, (mimeo).

Jacobsen, K. D. Informasjonstilgang og likebehandling i den offentlige virksomhet, *Tidsskrift for samfunnsforskning,* No. 2, 1965.

Kreiner, K. En empirisk undersøgelse af kollektive beslutningsprocesser i en uddannelsesorganisation, Copenhagen 1972 (mimeo).

Kuhn, T. S. *The Structure of Scientific Revolutions,* University of Chicago Press, 1962.

Lazarsfeld, P. F., Berelson, B., and Gaudet, H. *The People's Choice,* Columbia University Press, N. Y., 1960 (2nd edition).

Lewis, Lionel S. "Faculty Support of Academic Freedom and Self-Government", *Social Problems,* Spring 1966, Vol. 13. No. 4.

Lindbekk, Tore. *Mobilitets- og stillingsstrukturer innenfor tre akademiske profesjoner, 1910–63,* Universitetsforlaget, Oslo 1967.

Lindblom, C. E. *The Intelligence of Democracy,* N. Y., The Free Press, 1965.

Linder, Staffan B. *The Harried Leisure Class,* Columbia University Press, 1970.

Long, N. The Local Community as an Ecology of Games, *American Journal of Sociology,* Vol. 44, November 1958, pp. 251–261.

McNeil, K., and Thompson, J. D. "The Regeneration of Social Organizations" *American Sociological Review,* 36 (1971) pp. 624–637.

March, James G. "The Power of Power", *Varieties of Political Theory,* David Easton Ed., Englewood Cliffs, N. J., Prentice-Hall, Inc., 1966.

March, J. G. "Model Bias in Social Action", *Review of Educational Research,* 42: 413–429, Fall, 1972.

26

March, J. G., and Olsen, J.P. The uncertainty of the past. Organizational learning under ambiguity, *European Journal of Political Research*, 3, 1975.

March, James G. and Pate, Elisabeth. *A Boolean Treatment of Seeing, Linking, and Trusting*, Unpublished manuscript, Stanford, 1974.

March, J. G., and Simon, H. A. *Organizations*, N. Y., John Wiley & Sons, 1958.

Marx, K., and Engels, F. *The German Ideology*, London, Lawrence and Wishare, 1970.

Meyer, J. W. The Charter: Conditions of diffuse socialization in School, in Scott, W. R. (ed), *Social Structures and Social Processes*, New York, 1970.

Mintzberg, Henry. *The Nature of Managerial Work*, New York, Harper and Row, 1973.

Mood, Alexander (ed.). *More Scholars for the Dollar*, New York: McGraw-Hill, Carnegie Commission on the Future of Higher Education, 1971.

Mosher, Frederick (ed.). *"Government Reorganizations, Cases and Commentary"*, The Inter-University Case Program, Indianapolis, 1967.

Newcomb, T. M. Individual Systems of Orientation, in Koch, S. (ed.), *Psychology: A Study of a Science*, McGraw-Hill, 1959.

Olsen, J. P. «Universitetet — En organisasjon i endring», Oslo 1968, (mimeo).

Olsen, J. P. "A Study of Choice in an Academic Organization", Bergen 1970 (mimeo).

Olsen, J. P. "Local Budgeting — Decision-Making or Ritual Act?" *Scandinavian Political Studies*, Vol. V, 1970 (a).

Olsen, J. P. Reorganization of Formal Authority in a Norwegian University, Bergen, 1971 (mimeo).

Olsen, J. P. Voting, "Sounding out", and the Governance of Modern Organizations, *Acta Sociologica*, Vol. 15, No. 3 1972.

Olson, M. *The Logic of Collective Action*, Schocken Books, N. Y. 1968 (paperback edition).

Parsons, T. Introduction to Max Weber, *The Theory of Social and Economic Organization*, The Free Press, N. Y. 1964.

Peltason, J. W. "Judicial process", *International Encyclopedia of the Social Sciences*, The MacMillan Company & The Free Press, 1968.

Peterson, Vance T. *Response to Mandate: A Study of Organizational Implementation of Mandated Change*. Unpublished Ph.D. dissertation, Stanford University, Stanford, Calif. 1975.

Pitkin, H. F. The concept of representation, University of California Press, 1967.

Pruitt, D. Definition of the Situation as a Determinant of International Action, in Kelman (ed.) *International Behavior*, Holt, Rinehart, and Winston, 1966, pp. 391—432.

Rawls, John. *A Theory of Justice*, Harvard University Press, Cambridge, 1971.

Riste, T., and Spangen, E. *Norsk fysikk. Omfang, struktur og vekst*. Universitetsforlaget, Oslo 1968.

Robinson, A., and Majak, R. R. The Theory of Decision-Making, in Charlesworth (ed.), *Contemporary Political Analysis*, Free Press, 1967.

Rogowski, R. "Social Structure and Stable Rule: A General Theory", Technical Report, No. 3 (69—3), Center of International Studies, Princeton University (mimeo).

Rokkan, S. Norway, Numerical Democracy and Corporate Pluralism, in Dahl (ed.), *Political Oppositions in Western Democracies*, Yale University Press, 1968 (3rd printing).

Rommetveit, Kåre. Framveksten av det medisinske fakultet ved Universitetet i Tromsø, Bergen, University of Bergen, 1971 (mimeo).

Rose, A. M. *The Power Structure,* New York, Oxford University Press, 1967.
Rosenau, James N. "The Premises and Promises of Decision-Making Analysis", in James C. Charlesworth (ed.), *Contemporary Political Analysis,* New York, The Free Press, 1967, p. 195.
Rousseau, Jean-Jaques. *Social Contract,* London, Oxford University Press, 1966, (First printed 1762).
Schattschneider, E. E. *The Semi-Sovereign People,* Holt, Rinehart and Winston, N. Y. 1960.
Schilling, W. R. The H-Bomb Decision: How to Decide Without Actually Choosing, in Welson, W. R., *The Politics of Science,* Oxford University Press, 1968.
Seip, J. A. «Det norske system» i den økonomiske liberalismes klassiske tid, *Historisk Tidsskrift,* Vol. 39 (1959), pp. 1—58.
Selznick, P. *TVA and the Grass Roots,* University of California Press, 1949.
Silverman, D. *The Theory of Organizations,* London, Heinemann, 1970.
Simmel, G. *Conflict and the Web of Group Affiliations,* Free Press, Glencoe, 1955.
Simon, H. A. "A Behavioral Model of Rational Choice", *Quarterly Journal of Economics,* Vol. 69, February 1955.
Simon, H. A. "On the Concept of Organizational Goal", *Administrative Science Quarterly,* June, 9, 1964, pp. 1—22.
Simon, H. A. "The Job of a College President", *The Educational Record,* Vol. 48, No. 1, Winter, 1967, pp. 68—78.
Skoie, Hans. "The Problems of a Small Scientific Community: The Norwegian Case", *Minerva,* Vol. VII, No. 3, Spring 1969.
Stava, Per. The Location of Norwegian District Colleges and Universities, Bergen, 1971, (mimeo).
Stjernø, Steinar. «Universitetspolitikken i Norge 1950—1970», Bergen, 1971, (mimeo).
Steinbruner, John D. *The Cybernetic Theory of Decision,* Princeton, New Jersey, Princeton University Press, 1974.
Stinchcombe, Arthur L. *Creating efficient industrial administration,* New York, Academic Press, 1974.
Szalai, Alexander (ed.) *The Use of Time: Daily Activities of Urban and Suburban Populations in Twelve Countries,* The Hague, Mouton, 1973.
Thompson, J., *Organizations in Action,* N. Y., McGraw-Hill, 1967.
Thompson, J., and McEwan, W. J. Organizational Goals and Environment Goal Setting as an Interaction Process, *American Sociological Review,* Vol. 23, February 1958, pp. 23—31.
Torgersen, Ulf. "The Market of Professional Manpower in Norway", Oslo, 1967 (mimeo).
Torgersen, Ulf. "Political Strategies and Employment Conditions: Some Comments on a Problem", Oslo, 1970 (mimeo).
Trow, M. The Democratization of Higher Education in America, *European Journal of Sociology,* Vol. XII, 1962, pp. 231—262.
Truman, David B. *Governmental Process,* New York, Alfred A. Knopf, 1965.
Tyler, R. W. *Basic Principles of Curriculum and Instruction,* Chicago 1949.
Valen, H., and Martinussen, W. *Velgerne og de politiske frontlinjer,* Gyldendal, Oslo, 1972.
Veblen, Torstein. *The Higher Learning in America,* New York, Hill and Wang, 1957.
Vickers, Geoffrey. *The Art of Judgment,* New York: Basic Books, 1965.
Weber, M. *Economy and Society,* Bedminster Press, N. Y., 1968.

401

Weick, K. E. *The Social Psychology of Organizing,* Addison-Wesley, 1969.

Weiner, Stephen S. *Educational decisions in an organized anarchy,* Unpublished Ph.D. thesis, Stanford University, Stanford, Calif., 1972.

Wetlesen, T. Schou. Universitetsbudsjettering, Oslo 1967 (mimeo).

Winter, Sidney G., Jr. Economic "natural selection" and the theory of the firm, *Yale Economic Essays,* 1964, 4: pp. 225—272.

Woodward, J. *Industrial Organization: Theory and Practice,* London, Oxford University Press, 1965.

Wootton, Graham. *Interest-groups,* Englewood Cliffs, N. J., Prentice-Hall, Inc. 1960.

Index

405

406

268–273, 284, 316–317, 323, 330, 352–353, 374, 378, 386. *See also* Activation
bounding, 251–252
expectations, 149
observation, 95
Participation, 18, 21, 25–29, 35–36, 38, 41–48, 52, 110, 160, 168, 175, 201–203, 225, 233–234, 239–240, 244, 252, 277–312, 323–324, 326, 328, 330–331, 333–334, 354, 373, 396. *See also* Activation
decision maker activity, 34
hierarchical, 28
rate of, 227, 234, 236, 274
specialized, 28
unsegmented, 28
Paté, E., 67
Pedagogical structure, 157–158, 162 –169, 171–172
Peer-rating, 389–390, 394
Perception, 61, 65–66, 73, 83, 87, 90–91, 199–200, 289, 291, 297, 300, 303, 306, 309, 320, 330, 379
Peterson, V. T., 39
Pitkin, H. F., 42
Planning, 11, 50, 67, 80, 176, 193– 196, 232, 239–240, 245, 248
as advertisements, 195
as excuses for interaction, 196
as games, 195–196
as symbols, 195
Play, 77–81
Policy gradualism, 271–272
Political philosophy, 42
Position, 273–274
Power, 11, 24, 38–39, 48–49, 94, 104, 133, 159–161, 175, 196–197, 204, 252, 280, 286, 288–290, 296, 311, 316, 341, 351, 386–396. *See also* Authority
actual, 198
distribution of, 159, 386–387
of junior faculty, 328
legitimate, 198
models of, 199, 210–212, 214
peer rating of, 389–390, 394–396
perceived, 198
of politics, 343
self rating of, 389–390, 394– 396
Preferences, 15, 19, 25, 61, 70–71, 74, 80, 82. *See also* Goals; Intention; Purpose

Private foundations, 178
Problems, 24–27, 31–37, 40–41, 47, 140–148, 174–175, 203, 225–227, 242–245, 248, 316–317, 351, 369, 375–379
activity of, 33–35
latency of, 33–35
solving of, 89, 314
Presence, 272–274. *See also* Activation
Purpose, 48, 69–71, 77. *See also* Goals. Intention; Preferences

Ranking of candidates, 113–114, 124, 130
Rational action, 45–46
Rational calculation, 54–56, 67
Rational decision models, 47, 82– 83, 85, 107, 110, 121, 131, 242– 243, 309. *See also* Style; Organizational choice
Rationality, 54, 69–71, 76–79, 89, 132, 151, 376
adaptive, 58, 59, 67
bounded, 82
Rationalization, 75–76
Reality, 18–19, 61–62, 64, 91
Relevance, 24–26, 63–64, 66, 86, 120, 149
Reorganization, 314–316, 321–329, 333–336, 377–378
of garbage can, 315, 318
Reputation, institutional, 178, 181– 184
Research Council for Scientific Research, 332
Research reputation, 178, 182–184
Resolution, 33–37
Rewards, 281–282, 285–286, 311– 312
Richmond Complex, 230–232, 237
Riste, T., 329
Robinson, A., 82–83
Rokkan, S., 378
Roles, 15, 140–141, 157, 185
Romelaer, P., 203
Rommetveit, K., 143, 150
Rose, A. M., 386
Rousseau, J. J., 278
Rules, 40, 42, 44, 56, 77, 82, 104, 174, 187, 209, 217, 280–282, 285. *See also* Attention structures
Rytina, R., 386

408